THE DEMONS

OBIN - SON OF BATMAN

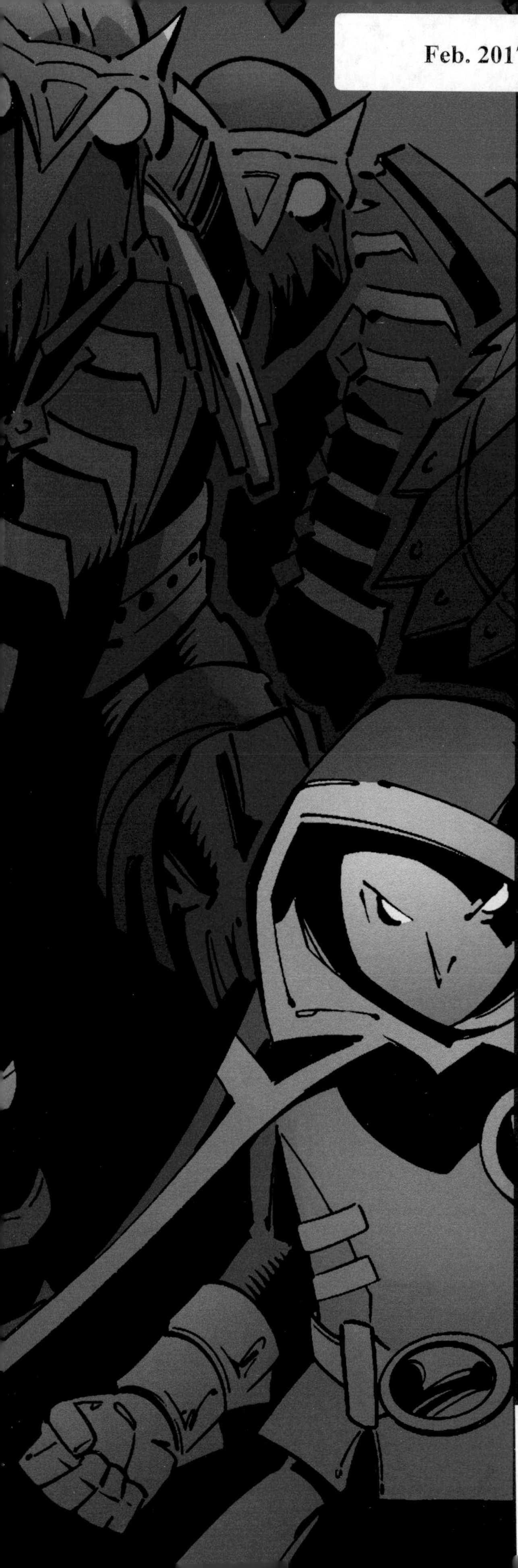

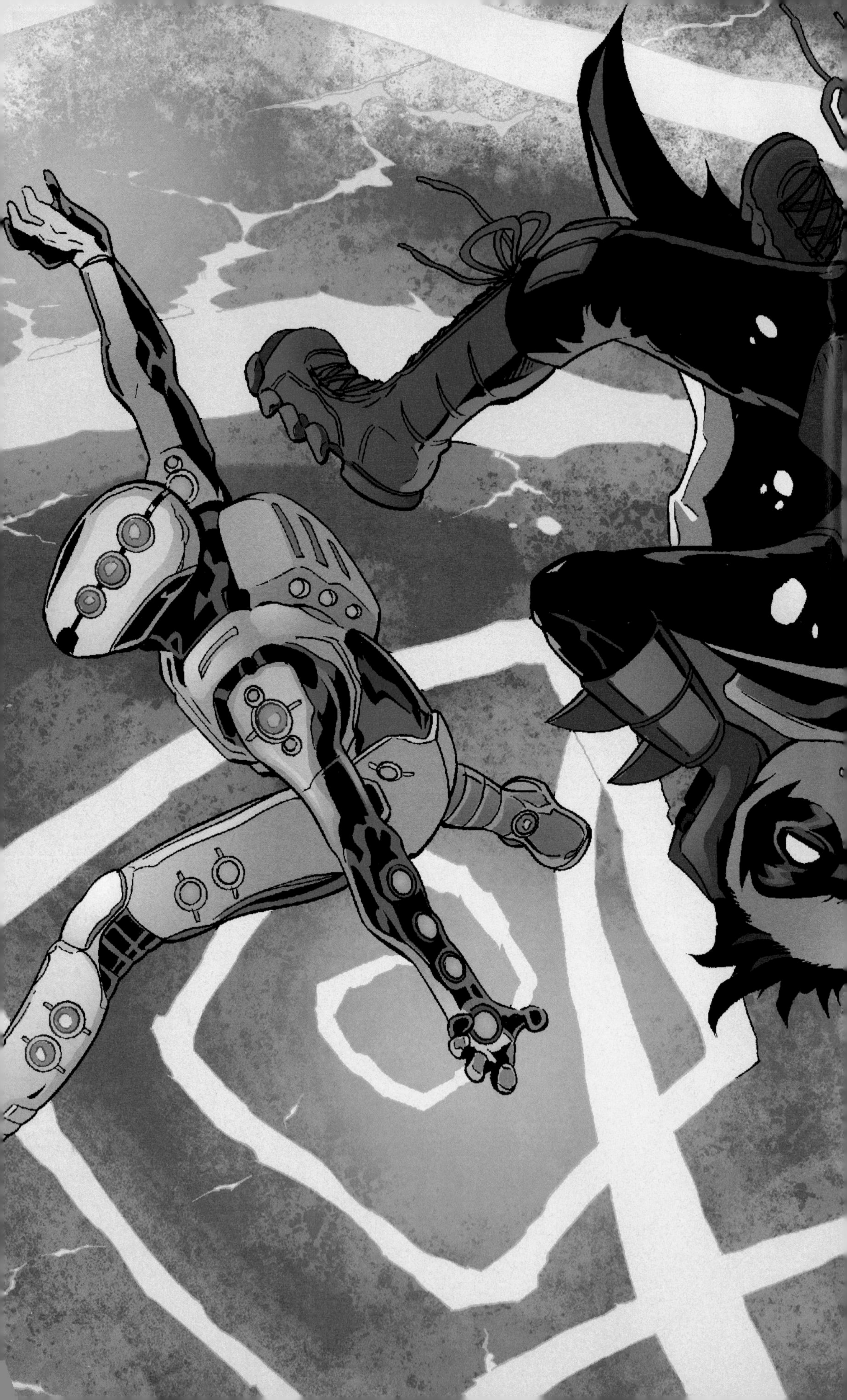

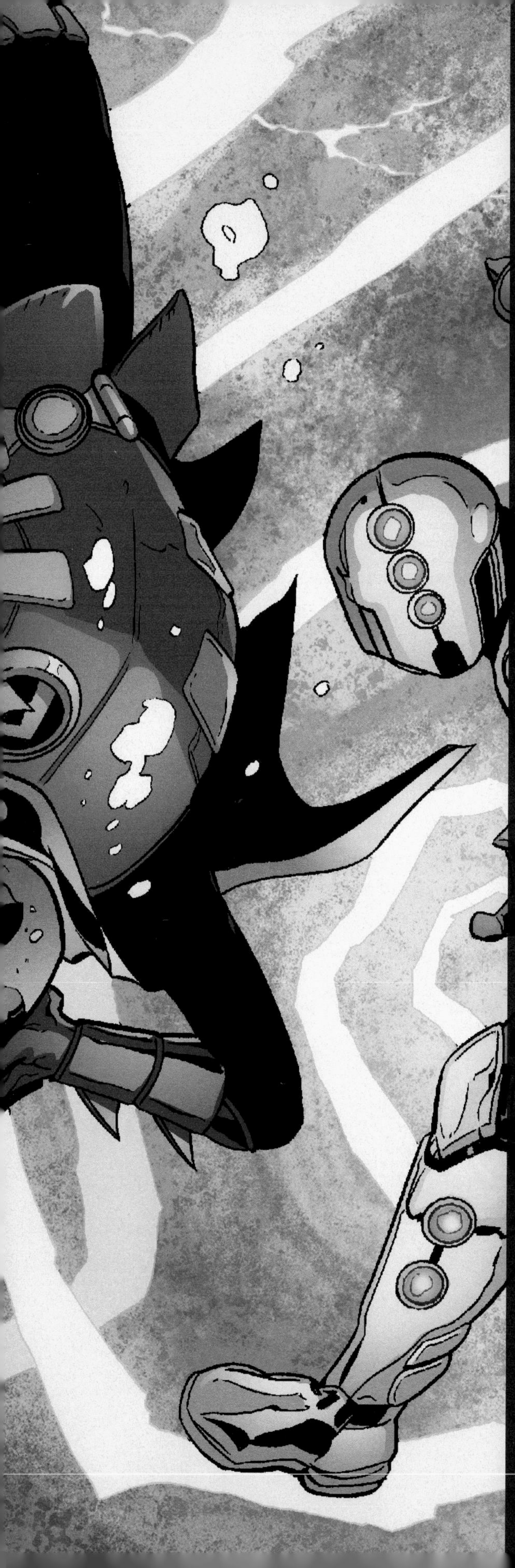

ROBIN – SON OF BATMAN

VOLUME 2

DAWN OF THE DEMONS

WRITTEN BY
PATRICK GLEASON
RAY FAWKES

PENCILS BY
PATRICK GLEASON
SCOTT MCDANIEL
RAMON BACHS

INKS BY
MICK GRAY
ANDY OWENS
RAMON BACHS

COLORS BY
JOHN KALISZ
CHRIS SOTOMAYOR
MAT LOPES

LETTERS BY
TOM NAPOLITANO
COREY BREEN
DERON BENNETT

COLLECTION COVER ARTISTS
PATRICK GLEASON,
MICK GRAY & JOHN KALISZ

BATMAN CREATED BY
BOB KANE WITH **BILL FINGER**

MARK DOYLE Editor – Original Series
REBECCA TAYLOR Associate Editor – Original Series
JEB WOODARD Group Editor – Collected Editions
STEVE COOK Design Director – Books
DAMIAN RYLAND Publication Design

BOB HARRAS Senior VP – Editor-in-Chief, DC Comics

DIANE NELSON President
DAN DiDIO Publisher
JIM LEE Publisher
GEOFF JOHNS President & Chief Creative Officer
AMIT DESAI Executive VP – Business & Marketing Strategy, Direct to Consumer & Global Franchise Management
SAM ADES Senior VP – Direct to Consumer
BOBBIE CHASE VP – Talent Development
MARK CHIARELLO Senior VP – Art, Design & Collected Editions
JOHN CUNNINGHAM Senior VP – Sales & Trade Marketing
ANNE DePIES Senior VP – Business Strategy, Finance & Administration
DON FALLETTI VP – Manufacturing Operations
LAWRENCE GANEM VP – Editorial Administration & Talent Relations
ALISON GILL Senior VP – Manufacturing & Operations
HANK KANALZ Senior VP – Editorial Strategy & Administration
JAY KOGAN VP – Legal Affairs
THOMAS LOFTUS VP – Business Affairs
JACK MAHAN VP – Business Affairs
NICK J. NAPOLITANO VP – Manufacturing Administration
EDDIE SCANNELL VP – Consumer Marketing
COURTNEY SIMMONS Senior VP – Publicity & Communications
JIM (SKI) SOKOLOWSKI VP – Comic Book Specialty & Trade Marketing
NANCY SPEARS VP – Mass, Book, Digital Sales & Trade Marketing

ROBIN – SON OF BATMAN VOLUME 2: DAWN OF THE DEMONS

Published by DC Comics. All new material Copyright © 2017 DC Comics. All Rights Reserved. Originally published in
single magazine form in ROBIN: SON OF BATMAN 7-13. Copyright © 2015, 2016 DC Comics. All Rights Reserved.
All characters, their distinctive likenesses and related elements featured in this publication are trademarks of DC
Comics. The stories, characters and incidents featured in this publication are entirely fictional.
DC Comics does not read or accept unsolicited submissions of ideas, stories or artwork.

DC Comics, 2900 West Alameda Ave., Burbank, CA 91505
Printed by LSC Communications, Kendallville, IN, USA. 12/30/16. First Printing.
ISBN: 978-1-4012-6789-6

Library of Congress Cataloging-in-Publication Data is available.

PEFC Certified

Printed on paper from
sustainably managed
forests, controlled
sources

PEFC/29-31-337   www.pefc.org

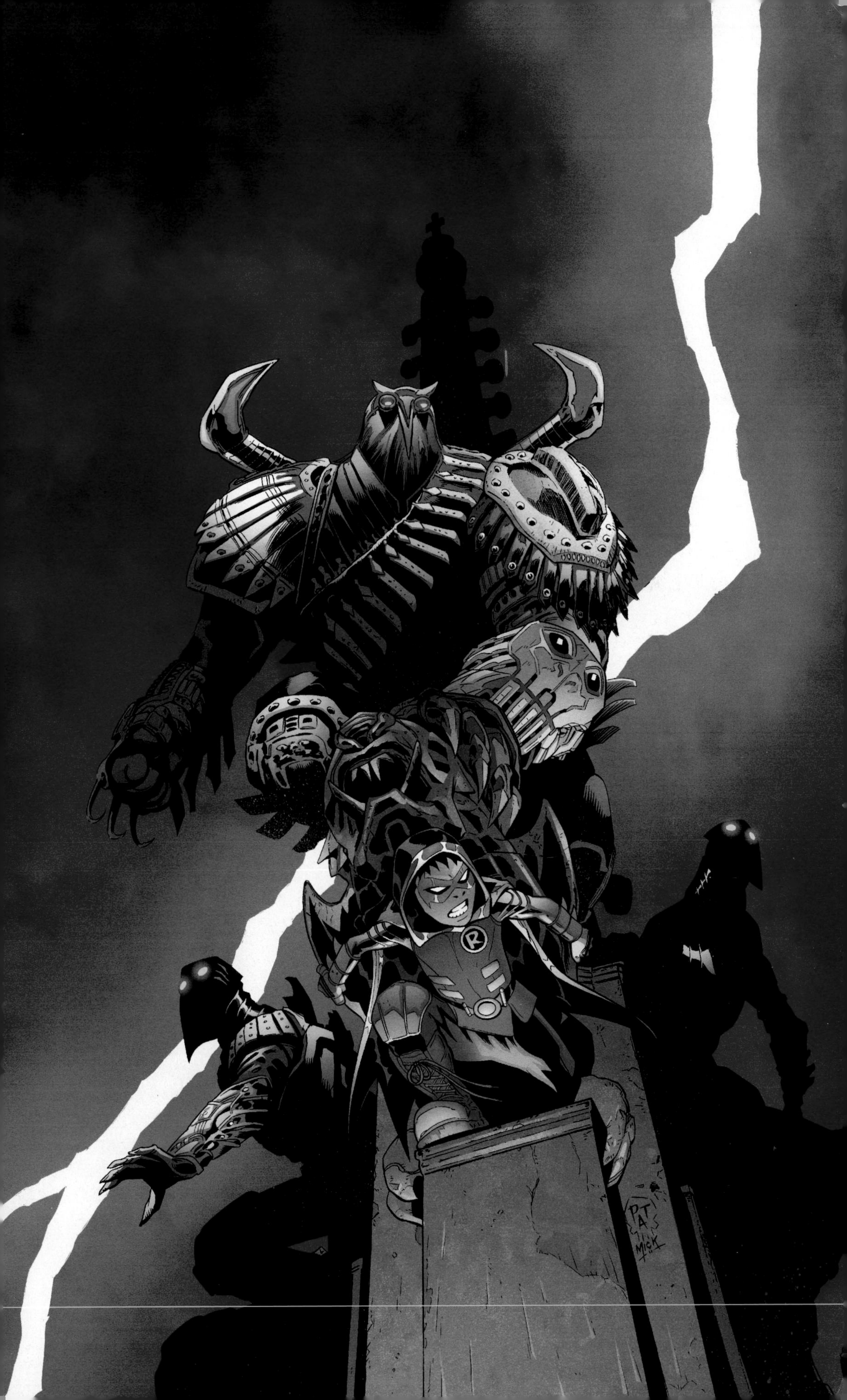

PATRICK GLEASON, MICK GRAY & JOHN KALISZ cover

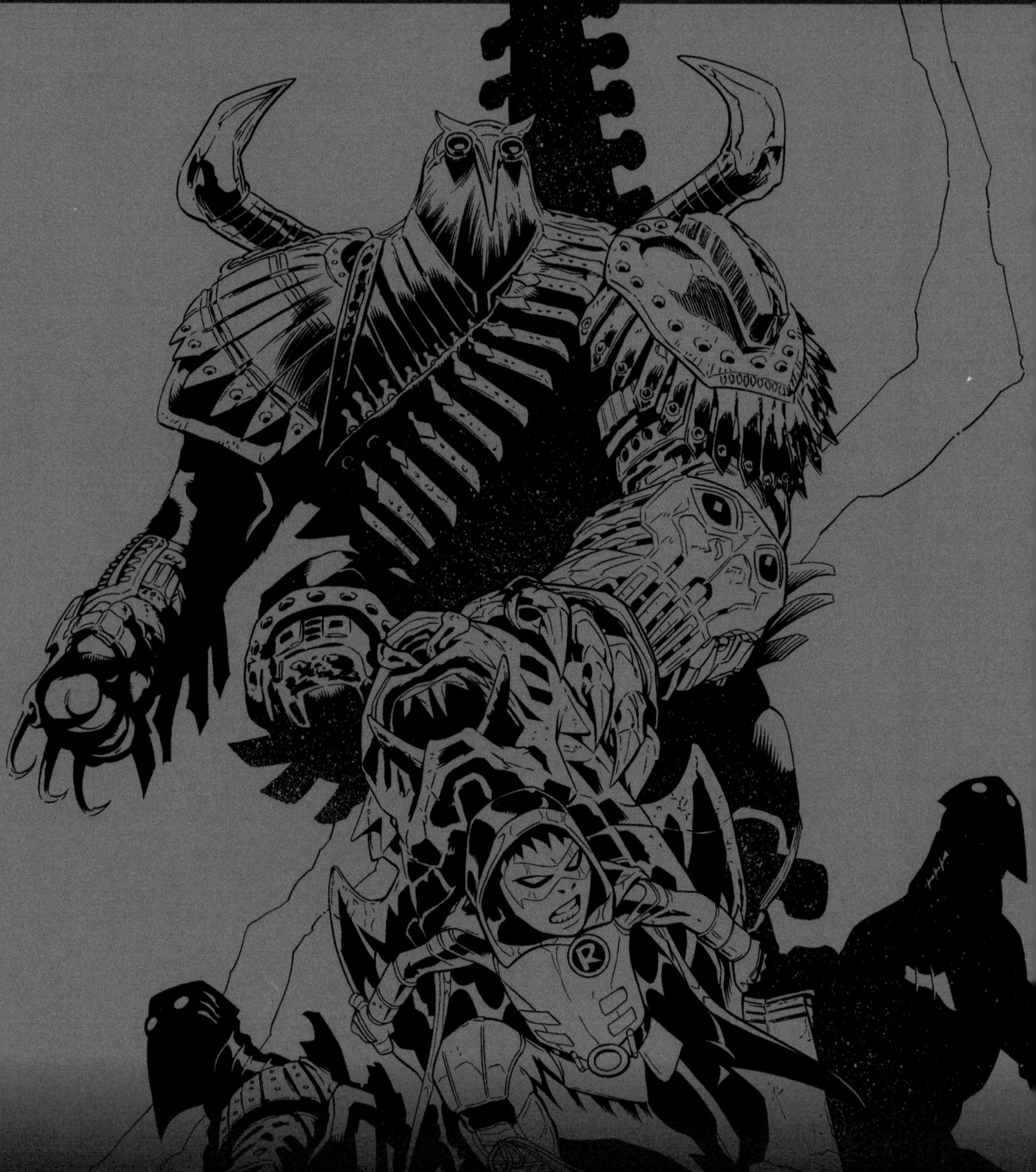

PREVIOUSLY IN ROBIN WAR...

There are amateur Robins in Gotham. In an effort to control the teen vigilante movement, Gotham's Councilwoman Athene Noctua has put laws in place that make the wearing or possessing of Robin merchandise illegal. The vigilantes were driven underground, where they were found by the real Robin—Damian Wayne—and the three men who once called themselves Robin—Dick Grayson, Jason Todd and Tim Drake. In an effort to protect the untrained Robins, Dick Grayson tipped off the Gotham police to their location, leading to the arrest of the entire group, including Damian, Jason, and Tim. Dick's intentions were to keep the children safe, but now they are fighting the elite Talons of the Court of Owls with Dick off on his own mysterious mission...

ROBIN WAR was originally published in ROBIN WAR #1 GRAYSON #15, DETECTIVE COMICS #47, WE ARE ROBIN #7, ROBIN: SON OF BATMAN #7, RED HOOD/ARSENAL #7,

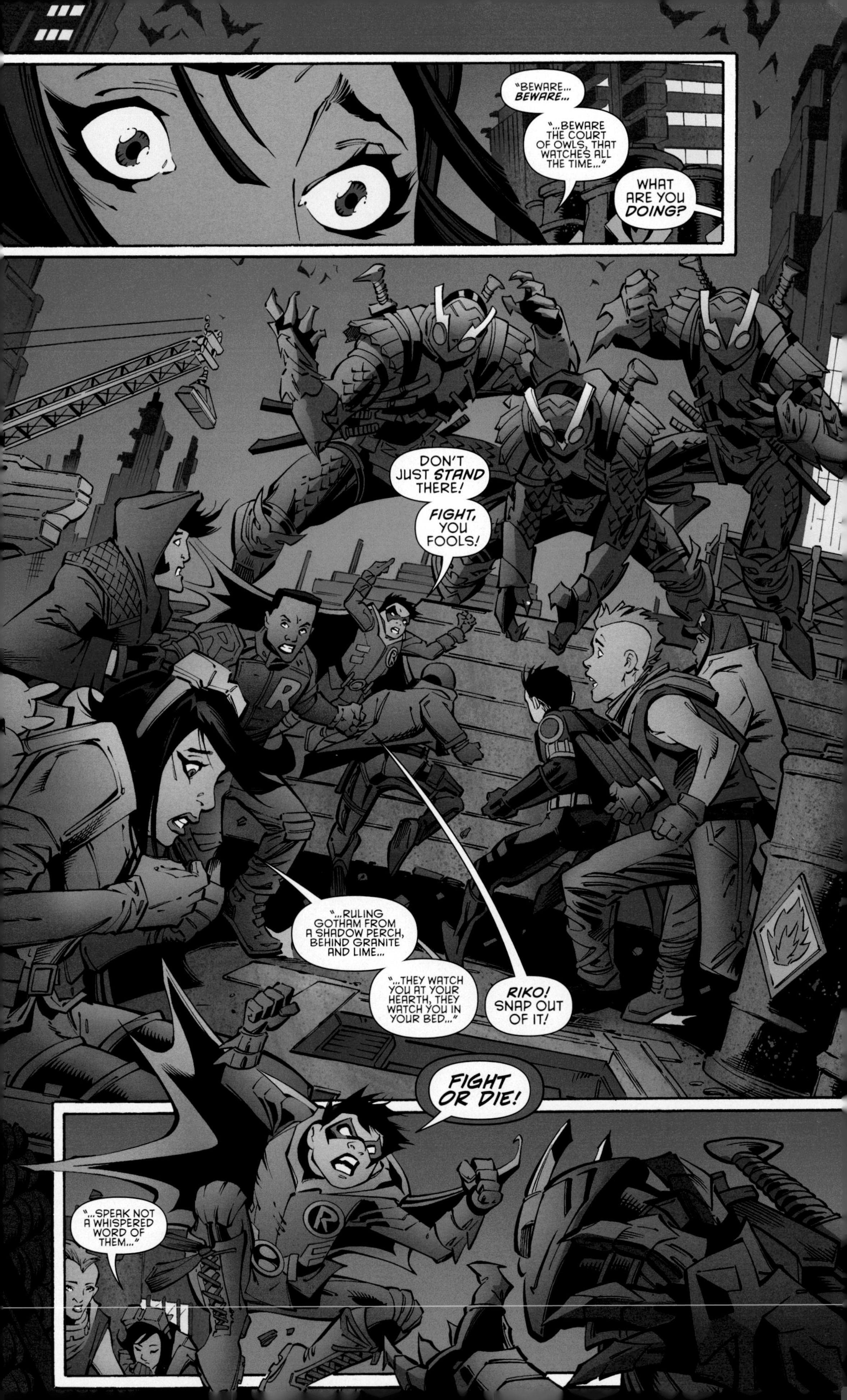
"BEWARE... BEWARE...
"...BEWARE THE COURT OF OWLS, THAT WATCHES ALL THE TIME..."
WHAT ARE YOU DOING?
DON'T JUST STAND THERE!
FIGHT, YOU FOOLS!
"...RULING GOTHAM FROM A SHADOW PERCH, BEHIND GRANITE AND LIME...
"...THEY WATCH YOU AT YOUR HEARTH, THEY WATCH YOU IN YOUR BED..."
RIKO! SNAP OUT OF IT!
FIGHT OR DIE!
"...SPEAK NOT A WHISPERED WORD OF THEM..."

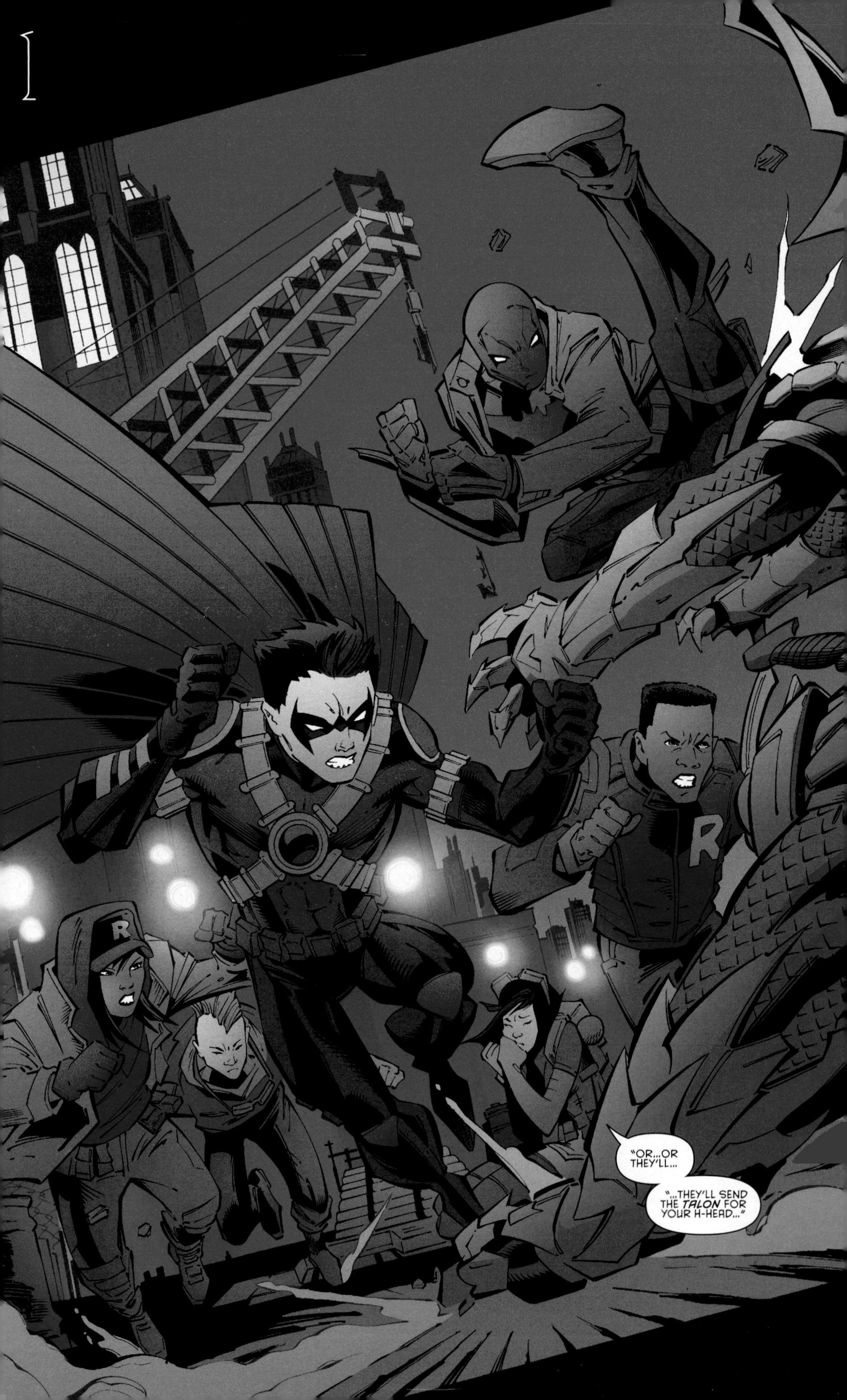
"OR...OR THEY'LL...
"...THEY'LL SEND THE *TALON* FOR YOUR H-HEAD..."

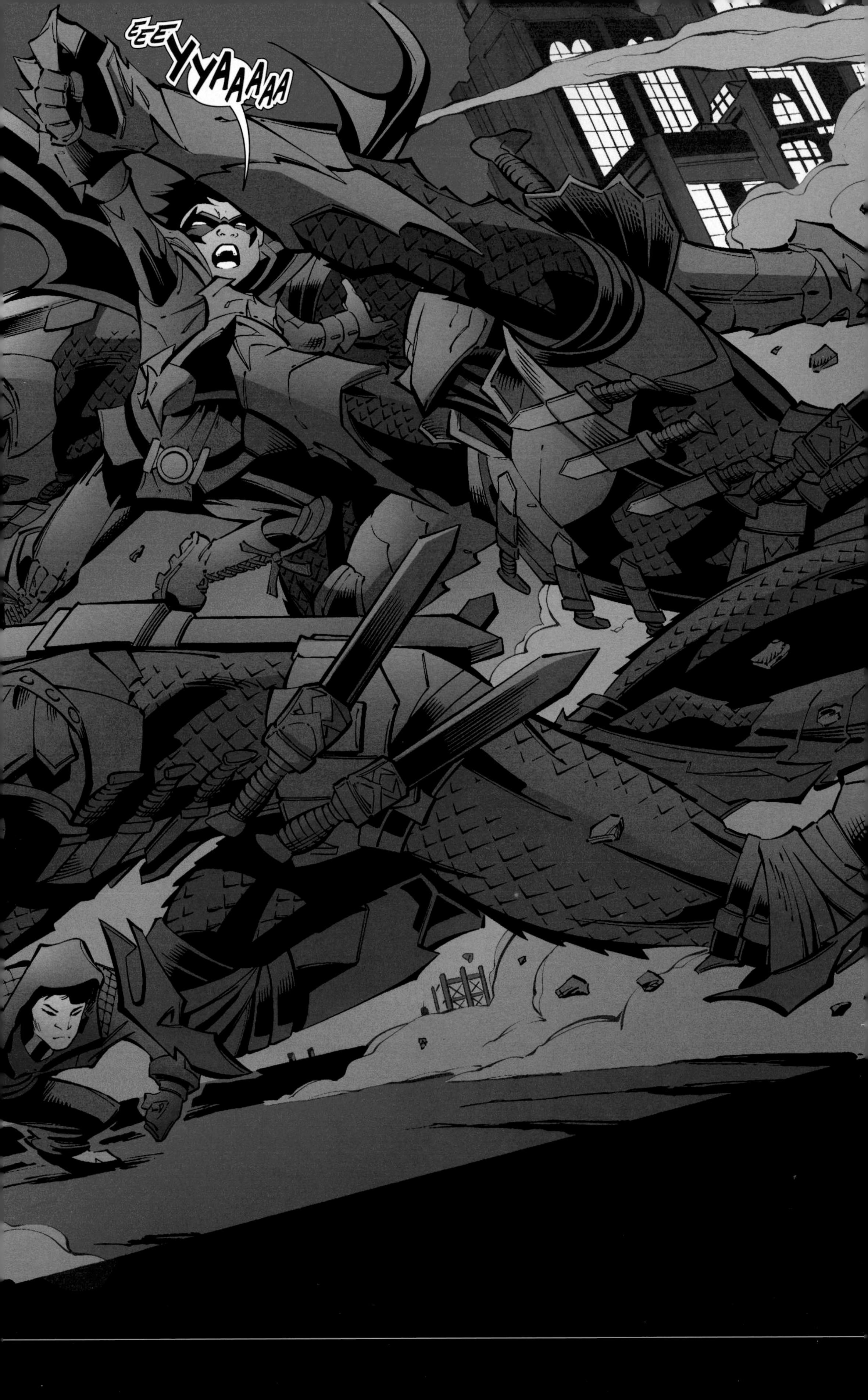
EEEYYAAAAAA

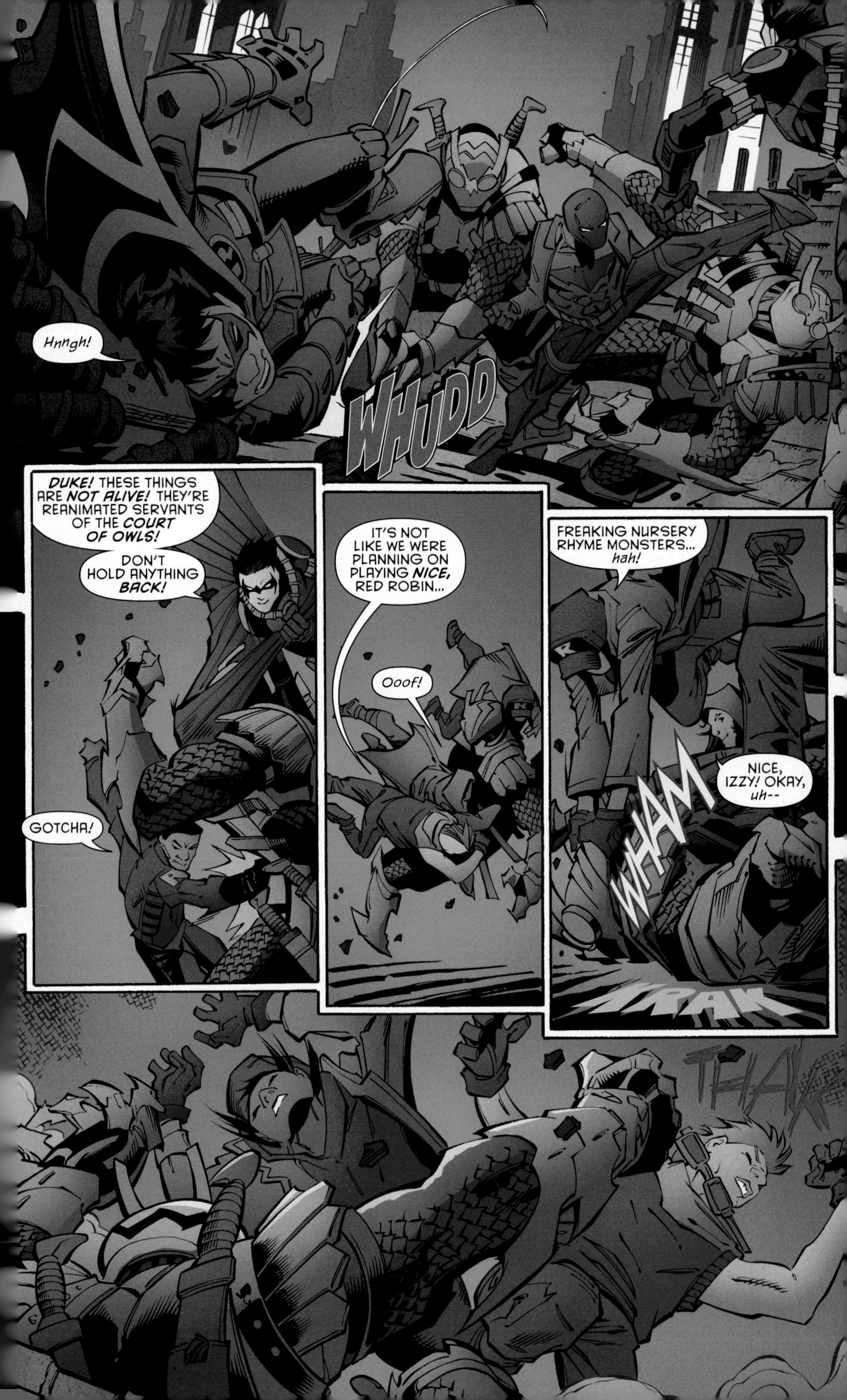
Hnngh!
WHUDD
DUKE! THESE THINGS ARE NOT ALIVE! THEY'RE REANIMATED SERVANTS OF THE COURT OF OWLS!
DON'T HOLD ANYTHING BACK!
GOTCHA!
IT'S NOT LIKE WE WERE PLANNING ON PLAYING NICE, RED ROBIN...
Ooof!
FREAKING NURSERY RHYME MONSTERS... hah!
NICE, IZZY! OKAY, uh--
WHAM
KRAK
THAK

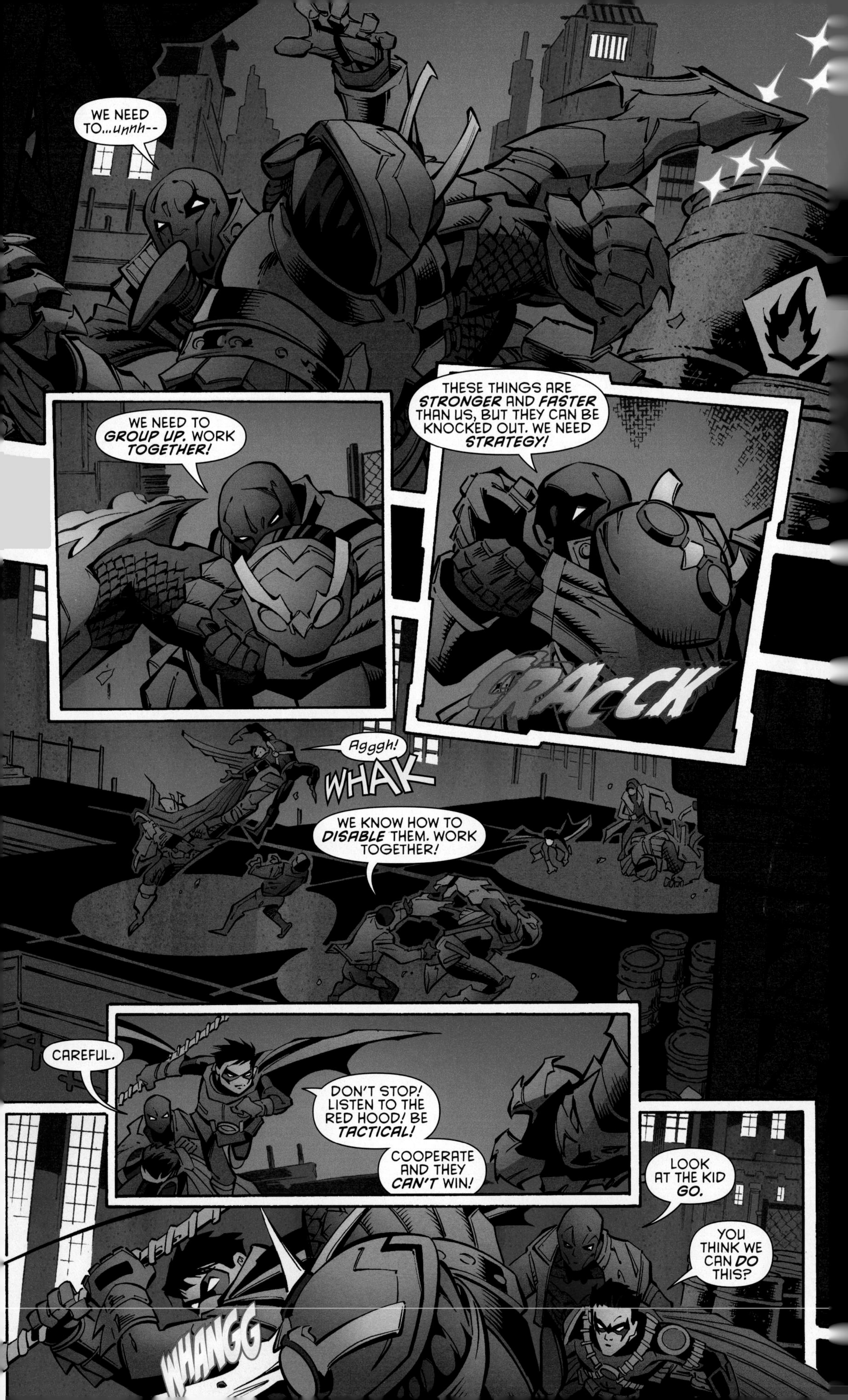
WE NEED TO...unnh--
WE NEED TO GROUP UP. WORK TOGETHER!
THESE THINGS ARE STRONGER AND FASTER THAN US, BUT THEY CAN BE KNOCKED OUT. WE NEED STRATEGY!
CRACCK
Agggh!
WHAK
WE KNOW HOW TO DISABLE THEM. WORK TOGETHER!
CAREFUL.
DON'T STOP! LISTEN TO THE RED HOOD! BE TACTICAL!
COOPERATE AND THEY CAN'T WIN!
LOOK AT THE KID GO.
YOU THINK WE CAN DO THIS?
WHANGG

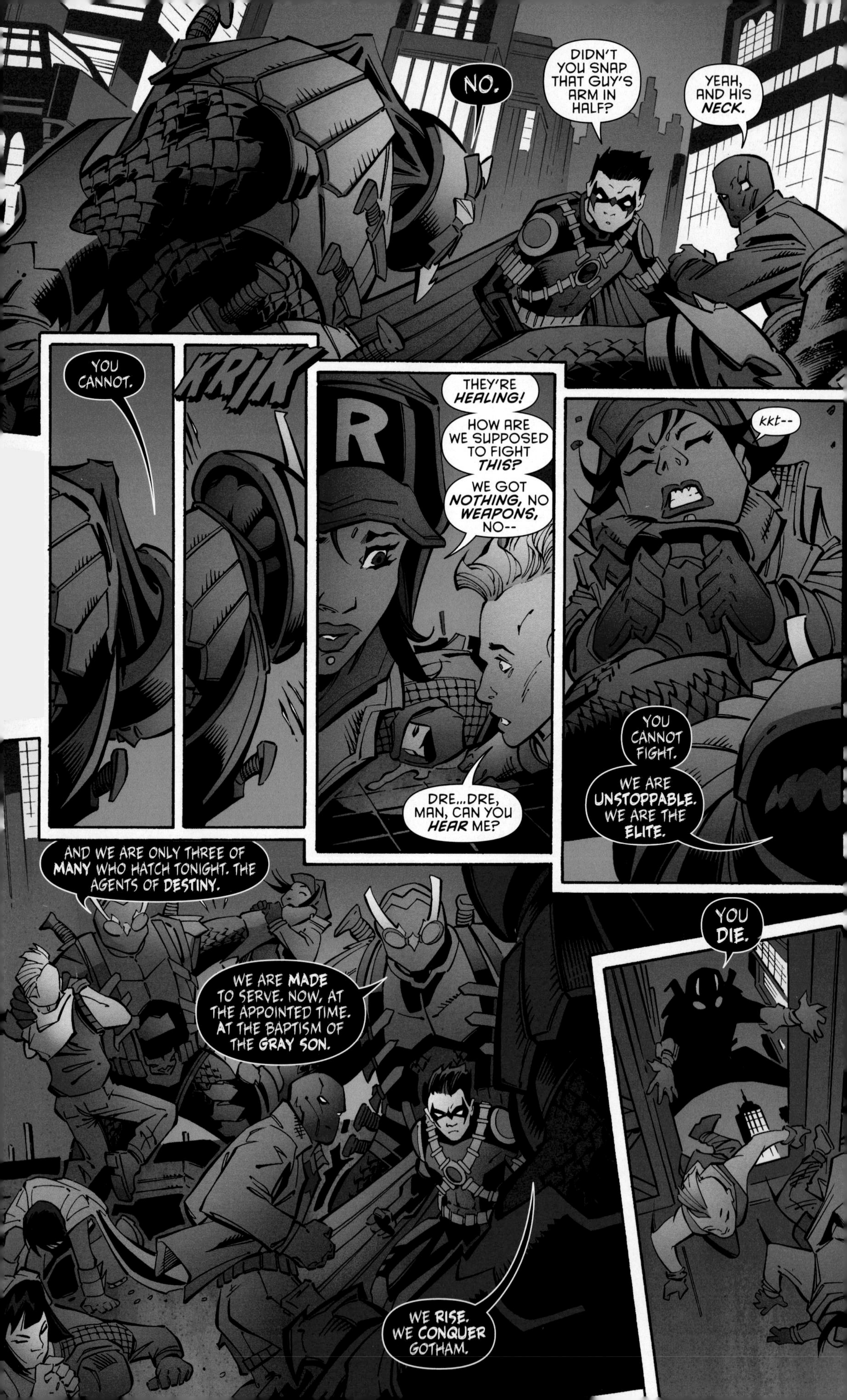
NO.
DIDN'T YOU SNAP THAT GUY'S ARM IN HALF?
YEAH, AND HIS *NECK.*
YOU CANNOT.
KRIK
THEY'RE *HEALING!*
HOW ARE WE SUPPOSED TO FIGHT *THIS?*
WE GOT *NOTHING,* NO *WEAPONS,* NO--
DRE...DRE, MAN, CAN YOU *HEAR* ME?
kkt--
YOU CANNOT FIGHT.
WE ARE **UNSTOPPABLE.** WE ARE THE **ELITE.**
AND WE ARE ONLY THREE OF **MANY** WHO HATCH TONIGHT. THE AGENTS OF **DESTINY.**
WE ARE **MADE** TO SERVE. NOW, AT THE APPOINTED TIME. AT THE BAPTISM OF THE **GRAY SON.**
YOU **DIE.**
WE **RISE.** WE **CONQUER** GOTHAM.

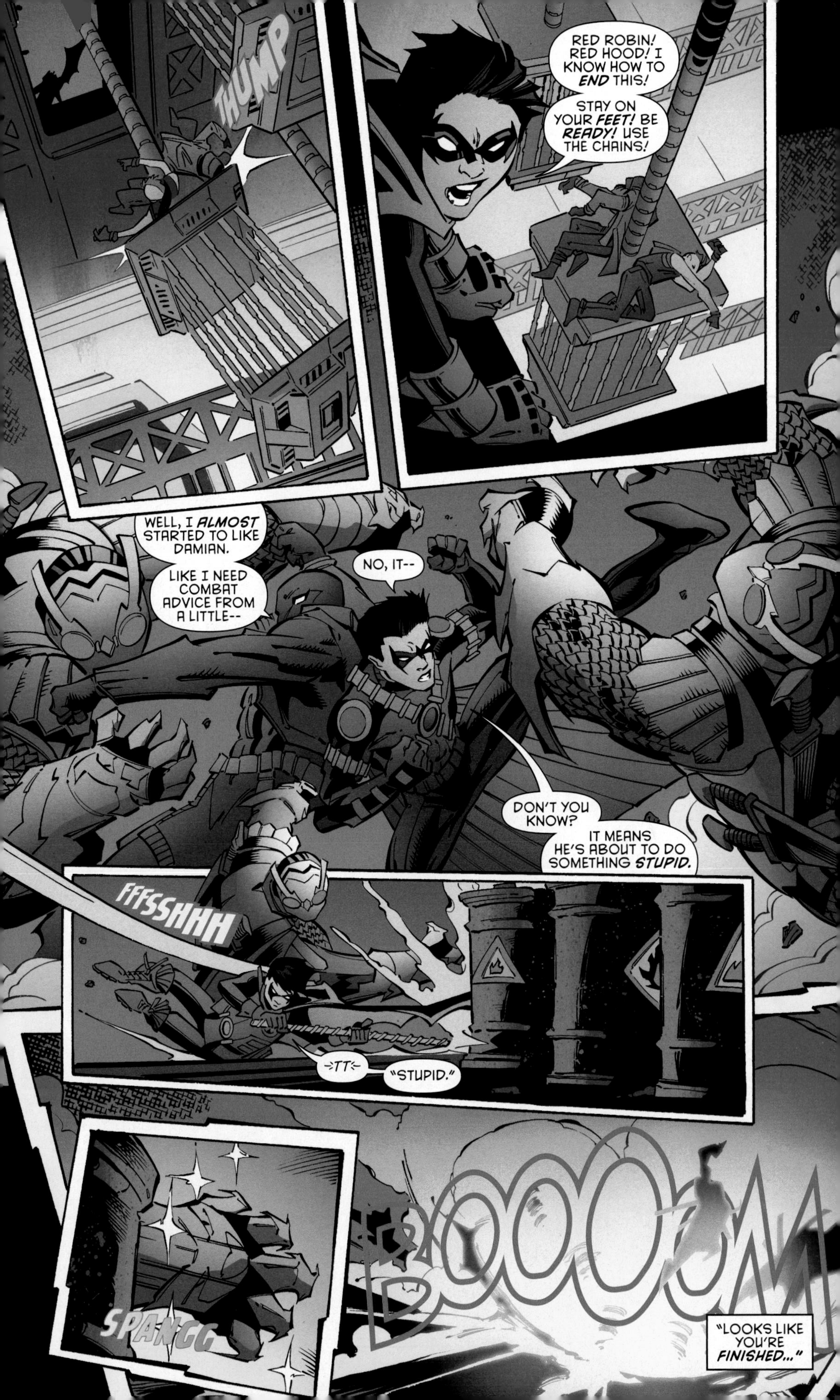
THUMP
RED ROBIN! RED HOOD! I KNOW HOW TO END THIS!
STAY ON YOUR FEET! BE READY! USE THE CHAINS!
WELL, I ALMOST STARTED TO LIKE DAMIAN.
LIKE I NEED COMBAT ADVICE FROM A LITTLE--
NO, IT--
DON'T YOU KNOW?
IT MEANS HE'S ABOUT TO DO SOMETHING STUPID.
FFFSSHHH
-TT-
"STUPID."
SPANGG
BOOOOOM
"LOOKS LIKE YOU'RE FINISHED..."

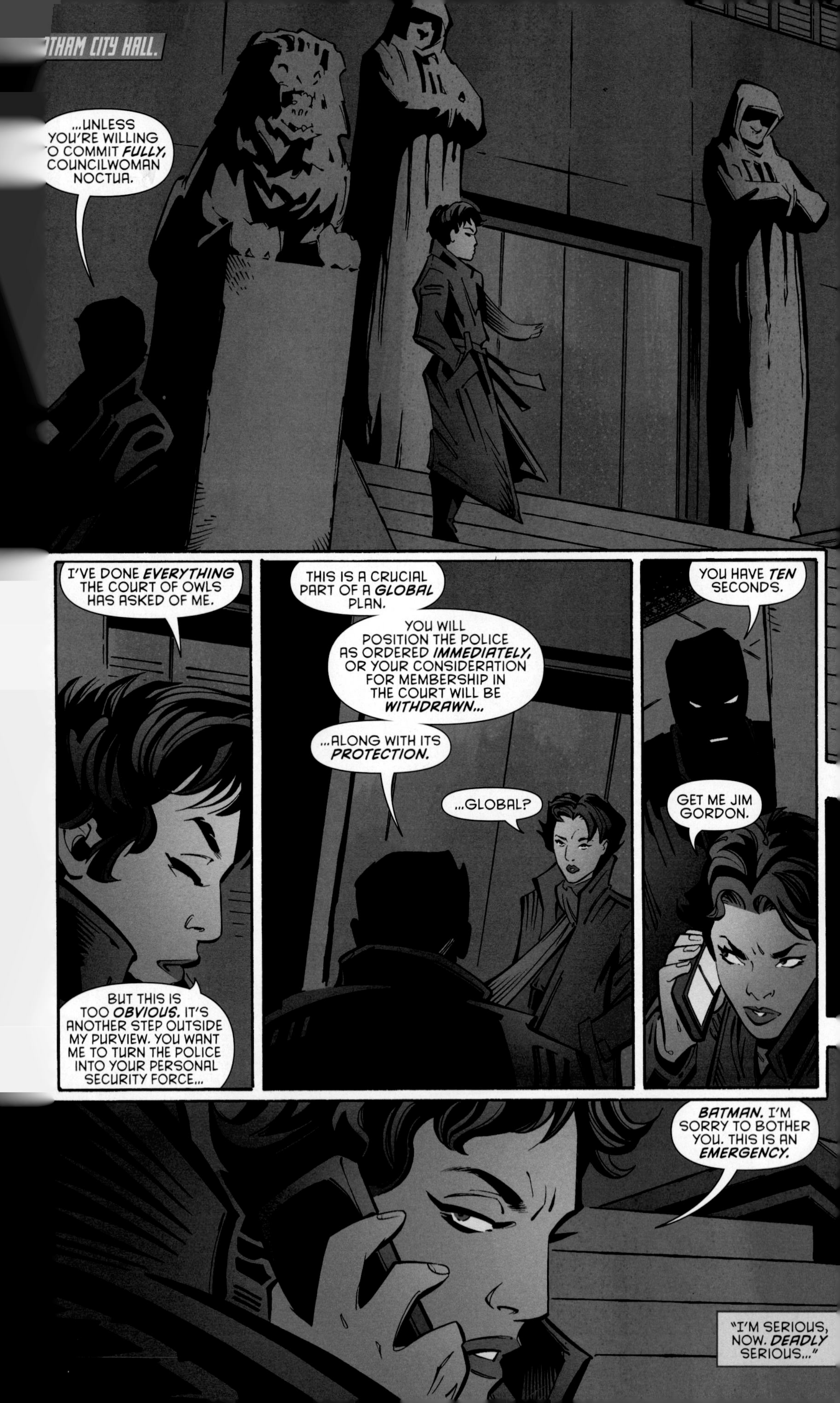
...THAM CITY HALL.
...UNLESS YOU'RE WILLING TO COMMIT FULLY, COUNCILWOMAN NOCTUA.
I'VE DONE EVERYTHING THE COURT OF OWLS HAS ASKED OF ME.
BUT THIS IS TOO OBVIOUS. IT'S ANOTHER STEP OUTSIDE MY PURVIEW. YOU WANT ME TO TURN THE POLICE INTO YOUR PERSONAL SECURITY FORCE...
THIS IS A CRUCIAL PART OF A GLOBAL PLAN.
YOU WILL POSITION THE POLICE AS ORDERED IMMEDIATELY, OR YOUR CONSIDERATION FOR MEMBERSHIP IN THE COURT WILL BE WITHDRAWN...
...ALONG WITH ITS PROTECTION.
...GLOBAL?
YOU HAVE TEN SECONDS.
GET ME JIM GORDON.
BATMAN. I'M SORRY TO BOTHER YOU. THIS IS AN EMERGENCY.
"I'M SERIOUS, NOW. DEADLY SERIOUS..."

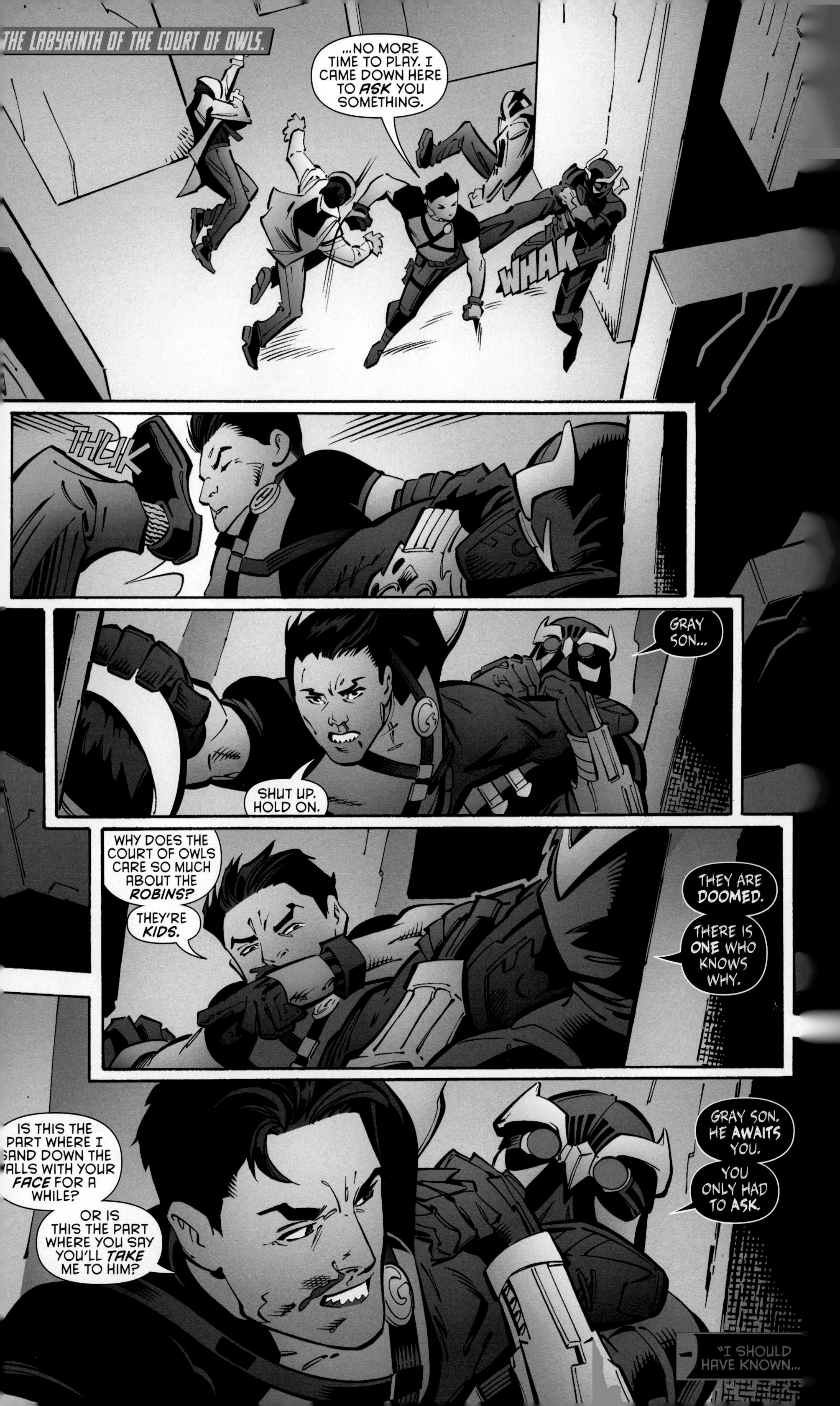
THE LABYRINTH OF THE COURT OF OWLS.
...NO MORE TIME TO PLAY. I CAME DOWN HERE TO ASK YOU SOMETHING.
WHAK
THUK
GRAY SON...
SHUT UP. HOLD ON.
WHY DOES THE COURT OF OWLS CARE SO MUCH ABOUT THE ROBINS?
THEY'RE KIDS.
THEY ARE DOOMED.
THERE IS ONE WHO KNOWS WHY.
IS THIS THE PART WHERE I SAND DOWN THE WALLS WITH YOUR FACE FOR A WHILE?
OR IS THIS THE PART WHERE YOU SAY YOU'LL TAKE ME TO HIM?
GRAY SON. HE AWAITS YOU.
YOU ONLY HAD TO ASK.
"I SHOULD HAVE KNOWN...

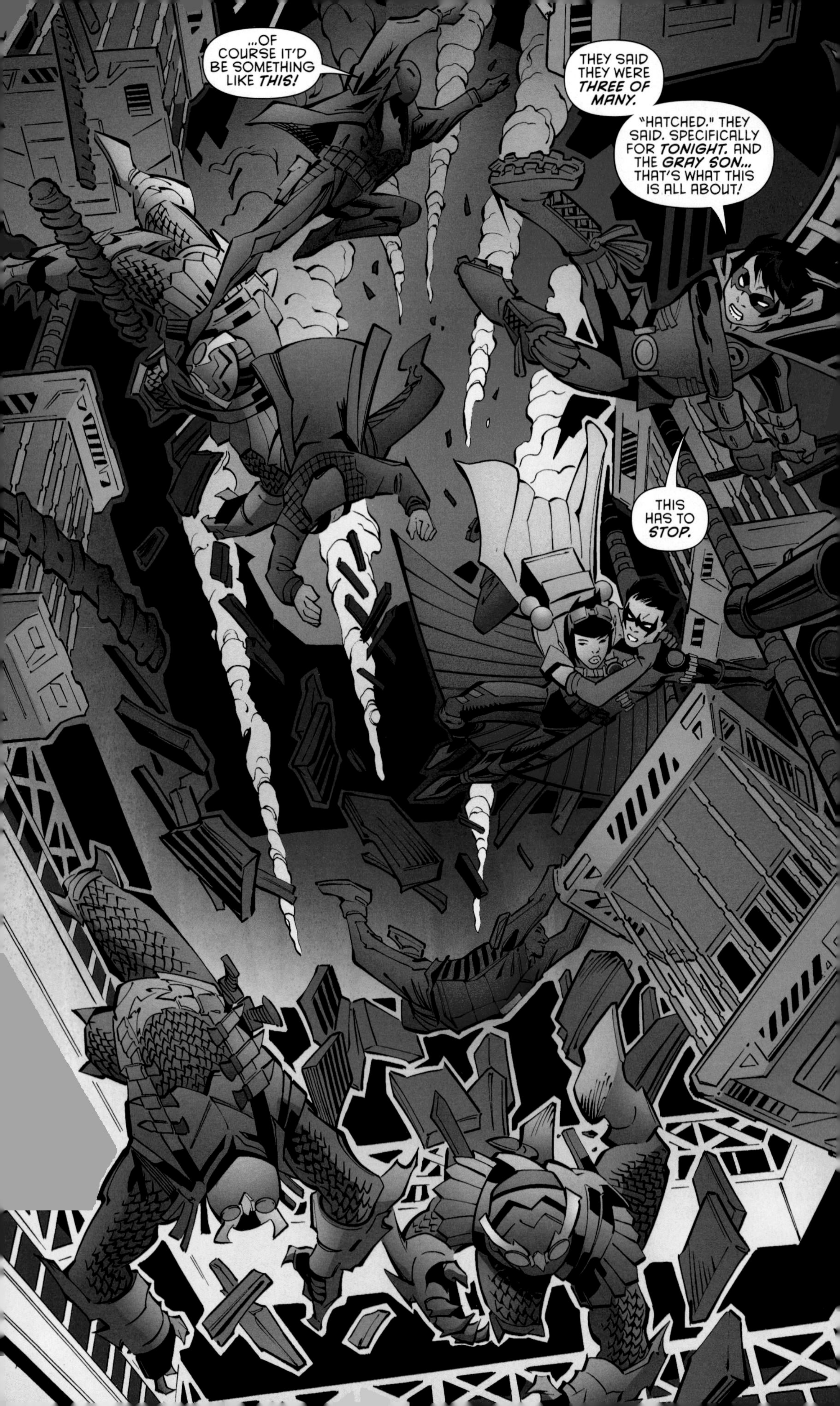
...OF COURSE IT'D BE SOMETHING LIKE *THIS!*
THEY SAID THEY WERE *THREE OF MANY.*
"HATCHED." THEY SAID. SPECIFICALLY FOR *TONIGHT.* AND THE *GRAY SON...* THAT'S WHAT THIS IS ALL ABOUT!
THIS HAS TO *STOP.*

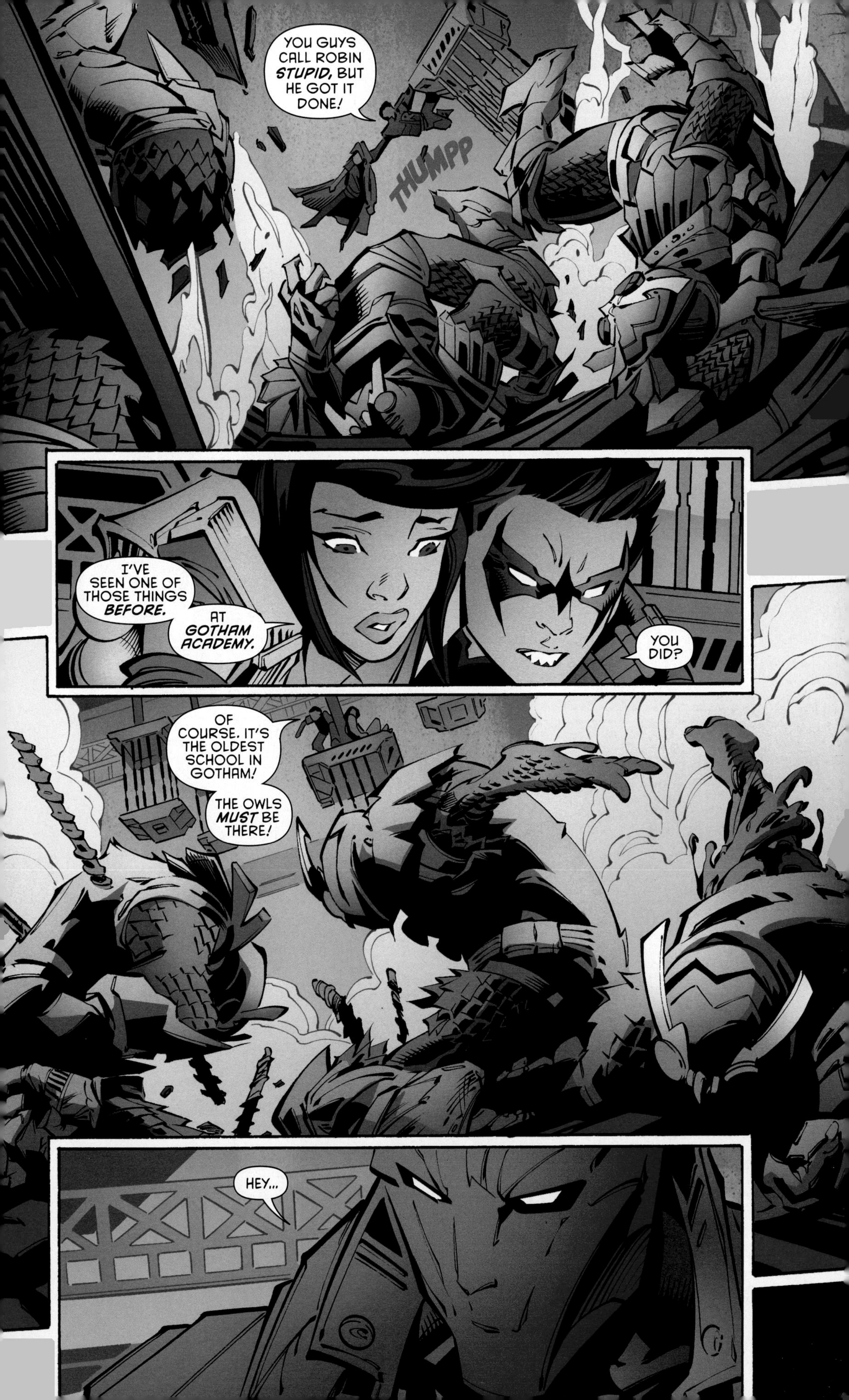
YOU GUYS CALL ROBIN STUPID, BUT HE GOT IT DONE!
THUMPP
I'VE SEEN ONE OF THOSE THINGS BEFORE.
AT GOTHAM ACADEMY.
YOU DID?
OF COURSE. IT'S THE OLDEST SCHOOL IN GOTHAM!
THE OWLS MUST BE THERE!
HEY...

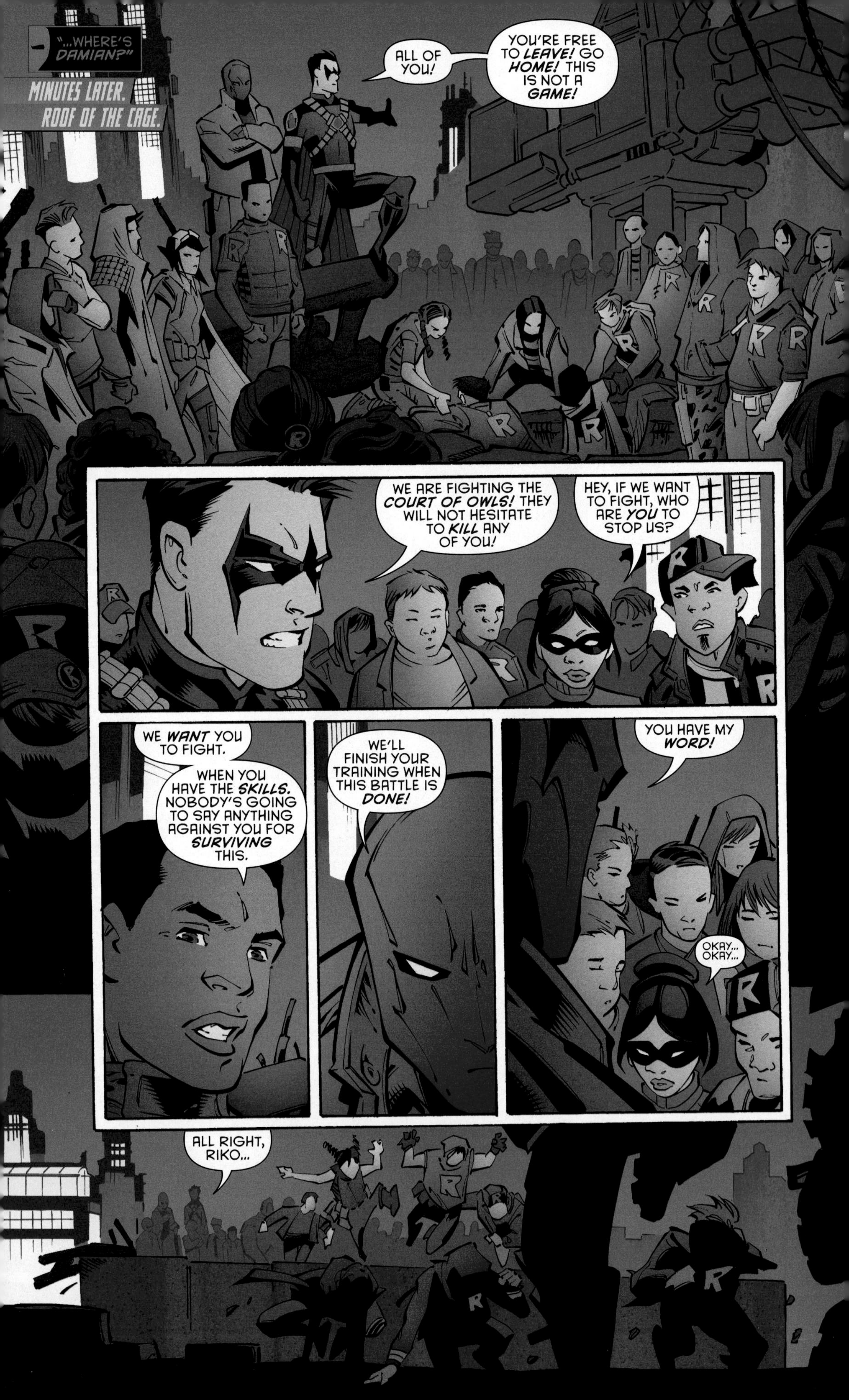
"...WHERE'S DAMIAN?"
MINUTES LATER.
ROOF OF THE CAGE.
YOU'RE FREE TO LEAVE! GO HOME! THIS IS NOT A GAME!
ALL OF YOU!
WE ARE FIGHTING THE COURT OF OWLS! THEY WILL NOT HESITATE TO KILL ANY OF YOU!
HEY, IF WE WANT TO FIGHT, WHO ARE YOU TO STOP US?
WE WANT YOU TO FIGHT.
WHEN YOU HAVE THE SKILLS. NOBODY'S GOING TO SAY ANYTHING AGAINST YOU FOR SURVIVING THIS.
WE'LL FINISH YOUR TRAINING WHEN THIS BATTLE IS DONE!
YOU HAVE MY WORD!
OKAY... OKAY...
ALL RIGHT, RIKO...

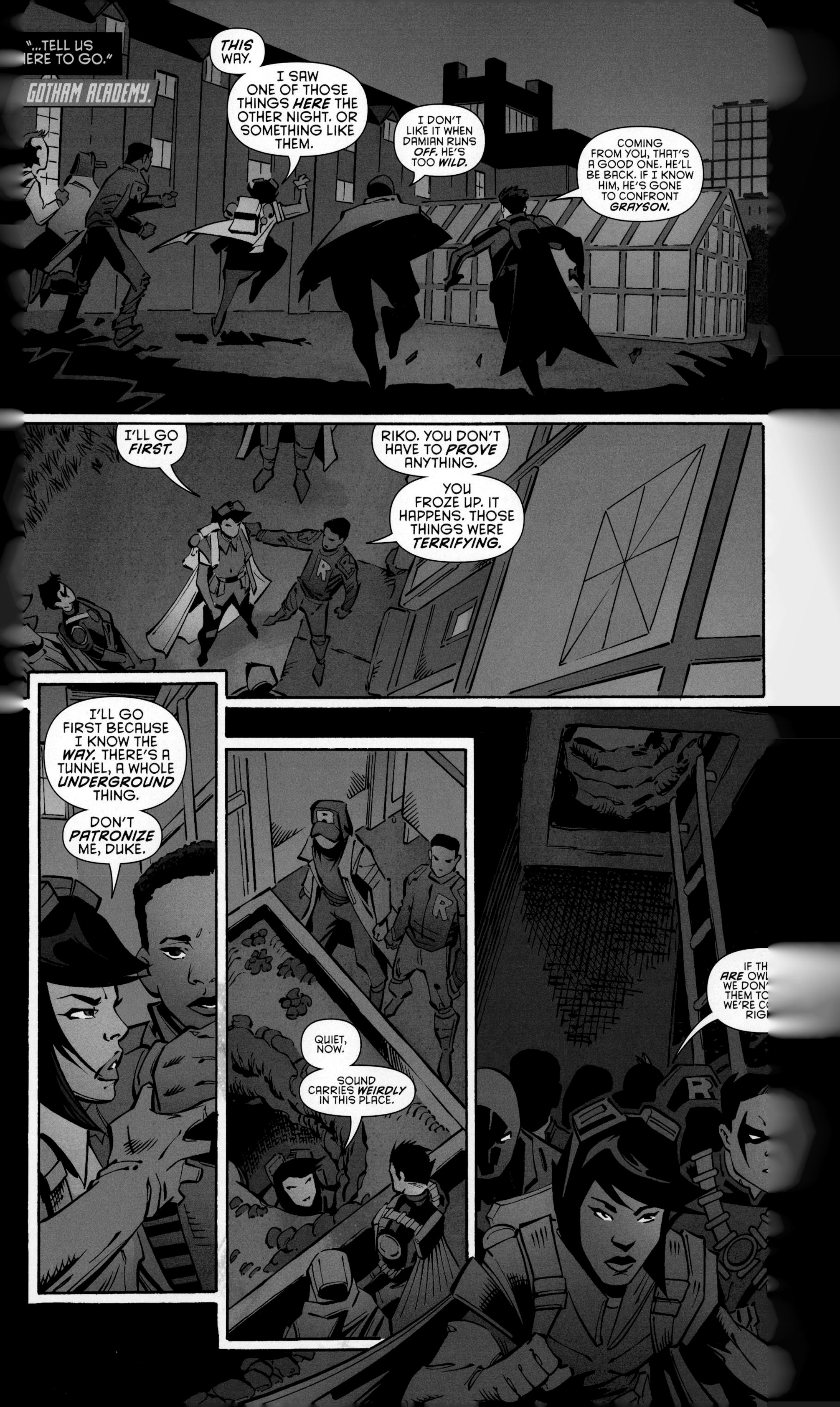

"...TELL US
ERE TO GO."
GOTHAM ACADEMY.
THIS WAY.
I SAW ONE OF THOSE THINGS HERE THE OTHER NIGHT. OR SOMETHING LIKE THEM.
I DON'T LIKE IT WHEN DAMIAN RUNS OFF. HE'S TOO WILD.
COMING FROM YOU, THAT'S A GOOD ONE. HE'LL BE BACK. IF I KNOW HIM, HE'S GONE TO CONFRONT GRAYSON.
I'LL GO FIRST.
RIKO. YOU DON'T HAVE TO PROVE ANYTHING.
YOU FROZE UP. IT HAPPENS. THOSE THINGS WERE TERRIFYING.
I'LL GO FIRST BECAUSE I KNOW THE WAY. THERE'S A TUNNEL, A WHOLE UNDERGROUND THING.
DON'T PATRONIZE ME, DUKE.
QUIET, NOW.
SOUND CARRIES WEIRDLY IN THIS PLACE.

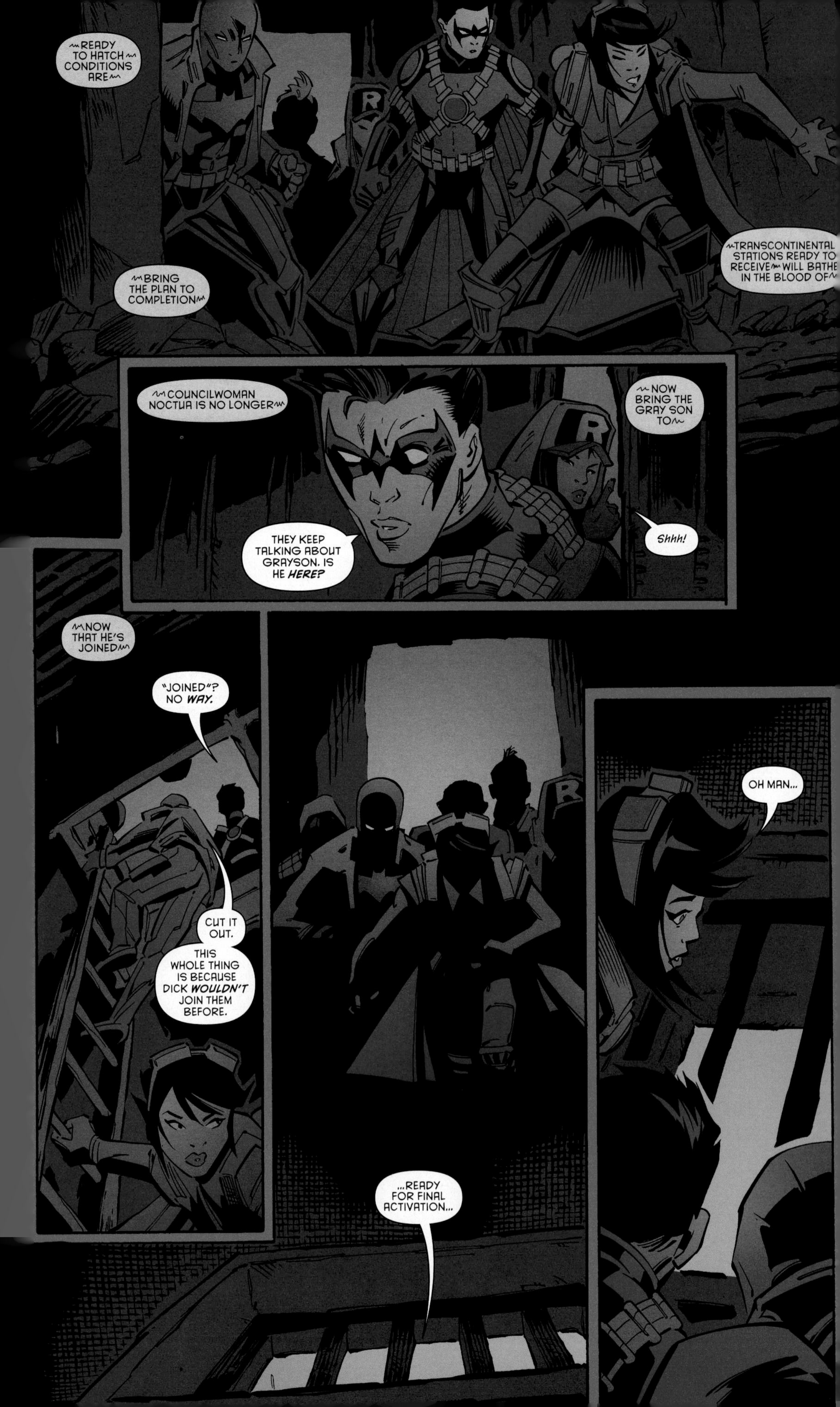
~READY TO HATCH~ CONDITIONS ARE~
~BRING THE PLAN TO COMPLETION~
~TRANSCONTINENTAL STATIONS READY TO RECEIVE~ WILL BATHE IN THE BLOOD OF~
~COUNCILWOMAN NOCTUA IS NO LONGER~
~NOW BRING THE GRAY SON TO~
THEY KEEP TALKING ABOUT GRAYSON. IS HE *HERE?*
Shhh!
~NOW THAT HE'S JOINED~
"JOINED"? NO *WAY.*
CUT IT OUT.
THIS WHOLE THING IS BECAUSE DICK *WOULDN'T* JOIN THEM BEFORE.
OH MAN...
...READY FOR FINAL ACTIVATION...

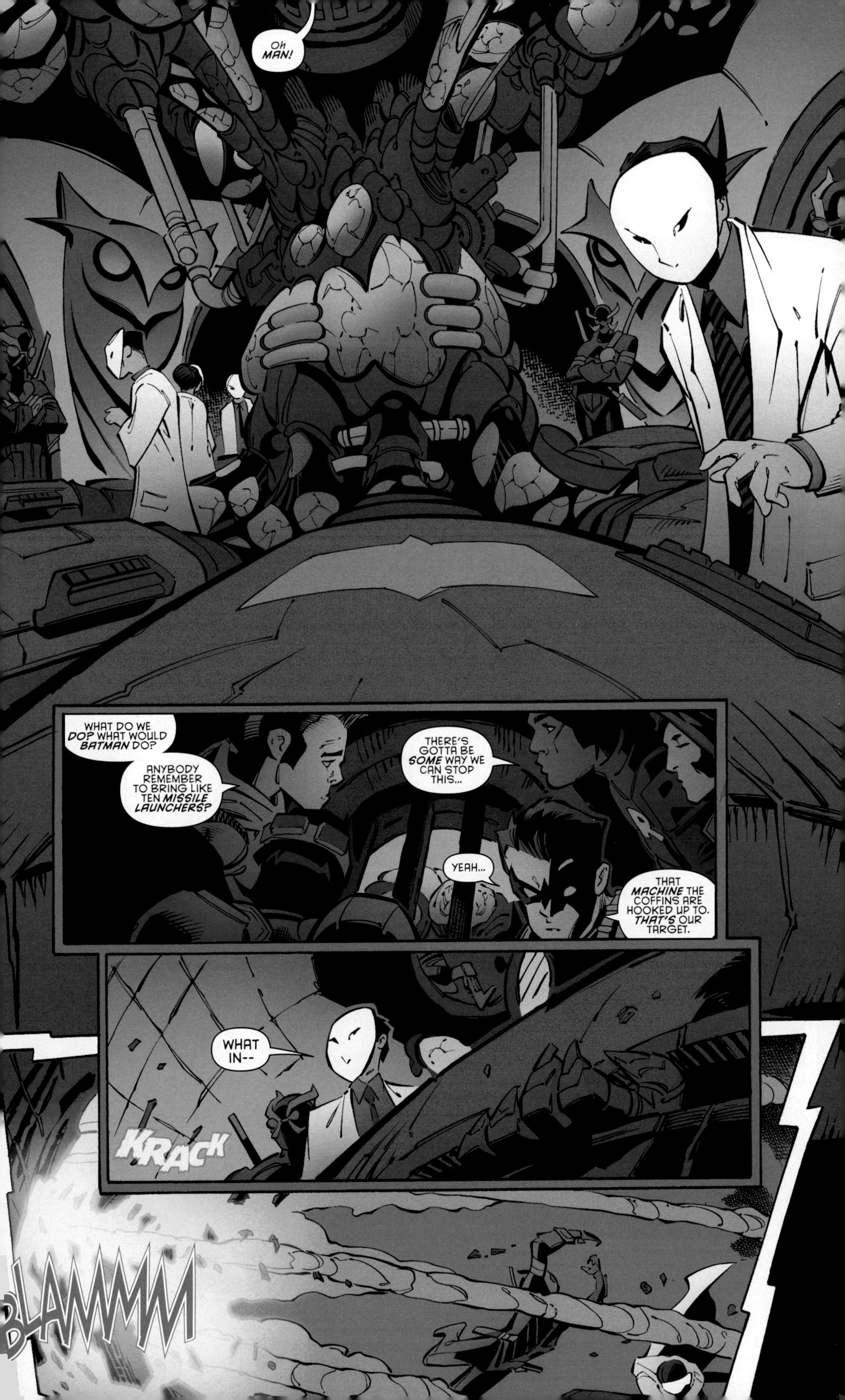
Oh MAN!
WHAT DO WE DO? WHAT WOULD BATMAN DO?
ANYBODY REMEMBER TO BRING LIKE TEN MISSILE LAUNCHERS?
THERE'S GOTTA BE SOME WAY WE CAN STOP THIS...
YEAH...
THAT MACHINE THE COFFINS ARE HOOKED UP TO. THAT'S OUR TARGET.
WHAT IN--
KRACK
BLAMMM

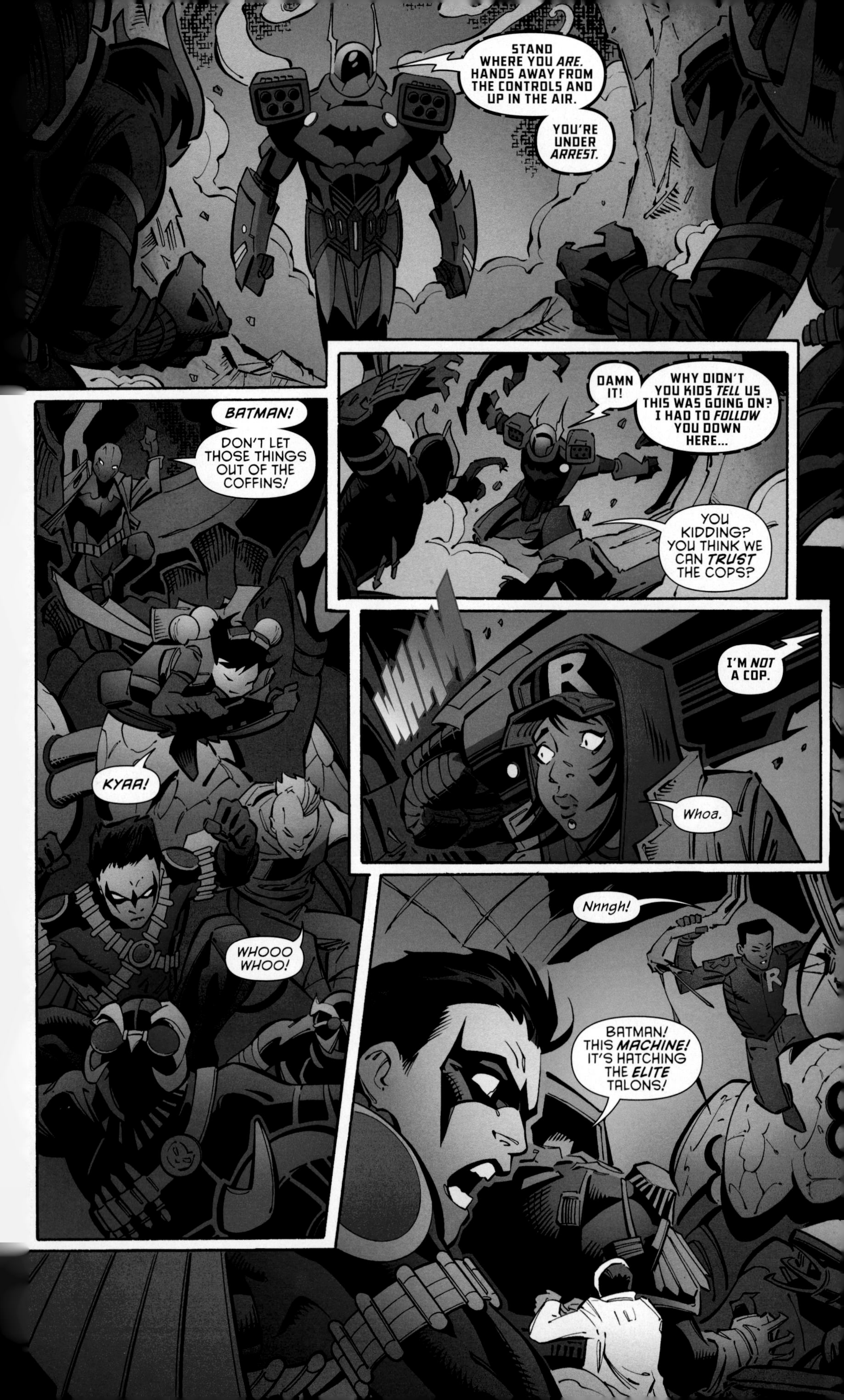
STAND WHERE YOU *ARE*. HANDS AWAY FROM THE CONTROLS AND UP IN THE AIR.
YOU'RE UNDER *ARREST*.
BATMAN!
DON'T LET THOSE THINGS OUT OF THE COFFINS!
DAMN IT!
WHY DIDN'T YOU KIDS *TELL* US THIS WAS GOING ON? I HAD TO *FOLLOW* YOU DOWN HERE...
YOU KIDDING? YOU THINK WE CAN *TRUST* THE COPS?
WHAM
I'M *NOT* A COP.
Whoa.
KYAA!
WHOOO WHOO!
Nnngh!
BATMAN! THIS *MACHINE!* IT'S HATCHING THE *ELITE* TALONS!

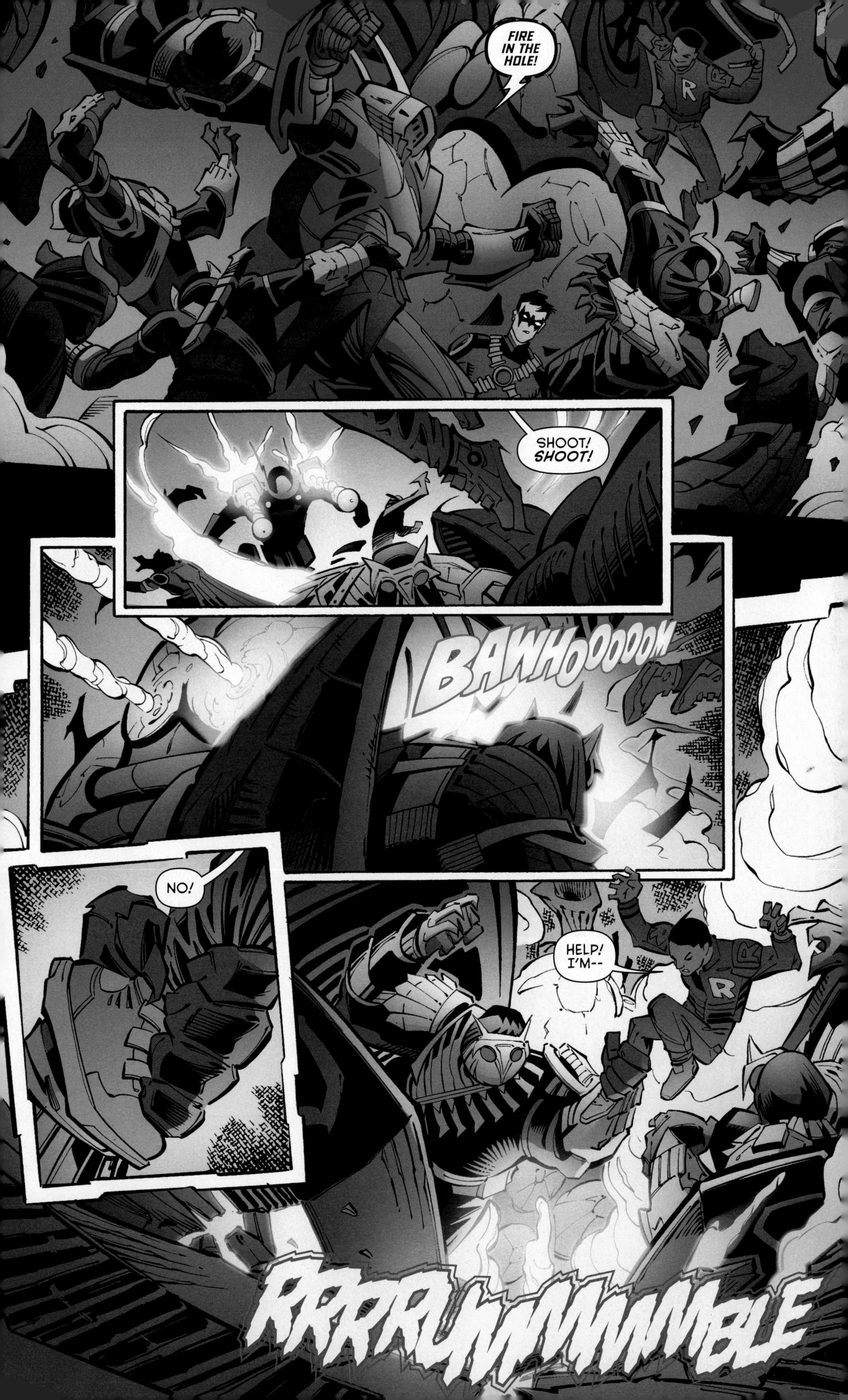
FIRE IN THE HOLE!
SHOOT! SHOOT!
BAWHOOOOOM
NO!
HELP! I'M--
RRRRUMMMMMBLE

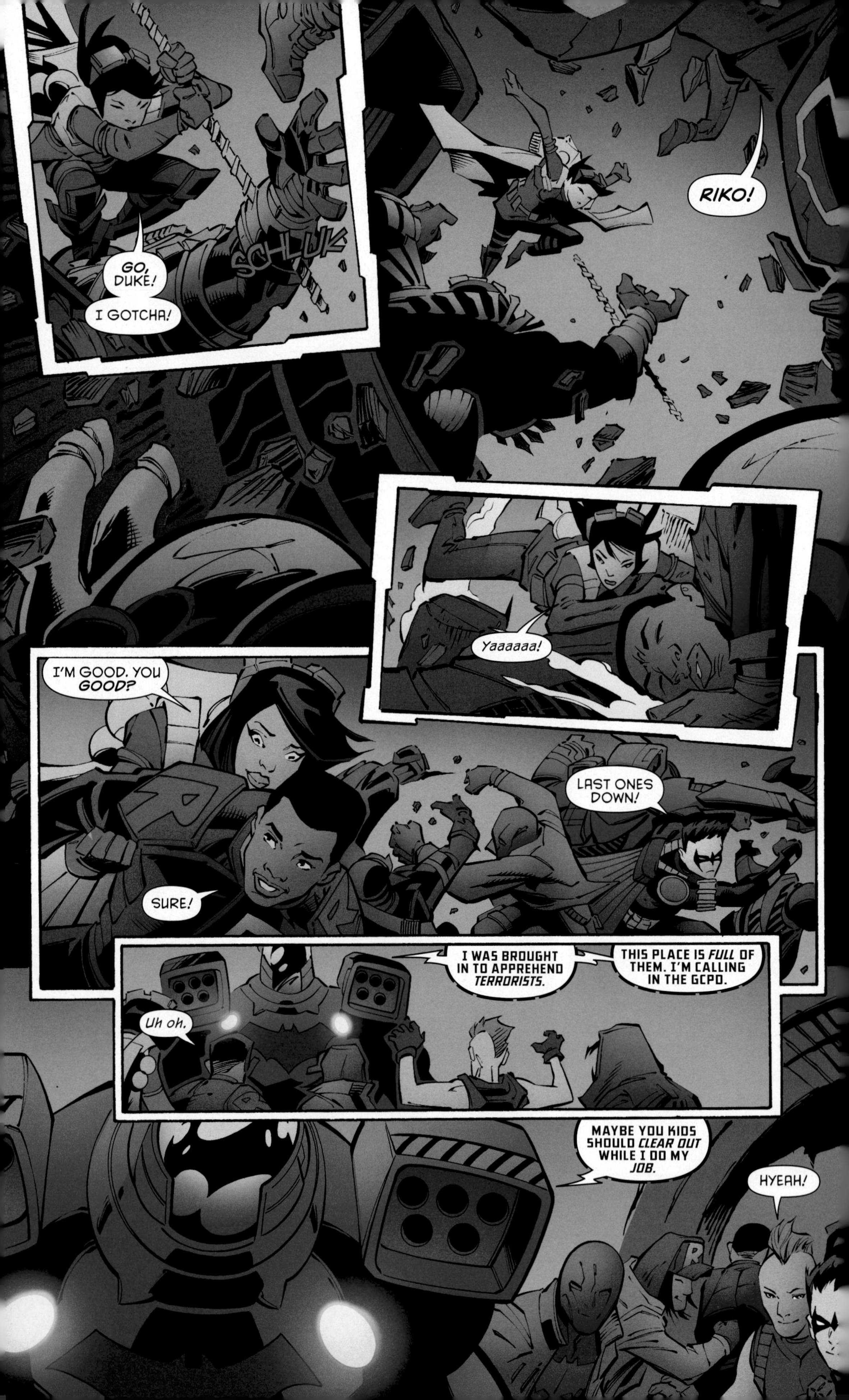
GO, DUKE!
I GOTCHA!
SCHLUK
RIKO!
Yaaaaaa!
I'M GOOD. YOU GOOD?
SURE!
LAST ONES DOWN!
Uh oh.
I WAS BROUGHT IN TO APPREHEND TERRORISTS.
THIS PLACE IS FULL OF THEM. I'M CALLING IN THE GCPD.
MAYBE YOU KIDS SHOULD CLEAR OUT WHILE I DO MY JOB.
HYEAH!

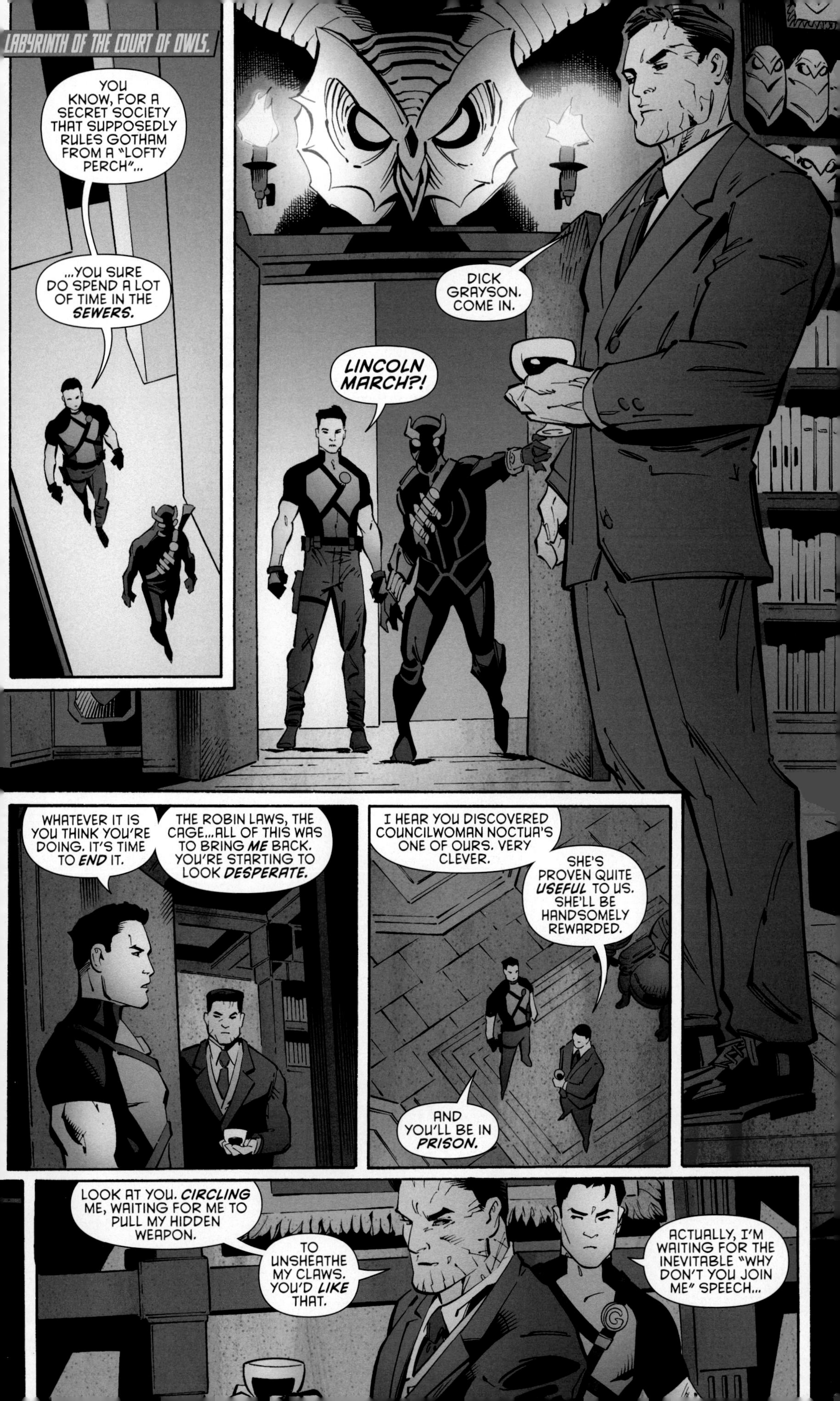
LABYRINTH OF THE COURT OF OWLS.
YOU KNOW, FOR A SECRET SOCIETY THAT SUPPOSEDLY RULES GOTHAM FROM A "LOFTY PERCH"...
...YOU SURE DO SPEND A LOT OF TIME IN THE SEWERS.
DICK GRAYSON. COME IN.
LINCOLN MARCH?!
WHATEVER IT IS YOU THINK YOU'RE DOING. IT'S TIME TO END IT.
THE ROBIN LAWS, THE CAGE...ALL OF THIS WAS TO BRING ME BACK. YOU'RE STARTING TO LOOK DESPERATE.
I HEAR YOU DISCOVERED COUNCILWOMAN NOCTUA'S ONE OF OURS. VERY CLEVER.
SHE'S PROVEN QUITE USEFUL TO US. SHE'LL BE HANDSOMELY REWARDED.
AND YOU'LL BE IN PRISON.
LOOK AT YOU. CIRCLING ME, WAITING FOR ME TO PULL MY HIDDEN WEAPON.
TO UNSHEATHE MY CLAWS. YOU'D LIKE THAT.
ACTUALLY, I'M WAITING FOR THE INEVITABLE "WHY DON'T YOU JOIN ME" SPEECH...

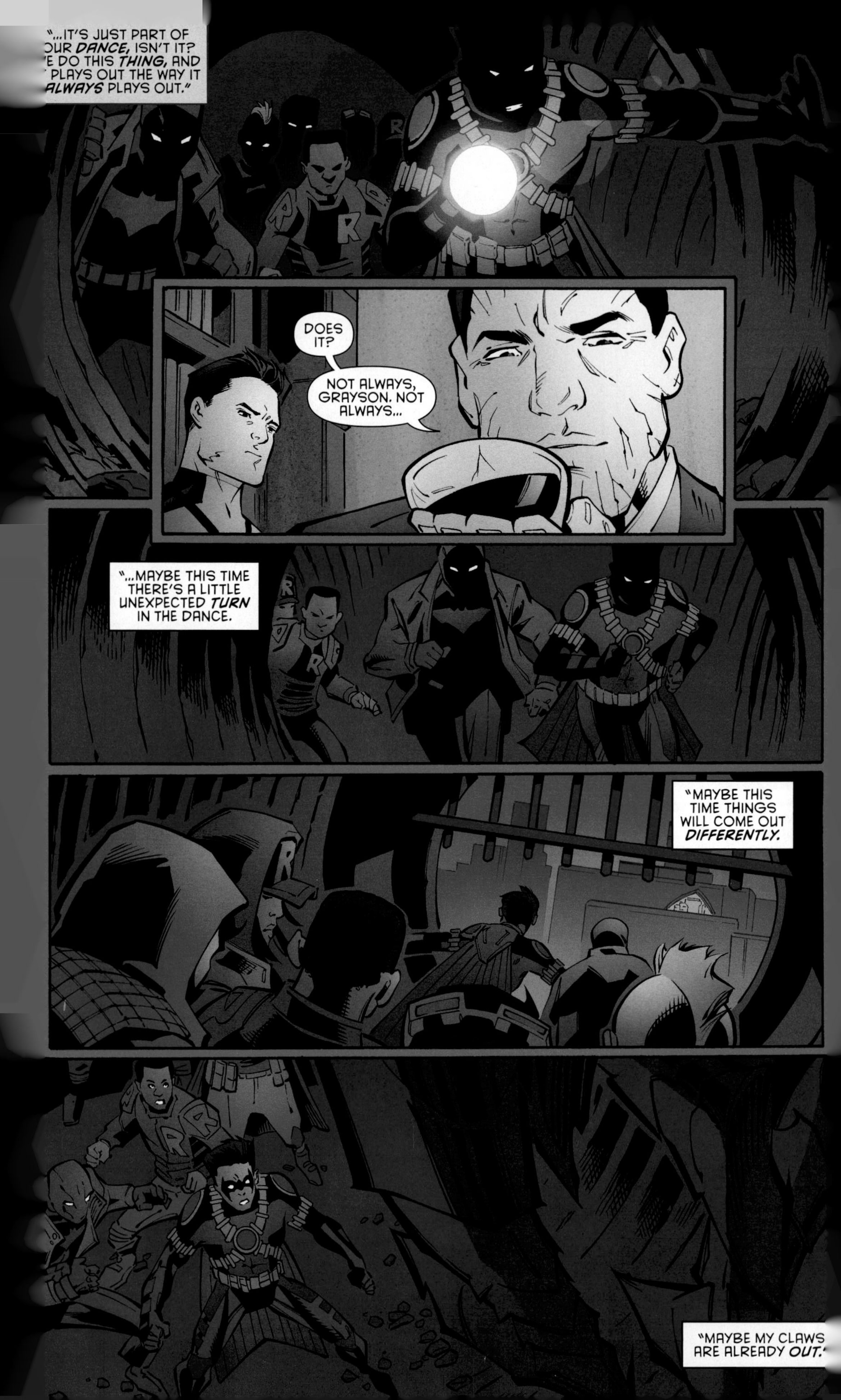

"...IT'S JUST PART OF OUR DANCE, ISN'T IT? WE DO THIS THING, AND IT PLAYS OUT THE WAY IT ALWAYS PLAYS OUT."
DOES IT?
NOT ALWAYS, GRAYSON. NOT ALWAYS...
"...MAYBE THIS TIME THERE'S A LITTLE UNEXPECTED TURN IN THE DANCE.
"MAYBE THIS TIME THINGS WILL COME OUT DIFFERENTLY.
"MAYBE MY CLAWS ARE ALREADY OUT."

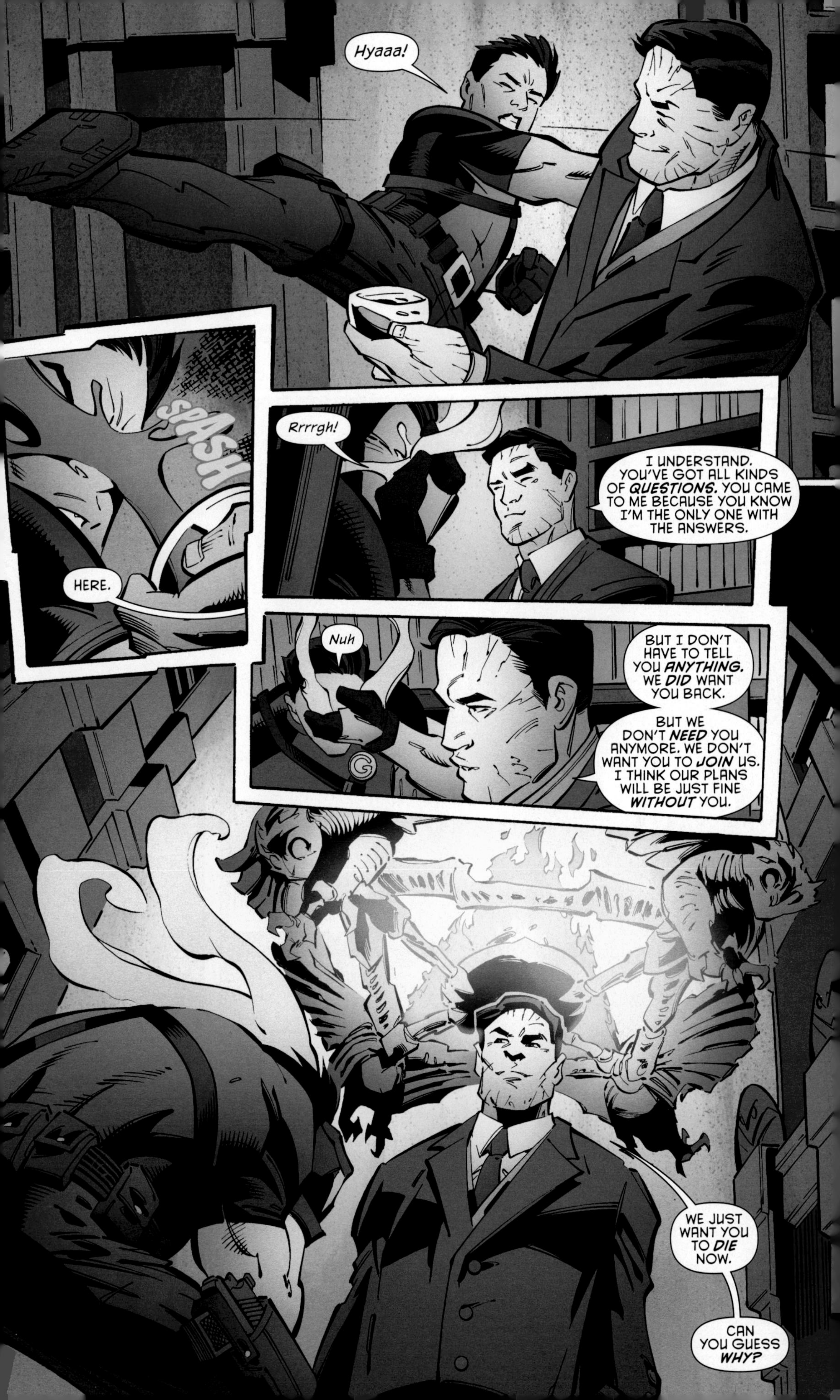
Hyaaa!
SPASH
HERE.
Rrrrgh!
I UNDERSTAND. YOU'VE GOT ALL KINDS OF QUESTIONS. YOU CAME TO ME BECAUSE YOU KNOW I'M THE ONLY ONE WITH THE ANSWERS.
Nuh
BUT I DON'T HAVE TO TELL YOU ANYTHING. WE DID WANT YOU BACK.
BUT WE DON'T NEED YOU ANYMORE. WE DON'T WANT YOU TO JOIN US. I THINK OUR PLANS WILL BE JUST FINE WITHOUT YOU.
WE JUST WANT YOU TO DIE NOW.
CAN YOU GUESS WHY?

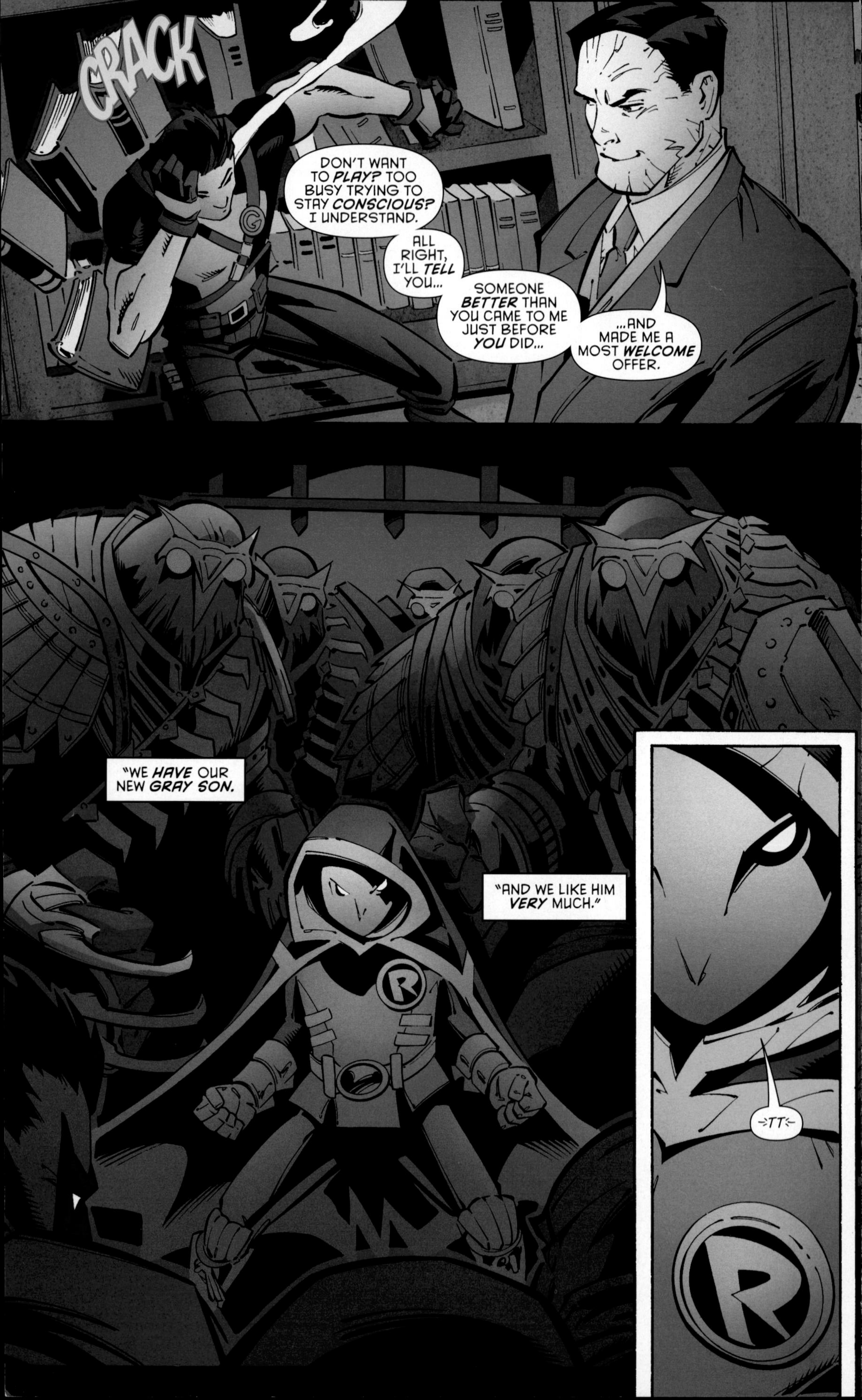
CRACK
DON'T WANT TO PLAY? TOO BUSY TRYING TO STAY CONSCIOUS? I UNDERSTAND.
ALL RIGHT, I'LL TELL YOU...
SOMEONE BETTER THAN YOU CAME TO ME JUST BEFORE YOU DID...
...AND MADE ME A MOST WELCOME OFFER.
"WE HAVE OUR NEW GRAY SON.
"AND WE LIKE HIM VERY MUCH."
TT

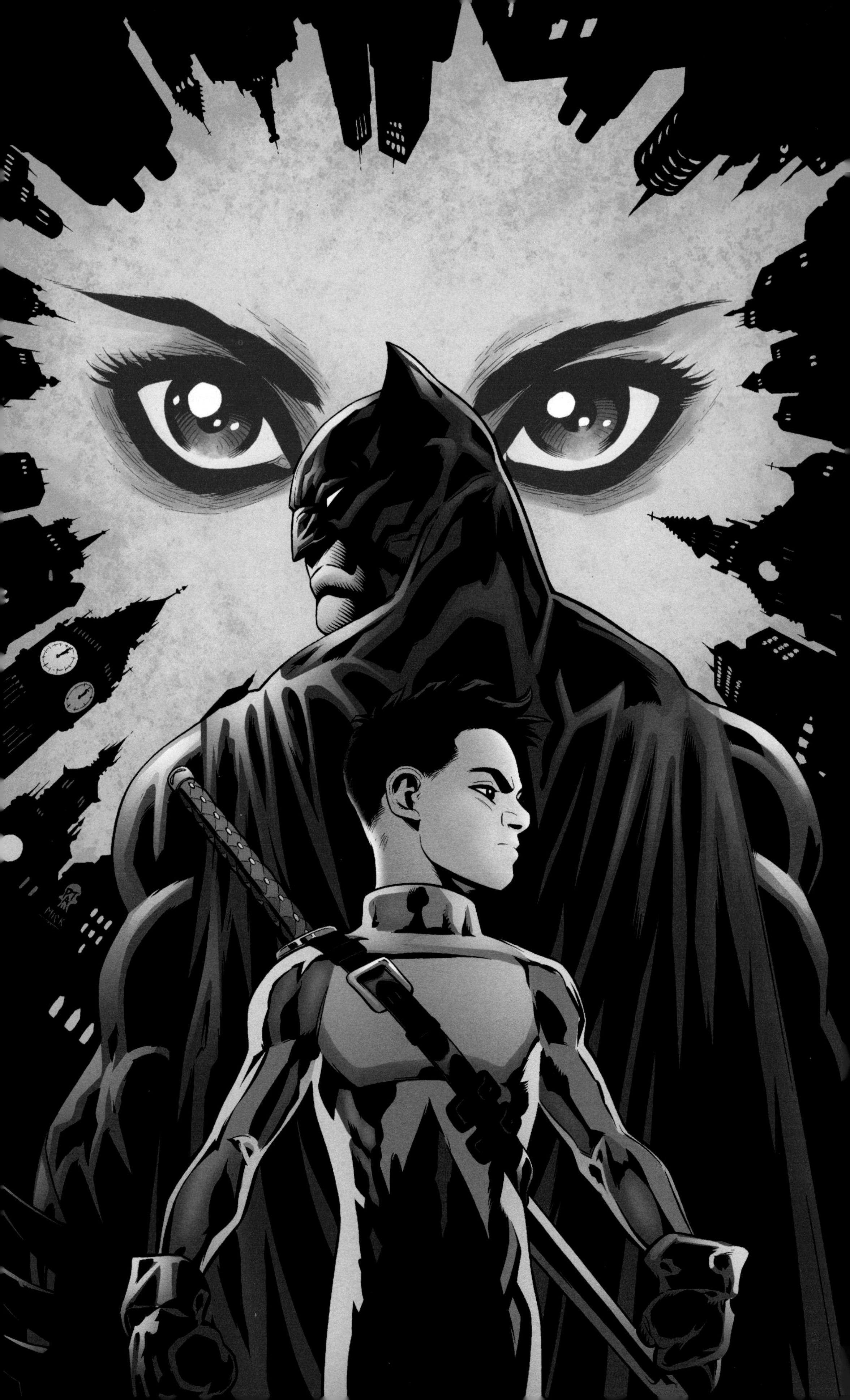

BETTER ANGELS

PATRICK GLEASON writer & penciller **MICK GRAY** inker **JOHN KALISZ** colorist **TOM NAPOLITANO** letterer **PATRICK GLEASON, MICK GRAY & JOHN KALISZ** cover

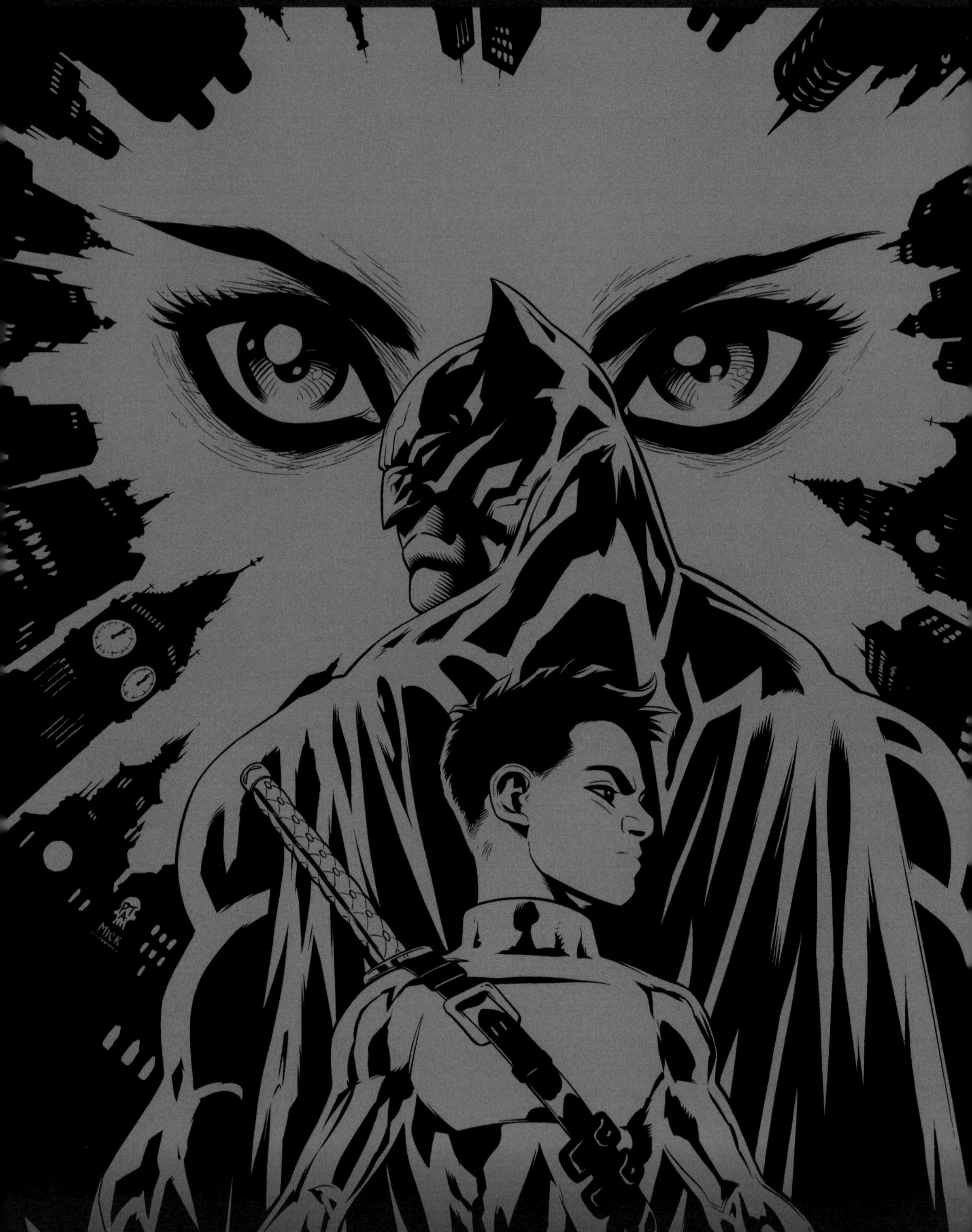

PREVIOUSLY IN ROBIN WAR...

As the war between the Court of Owls and the Robins escalated, a seemingly evil Damian fought a pitched battle with Duke, leader of the Robin vigilante movement. Despite a severe beating from Damian, Duke convinced the son of Batman that he was the true Robin and freed him from the Owls' talons. Unbeknownst to everyone, Dick joined the Court of Owls in order to bring an end to the Robin Laws and peace to Gotham City once again.

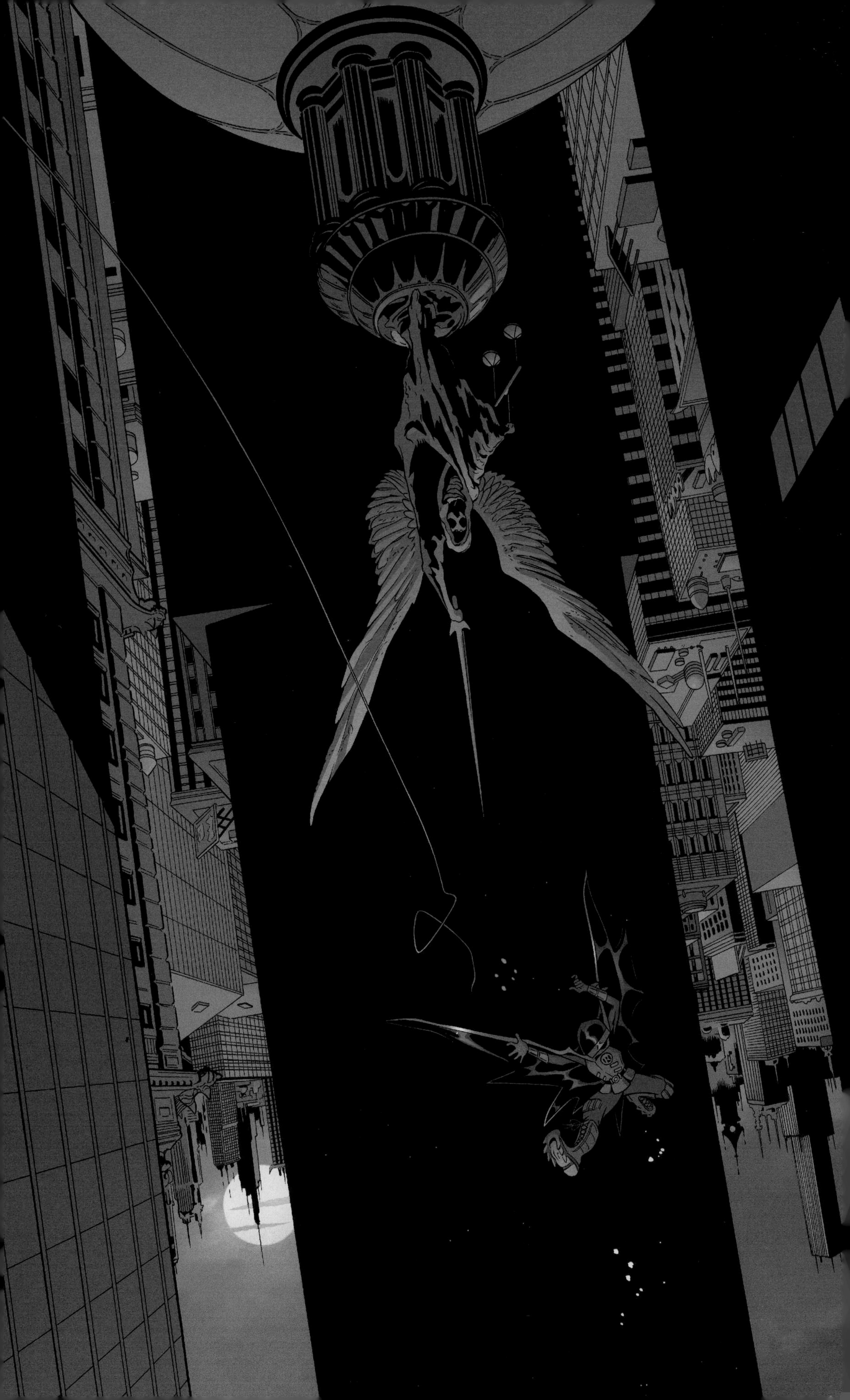

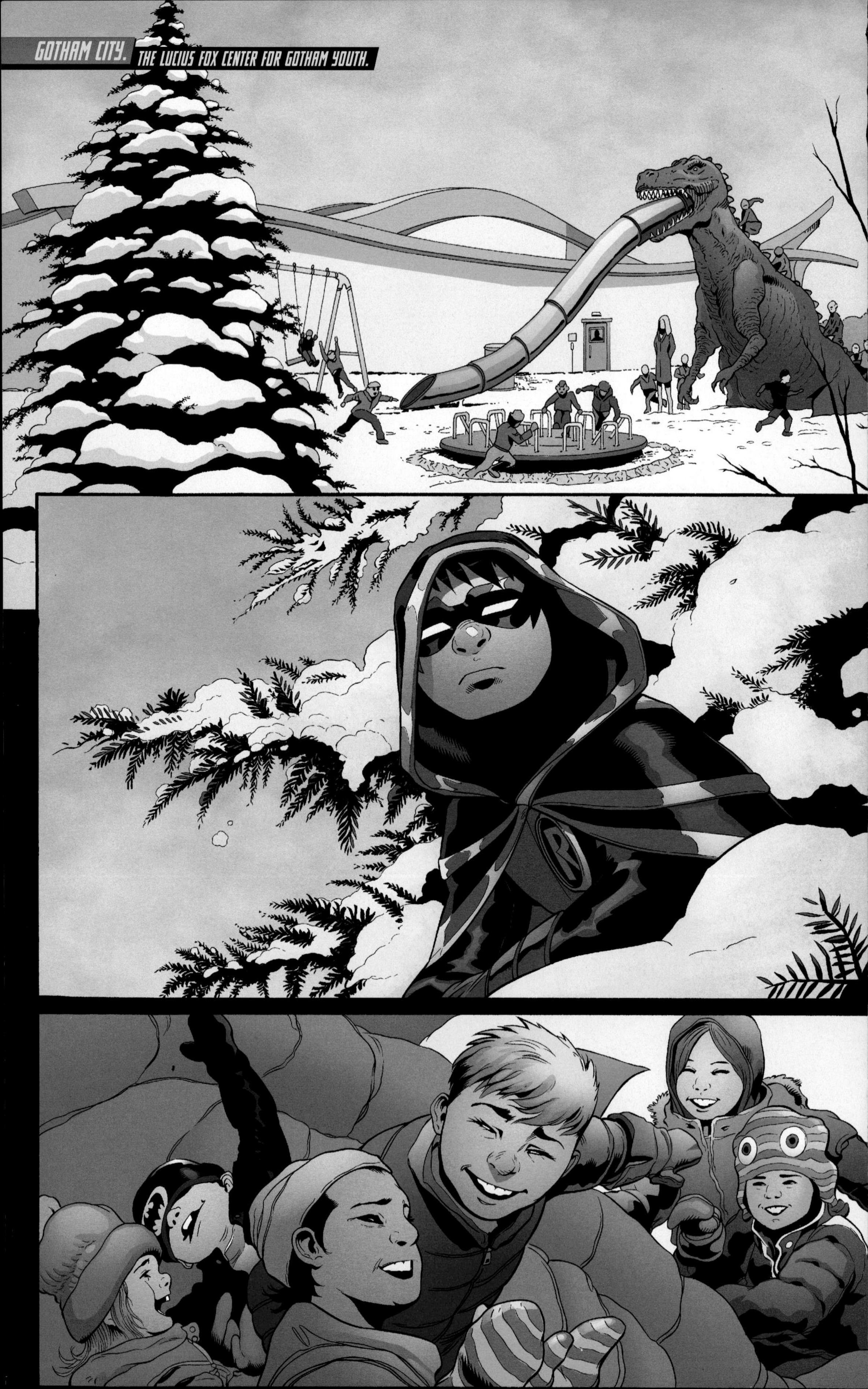
GOTHAM CITY.
THE LUCIUS FOX CENTER FOR GOTHAM YOUTH.

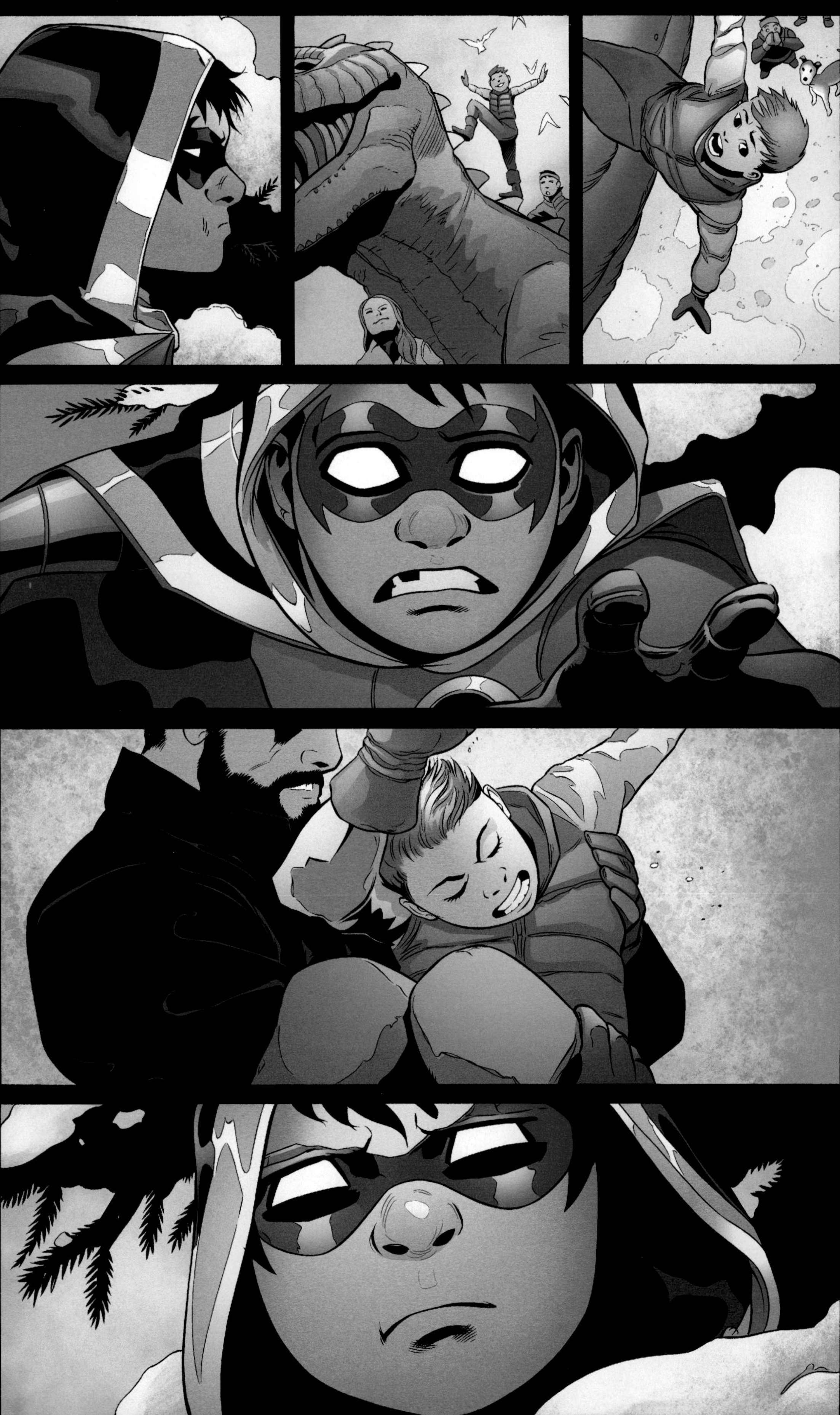

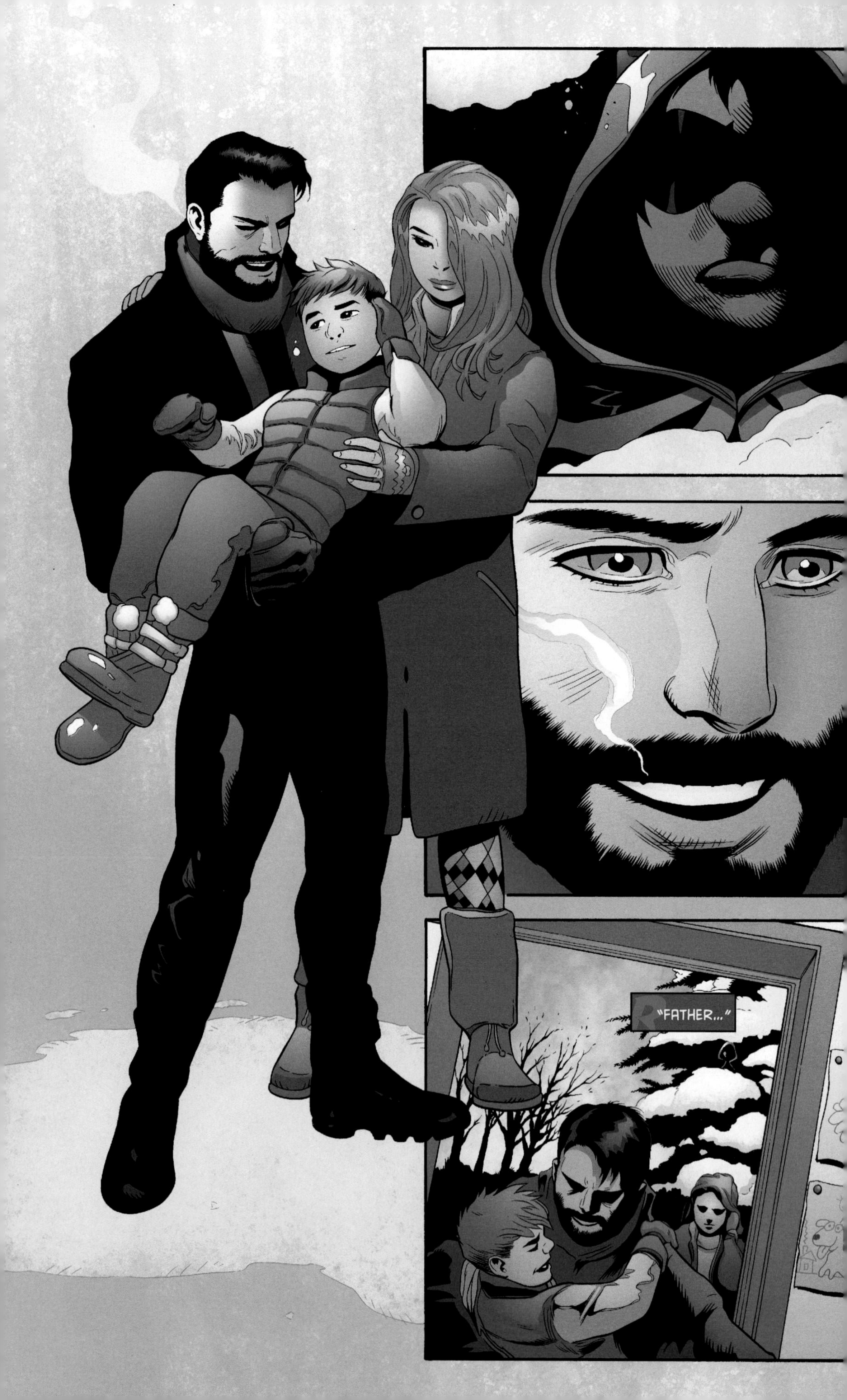
"FATHER..."

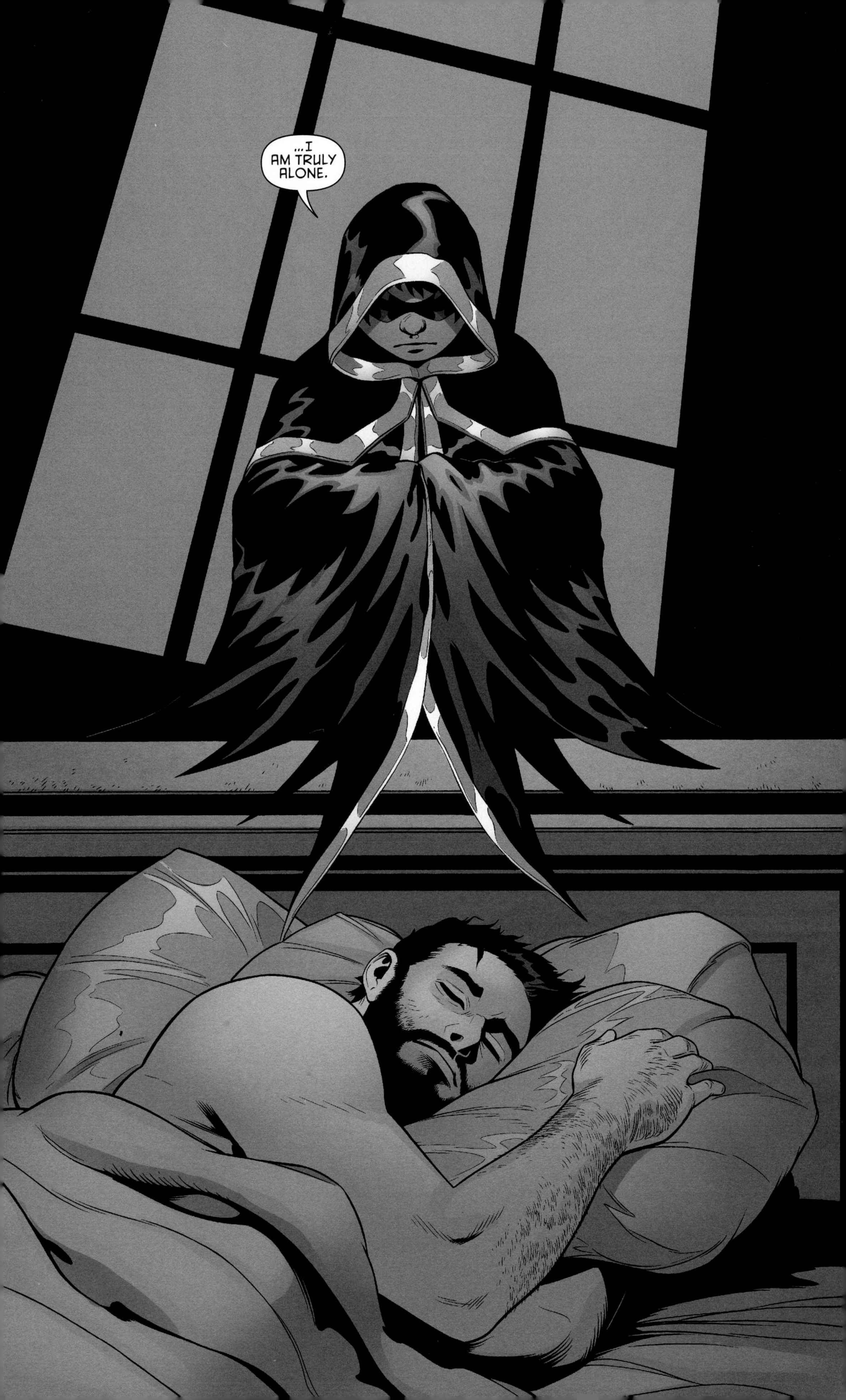
...I AM TRULY ALONE.

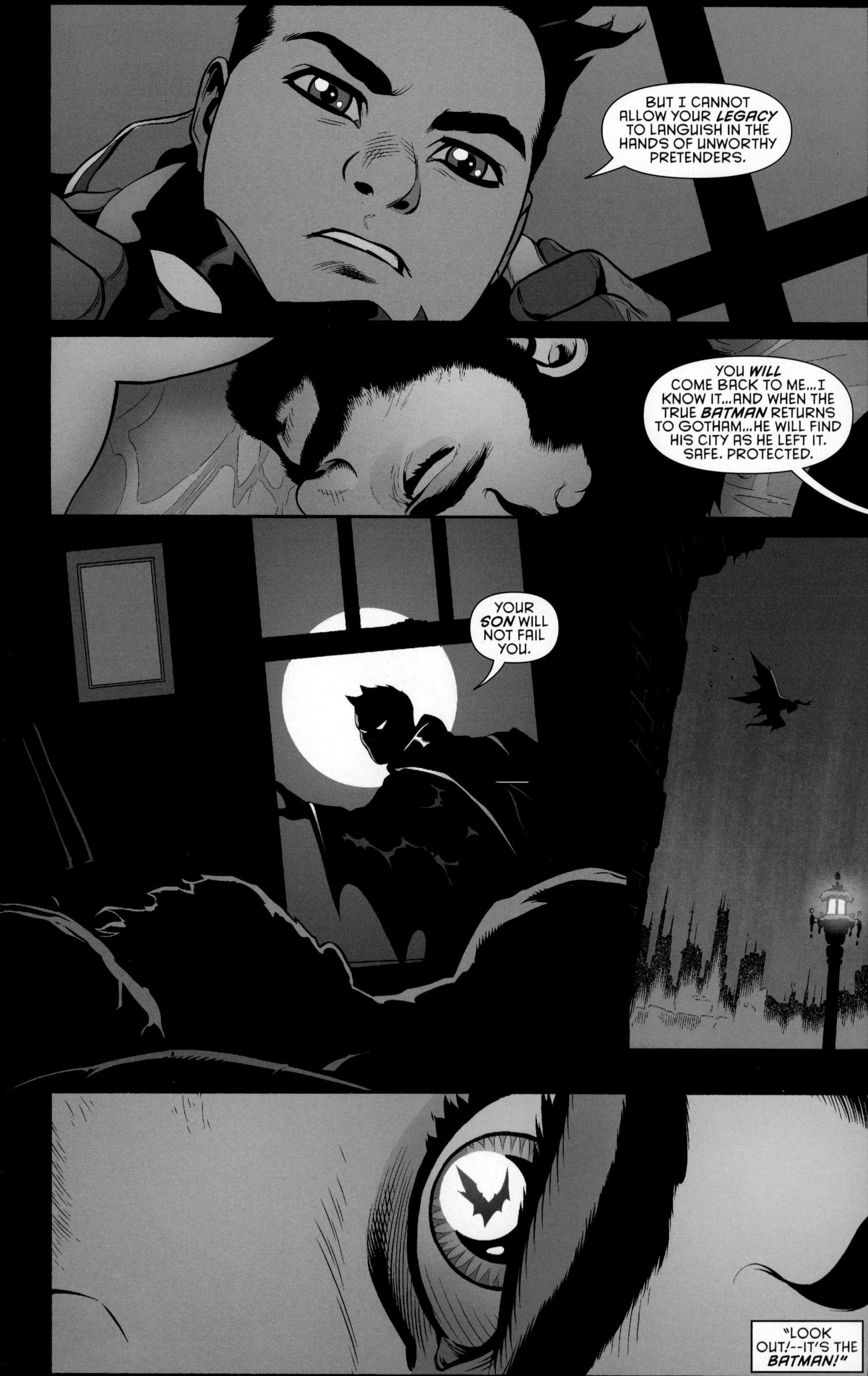
BUT I CANNOT ALLOW YOUR LEGACY TO LANGUISH IN THE HANDS OF UNWORTHY PRETENDERS.
YOU WILL COME BACK TO ME...I KNOW IT...AND WHEN THE TRUE BATMAN RETURNS TO GOTHAM...HE WILL FIND HIS CITY AS HE LEFT IT. SAFE. PROTECTED.
YOUR SON WILL NOT FAIL YOU.
"LOOK OUT!--IT'S THE BATMAN!"

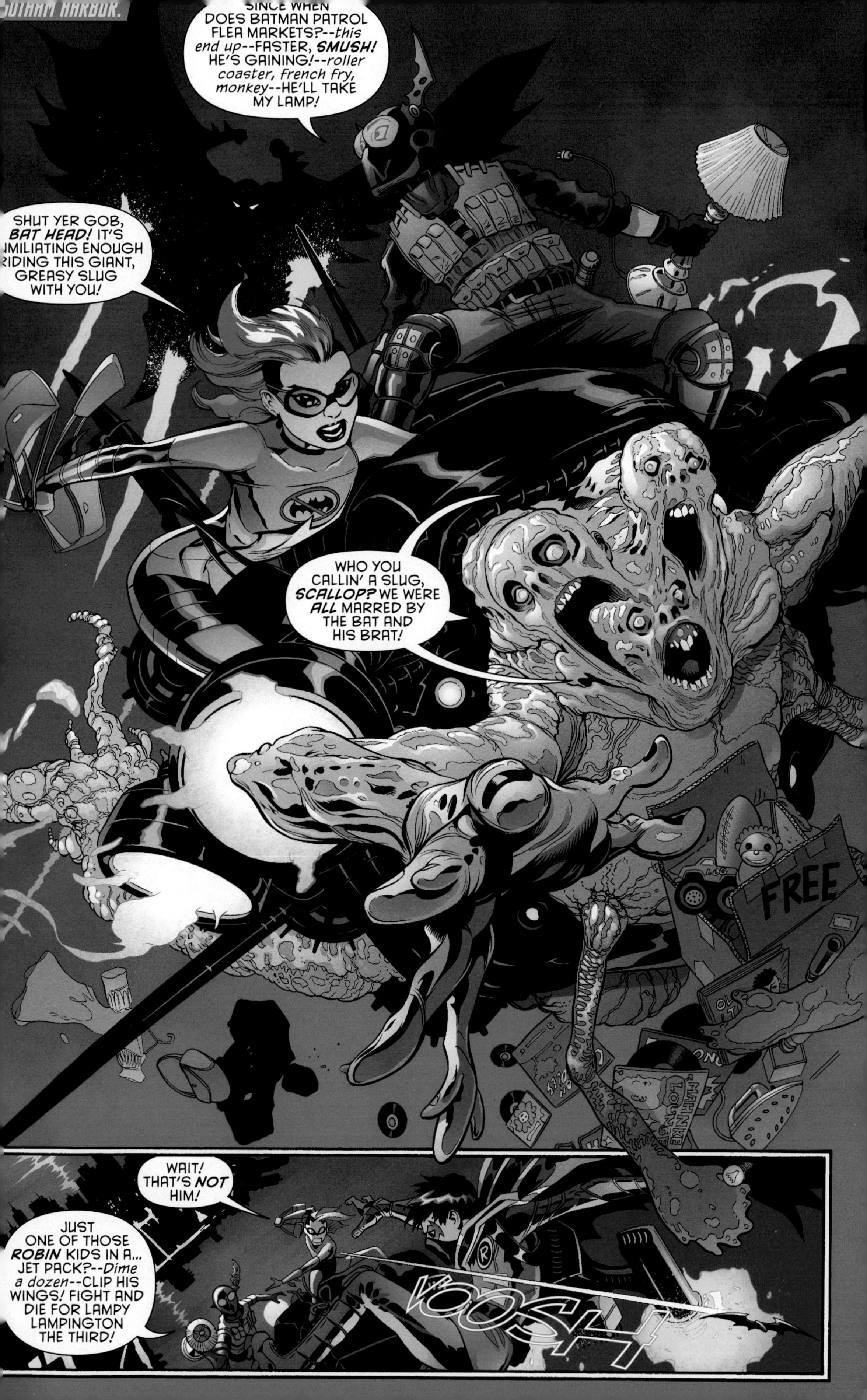
OTHAM HARBOR.
SINCE WHEN DOES BATMAN PATROL FLEA MARKETS?--*this end up*--FASTER, ***SMUSH!*** HE'S GAINING!--*roller coaster, french fry, monkey*--HE'LL TAKE MY LAMP!
SHUT YER GOB, ***BAT HEAD!*** IT'S MILIATING ENOUGH RIDING THIS GIANT, GREASY SLUG WITH YOU!
WHO YOU CALLIN' A SLUG, ***SCALLOP?*** WE WERE ***ALL*** MARRED BY THE BAT AND HIS BRAT!
FREE
WAIT! THAT'S ***NOT*** HIM!
JUST ONE OF THOSE ***ROBIN*** KIDS IN A... JET PACK?--*Dime a dozen*--CLIP HIS WINGS! FIGHT AND DIE FOR LAMPY LAMPINGTON THE THIRD!
VOOSH

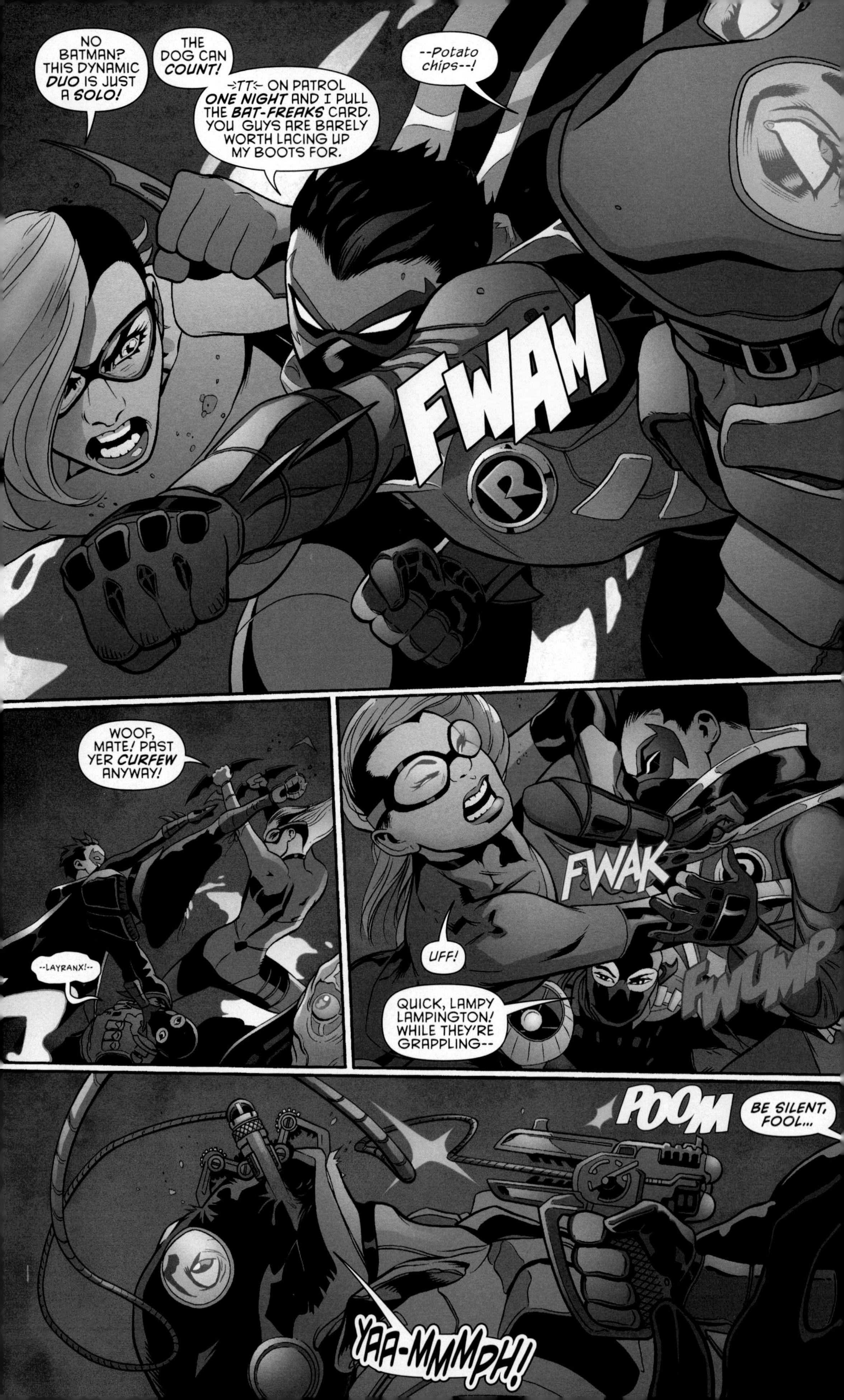
NO BATMAN? THIS DYNAMIC DUO IS JUST A SOLO!
THE DOG CAN COUNT!
TT ON PATROL ONE NIGHT AND I PULL THE BAT-FREAKS CARD. YOU GUYS ARE BARELY WORTH LACING UP MY BOOTS FOR.
--Potato chips--!
FWAM
WOOF, MATE! PAST YER CURFEW ANYWAY!
--LAYRANX!--
FWAK
UFF!
FWUMP
QUICK, LAMPY LAMPINGTON! WHILE THEY'RE GRAPPLING--
POOM
BE SILENT, FOOL...
YAA-MMMPH!

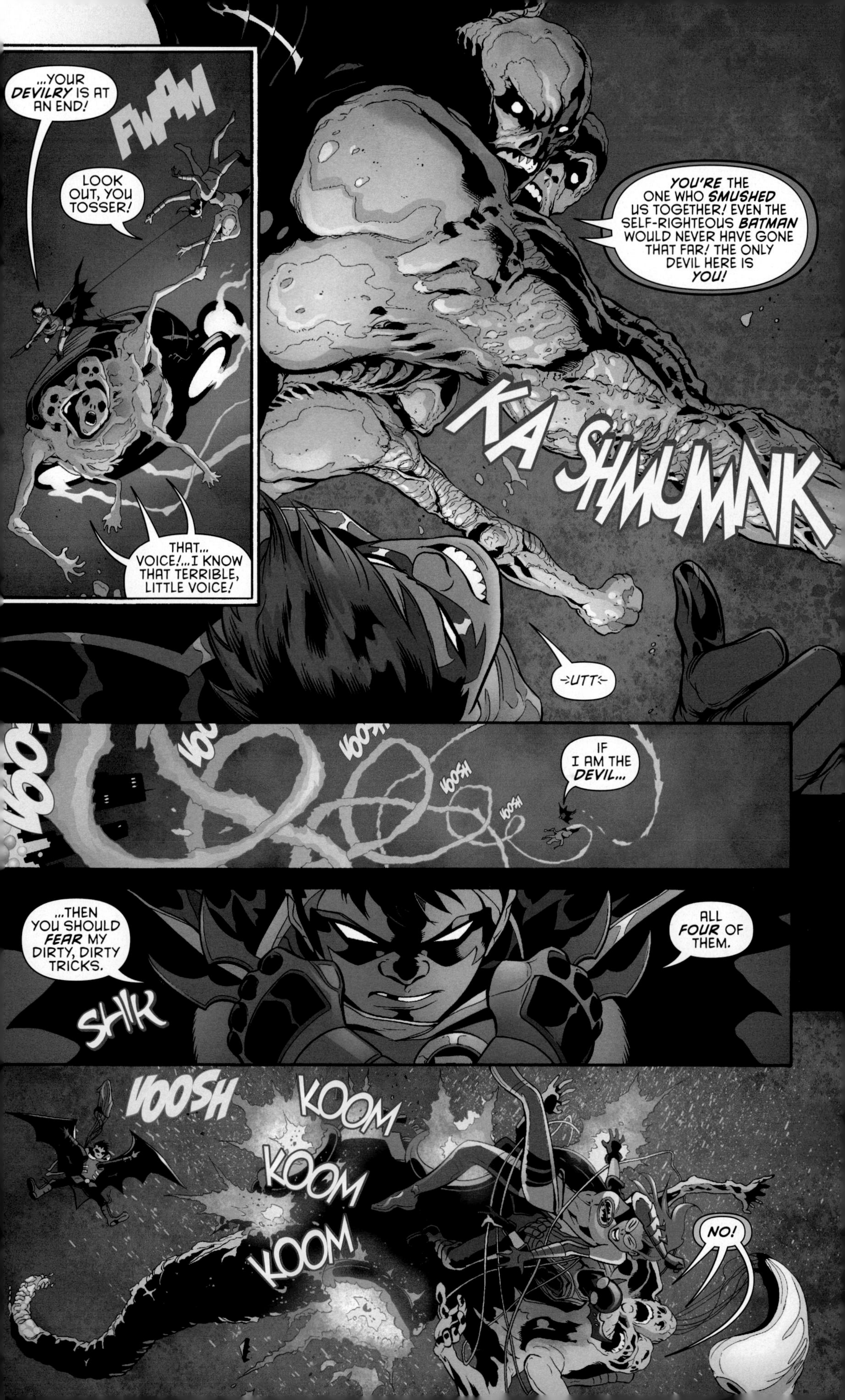
...YOUR DEVILRY IS AT AN END!
FWAM
LOOK OUT, YOU TOSSER!
THAT... VOICE!...I KNOW THAT TERRIBLE, LITTLE VOICE!
YOU'RE THE ONE WHO SMUSHED US TOGETHER! EVEN THE SELF-RIGHTEOUS BATMAN WOULD NEVER HAVE GONE THAT FAR! THE ONLY DEVIL HERE IS YOU!
KA SHMUMNK
UTT
VOOSH
VOOSH
VOOSH
IF I AM THE DEVIL...
...THEN YOU SHOULD FEAR MY DIRTY, DIRTY TRICKS.
ALL FOUR OF THEM.
SHIK
VOOSH
KOOM
KOOM
KOOM
NO!

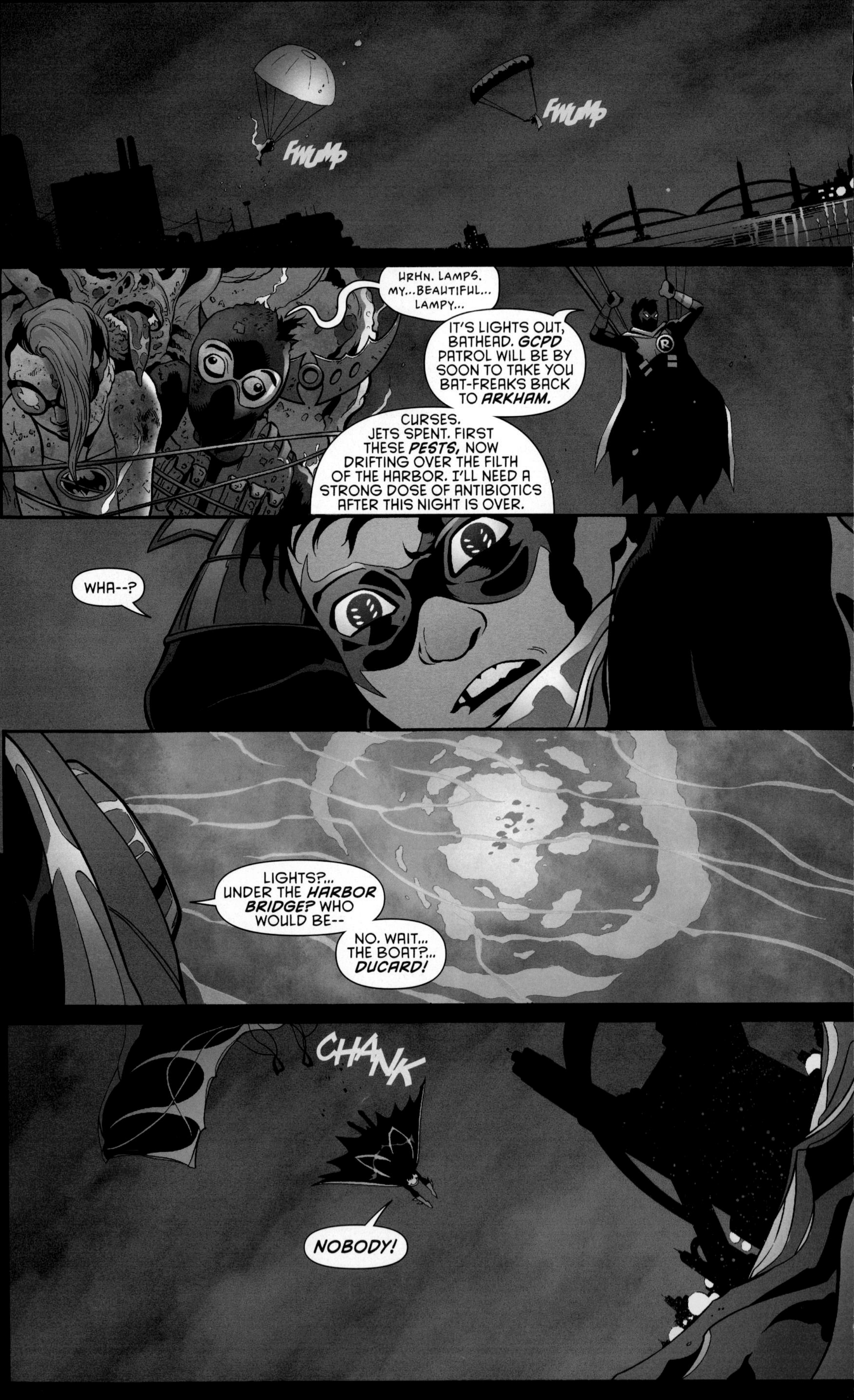
FWUMP
FWUMP
URHN. LAMPS. MY...BEAUTIFUL... LAMPY...
IT'S LIGHTS OUT, BATHEAD. GCPD PATROL WILL BE BY SOON TO TAKE YOU BAT-FREAKS BACK TO ARKHAM.
CURSES. JETS SPENT. FIRST THESE PESTS, NOW DRIFTING OVER THE FILTH OF THE HARBOR. I'LL NEED A STRONG DOSE OF ANTIBIOTICS AFTER THIS NIGHT IS OVER.
WHA--?
LIGHTS?... UNDER THE HARBOR BRIDGE? WHO WOULD BE--
NO. WAIT... THE BOAT?... DUCARD!
CHANK
NOBODY!

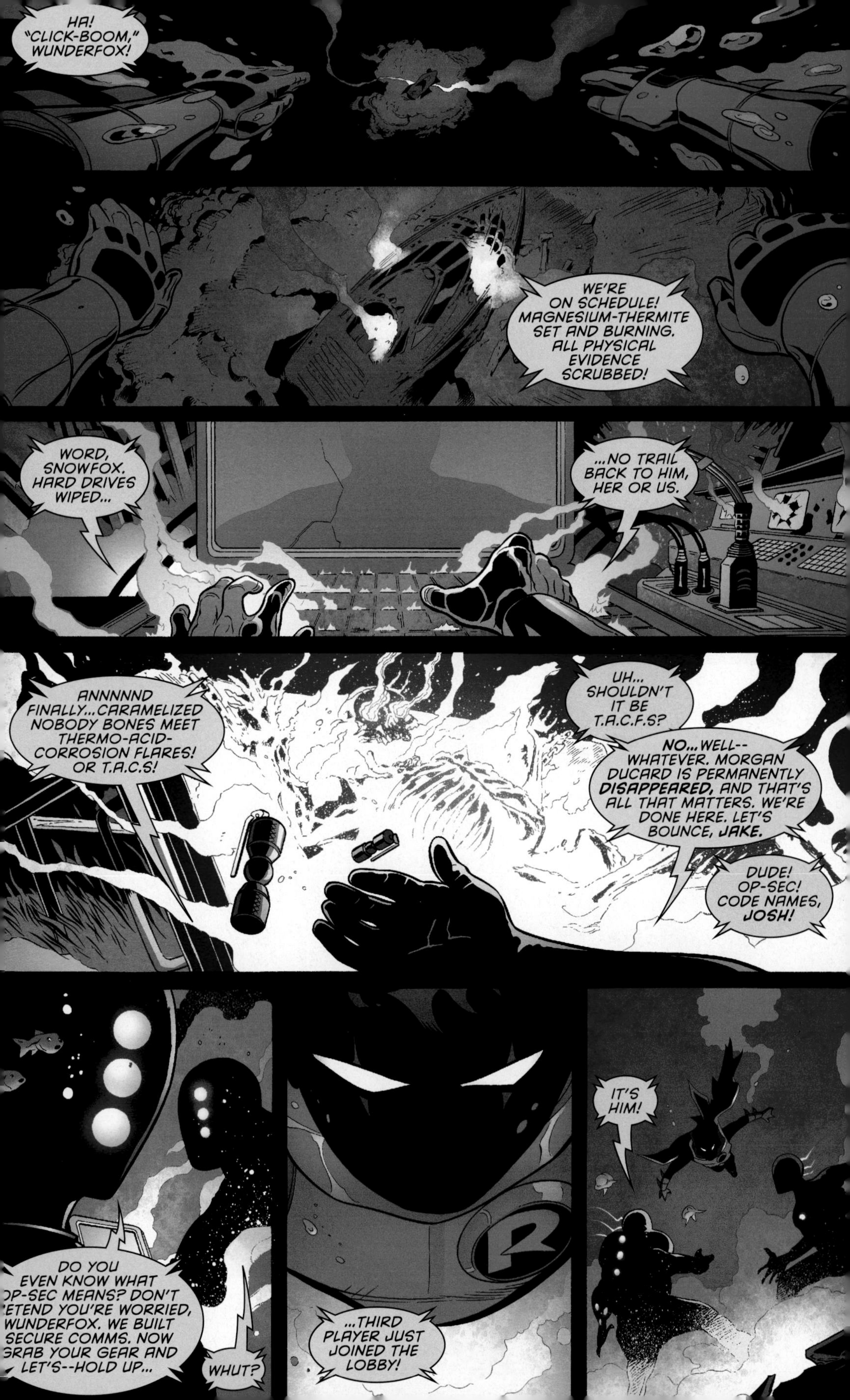
HA! "CLICK-BOOM," WUNDERFOX!
WE'RE ON SCHEDULE! MAGNESIUM-THERMITE SET AND BURNING. ALL PHYSICAL EVIDENCE SCRUBBED!
WORD, SNOWFOX. HARD DRIVES WIPED...
...NO TRAIL BACK TO HIM, HER OR US.
ANNNNND FINALLY...CARAMELIZED NOBODY BONES MEET THERMO-ACID-CORROSION FLARES! OR T.A.C.S!
UH... SHOULDN'T IT BE T.A.C.F.S?
NO...WELL--WHATEVER. MORGAN DUCARD IS PERMANENTLY DISAPPEARED, AND THAT'S ALL THAT MATTERS. WE'RE DONE HERE. LET'S BOUNCE, JAKE.
DUDE! OP-SEC! CODE NAMES, JOSH!
DO YOU EVEN KNOW WHAT OP-SEC MEANS? DON'T PRETEND YOU'RE WORRIED, WUNDERFOX. WE BUILT SECURE COMMS. NOW GRAB YOUR GEAR AND LET'S--HOLD UP...
WHUT?
...THIRD PLAYER JUST JOINED THE LOBBY!
IT'S HIM!

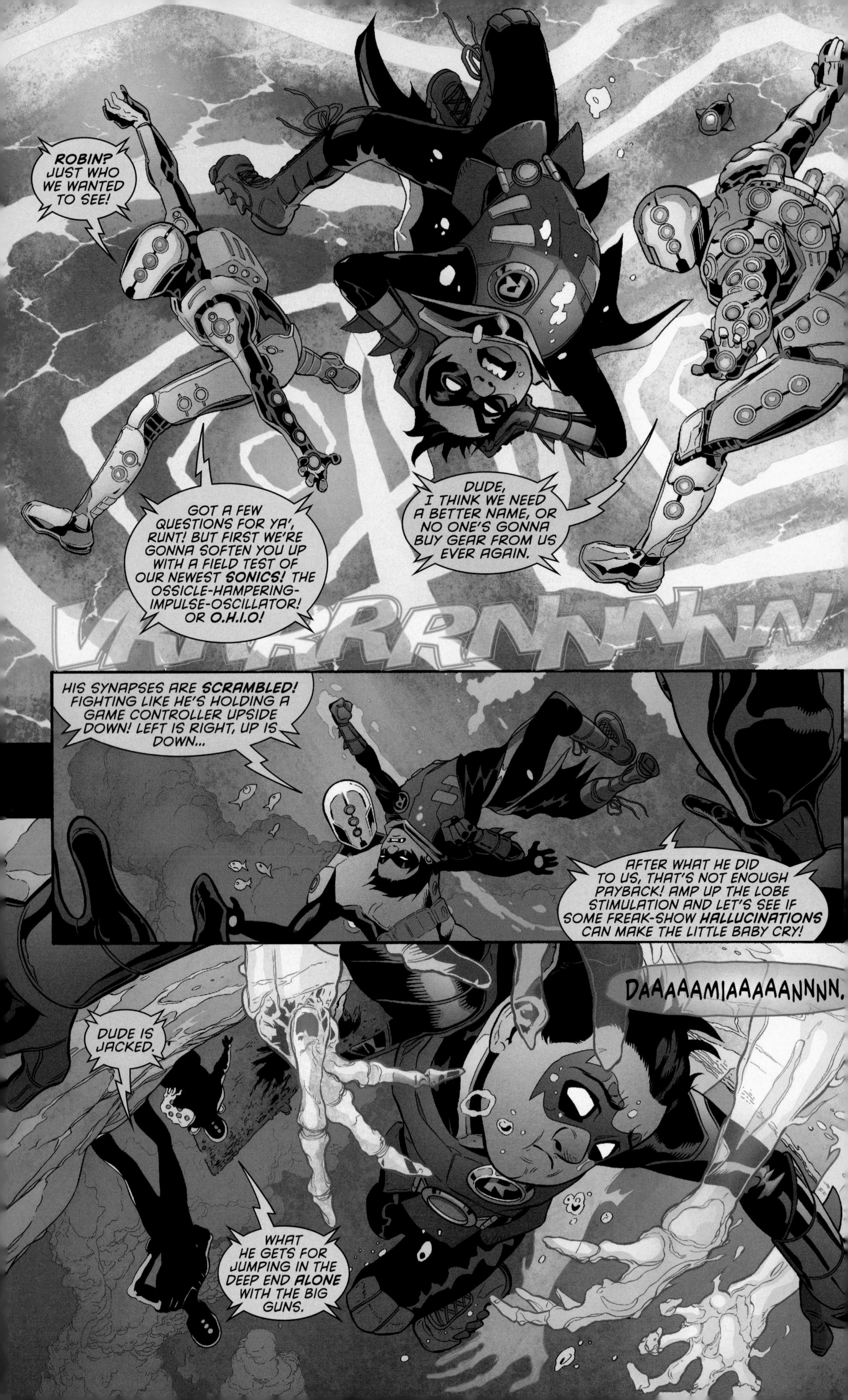
ROBIN? JUST WHO WE WANTED TO SEE!
GOT A FEW QUESTIONS FOR YA', RUNT! BUT FIRST WE'RE GONNA SOFTEN YOU UP WITH A FIELD TEST OF OUR NEWEST SONICS! THE OSSICLE-HAMPERING-IMPULSE-OSCILLATOR! OR O.H.I.O!
DUDE, I THINK WE NEED A BETTER NAME, OR NO ONE'S GONNA BUY GEAR FROM US EVER AGAIN.
VRRRRNNNNNN
HIS SYNAPSES ARE SCRAMBLED! FIGHTING LIKE HE'S HOLDING A GAME CONTROLLER UPSIDE DOWN! LEFT IS RIGHT, UP IS DOWN...
AFTER WHAT HE DID TO US, THAT'S NOT ENOUGH PAYBACK! AMP UP THE LOBE STIMULATION AND LET'S SEE IF SOME FREAK-SHOW HALLUCINATIONS CAN MAKE THE LITTLE BABY CRY!
DAAAAAMIAAAAANNNN.
DUDE IS JACKED.
WHAT HE GETS FOR JUMPING IN THE DEEP END ALONE WITH THE BIG GUNS.

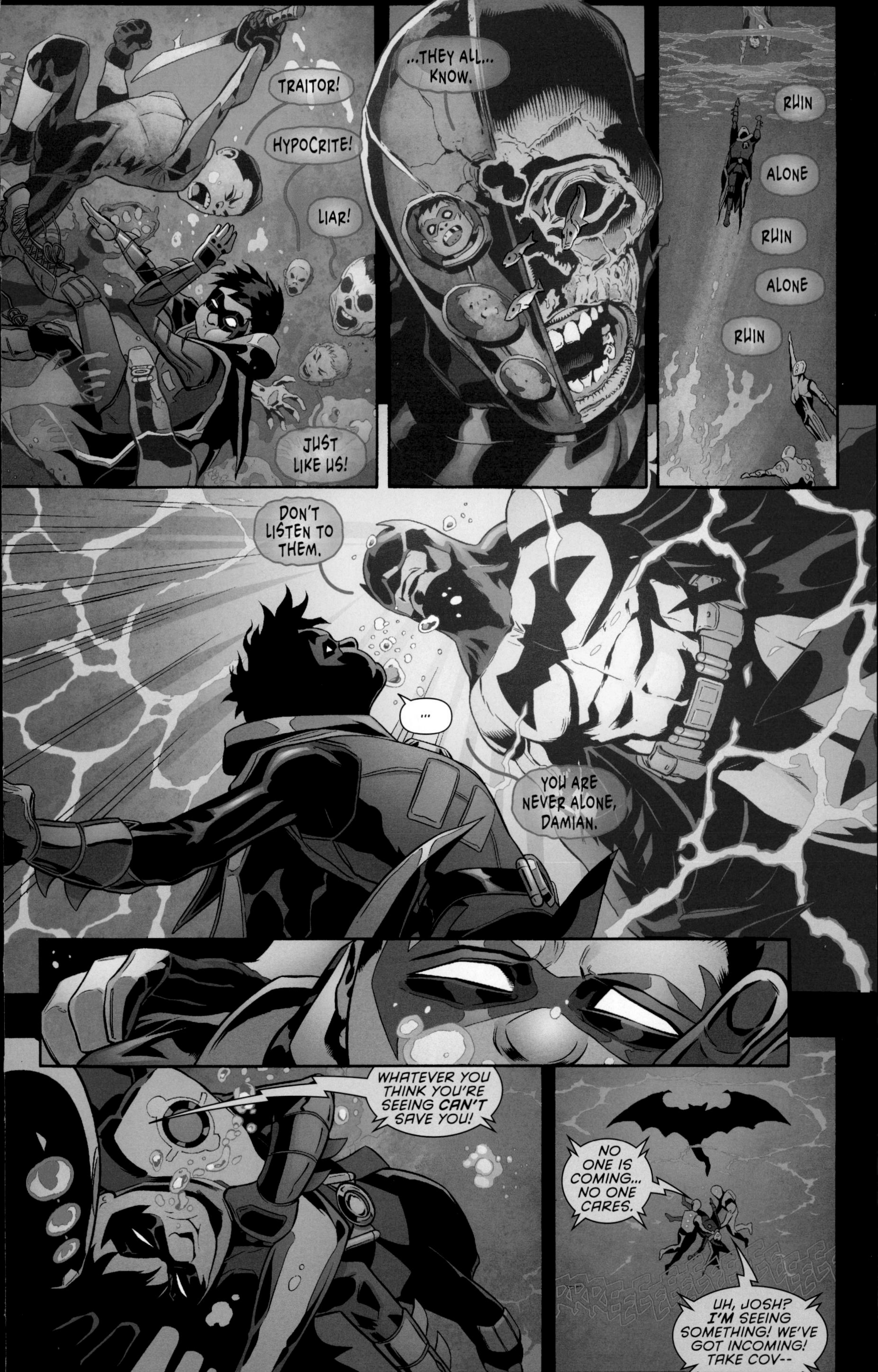
TRAITOR!
HYPOCRITE!
LIAR!
JUST LIKE US!
...THEY ALL... KNOW.
RUIN
ALONE
RUIN
ALONE
RUIN
DON'T LISTEN TO THEM.
...
YOU ARE NEVER ALONE, DAMIAN.
WHATEVER YOU THINK YOU'RE SEEING CAN'T SAVE YOU!
NO ONE IS COMING... NO ONE CARES.
UH, JOSH? I'M SEEING SOMETHING! WE'VE GOT INCOMING! TAKE COV--

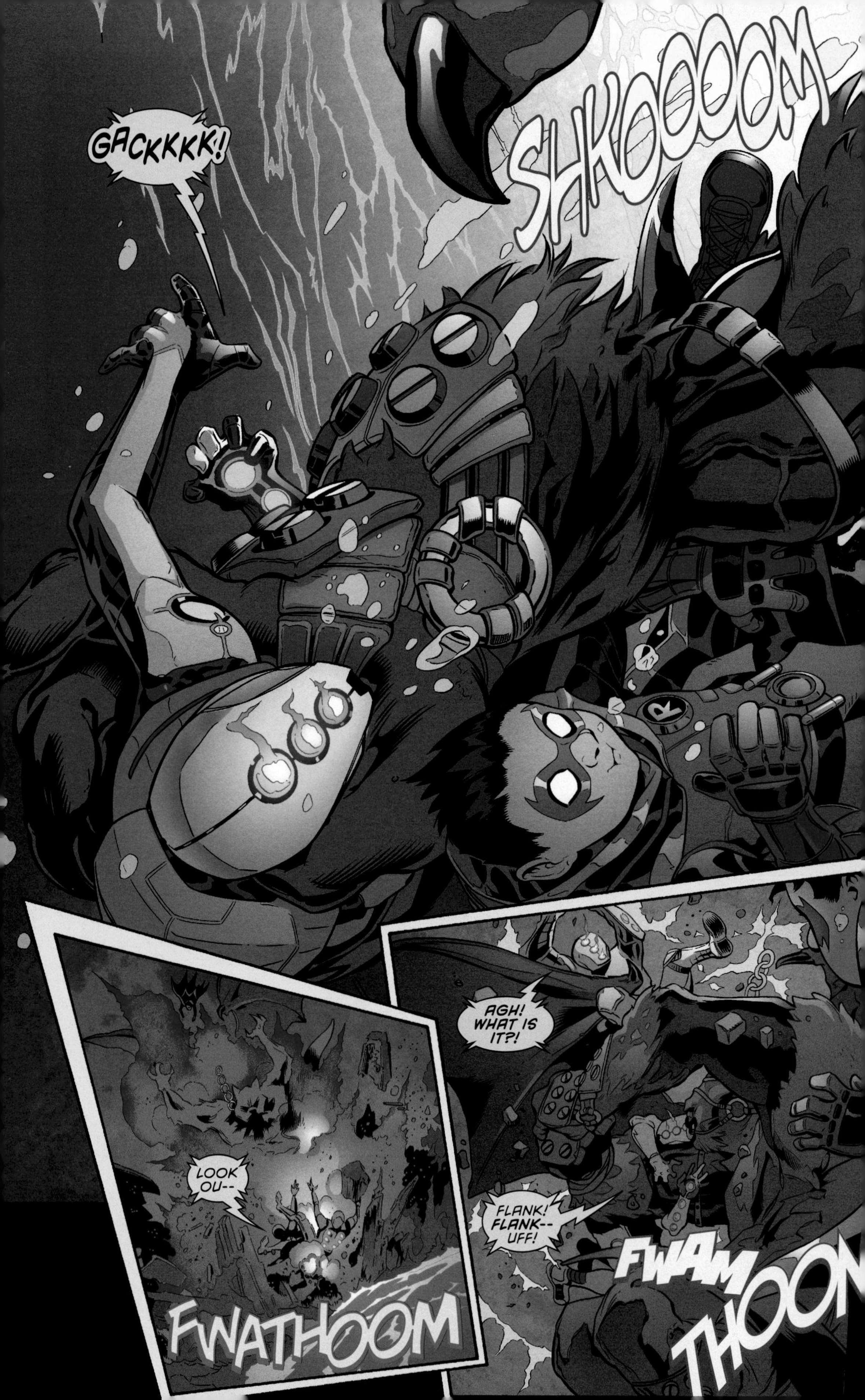
GACKKKK!
SHKOOOOM
LOOK OU--
FWATHOOM
AGH! WHAT IS IT?!
FLANK! FLANK-- UFF!
FWAM
THOOM

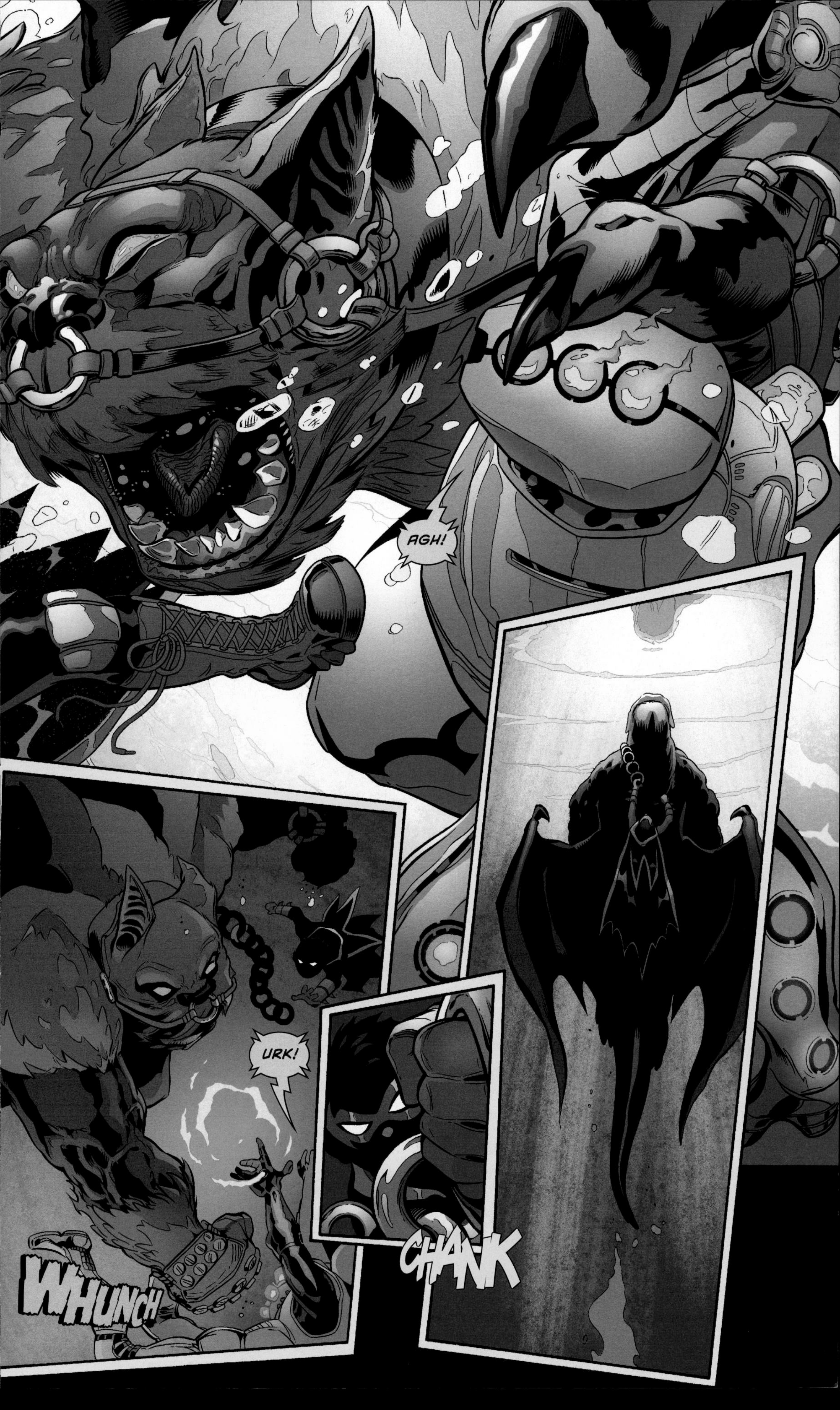
AGH!
URK!
WHUNCH
CHANK

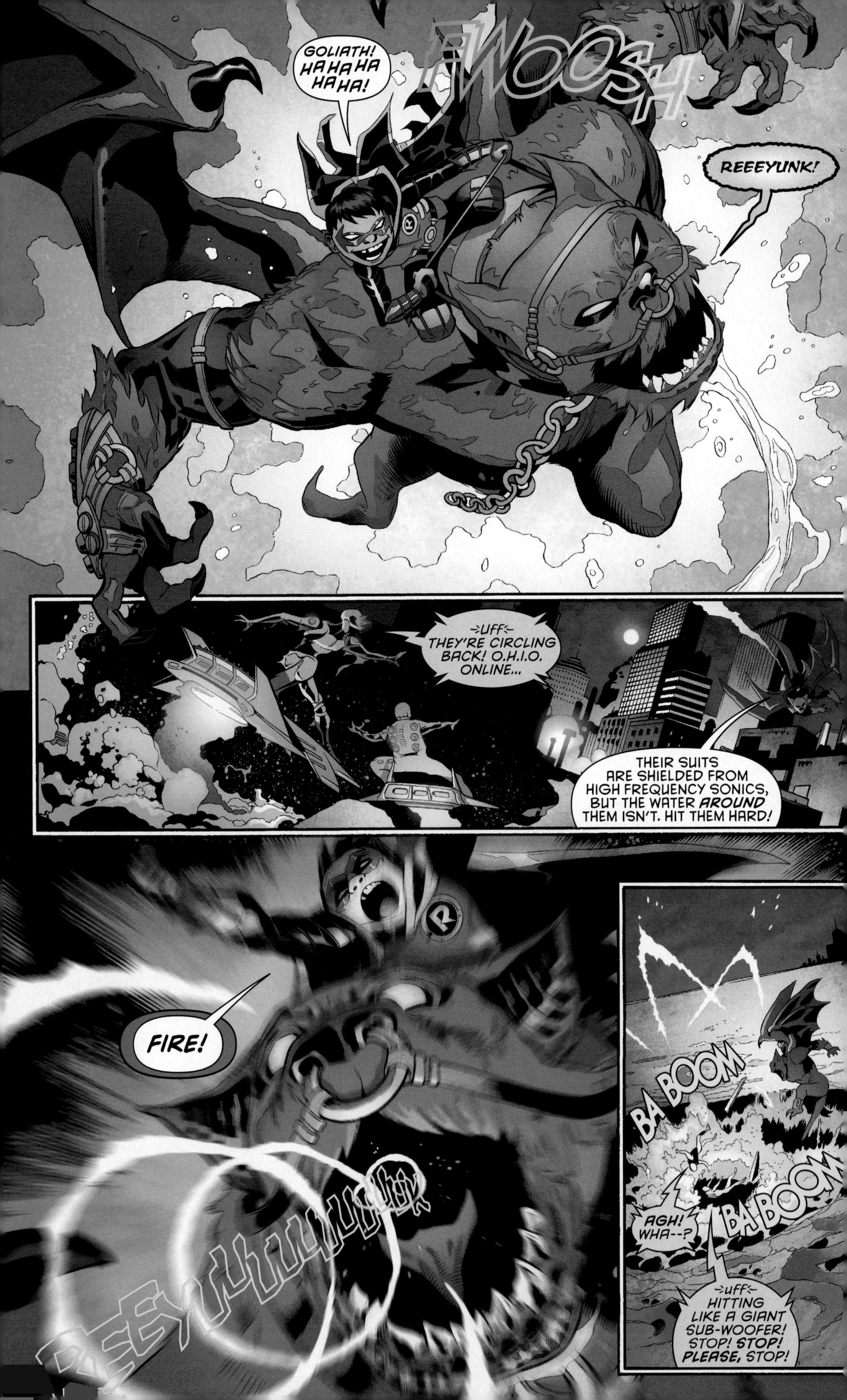
GOLIATH! HA HA HA HA HA!
FWOOSH
REEEYUNK!
~UFF~ THEY'RE CIRCLING BACK! O.H.I.O. ONLINE...
THEIR SUITS ARE SHIELDED FROM HIGH FREQUENCY SONICS, BUT THE WATER AROUND THEM ISN'T. HIT THEM HARD!
FIRE!
BA BOOM
AGH! WHA--?
BA BOOM
~UFF~ HITTING LIKE A GIANT SUB-WOOFER! STOP! STOP! PLEASE, STOP!

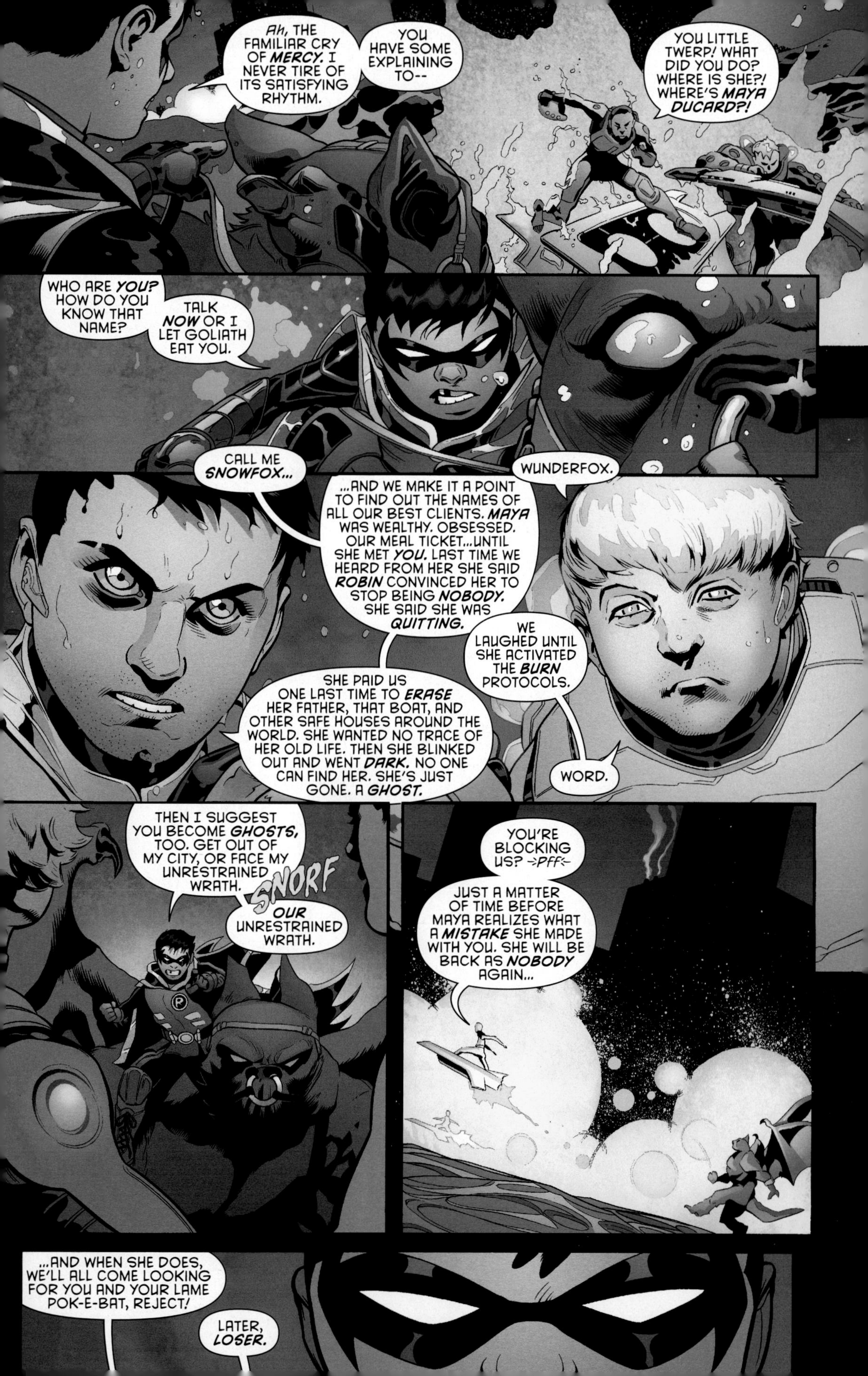
Ah, THE FAMILIAR CRY OF MERCY. I NEVER TIRE OF ITS SATISFYING RHYTHM.
YOU HAVE SOME EXPLAINING TO--
YOU LITTLE TWERP! WHAT DID YOU DO? WHERE IS SHE?! WHERE'S MAYA DUCARD?!
WHO ARE YOU? HOW DO YOU KNOW THAT NAME?
TALK NOW OR I LET GOLIATH EAT YOU.
CALL ME SNOWFOX...
WUNDERFOX.
...AND WE MAKE IT A POINT TO FIND OUT THE NAMES OF ALL OUR BEST CLIENTS. MAYA WAS WEALTHY. OBSESSED. OUR MEAL TICKET...UNTIL SHE MET YOU. LAST TIME WE HEARD FROM HER SHE SAID ROBIN CONVINCED HER TO STOP BEING NOBODY. SHE SAID SHE WAS QUITTING.
WE LAUGHED UNTIL SHE ACTIVATED THE BURN PROTOCOLS.
SHE PAID US ONE LAST TIME TO ERASE HER FATHER, THAT BOAT, AND OTHER SAFE HOUSES AROUND THE WORLD. SHE WANTED NO TRACE OF HER OLD LIFE. THEN SHE BLINKED OUT AND WENT DARK. NO ONE CAN FIND HER. SHE'S JUST GONE. A GHOST.
WORD.
THEN I SUGGEST YOU BECOME GHOSTS, TOO. GET OUT OF MY CITY, OR FACE MY UNRESTRAINED WRATH.
SNORF
OUR UNRESTRAINED WRATH.
YOU'RE BLOCKING US? -PFF-
JUST A MATTER OF TIME BEFORE MAYA REALIZES WHAT A MISTAKE SHE MADE WITH YOU. SHE WILL BE BACK AS NOBODY AGAIN...
...AND WHEN SHE DOES, WE'LL ALL COME LOOKING FOR YOU AND YOUR LAME POK-E-BAT, REJECT!
LATER, LOSER.

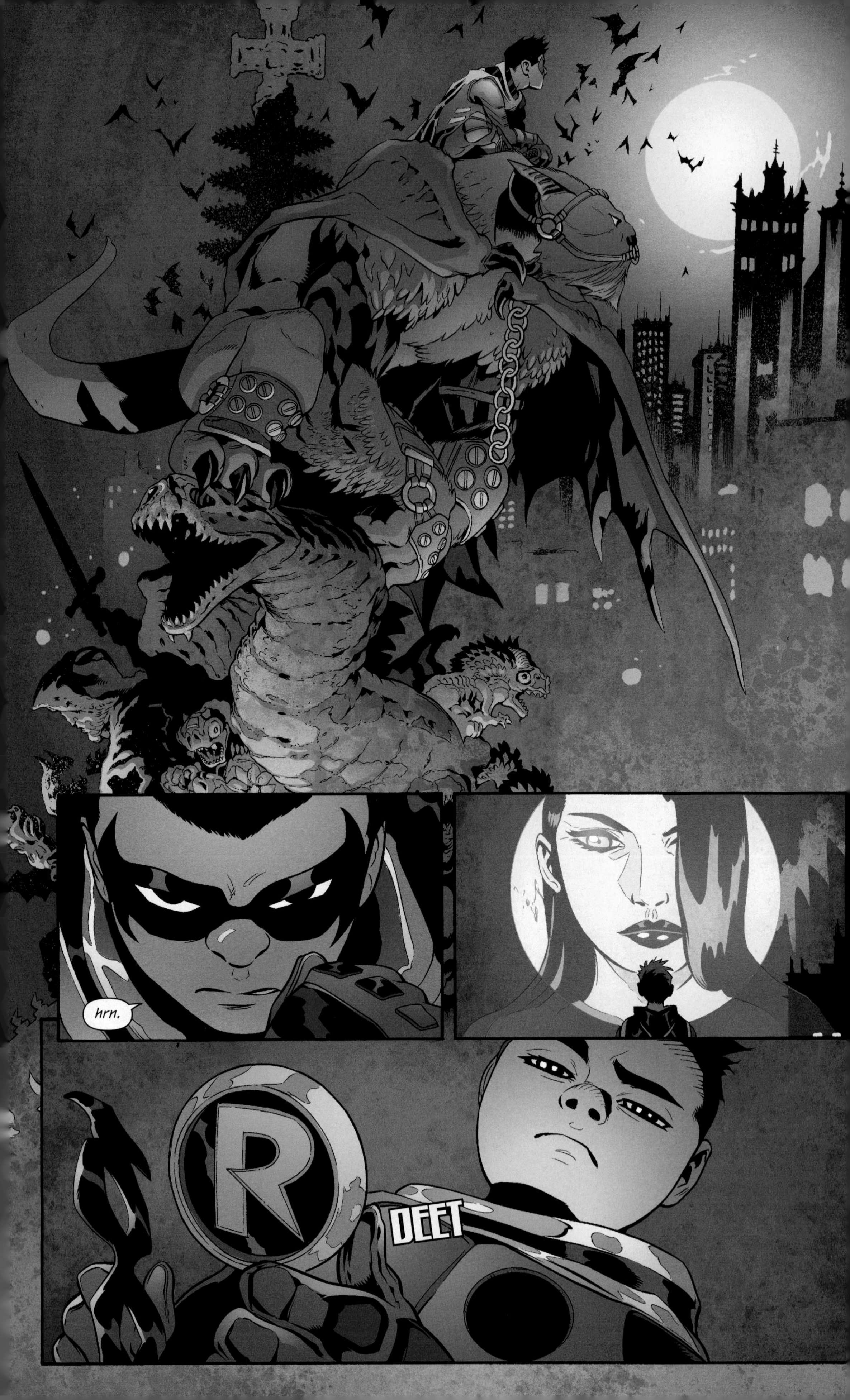
hrn.
DEET

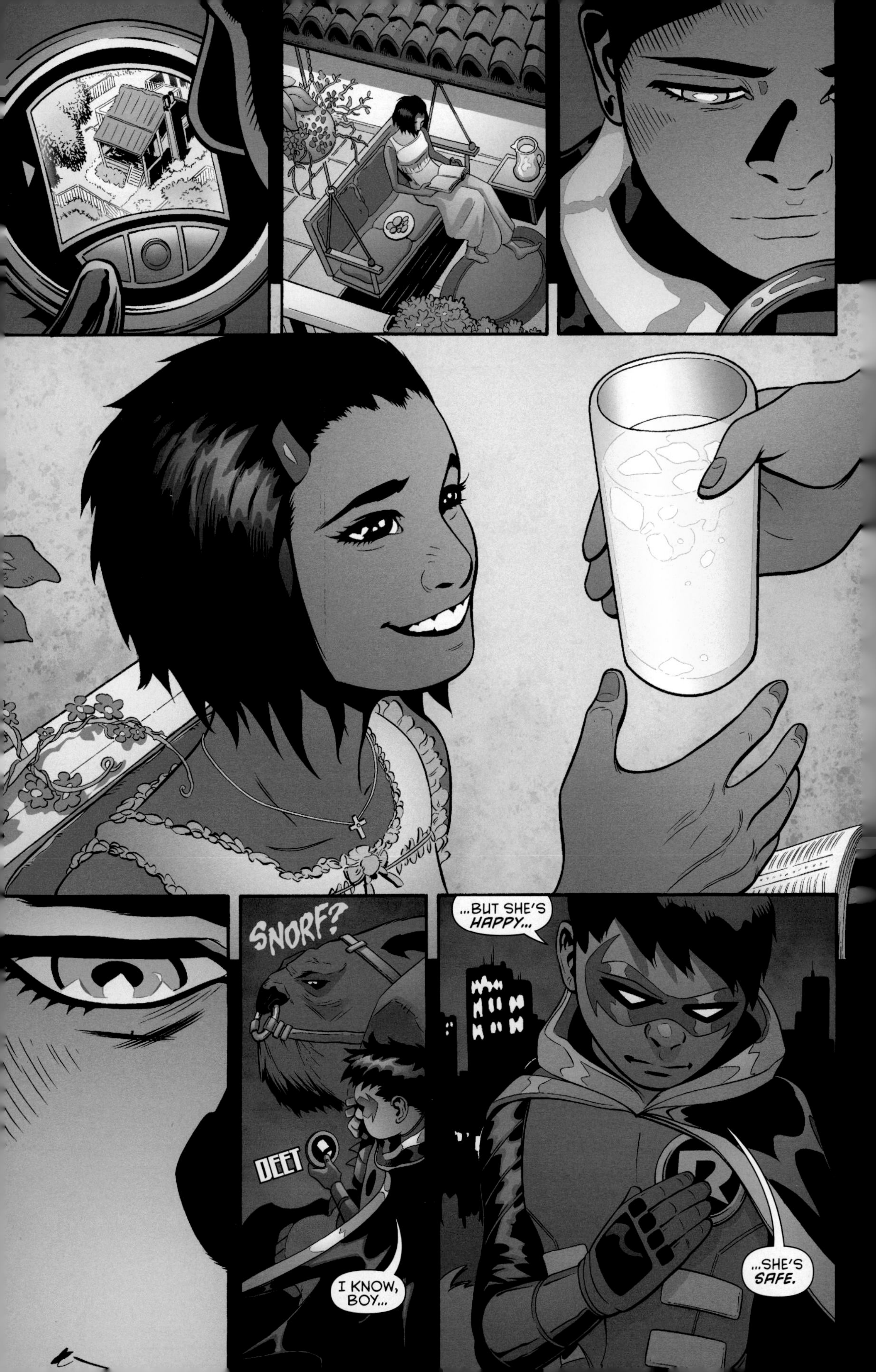
SNORF?
DEET
I KNOW, BOY...
...BUT SHE'S HAPPY...
...SHE'S SAFE.

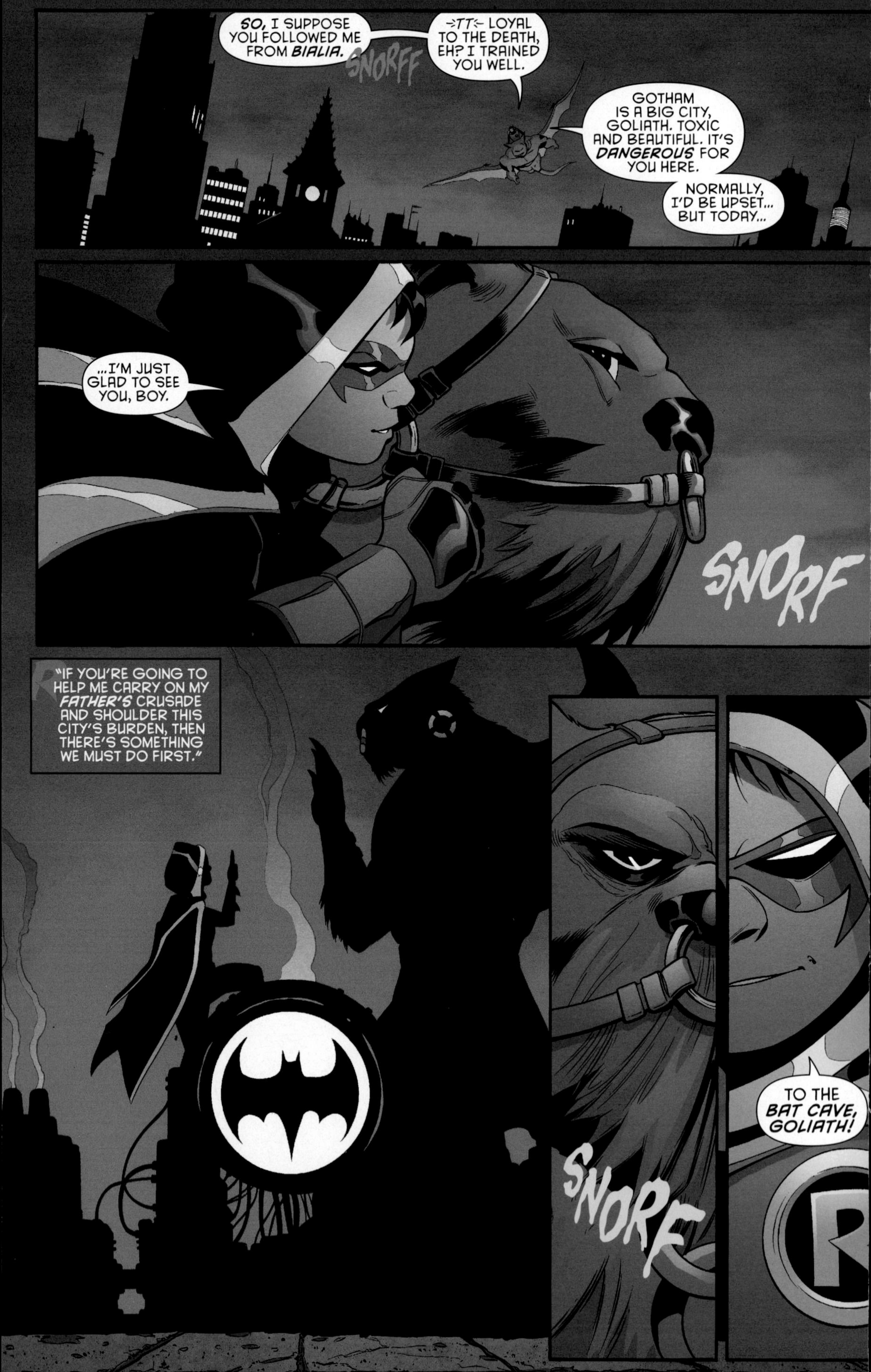

SO, I SUPPOSE YOU FOLLOWED ME FROM BIALIA.
SNORFF
»TT« LOYAL TO THE DEATH, EH? I TRAINED YOU WELL.
GOTHAM IS A BIG CITY, GOLIATH. TOXIC AND BEAUTIFUL. IT'S DANGEROUS FOR YOU HERE.
NORMALLY, I'D BE UPSET... BUT TODAY...
...I'M JUST GLAD TO SEE YOU, BOY.
SNORF
"IF YOU'RE GOING TO HELP ME CARRY ON MY FATHER'S CRUSADE AND SHOULDER THIS CITY'S BURDEN, THEN THERE'S SOMETHING WE MUST DO FIRST."
TO THE BAT CAVE, GOLIATH!
SNORF

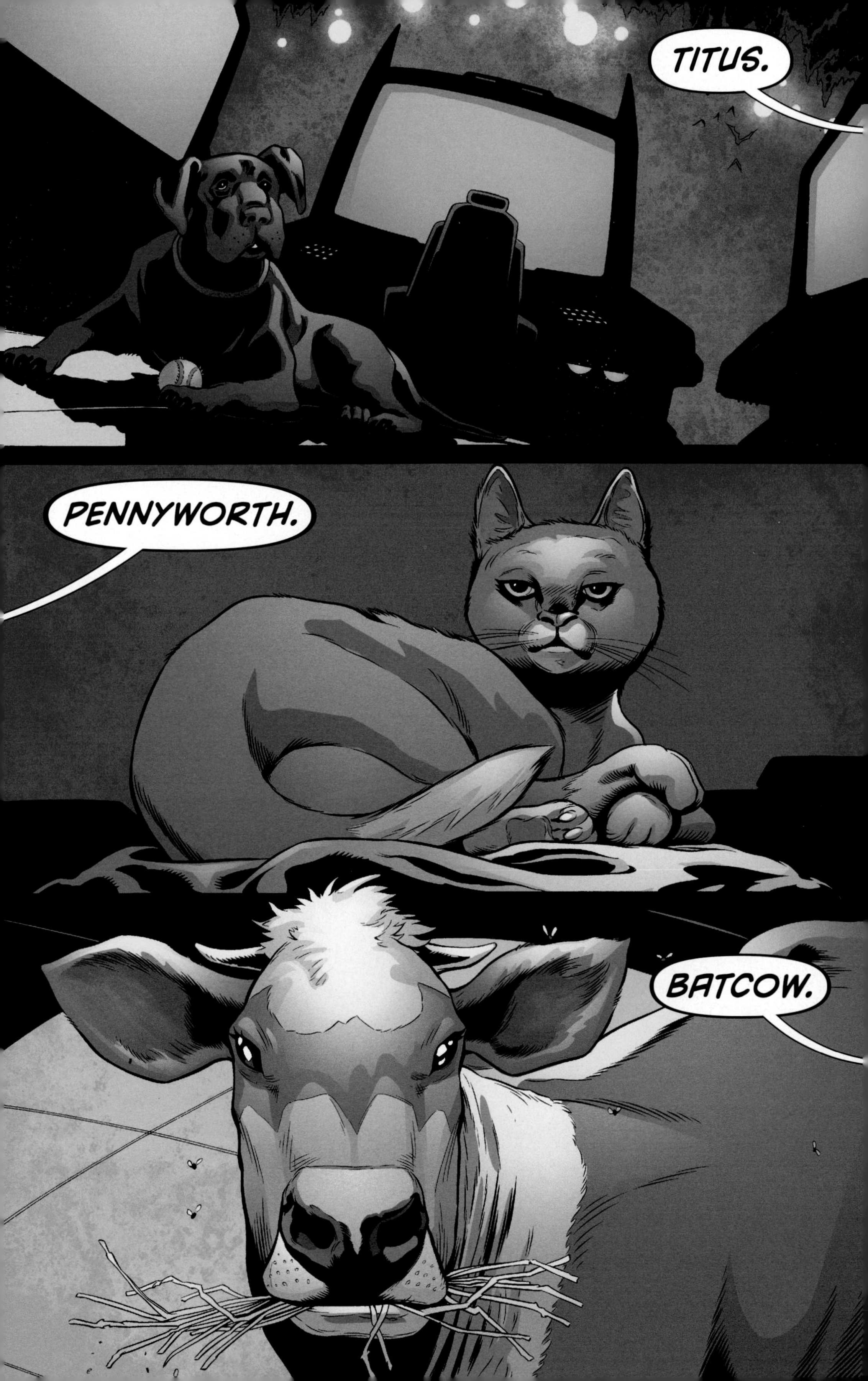
TITUS.
PENNYWORTH.
BATCOW.

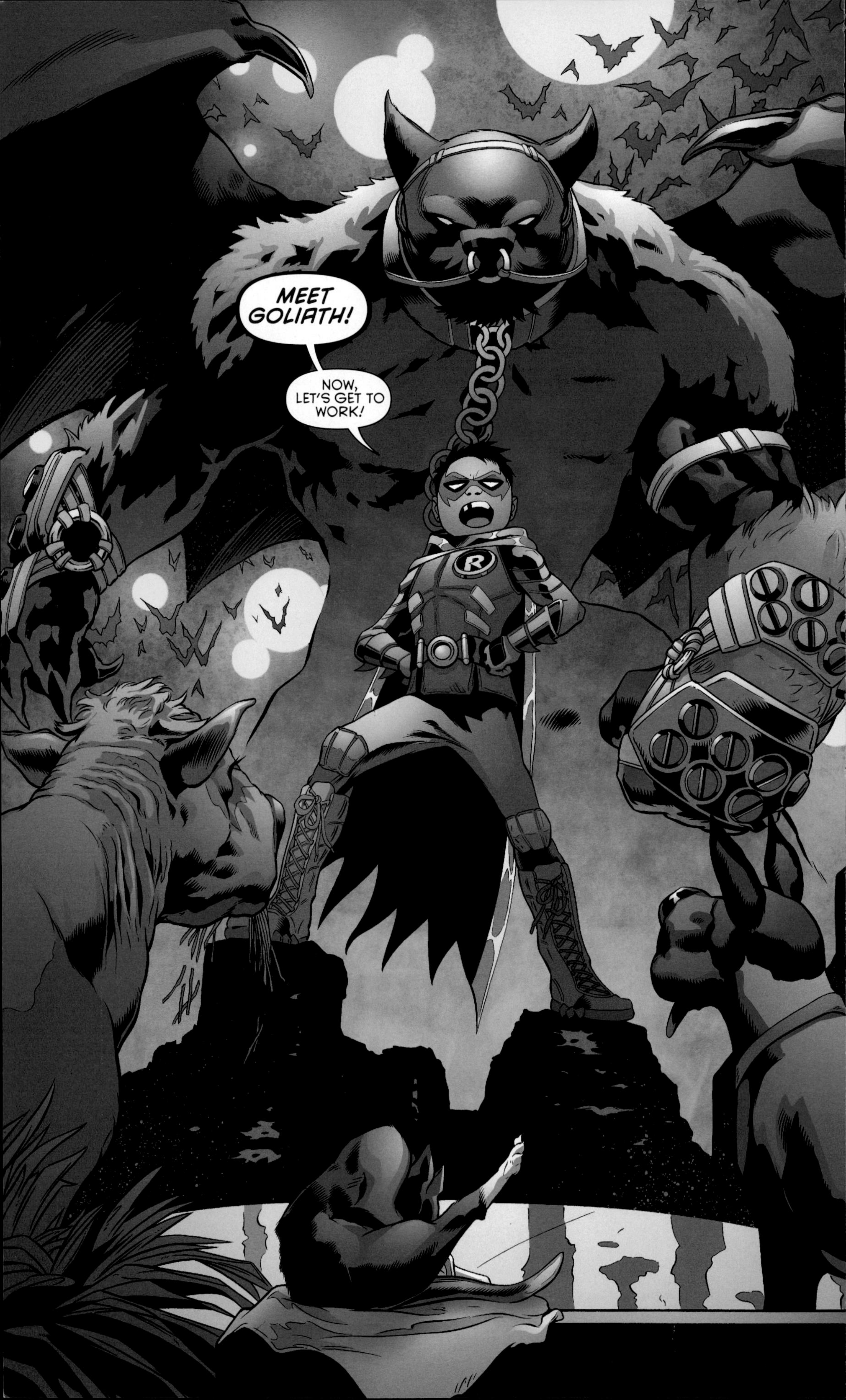
MEET GOLIATH!
NOW, LET'S GET TO WORK!

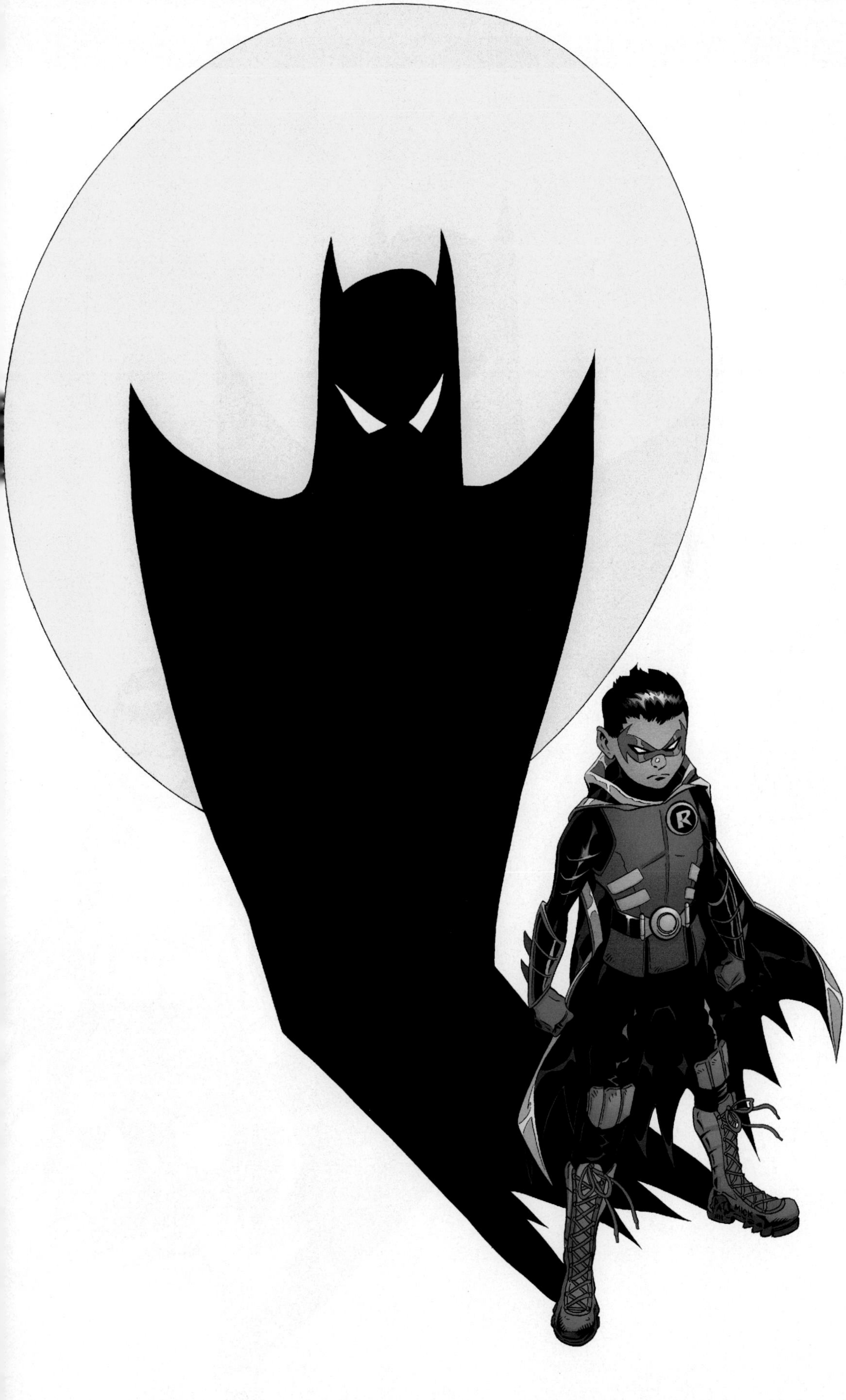

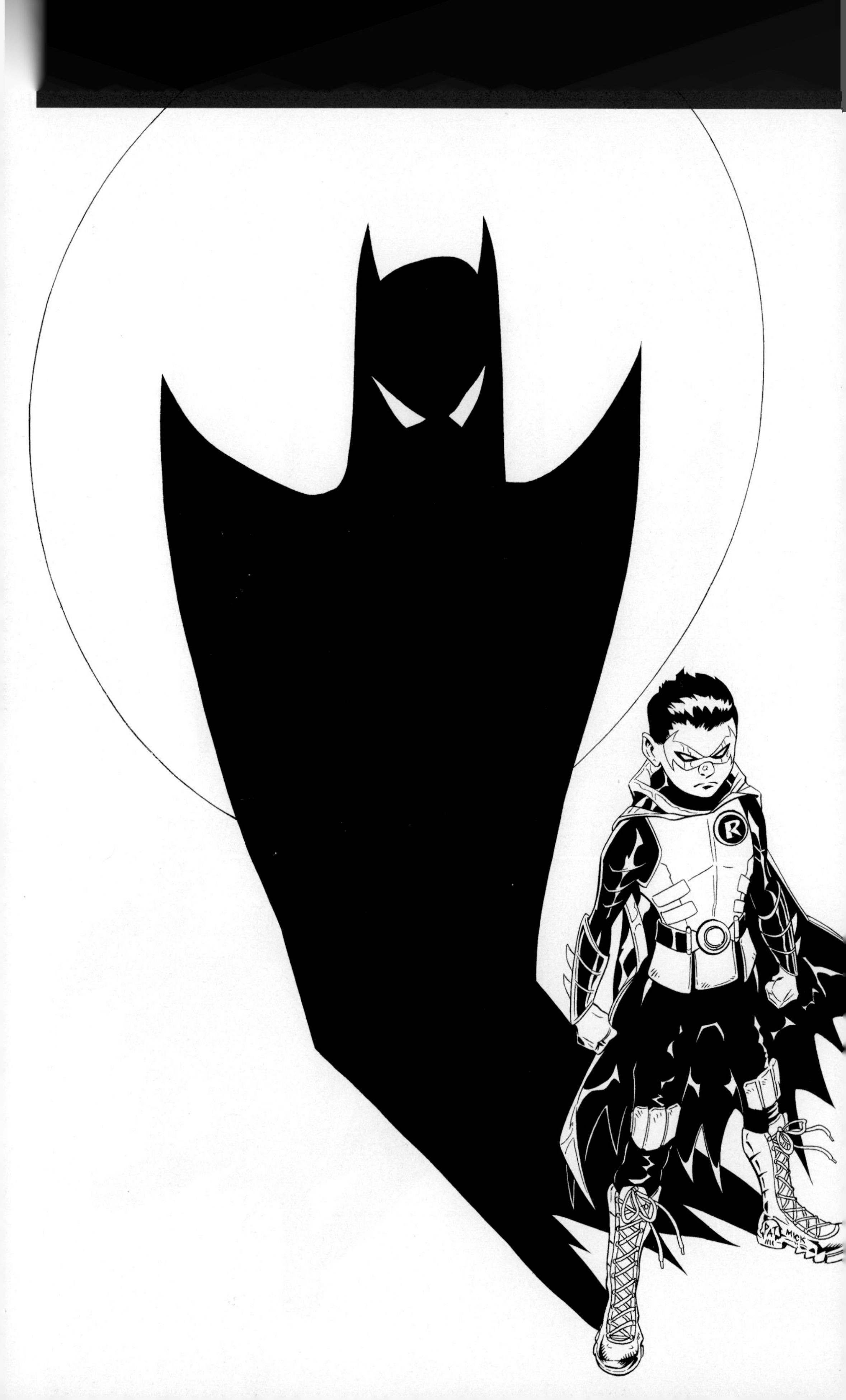
PAT MICK

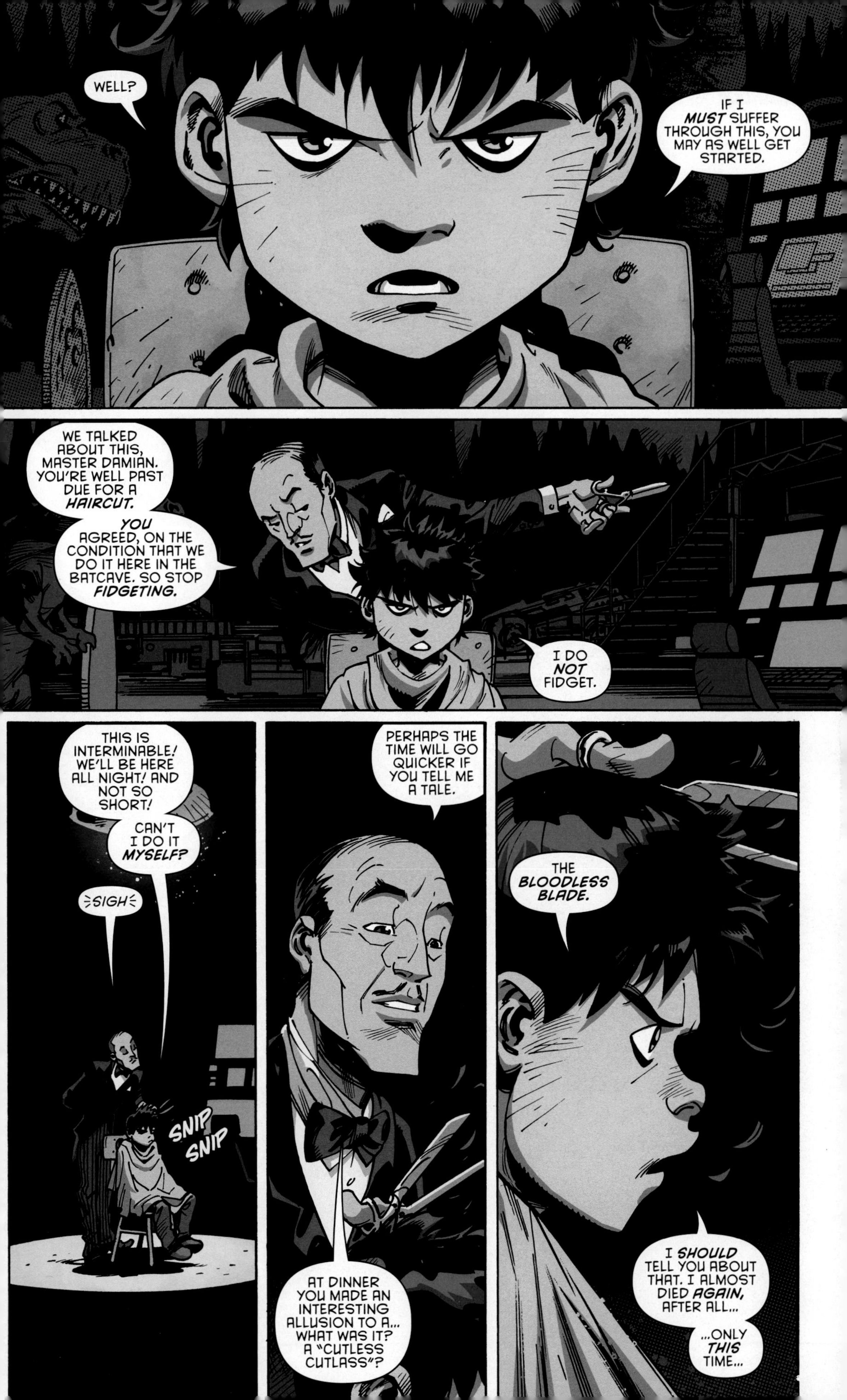

WELL?
IF I *MUST* SUFFER THROUGH THIS, YOU MAY AS WELL GET STARTED.
WE TALKED ABOUT THIS, MASTER DAMIAN. YOU'RE WELL PAST DUE FOR A *HAIRCUT.*
YOU AGREED, ON THE CONDITION THAT WE DO IT HERE IN THE BATCAVE. SO STOP *FIDGETING.*
I DO *NOT* FIDGET.
THIS IS INTERMINABLE! WE'LL BE HERE ALL NIGHT! AND NOT SO SHORT!
CAN'T I DO IT *MYSELF?*
SIGH
SNIP SNIP
PERHAPS THE TIME WILL GO QUICKER IF YOU TELL ME A TALE.
AT DINNER YOU MADE AN INTERESTING ALLUSION TO A... WHAT WAS IT? A "CUTLESS CUTLASS"?
THE *BLOODLESS BLADE.*
I *SHOULD* TELL YOU ABOUT THAT. I ALMOST DIED *AGAIN,* AFTER ALL...
...ONLY *THIS* TIME...

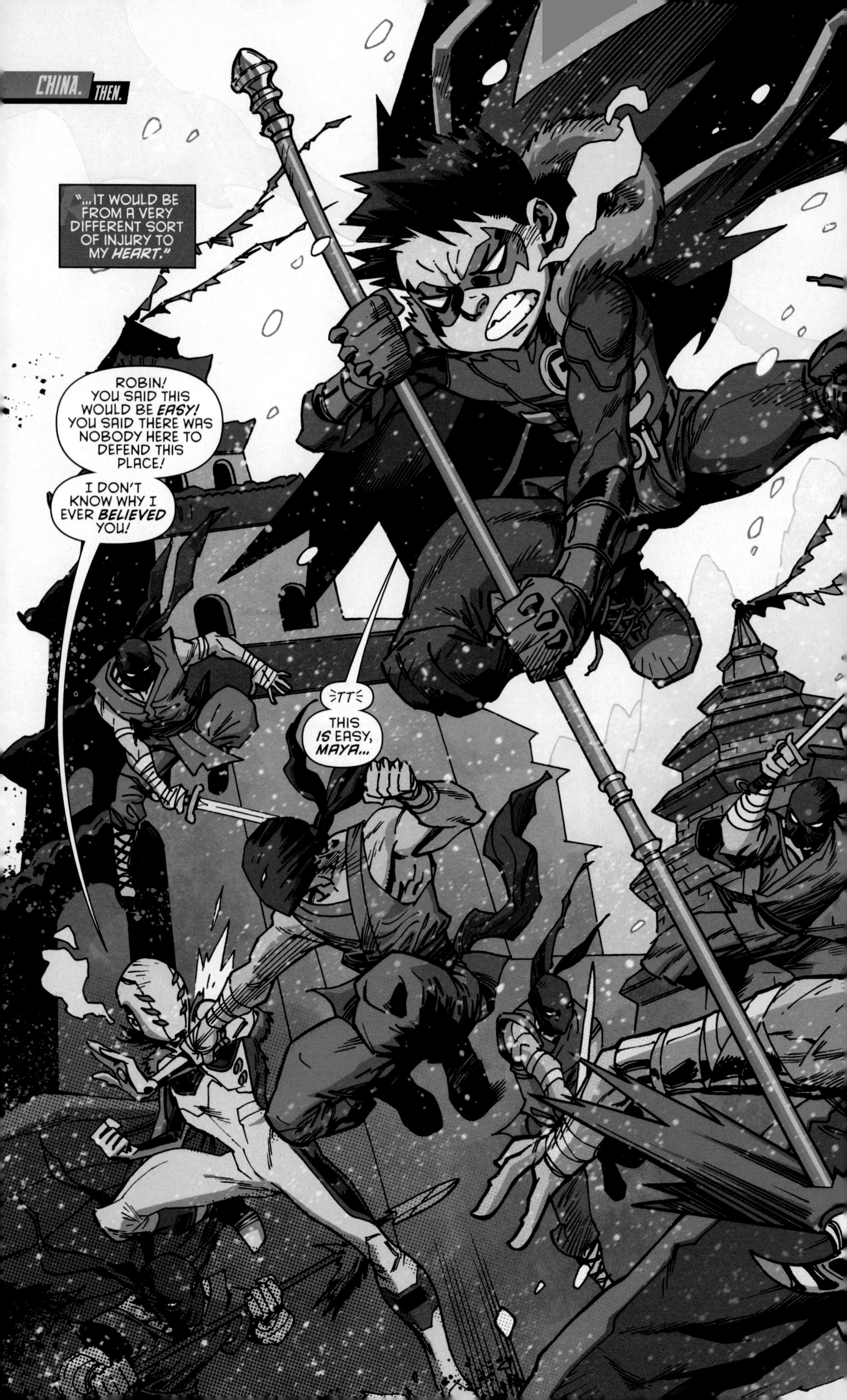
CHINA. THEN.
"...IT WOULD BE FROM A VERY DIFFERENT SORT OF INJURY TO MY *HEART*."
ROBIN! YOU SAID THIS WOULD BE *EASY!* YOU SAID THERE WAS NOBODY HERE TO DEFEND THIS PLACE!
I DON'T KNOW WHY I EVER *BELIEVED* YOU!
TT
THIS *IS* EASY, *MAYA*...

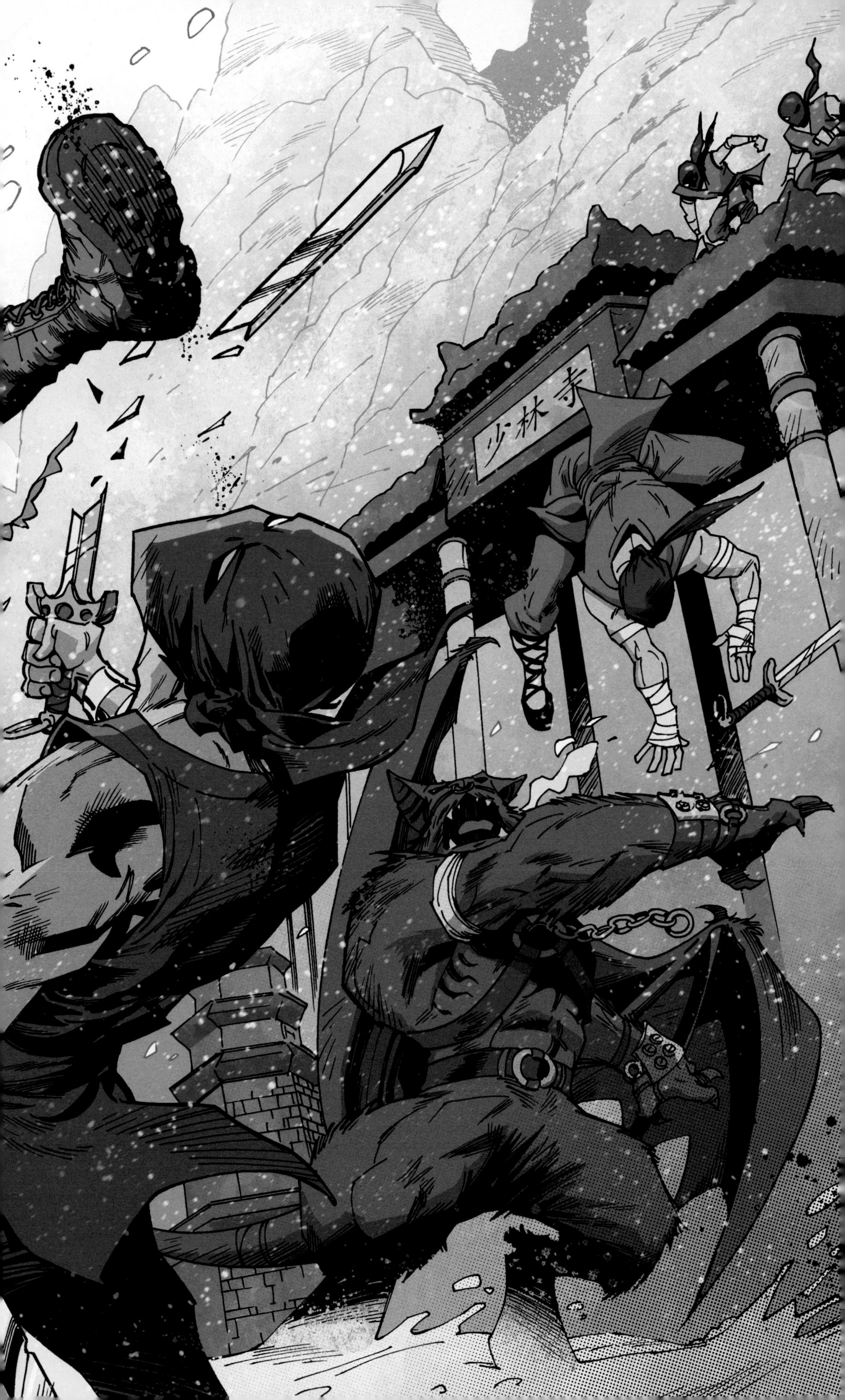
少林寺

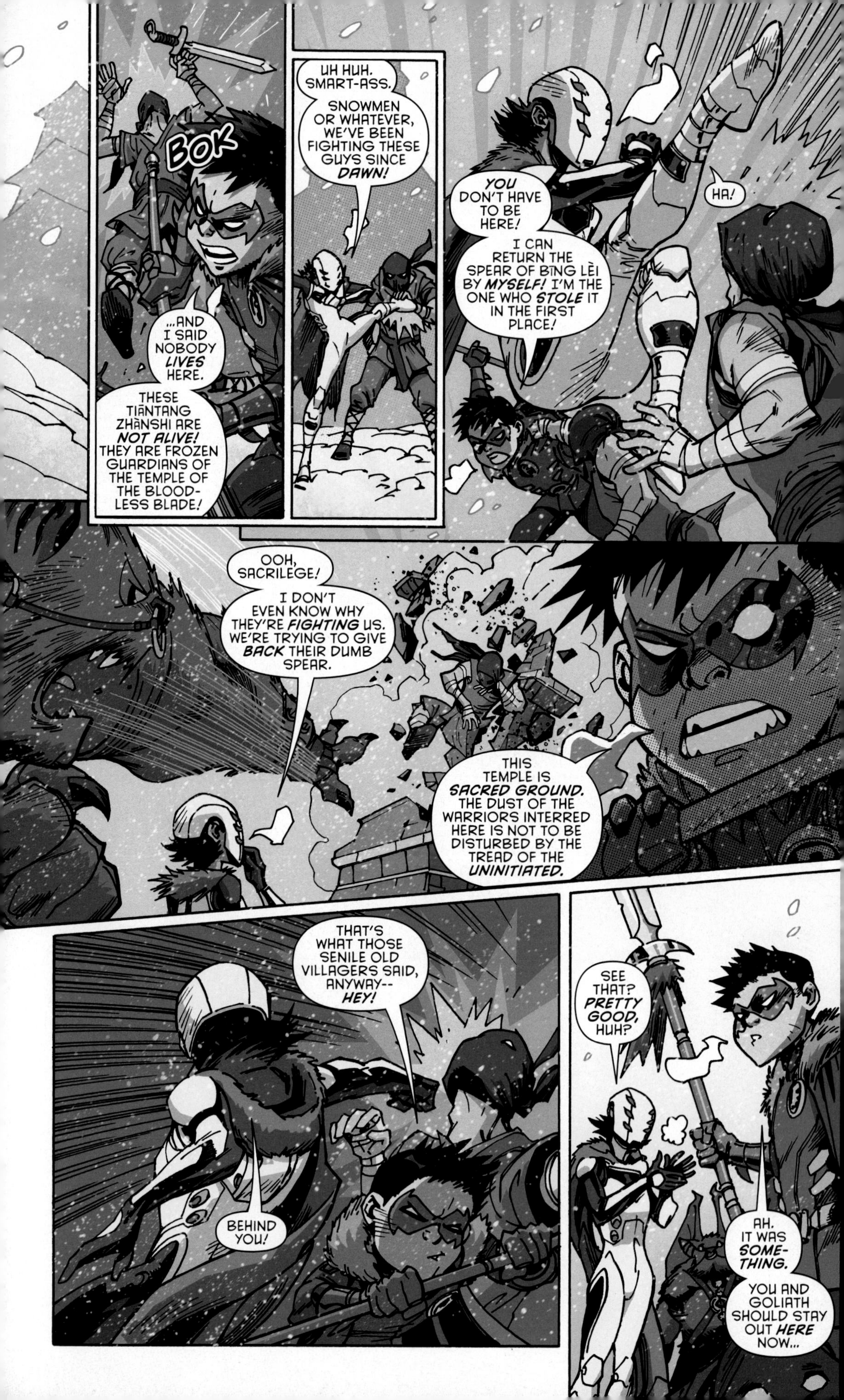
BOK
...AND I SAID NOBODY LIVES HERE.
THESE TIĀNTANG ZHĀNSHI ARE NOT ALIVE! THEY ARE FROZEN GUARDIANS OF THE TEMPLE OF THE BLOODLESS BLADE!
UH HUH. SMART-ASS.
SNOWMEN OR WHATEVER, WE'VE BEEN FIGHTING THESE GUYS SINCE DAWN!
YOU DON'T HAVE TO BE HERE!
I CAN RETURN THE SPEAR OF BĪNG LÈI BY MYSELF! I'M THE ONE WHO STOLE IT IN THE FIRST PLACE!
HA!
OOH, SACRILEGE!
I DON'T EVEN KNOW WHY THEY'RE FIGHTING US. WE'RE TRYING TO GIVE BACK THEIR DUMB SPEAR.
THIS TEMPLE IS SACRED GROUND. THE DUST OF THE WARRIORS INTERRED HERE IS NOT TO BE DISTURBED BY THE TREAD OF THE UNINITIATED.
THAT'S WHAT THOSE SENILE OLD VILLAGERS SAID, ANYWAY-- HEY!
BEHIND YOU!
SEE THAT? PRETTY GOOD, HUH?
AH. IT WAS SOMETHING.
YOU AND GOLIATH SHOULD STAY OUT HERE NOW...

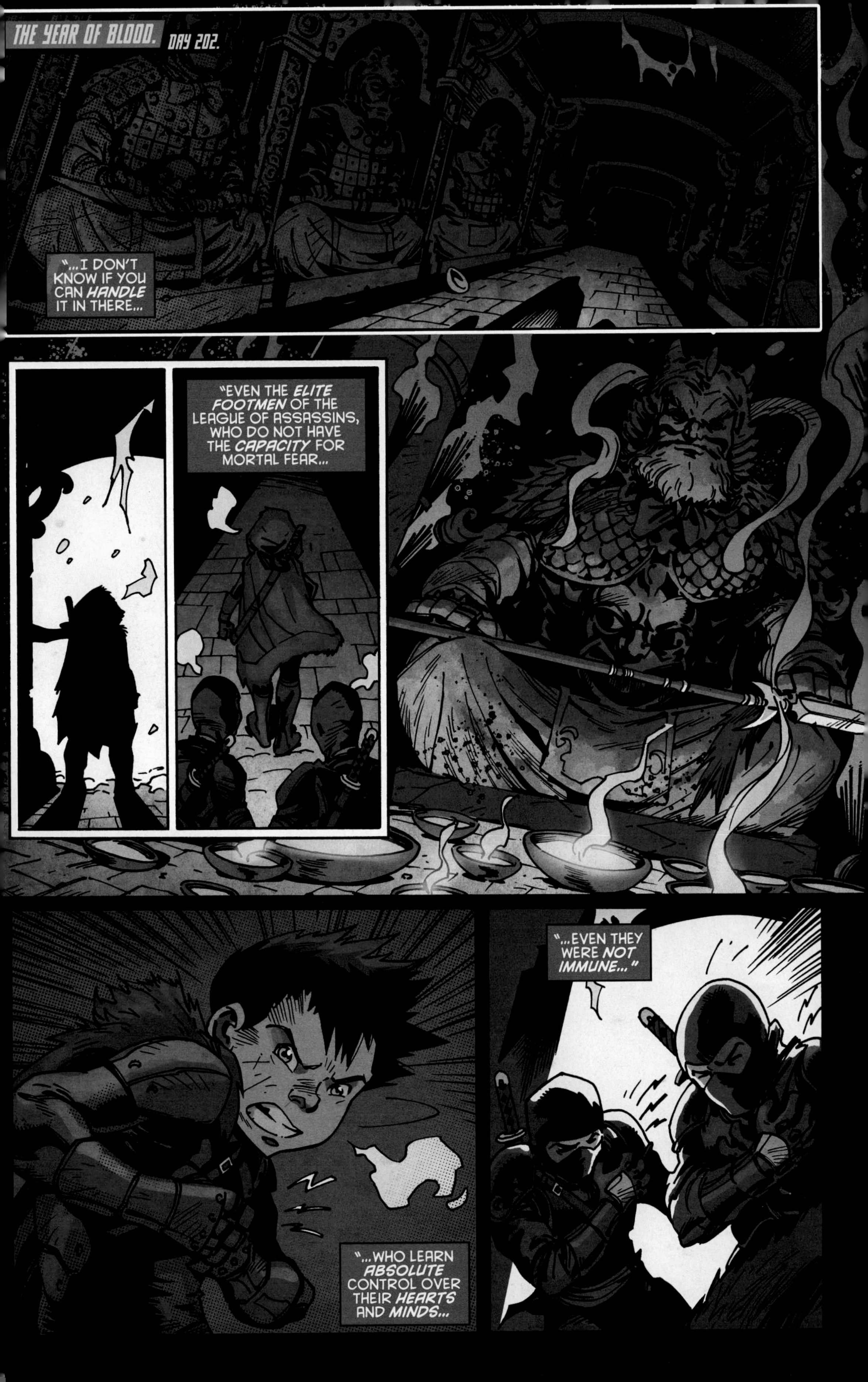
THE YEAR OF BLOOD. DAY 202.
"...I DON'T KNOW IF YOU CAN HANDLE IT IN THERE...
"EVEN THE ELITE FOOTMEN OF THE LEAGUE OF ASSASSINS, WHO DO NOT HAVE THE CAPACITY FOR MORTAL FEAR...
"...WHO LEARN ABSOLUTE CONTROL OVER THEIR HEARTS AND MINDS...
"...EVEN THEY WERE NOT IMMUNE..."

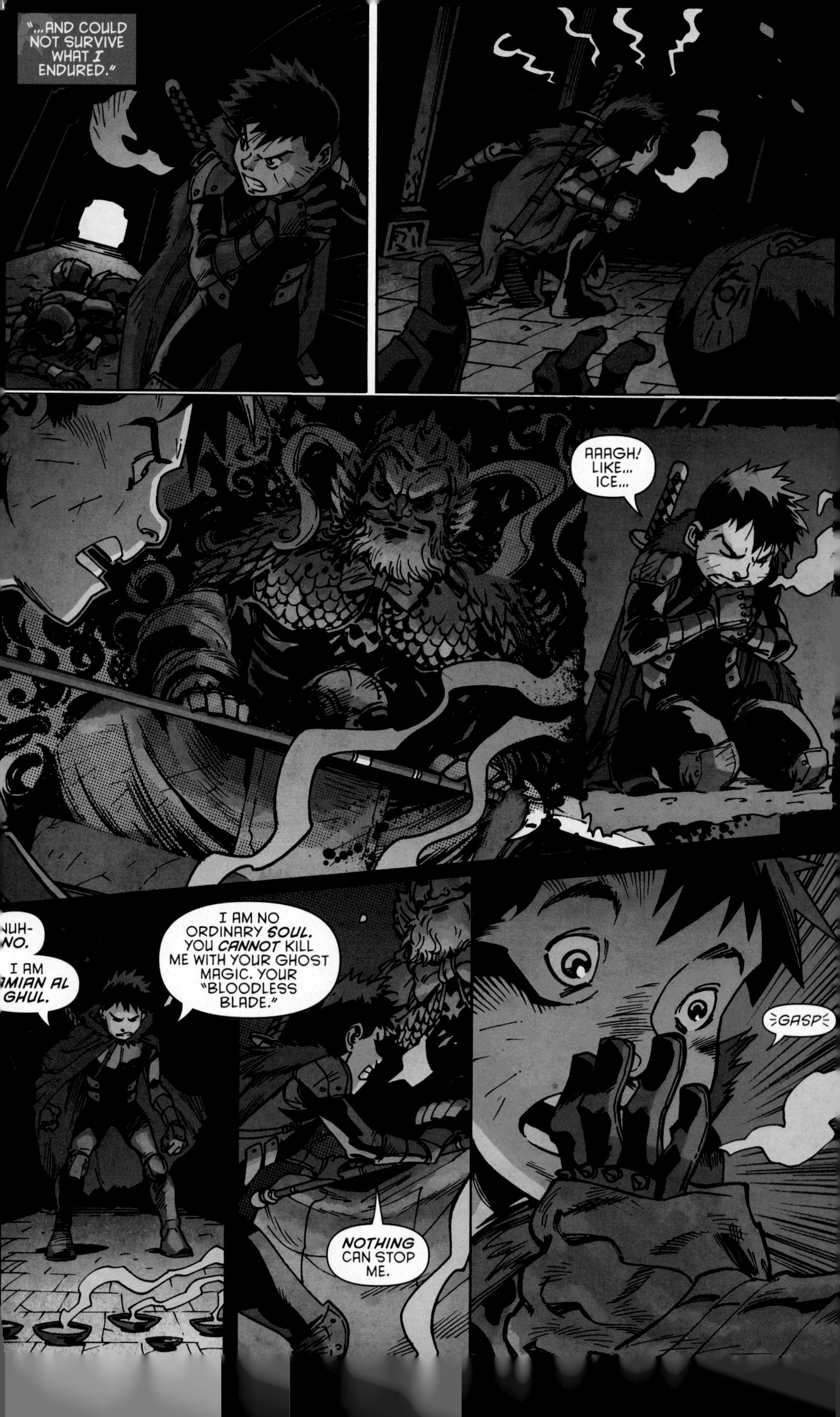
"...AND COULD NOT SURVIVE WHAT I ENDURED."
AAAGH! LIKE... ICE...
NUH- NO.
I AM AMIAN AL GHUL.
I AM NO ORDINARY SOUL. YOU CANNOT KILL ME WITH YOUR GHOST MAGIC. YOUR "BLOODLESS BLADE."
NOTHING CAN STOP ME.
GASP

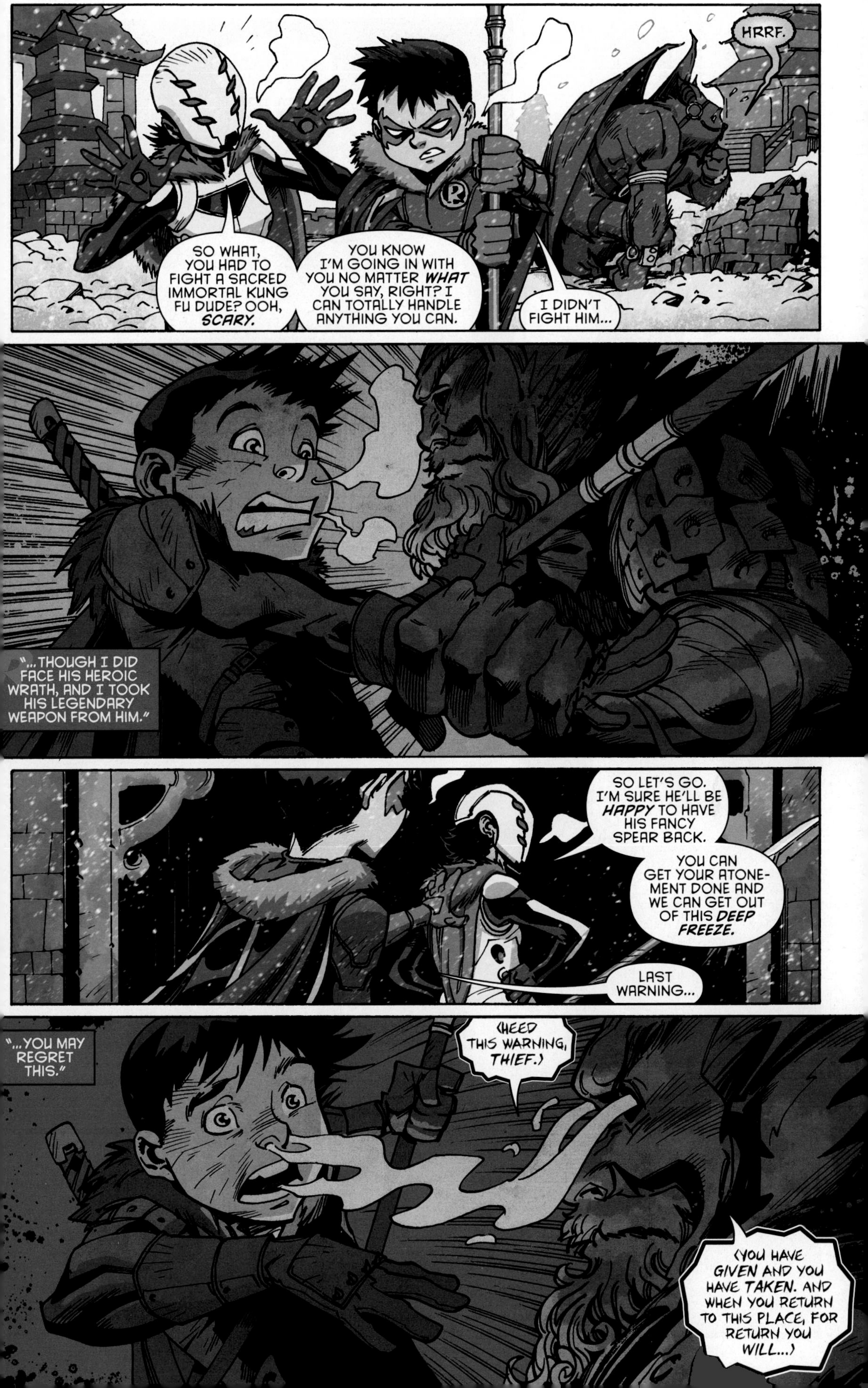

HRRF.
SO WHAT, YOU HAD TO FIGHT A SACRED IMMORTAL KUNG FU DUDE? OOH, SCARY.
YOU KNOW I'M GOING IN WITH YOU NO MATTER WHAT YOU SAY, RIGHT? I CAN TOTALLY HANDLE ANYTHING YOU CAN.
I DIDN'T FIGHT HIM...
"...THOUGH I DID FACE HIS HEROIC WRATH, AND I TOOK HIS LEGENDARY WEAPON FROM HIM."
SO LET'S GO. I'M SURE HE'LL BE HAPPY TO HAVE HIS FANCY SPEAR BACK.
YOU CAN GET YOUR ATONEMENT DONE AND WE CAN GET OUT OF THIS DEEP FREEZE.
LAST WARNING...
"...YOU MAY REGRET THIS."
(HEED THIS WARNING, THIEF.)
(YOU HAVE GIVEN AND YOU HAVE TAKEN. AND WHEN YOU RETURN TO THIS PLACE, FOR RETURN YOU WILL...)

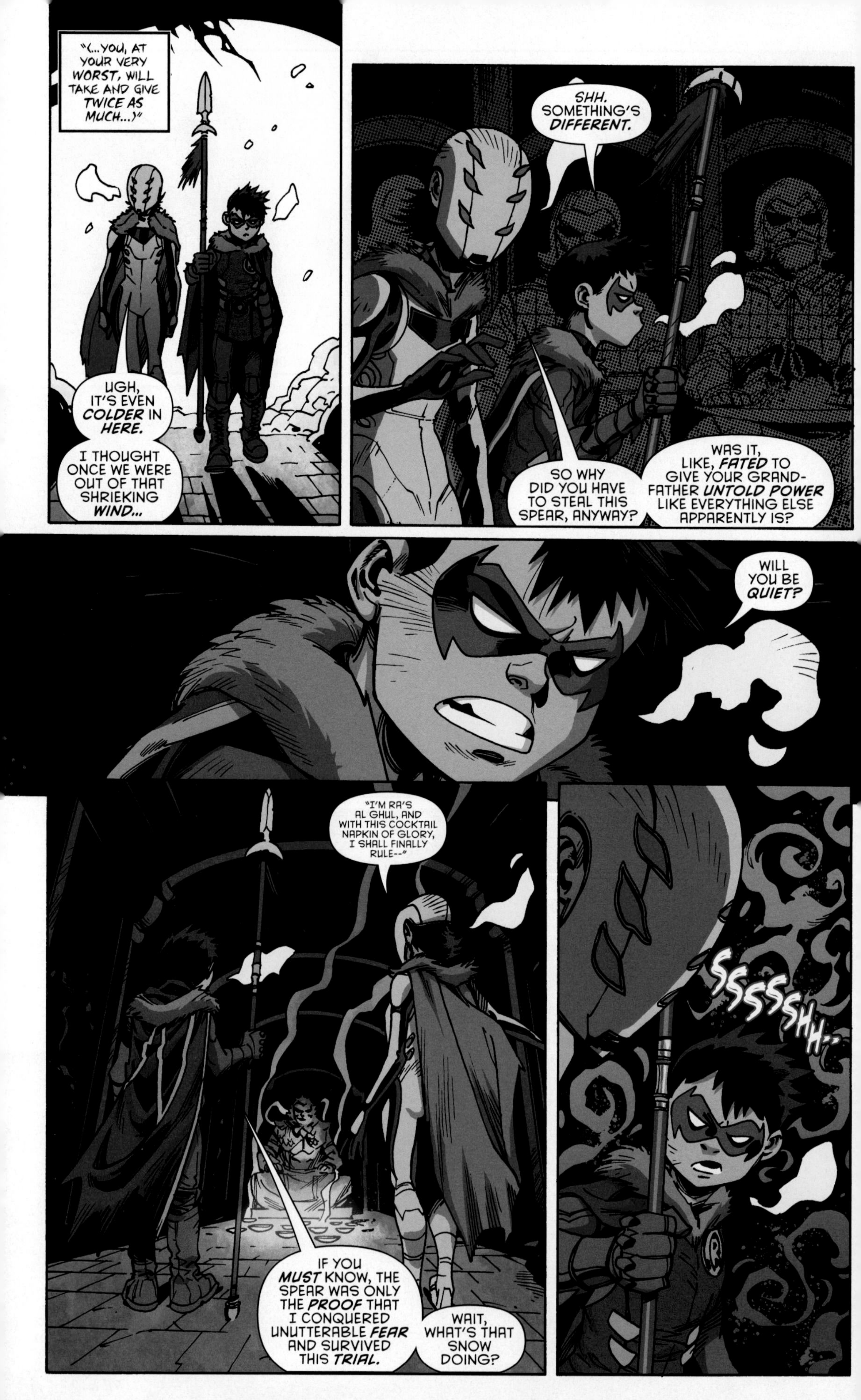
"(...YOU, AT YOUR VERY WORST, WILL TAKE AND GIVE TWICE AS MUCH...)"
UGH, IT'S EVEN COLDER IN HERE.
I THOUGHT ONCE WE WERE OUT OF THAT SHRIEKING WIND...
SHH. SOMETHING'S DIFFERENT.
SO WHY DID YOU HAVE TO STEAL THIS SPEAR, ANYWAY?
WAS IT, LIKE, FATED TO GIVE YOUR GRAND-FATHER UNTOLD POWER LIKE EVERYTHING ELSE APPARENTLY IS?
WILL YOU BE QUIET?
"I'M RA'S AL GHUL, AND WITH THIS COCKTAIL NAPKIN OF GLORY, I SHALL FINALLY RULE--"
IF YOU MUST KNOW, THE SPEAR WAS ONLY THE PROOF THAT I CONQUERED UNUTTERABLE FEAR AND SURVIVED THIS TRIAL.
WAIT, WHAT'S THAT SNOW DOING?
SSSSSHH..

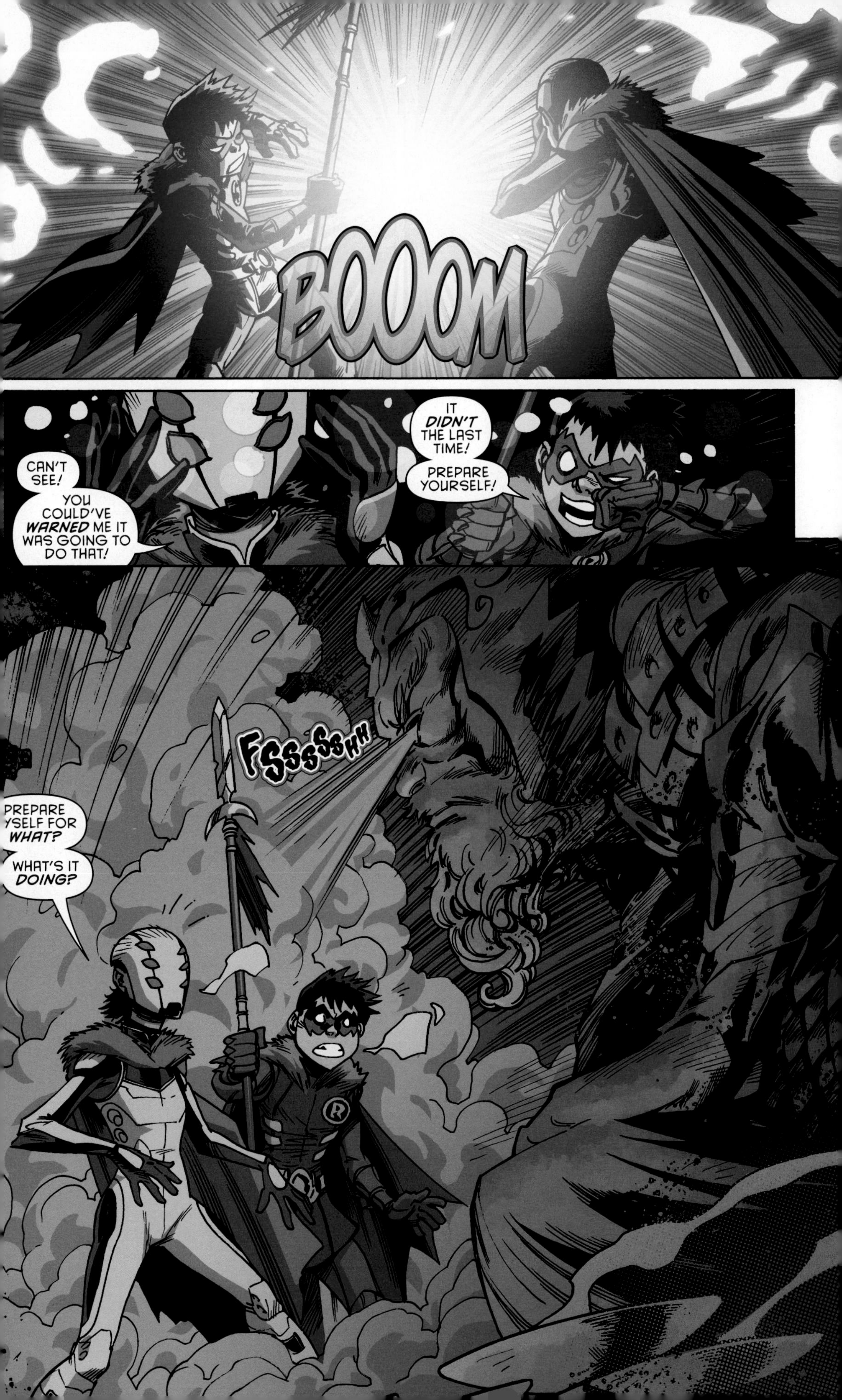
BOOOM
CAN'T SEE!
YOU COULD'VE WARNED ME IT WAS GOING TO DO THAT!
IT DIDN'T THE LAST TIME!
PREPARE YOURSELF!
FSSSSSHH
PREPARE YSELF FOR WHAT?
WHAT'S IT DOING?

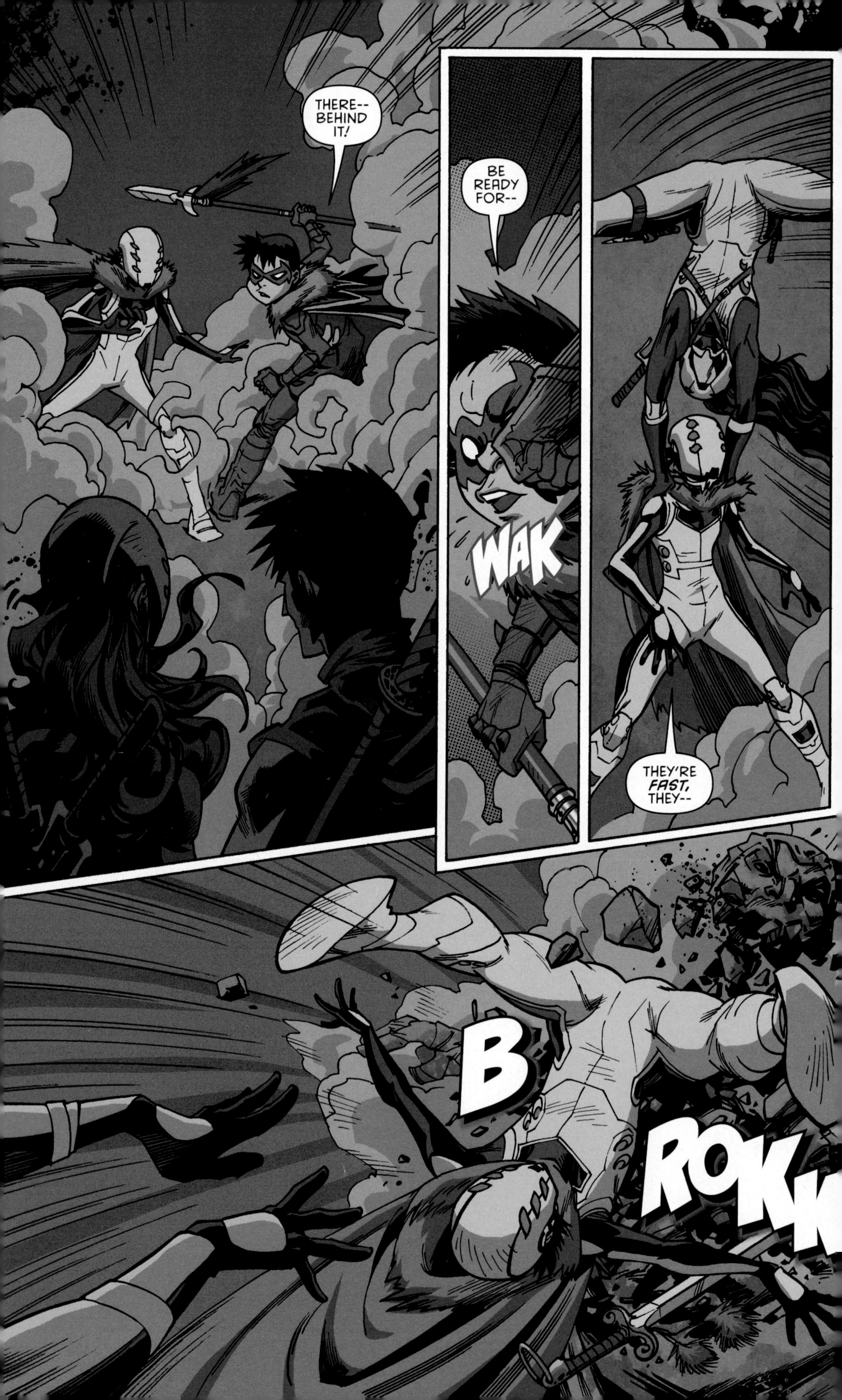
THERE-- BEHIND IT!
BE READY FOR--
WAK
THEY'RE *FAST,* THEY--
B
ROKK

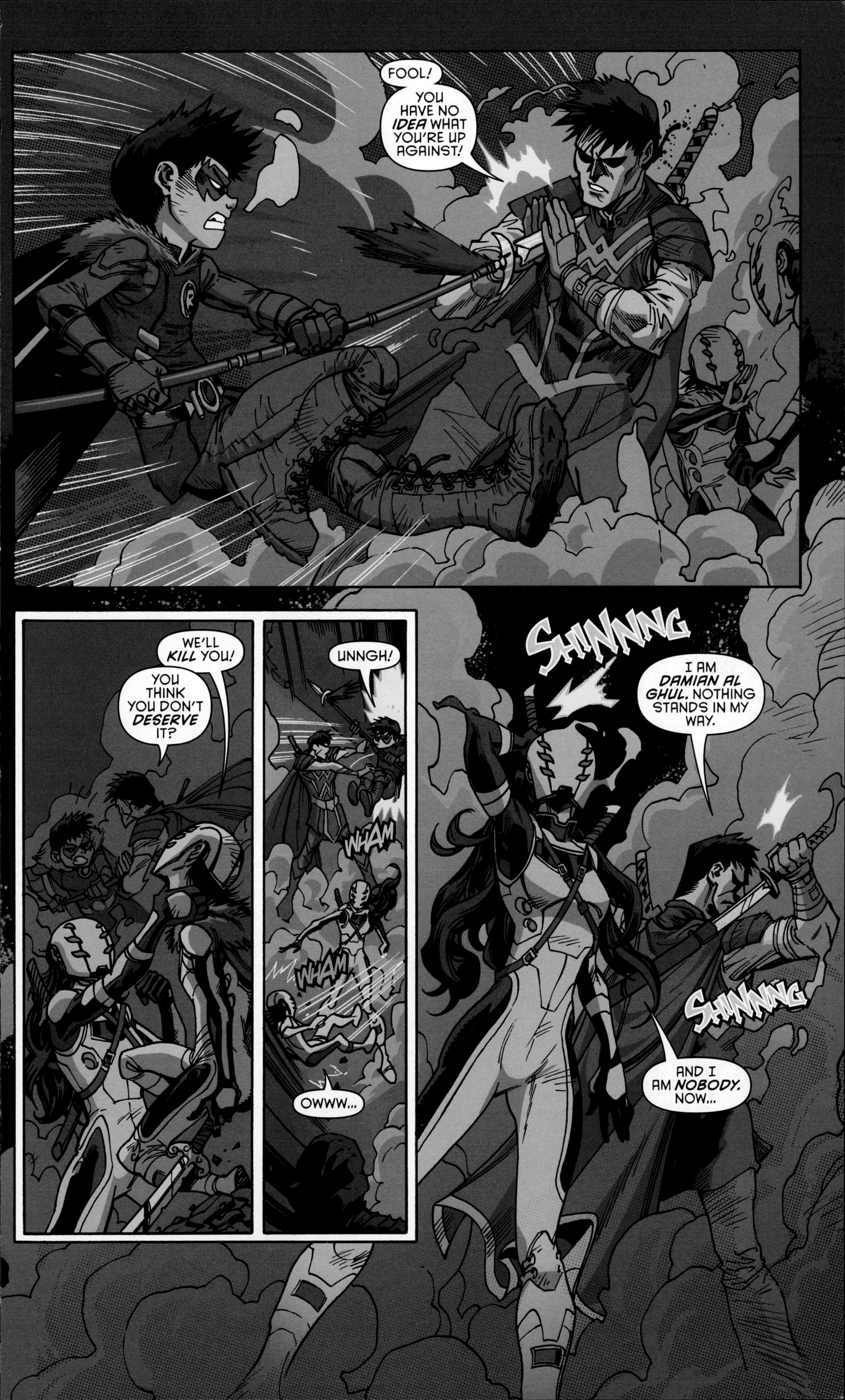
FOOL!
YOU HAVE NO IDEA WHAT YOU'RE UP AGAINST!
WE'LL KILL YOU!
YOU THINK YOU DON'T DESERVE IT?
UNNGH!
WHAM
WHAM
OWWW...
SHINNNG
I AM DAMIAN AL GHUL. NOTHING STANDS IN MY WAY.
SHINNNG
AND I AM NOBODY. NOW...

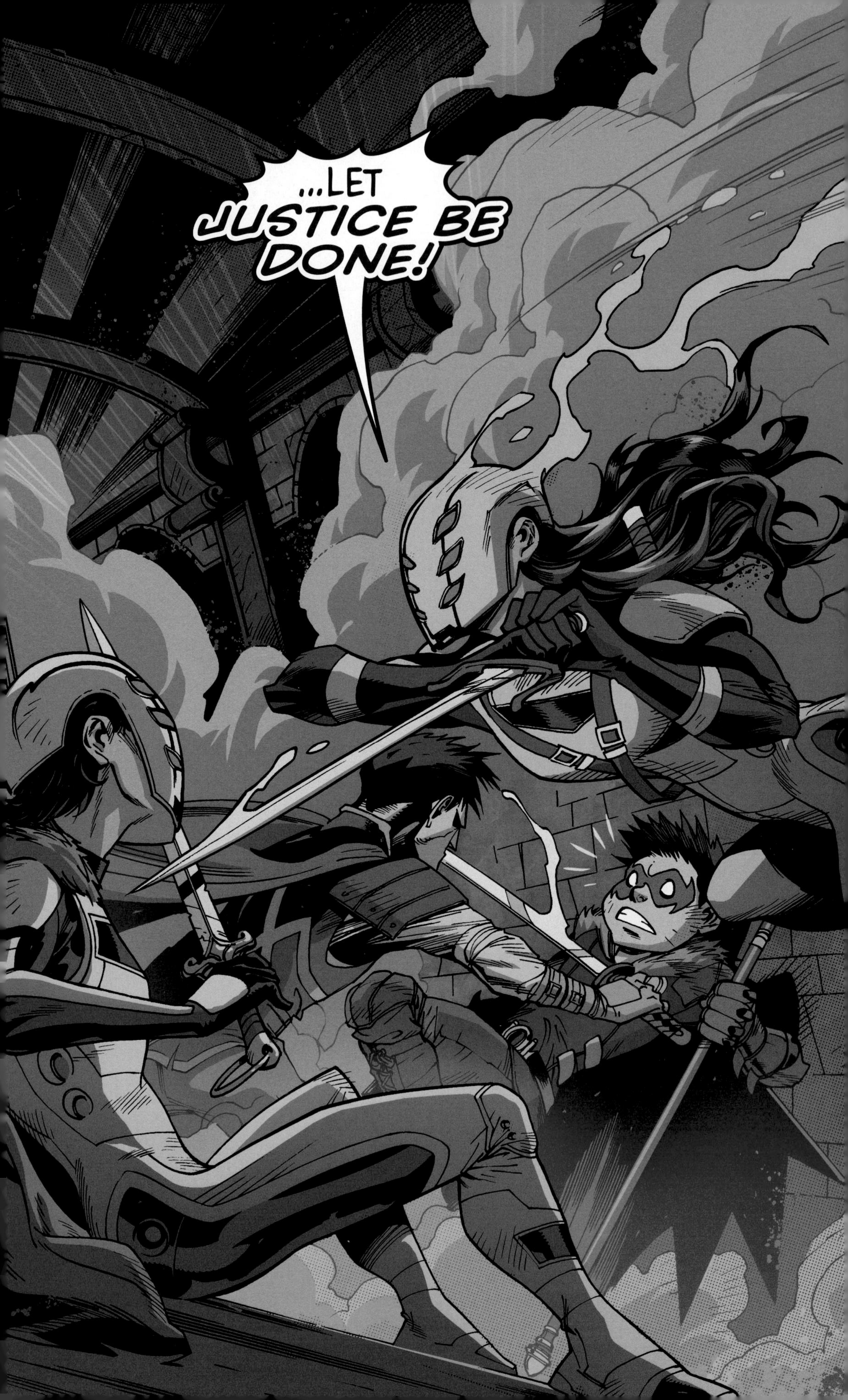
...LET JUSTICE BE DONE!

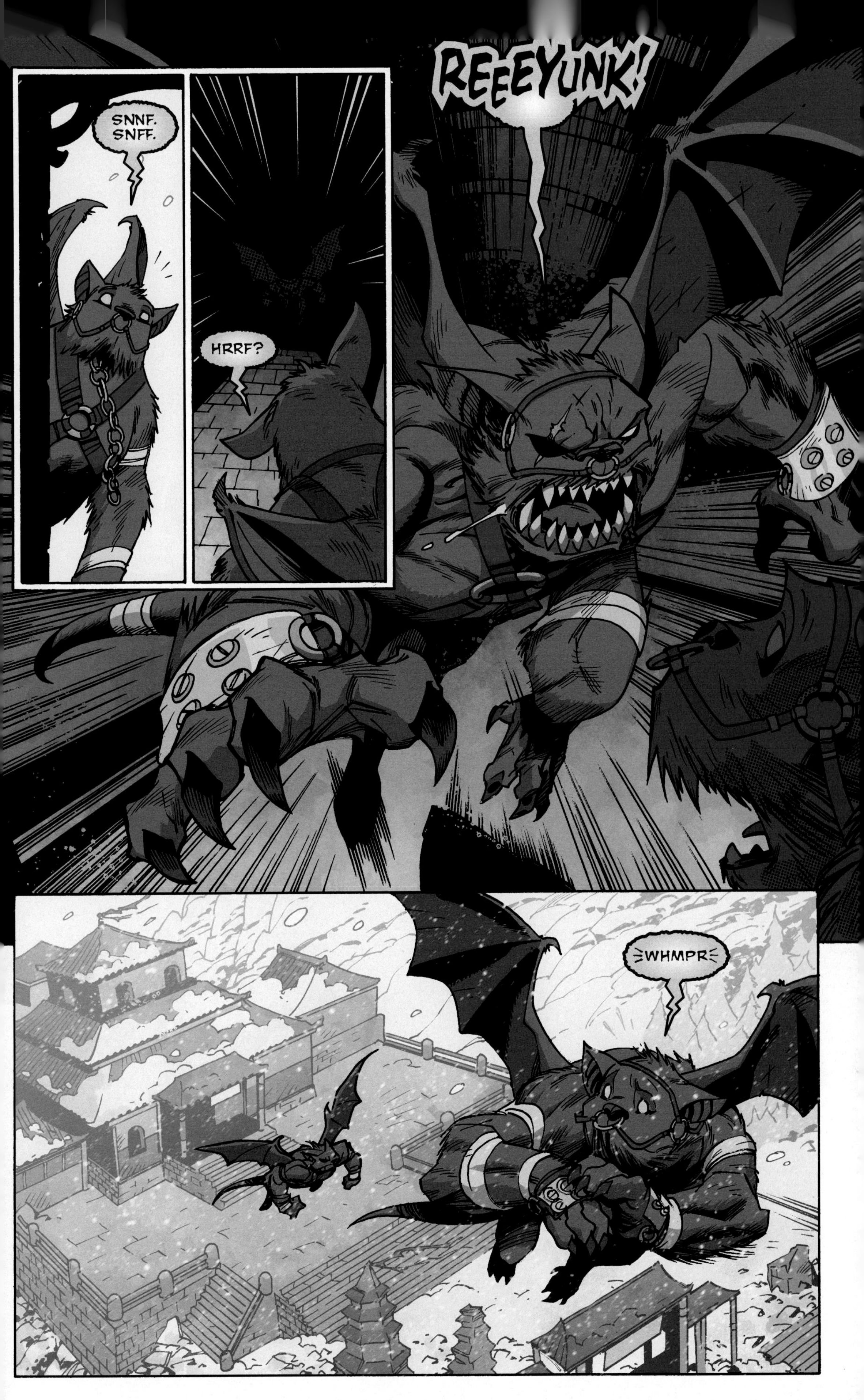
SNNF. SNFF.
HRRF?
REEEYUNK!
WHMPR

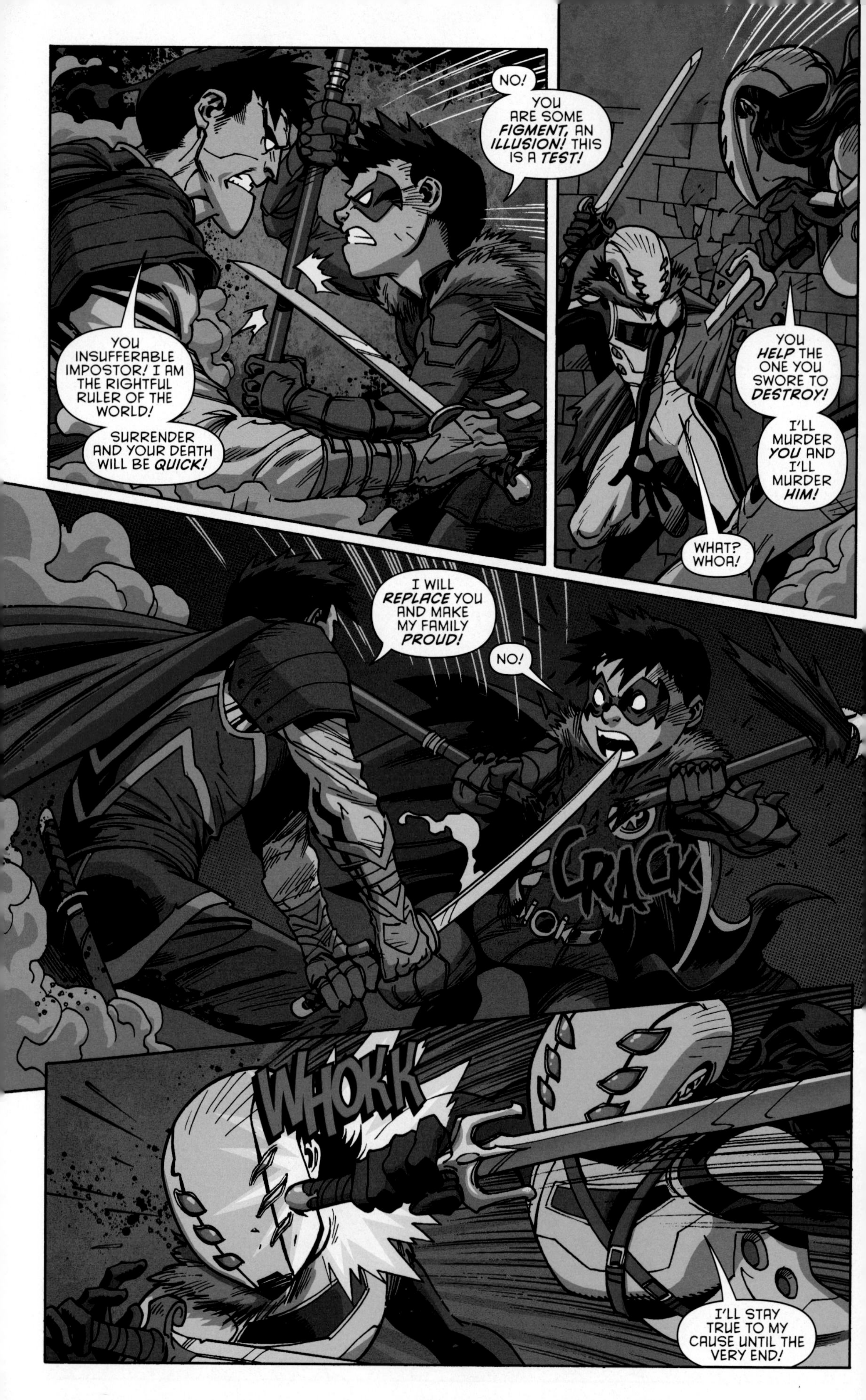
NO!
YOU ARE SOME FIGMENT, AN ILLUSION! THIS IS A TEST!
YOU INSUFFERABLE IMPOSTOR! I AM THE RIGHTFUL RULER OF THE WORLD!
SURRENDER AND YOUR DEATH WILL BE QUICK!
YOU HELP THE ONE YOU SWORE TO DESTROY!
I'LL MURDER YOU AND I'LL MURDER HIM!
WHAT? WHOA!
I WILL REPLACE YOU AND MAKE MY FAMILY PROUD!
NO!
CRACK
WHOKK
I'LL STAY TRUE TO MY CAUSE UNTIL THE VERY END!

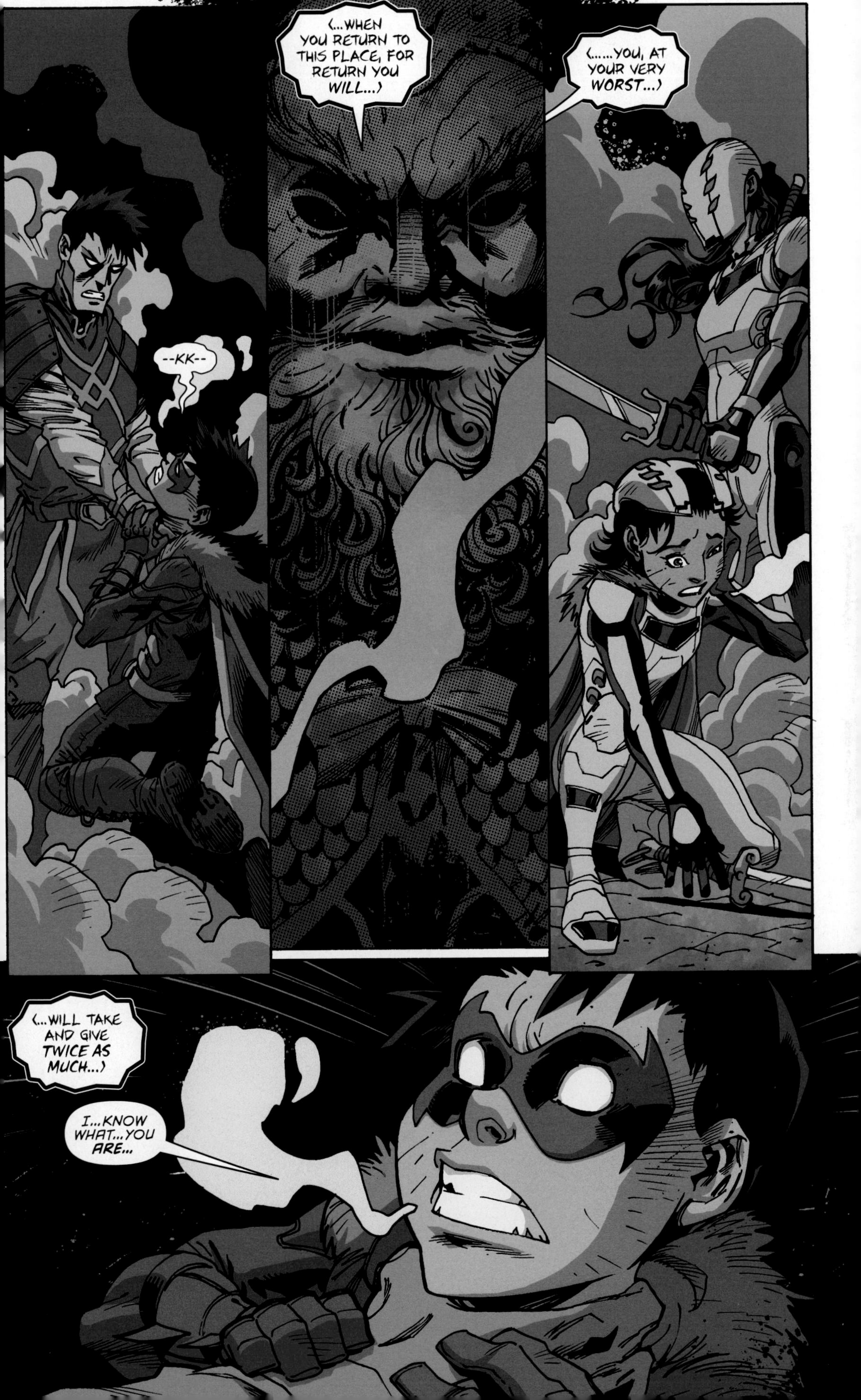
--KK--
(...WHEN YOU RETURN TO THIS PLACE, FOR RETURN YOU WILL...)
(......YOU, AT YOUR VERY WORST...)
(...WILL TAKE AND GIVE TWICE AS MUCH...)
I...KNOW WHAT...YOU ARE...

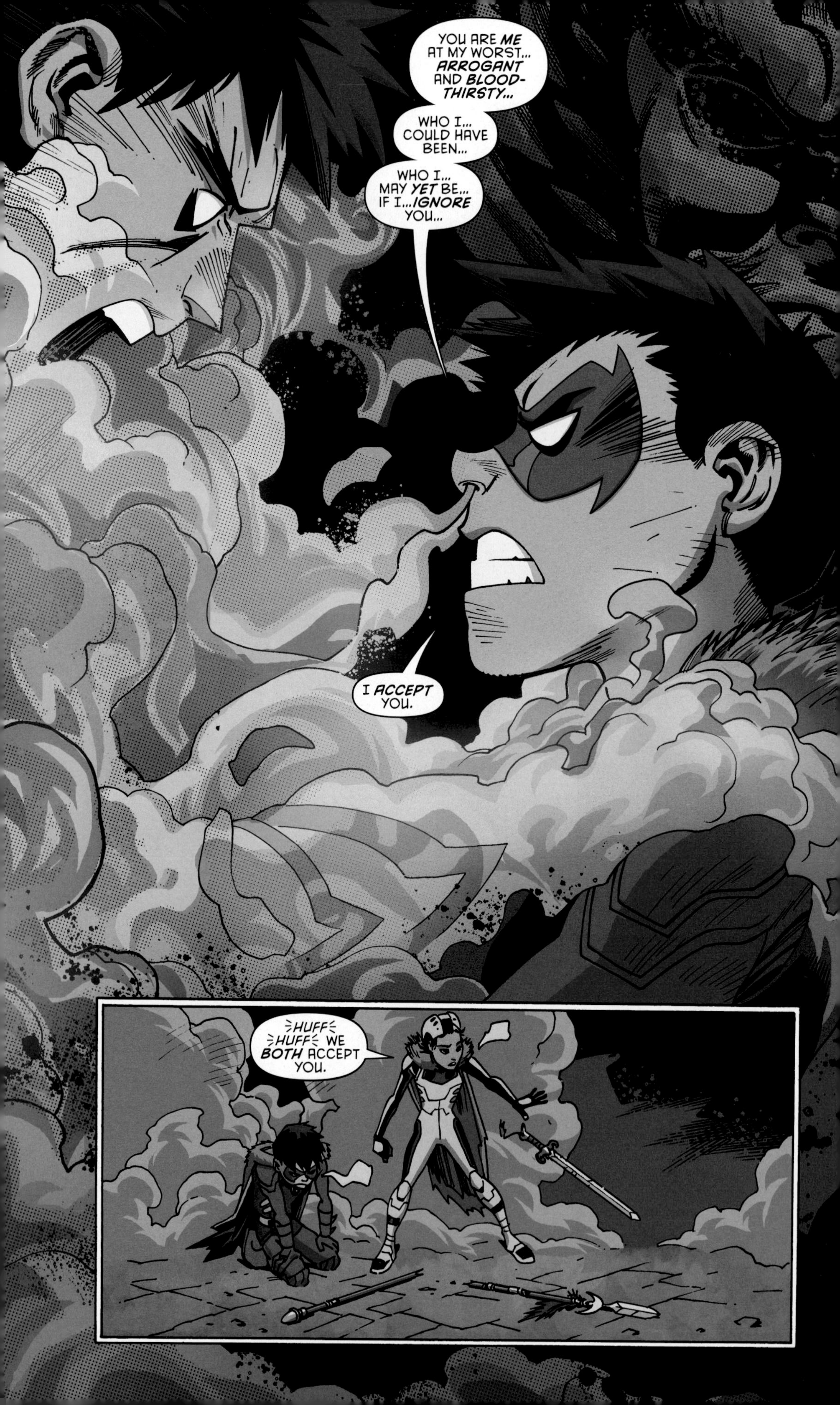
YOU ARE ME AT MY WORST... ARROGANT AND BLOOD-THIRSTY...
WHO I... COULD HAVE BEEN...
WHO I... MAY YET BE... IF I...IGNORE YOU...
I ACCEPT YOU.
HUFF HUFF WE BOTH ACCEPT YOU.

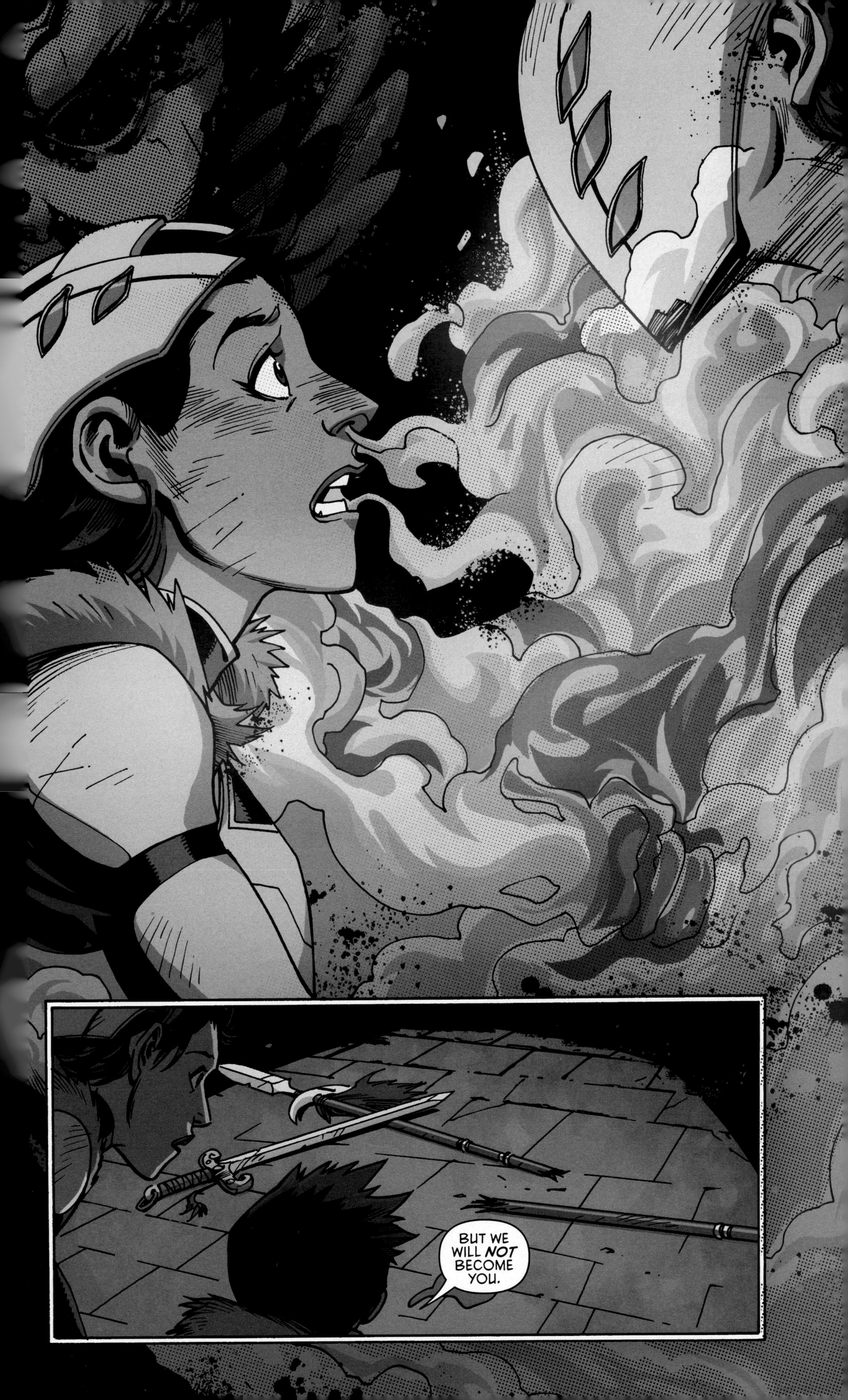
BUT WE WILL NOT BECOME YOU.

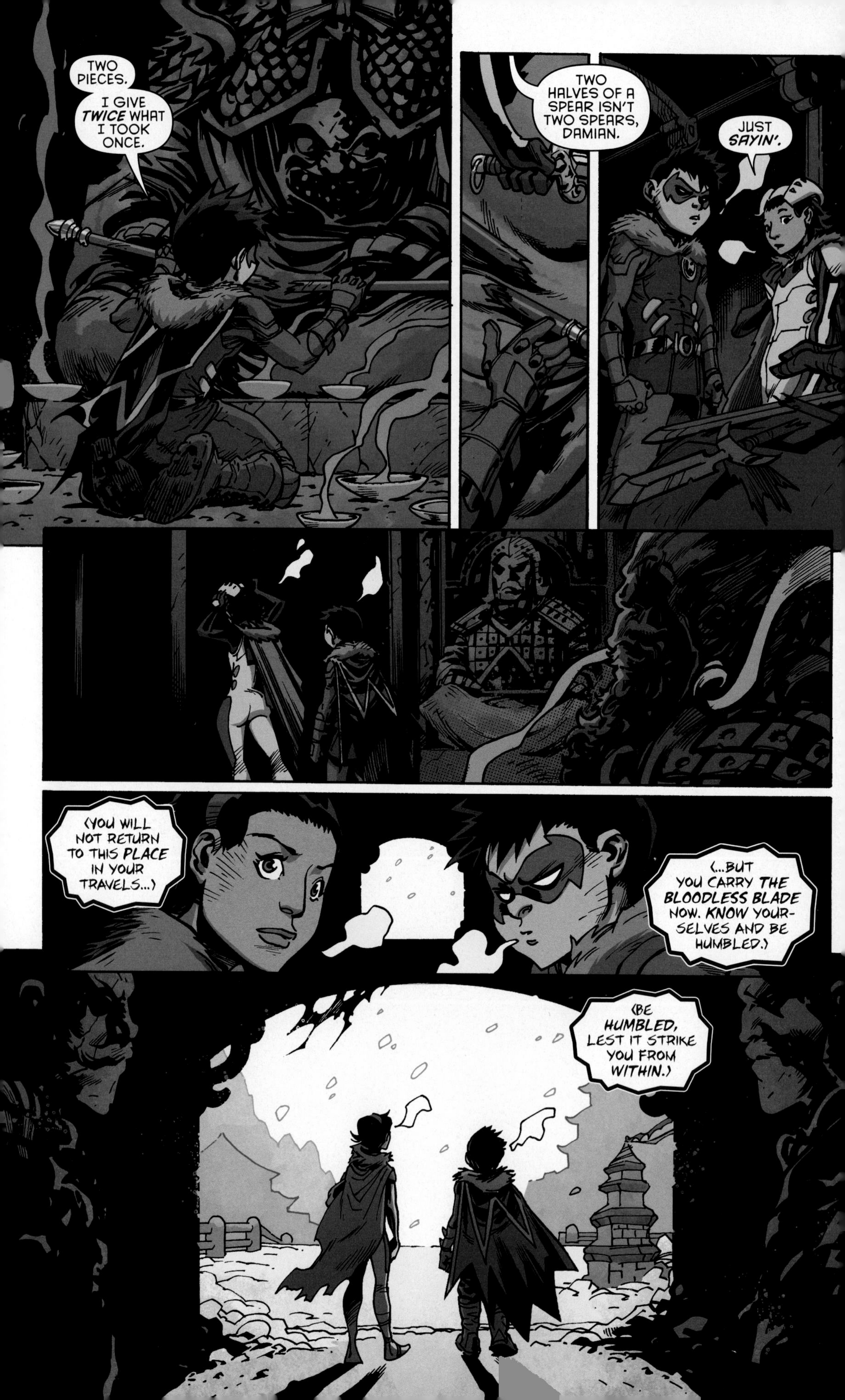
TWO PIECES.
I GIVE TWICE WHAT I TOOK ONCE.
TWO HALVES OF A SPEAR ISN'T TWO SPEARS, DAMIAN.
JUST SAYIN'.
(YOU WILL NOT RETURN TO THIS PLACE IN YOUR TRAVELS...)
(...BUT YOU CARRY THE BLOODLESS BLADE NOW. KNOW YOURSELVES AND BE HUMBLED.)
(BE HUMBLED, LEST IT STRIKE YOU FROM WITHIN.)

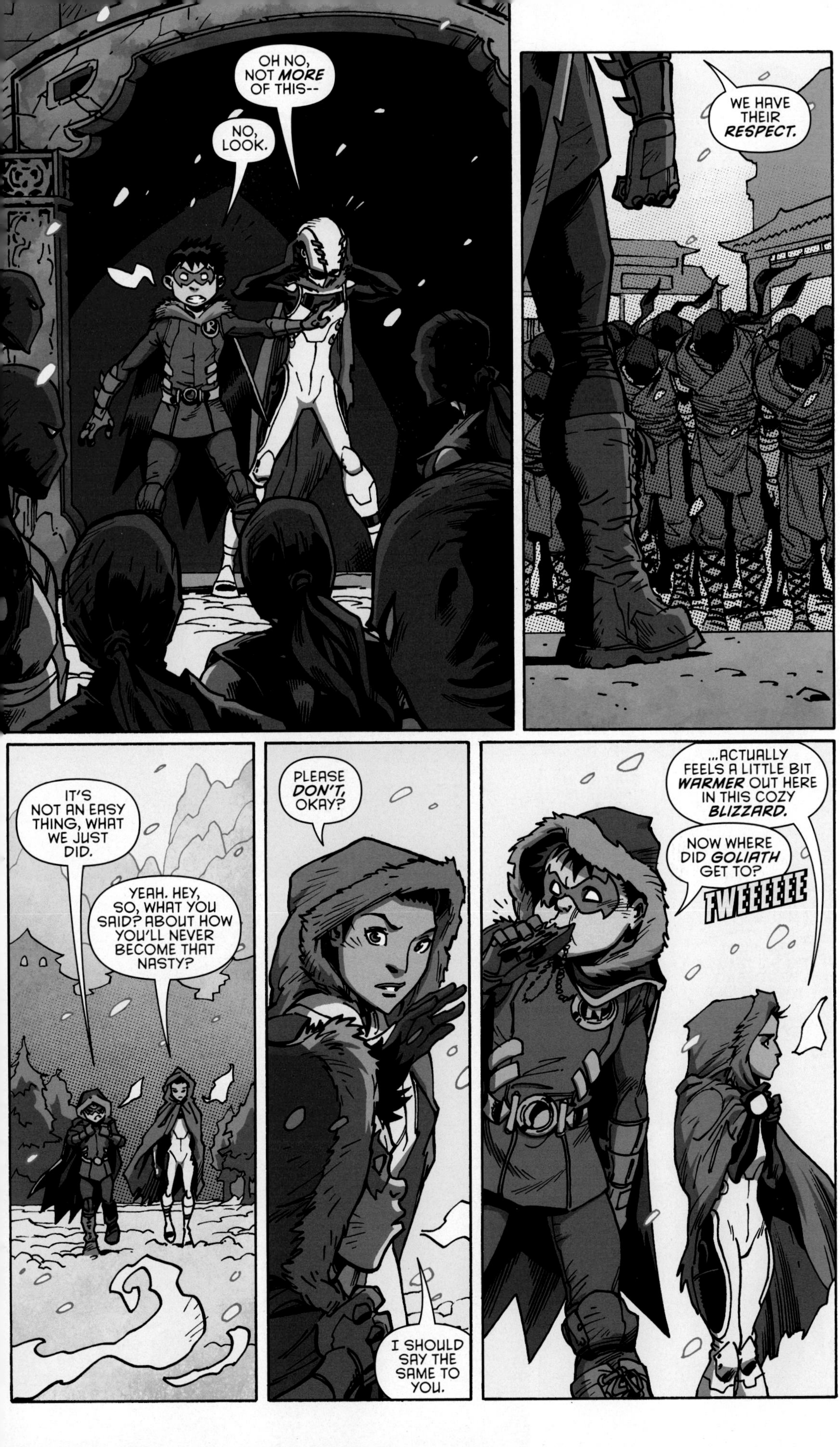
OH NO, NOT MORE OF THIS--
NO, LOOK.
WE HAVE THEIR RESPECT.
IT'S NOT AN EASY THING, WHAT WE JUST DID.
YEAH. HEY, SO, WHAT YOU SAID? ABOUT HOW YOU'LL NEVER BECOME THAT NASTY?
PLEASE DON'T, OKAY?
I SHOULD SAY THE SAME TO YOU.
...ACTUALLY FEELS A LITTLE BIT WARMER OUT HERE IN THIS COZY BLIZZARD.
NOW WHERE DID GOLIATH GET TO?
FWEEEEEE

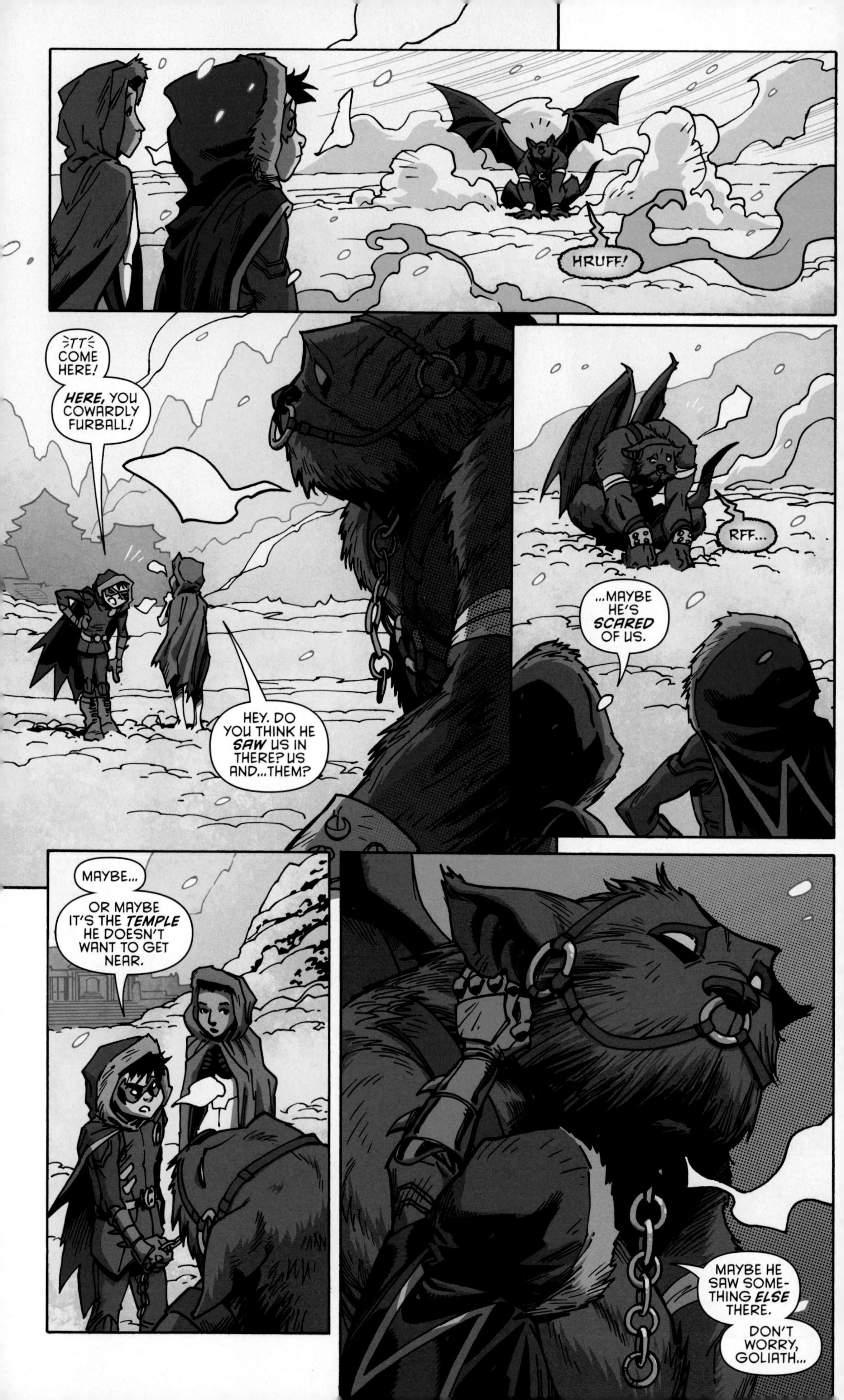
HRUFF!
TT
COME HERE!
HERE, YOU COWARDLY FURBALL!
HEY. DO YOU THINK HE SAW US IN THERE? US AND...THEM?
RFF...
...MAYBE HE'S SCARED OF US.
MAYBE...
OR MAYBE IT'S THE TEMPLE HE DOESN'T WANT TO GET NEAR.
MAYBE HE SAW SOMETHING ELSE THERE.
DON'T WORRY, GOLIATH...

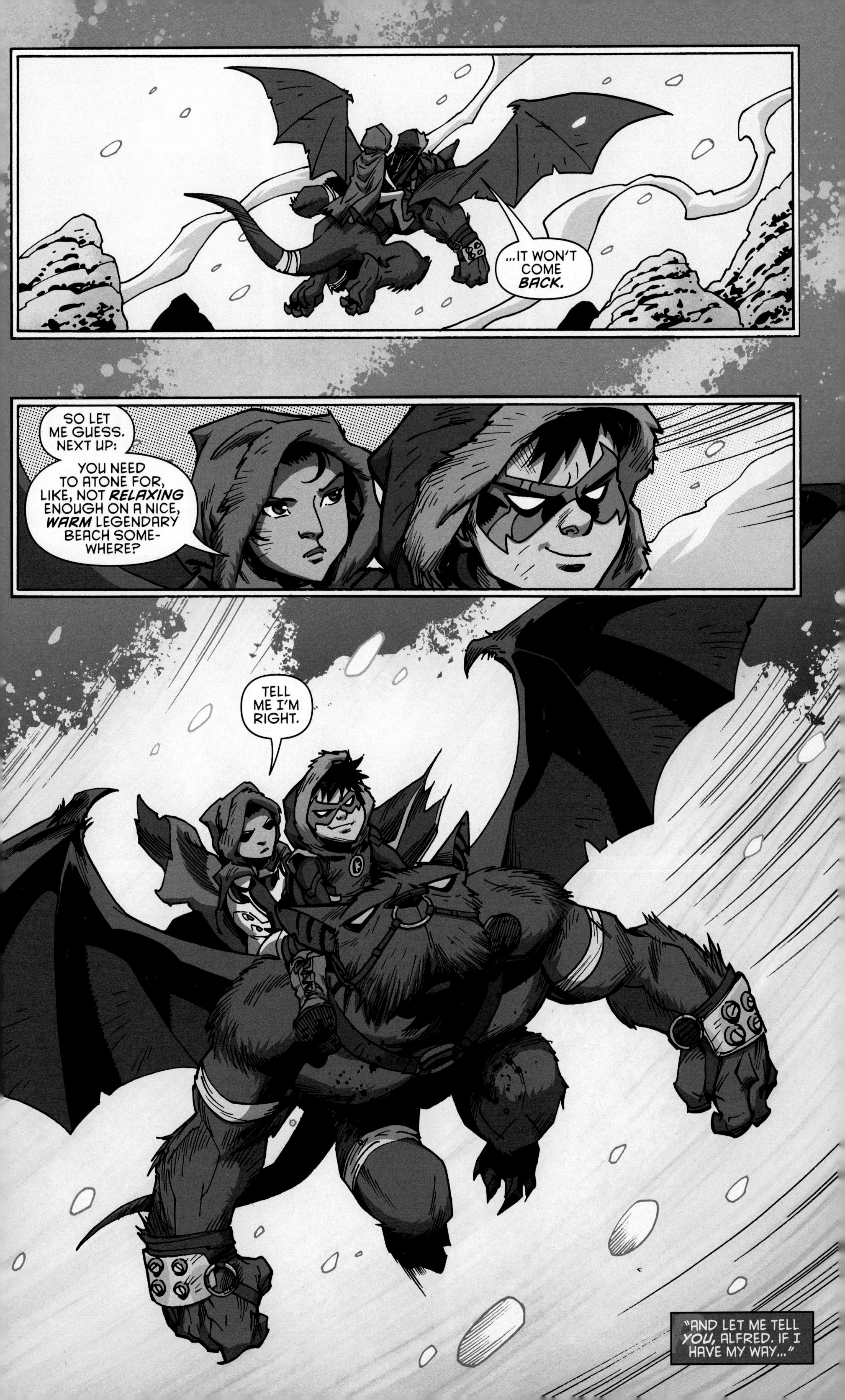
...IT WON'T COME BACK.
SO LET ME GUESS. NEXT UP:
YOU NEED TO ATONE FOR, LIKE, NOT RELAXING ENOUGH ON A NICE, WARM LEGENDARY BEACH SOME-WHERE?
TELL ME I'M RIGHT.
"AND LET ME TELL YOU, ALFRED. IF I HAVE MY WAY..."

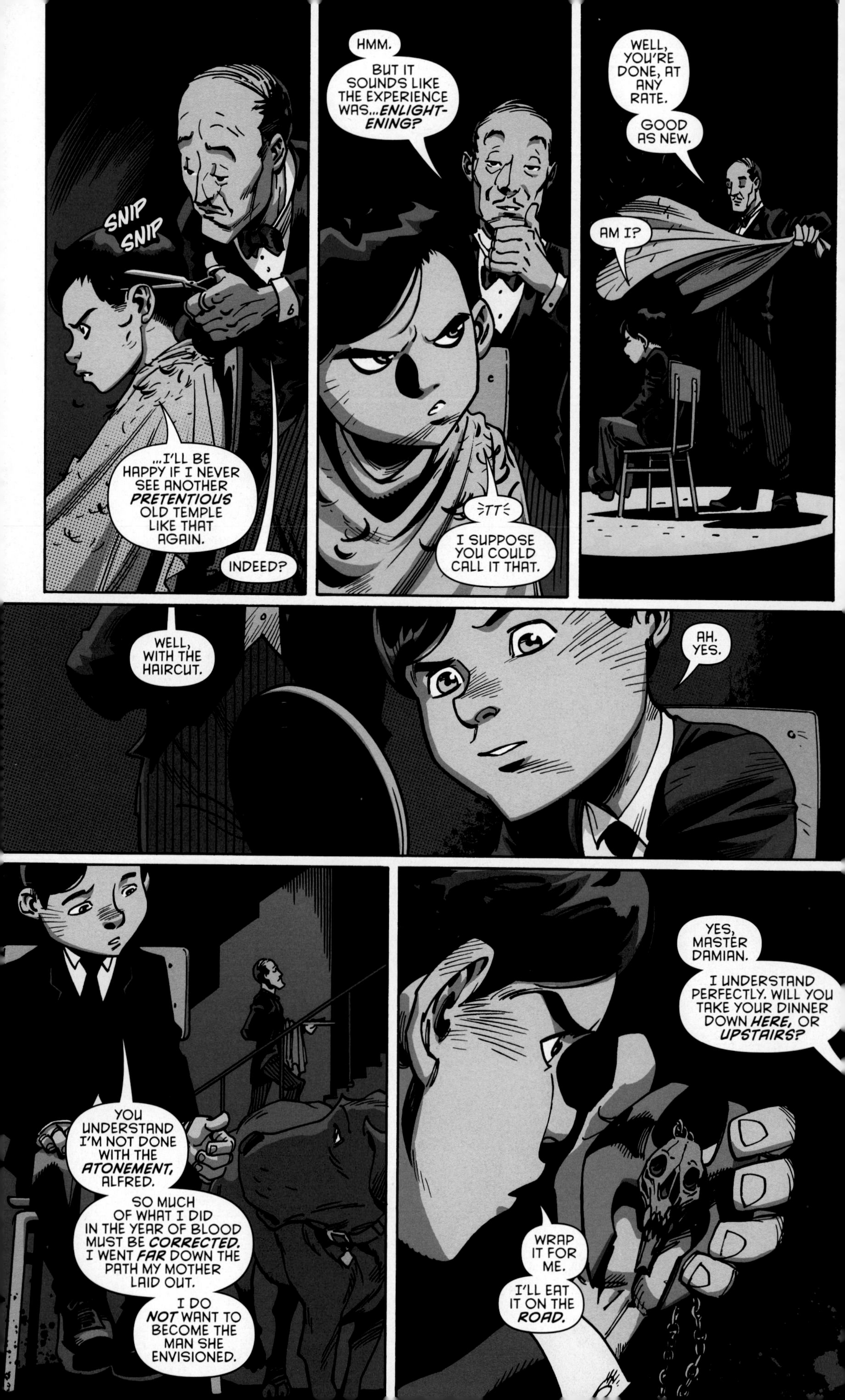
SNIP SNIP
...I'LL BE HAPPY IF I NEVER SEE ANOTHER PRETENTIOUS OLD TEMPLE LIKE THAT AGAIN.
INDEED?
HMM.
BUT IT SOUNDS LIKE THE EXPERIENCE WAS...ENLIGHT-ENING?
TT
I SUPPOSE YOU COULD CALL IT THAT.
WELL, YOU'RE DONE, AT ANY RATE.
GOOD AS NEW.
AM I?
WELL, WITH THE HAIRCUT.
AH. YES.
YOU UNDERSTAND I'M NOT DONE WITH THE ATONEMENT, ALFRED.
SO MUCH OF WHAT I DID IN THE YEAR OF BLOOD MUST BE CORRECTED. I WENT FAR DOWN THE PATH MY MOTHER LAID OUT.
I DO NOT WANT TO BECOME THE MAN SHE ENVISIONED.
YES, MASTER DAMIAN.
I UNDERSTAND PERFECTLY. WILL YOU TAKE YOUR DINNER DOWN HERE, OR UPSTAIRS?
WRAP IT FOR ME.
I'LL EAT IT ON THE ROAD.

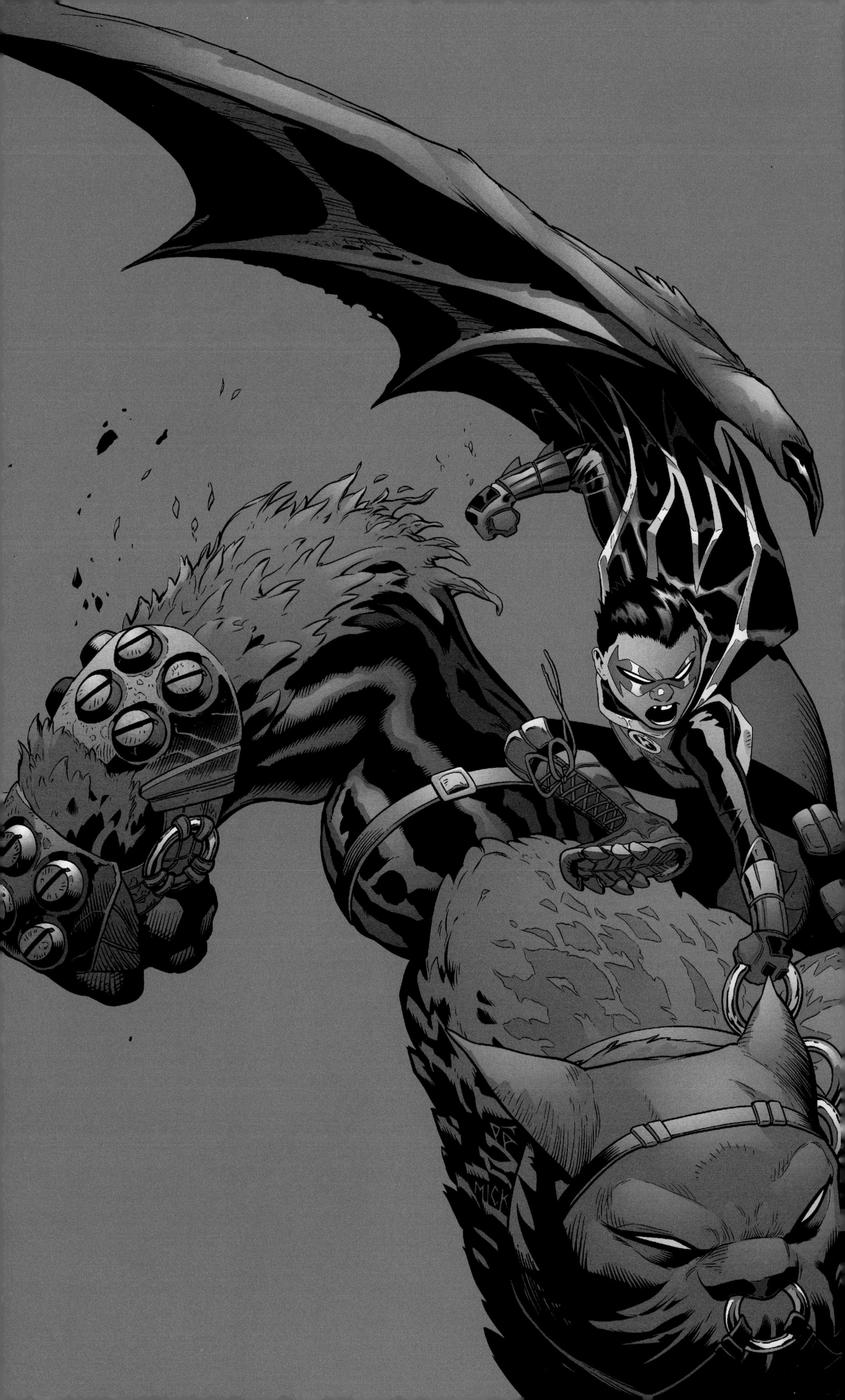

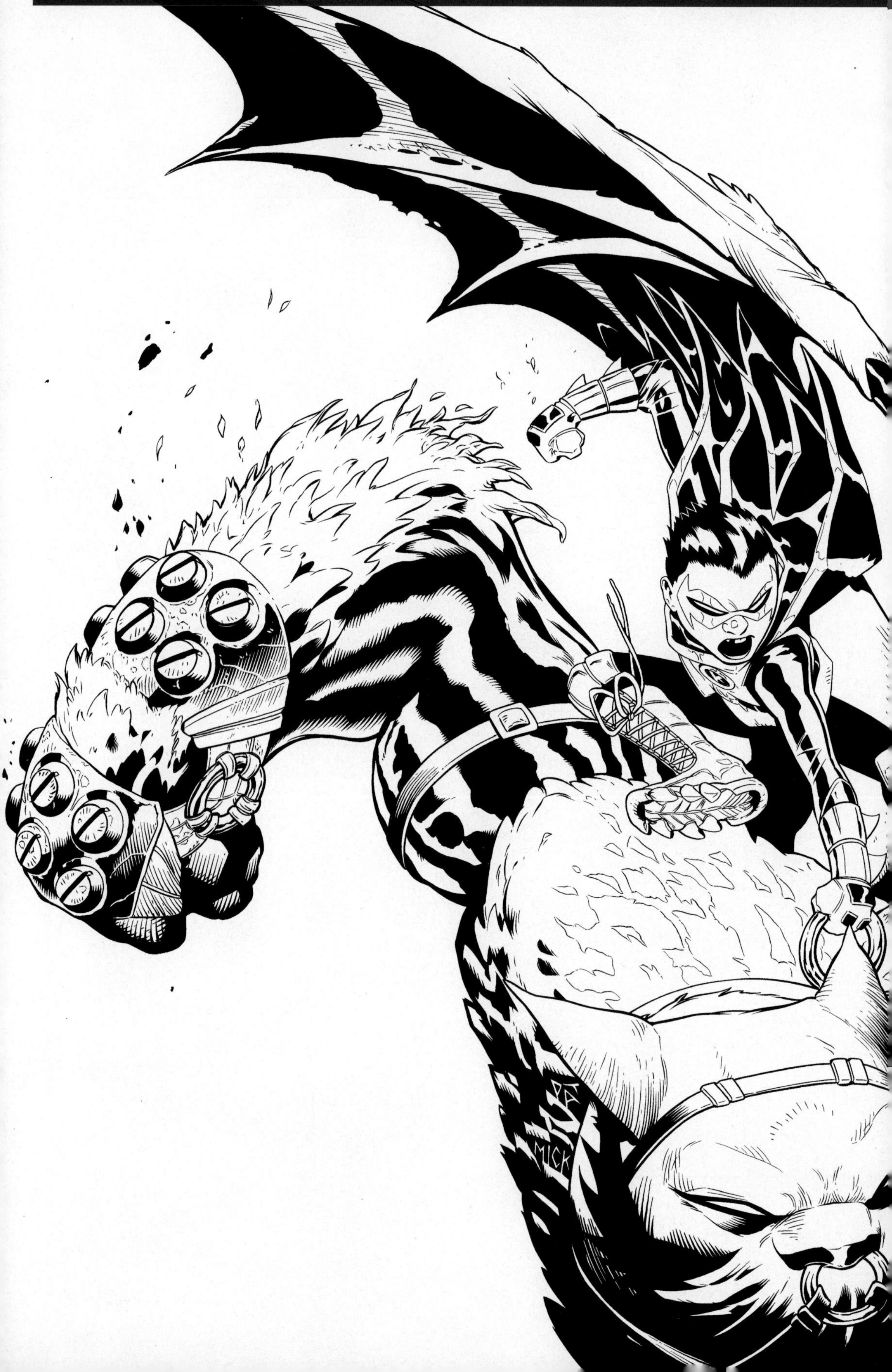

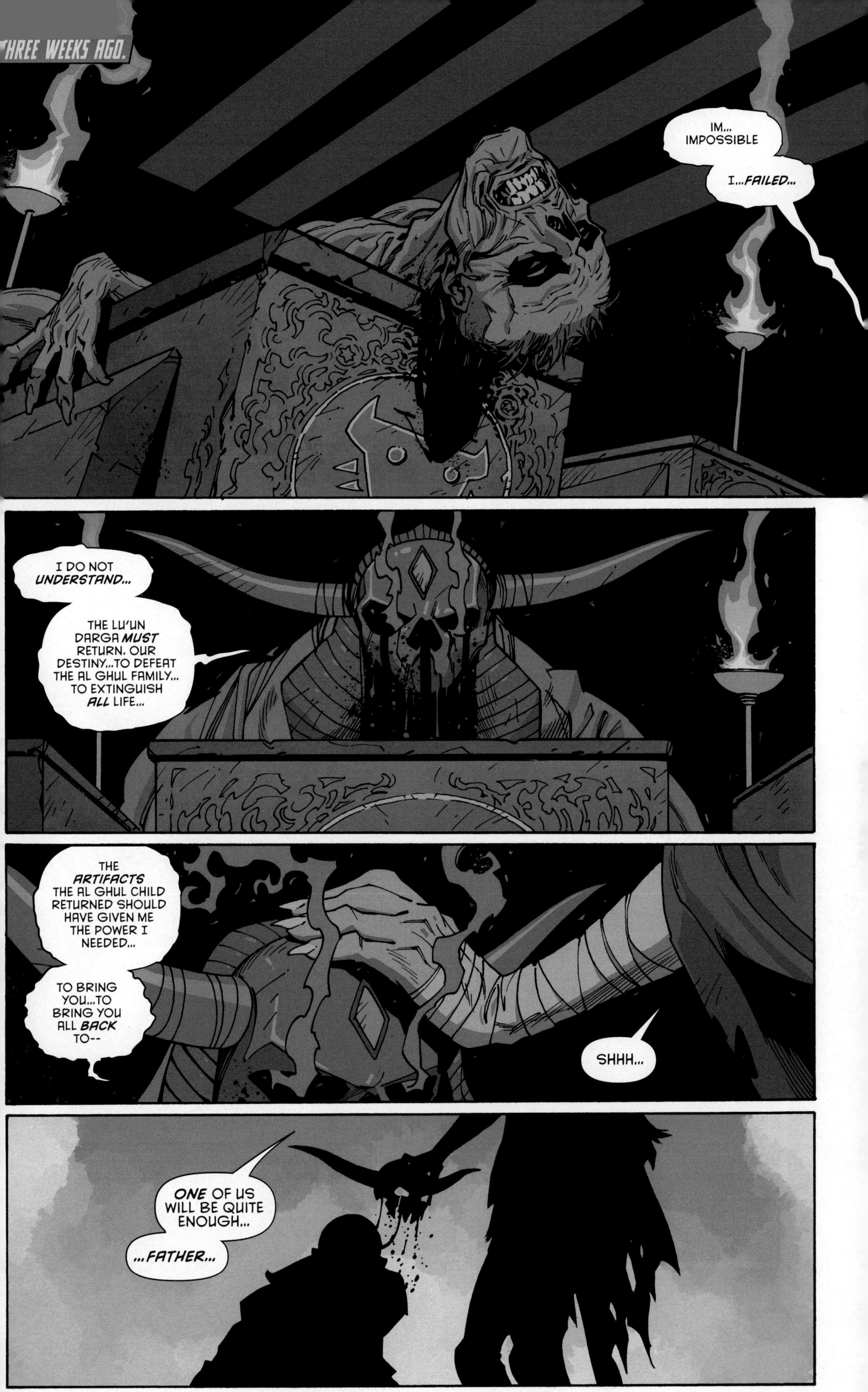
THREE WEEKS AGO.
IM... IMPOSSIBLE
I...FAILED...
I DO NOT UNDERSTAND...
THE LU'UN DARGA MUST RETURN. OUR DESTINY...TO DEFEAT THE AL GHUL FAMILY... TO EXTINGUISH ALL LIFE...
THE ARTIFACTS THE AL GHUL CHILD RETURNED SHOULD HAVE GIVEN ME THE POWER I NEEDED...
TO BRING YOU...TO BRING YOU ALL BACK TO--
SHHH...
ONE OF US WILL BE QUITE ENOUGH...
...FATHER...

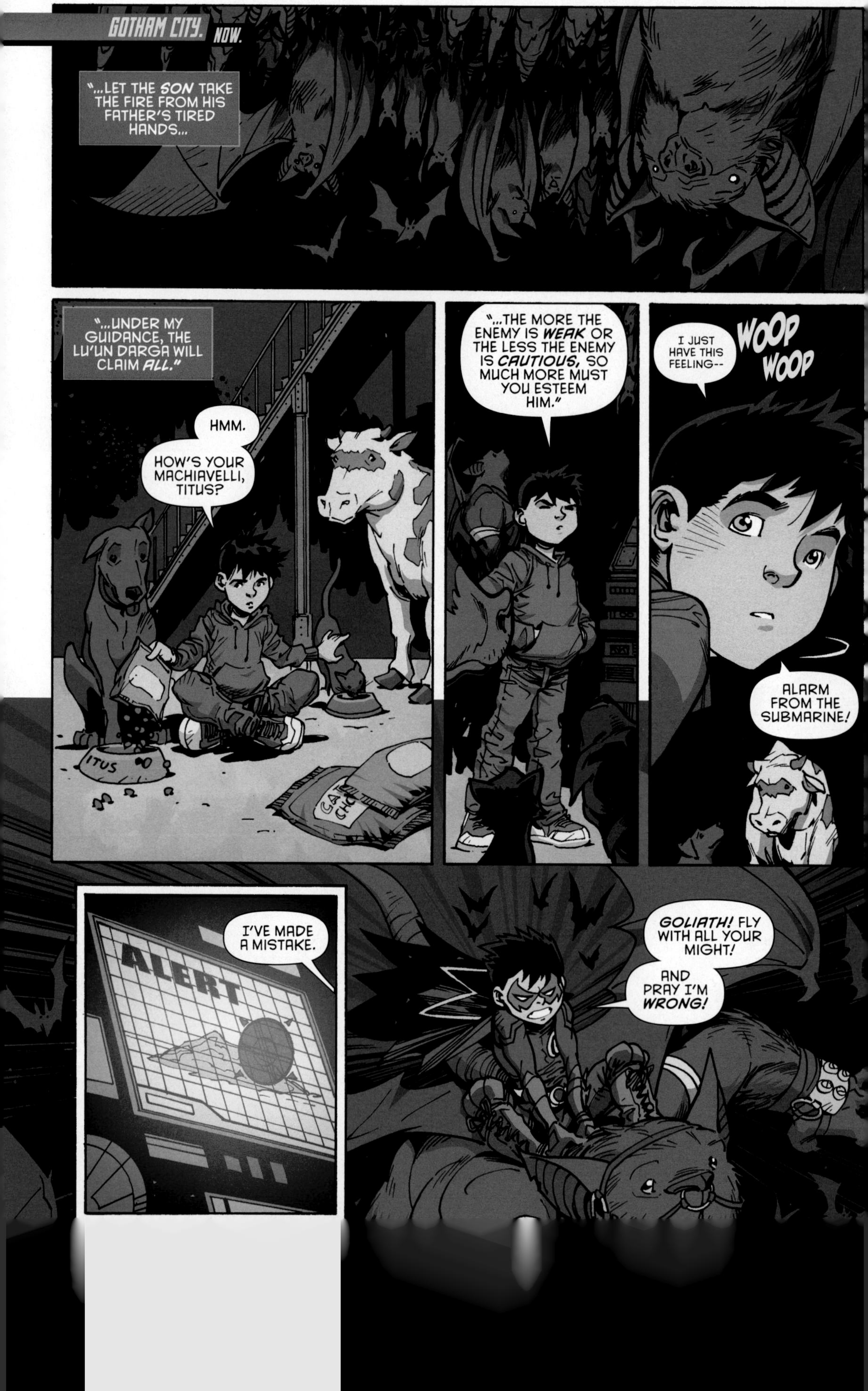
GOTHAM CITY. NOW.
"...LET THE SON TAKE THE FIRE FROM HIS FATHER'S TIRED HANDS...
"...UNDER MY GUIDANCE, THE LU'UN DARGA WILL CLAIM ALL."
HMM.
HOW'S YOUR MACHIAVELLI, TITUS?
ITUS
"...THE MORE THE ENEMY IS WEAK OR THE LESS THE ENEMY IS CAUTIOUS, SO MUCH MORE MUST YOU ESTEEM HIM."
I JUST HAVE THIS FEELING--
WOOP WOOP
ALARM FROM THE SUBMARINE!
ALERT
I'VE MADE A MISTAKE.
GOLIATH! FLY WITH ALL YOUR MIGHT!
AND PRAY I'M WRONG!

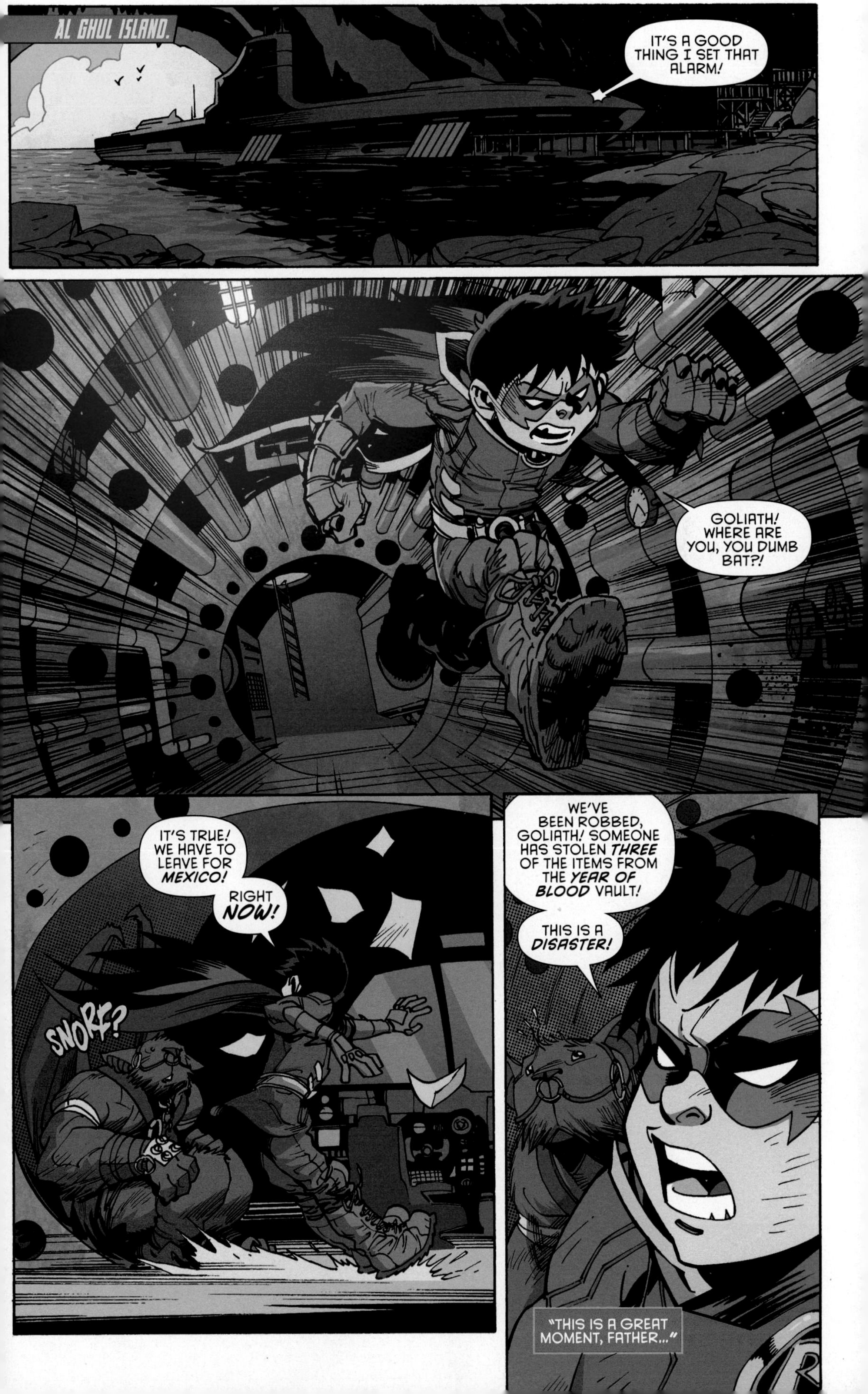
AL GHUL ISLAND.
IT'S A GOOD THING I SET THAT ALARM!
GOLIATH! WHERE ARE YOU, YOU DUMB BAT?!
IT'S TRUE! WE HAVE TO LEAVE FOR MEXICO!
RIGHT NOW!
SNORF?
WE'VE BEEN ROBBED, GOLIATH! SOMEONE HAS STOLEN THREE OF THE ITEMS FROM THE YEAR OF BLOOD VAULT!
THIS IS A DISASTER!
"THIS IS A GREAT MOMENT, FATHER..."

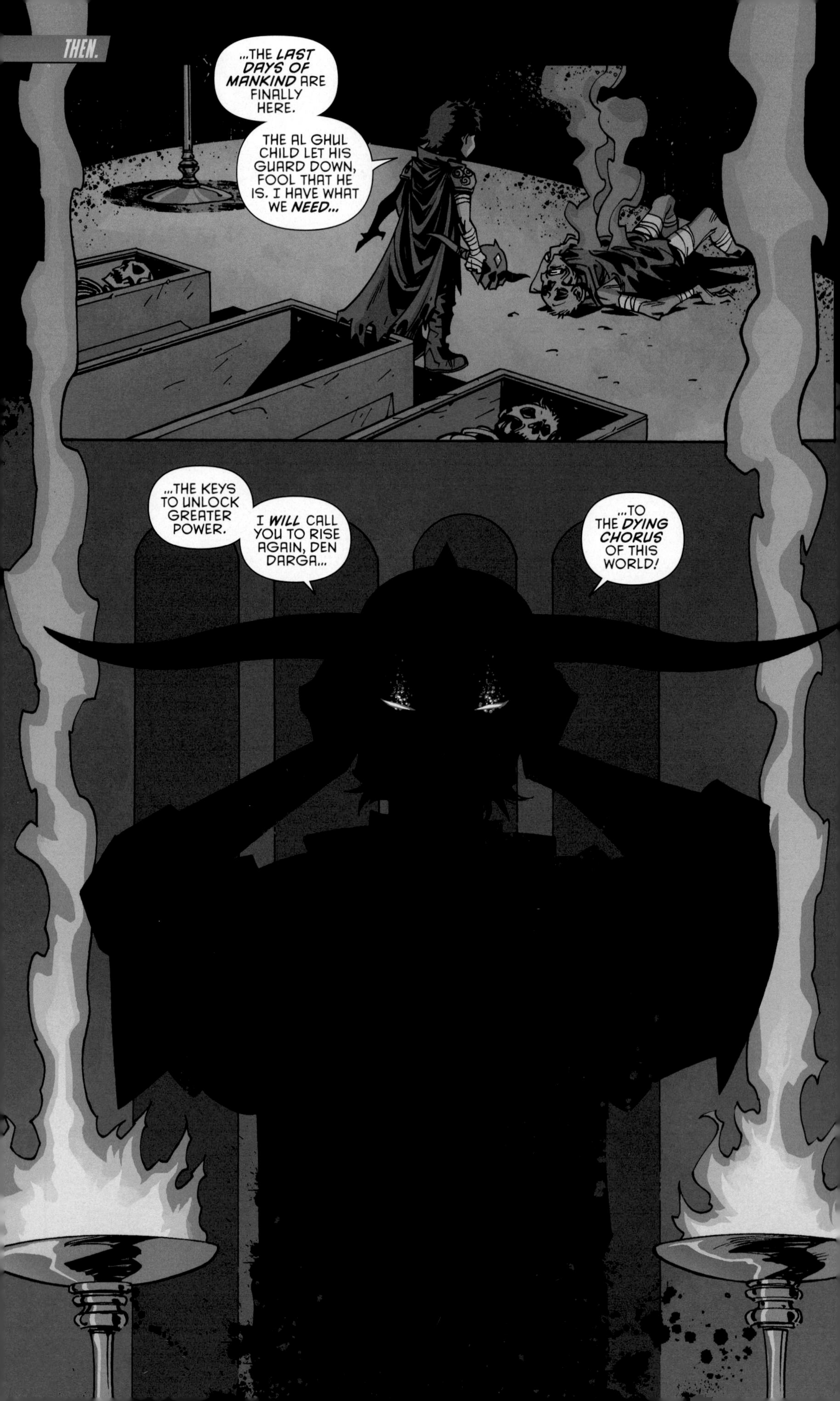
THEN.
...THE LAST DAYS OF MANKIND ARE FINALLY HERE.
THE AL GHUL CHILD LET HIS GUARD DOWN, FOOL THAT HE IS. I HAVE WHAT WE NEED...
...THE KEYS TO UNLOCK GREATER POWER.
I WILL CALL YOU TO RISE AGAIN, DEN DARGA...
...TO THE DYING CHORUS OF THIS WORLD!

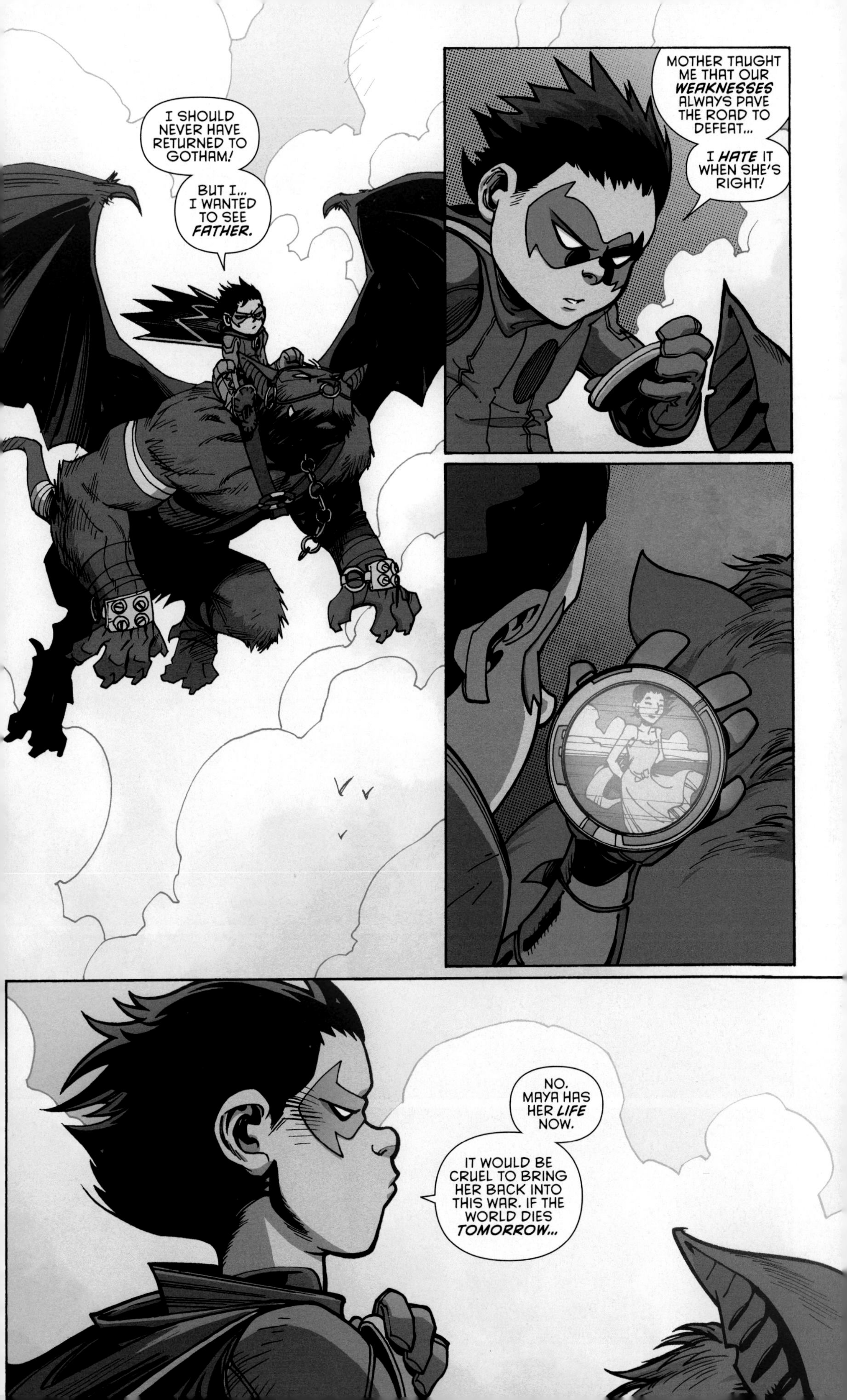
I SHOULD NEVER HAVE RETURNED TO GOTHAM!
BUT I... I WANTED TO SEE FATHER.
MOTHER TAUGHT ME THAT OUR WEAKNESSES ALWAYS PAVE THE ROAD TO DEFEAT...
I HATE IT WHEN SHE'S RIGHT!
NO. MAYA HAS HER LIFE NOW.
IT WOULD BE CRUEL TO BRING HER BACK INTO THIS WAR. IF THE WORLD DIES TOMORROW...

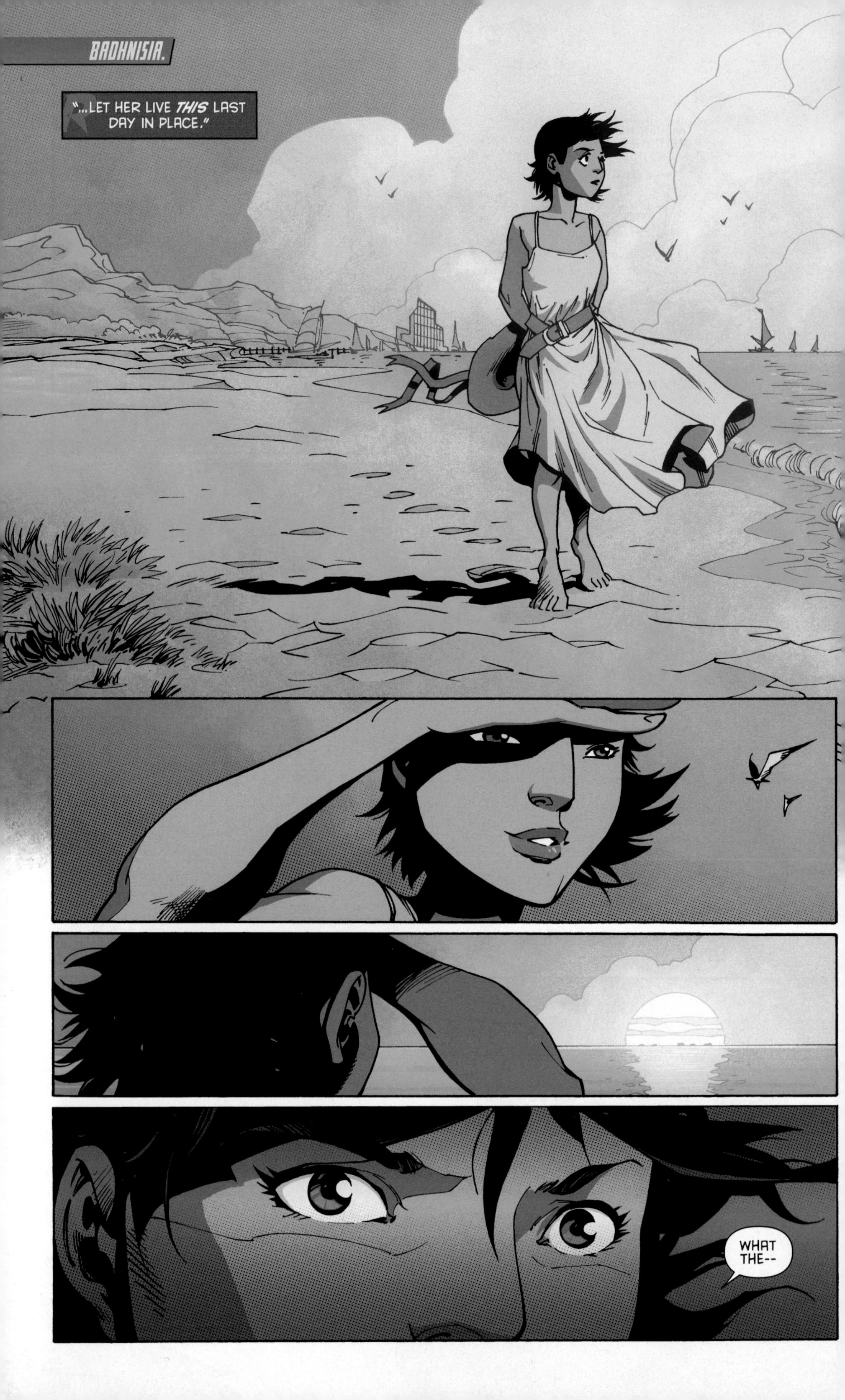
BADHNISIA.
"...LET HER LIVE THIS LAST DAY IN PLACE."
WHAT THE--

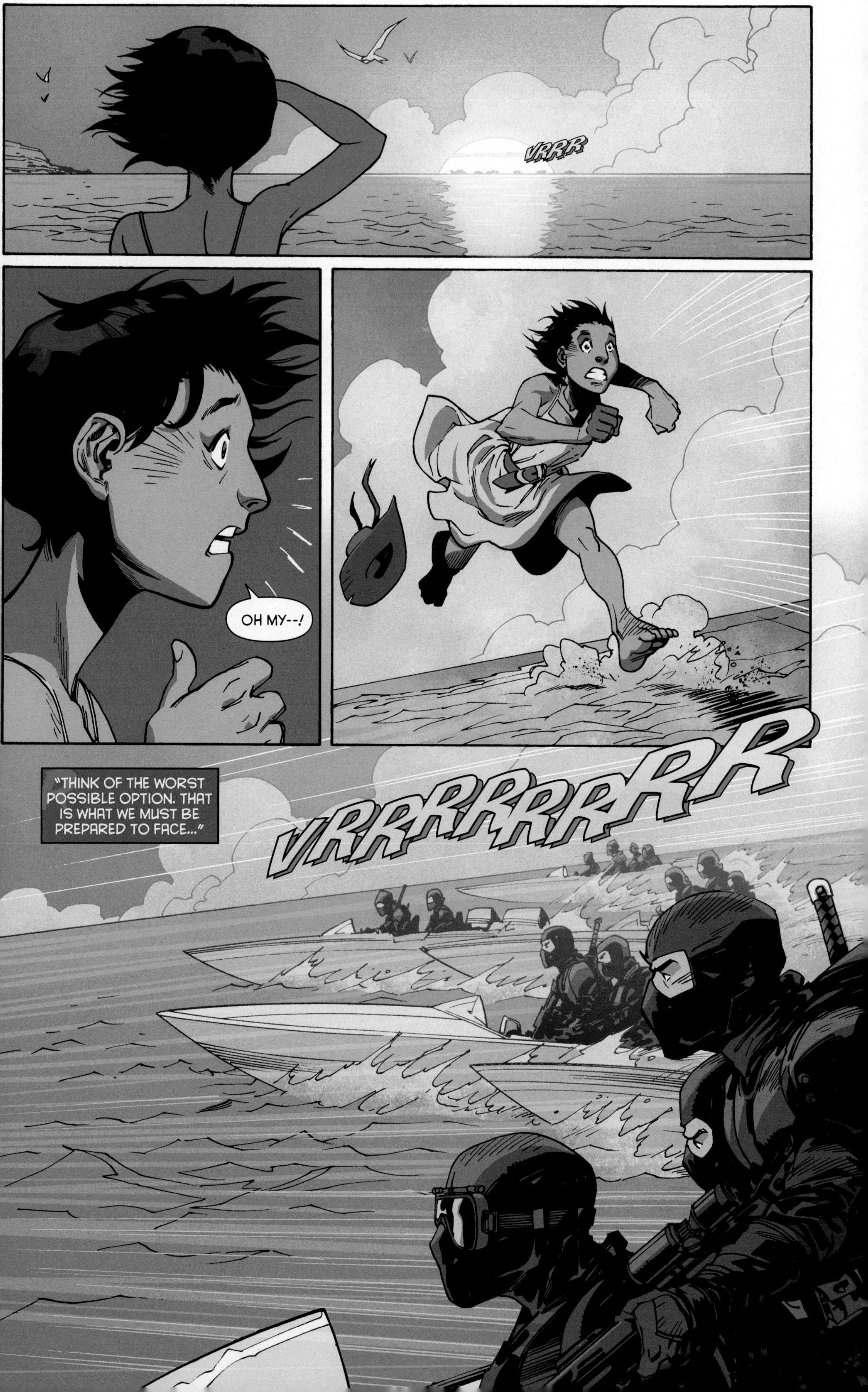
VRRR
OH MY--!
"THINK OF THE WORST POSSIBLE OPTION. THAT IS WHAT WE MUST BE PREPARED TO FACE..."
VRRRRRRRRR

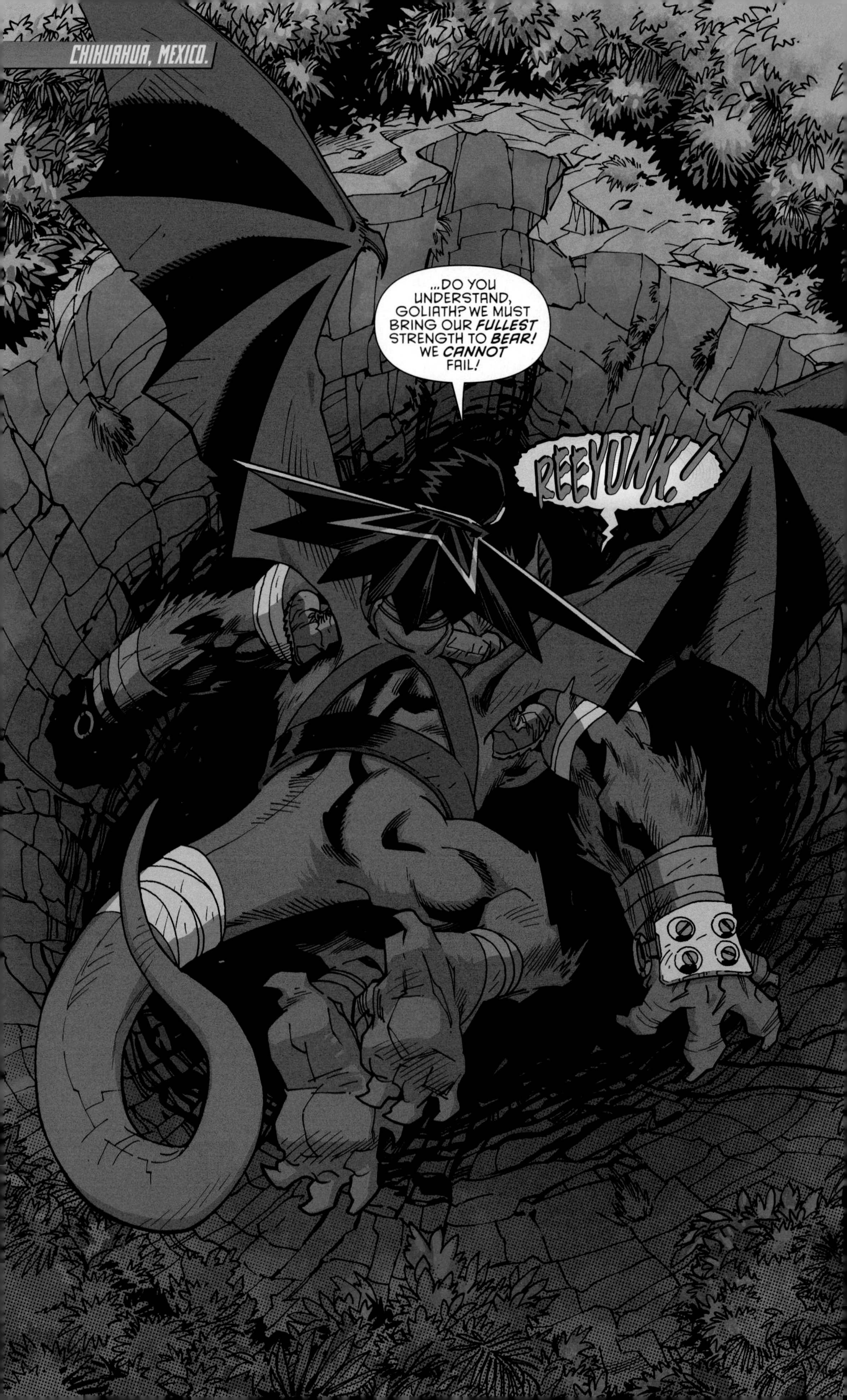
CHIHUAHUA, MEXICO.
...DO YOU UNDERSTAND, GOLIATH? WE MUST BRING OUR FULLEST STRENGTH TO BEAR! WE CANNOT FAIL!
REEYUNK!

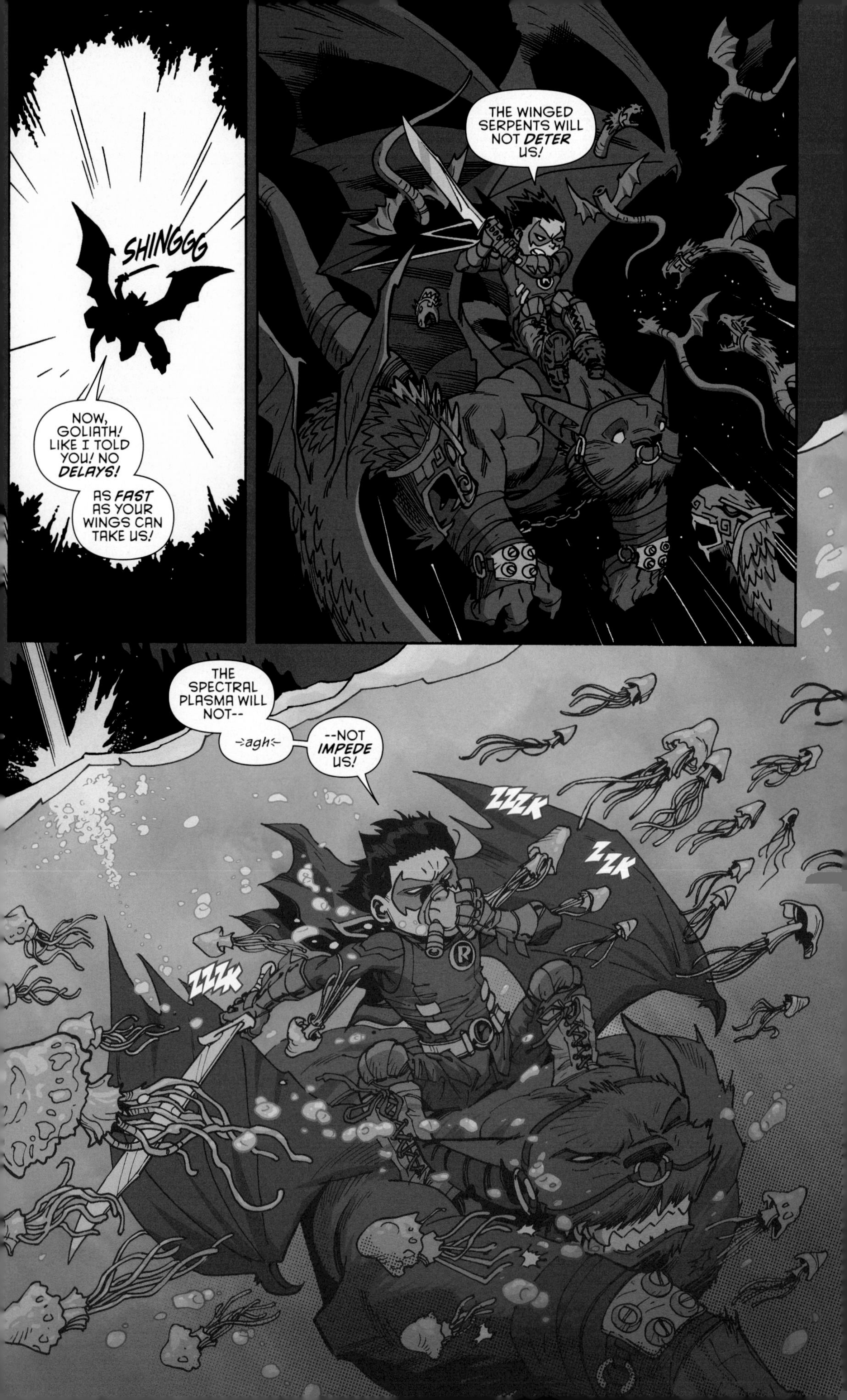
SHINGGG
NOW, GOLIATH! LIKE I TOLD YOU! NO DELAYS!
AS FAST AS YOUR WINGS CAN TAKE US!
THE WINGED SERPENTS WILL NOT DETER US!
THE SPECTRAL PLASMA WILL NOT--
agh
--NOT IMPEDE US!
ZZZK
ZZK
ZZZK

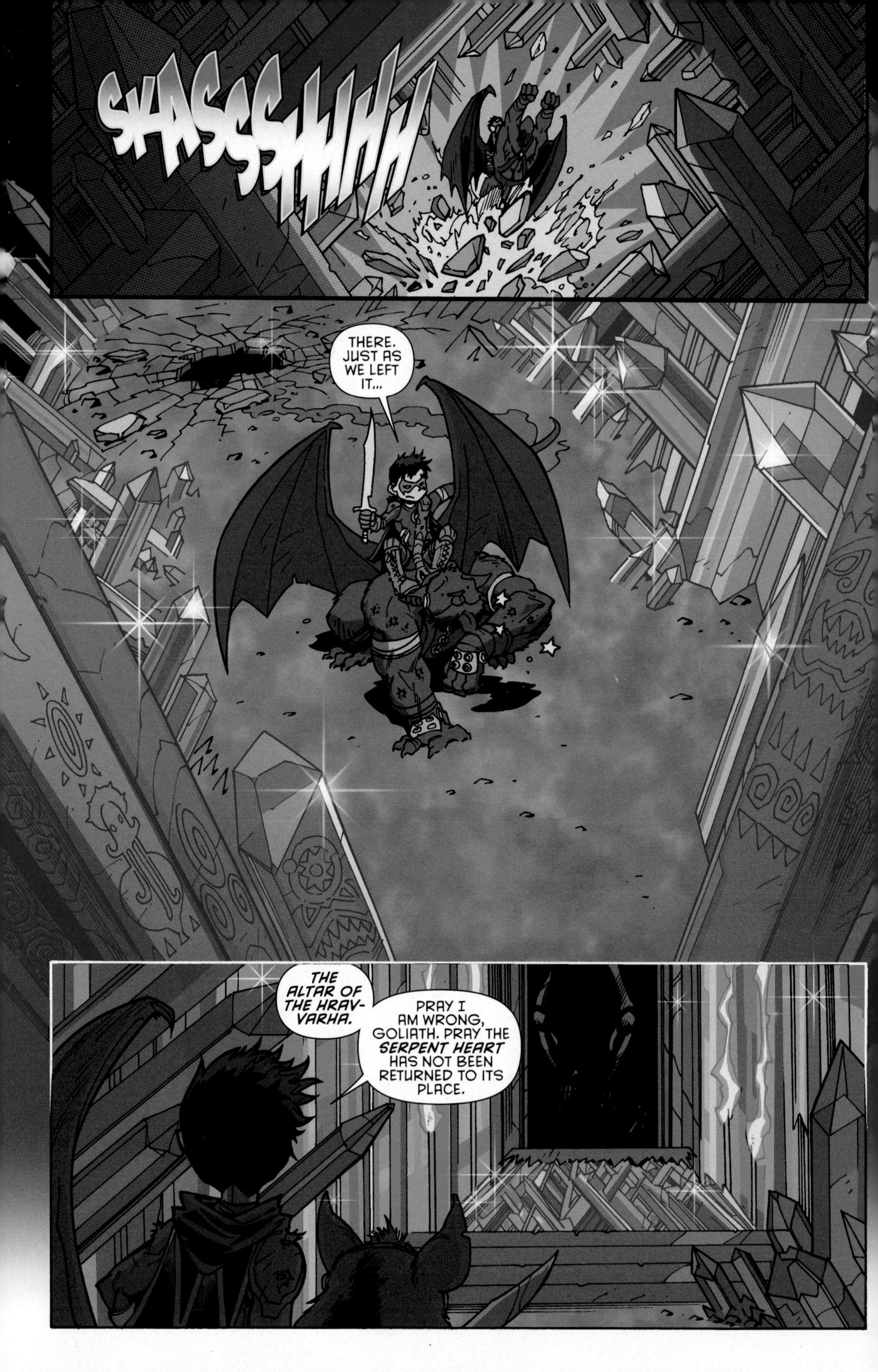
SKASSSHHHH
THERE. JUST AS WE LEFT IT...
THE ALTAR OF THE HRAV-VARHA.
PRAY I AM WRONG, GOLIATH. PRAY THE SERPENT HEART HAS NOT BEEN RETURNED TO ITS PLACE.

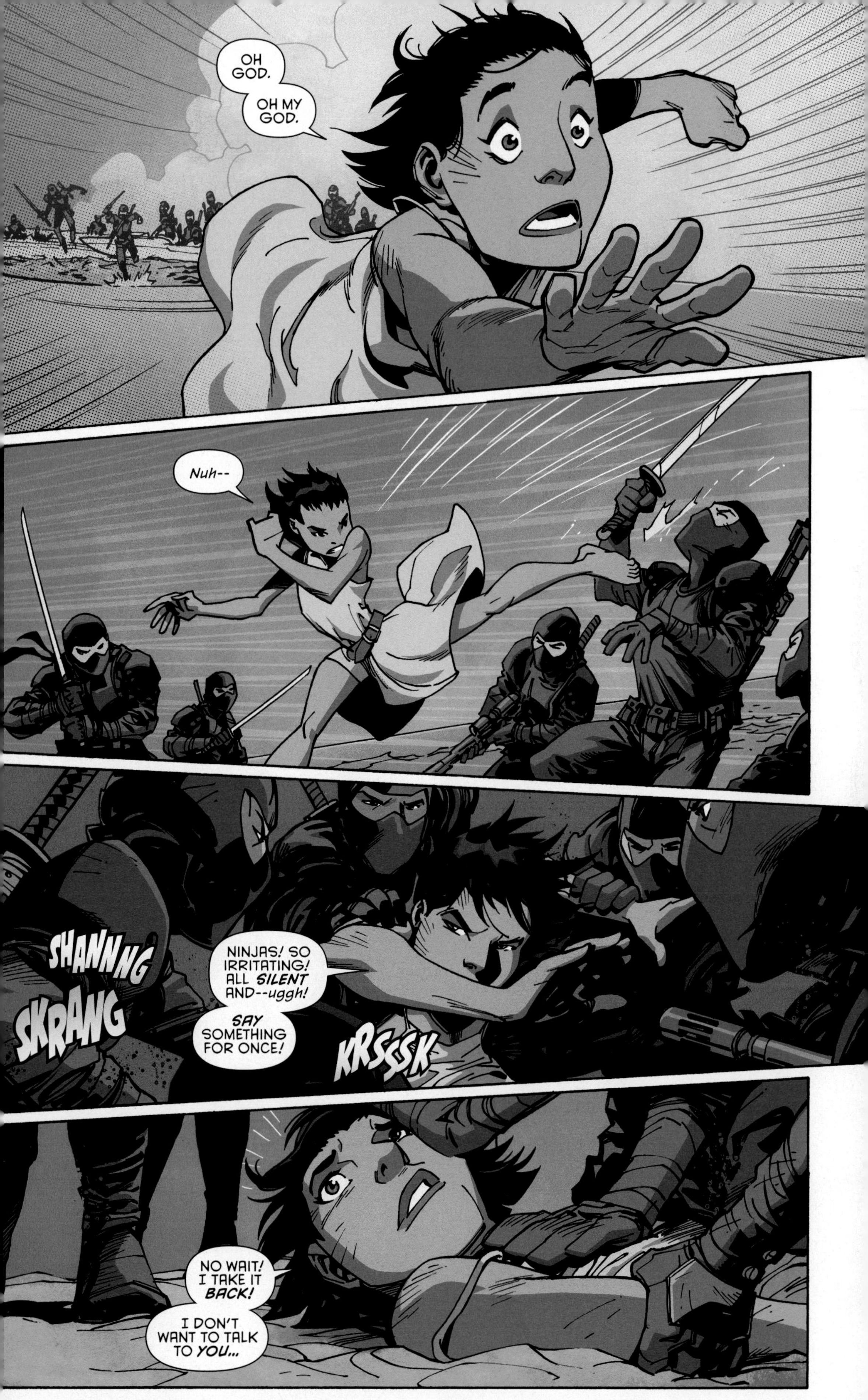
OH GOD.
OH MY GOD.
Nuh--
SHANNNG
SKRANG
NINJAS! SO IRRITATING! ALL SILENT AND--uggh!
SAY SOMETHING FOR ONCE!
KRSSSK
NO WAIT! I TAKE IT BACK!
I DON'T WANT TO TALK TO YOU...

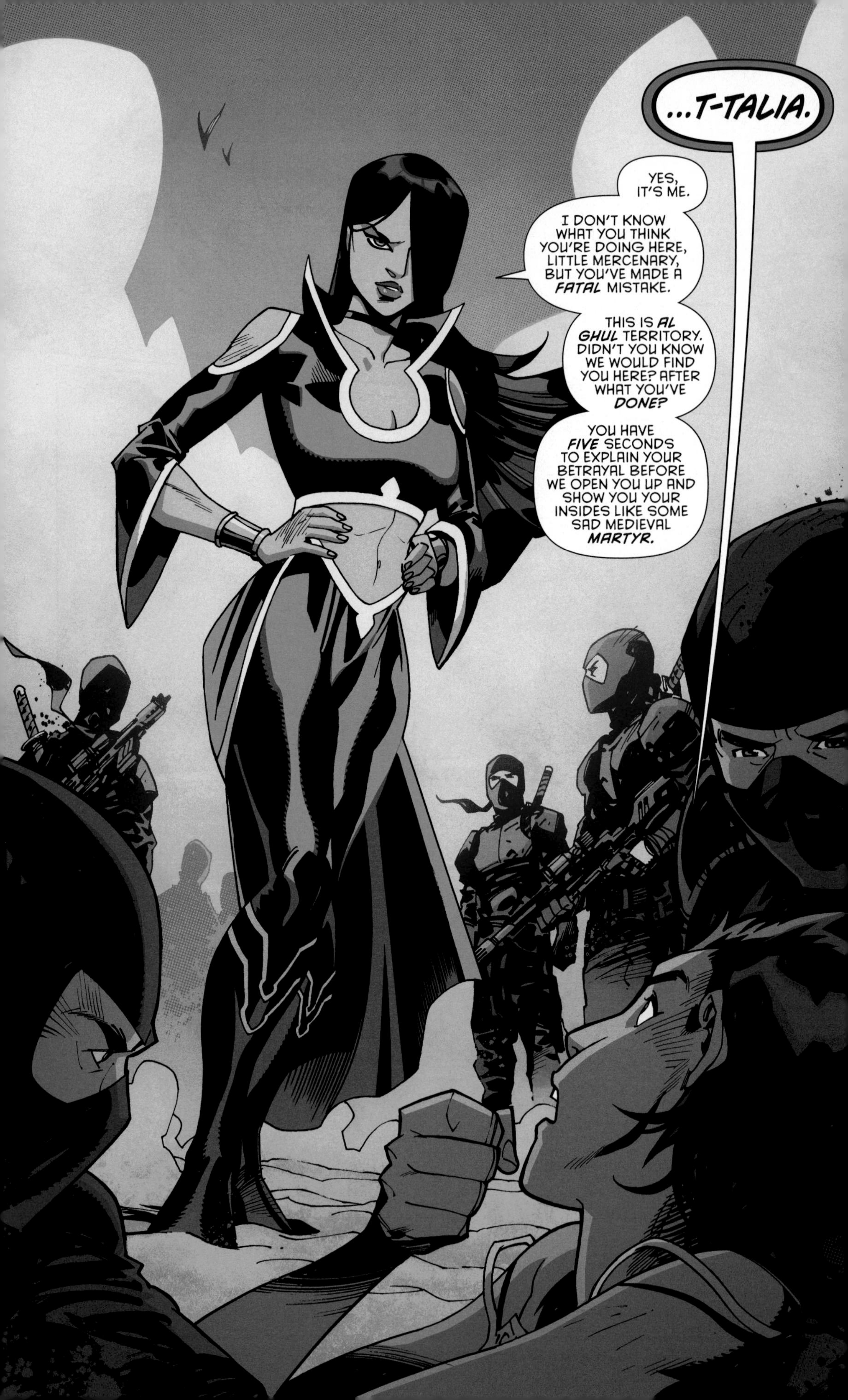
...T-TALIA.
YES, IT'S ME.
I DON'T KNOW WHAT YOU THINK YOU'RE DOING HERE, LITTLE MERCENARY, BUT YOU'VE MADE A FATAL MISTAKE.
THIS IS AL GHUL TERRITORY. DIDN'T YOU KNOW WE WOULD FIND YOU HERE? AFTER WHAT YOU'VE DONE?
YOU HAVE FIVE SECONDS TO EXPLAIN YOUR BETRAYAL BEFORE WE OPEN YOU UP AND SHOW YOU YOUR INSIDES LIKE SOME SAD MEDIEVAL MARTYR.

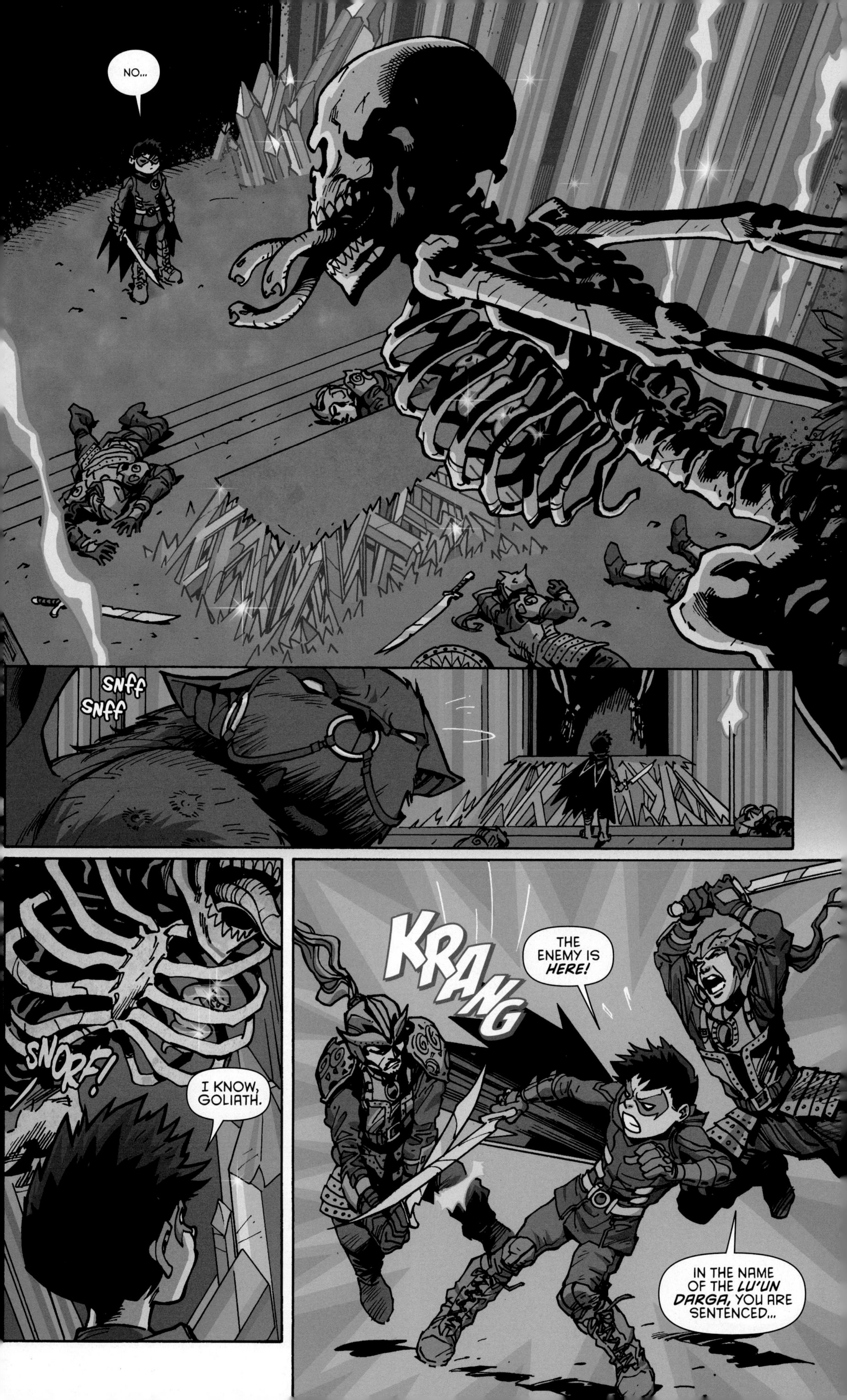
NO...
SNFF
SNFF
SNORF!
I KNOW, GOLIATH.
KRANG
THE ENEMY IS HERE!
IN THE NAME OF THE LU'UN DARGA, YOU ARE SENTENCED...

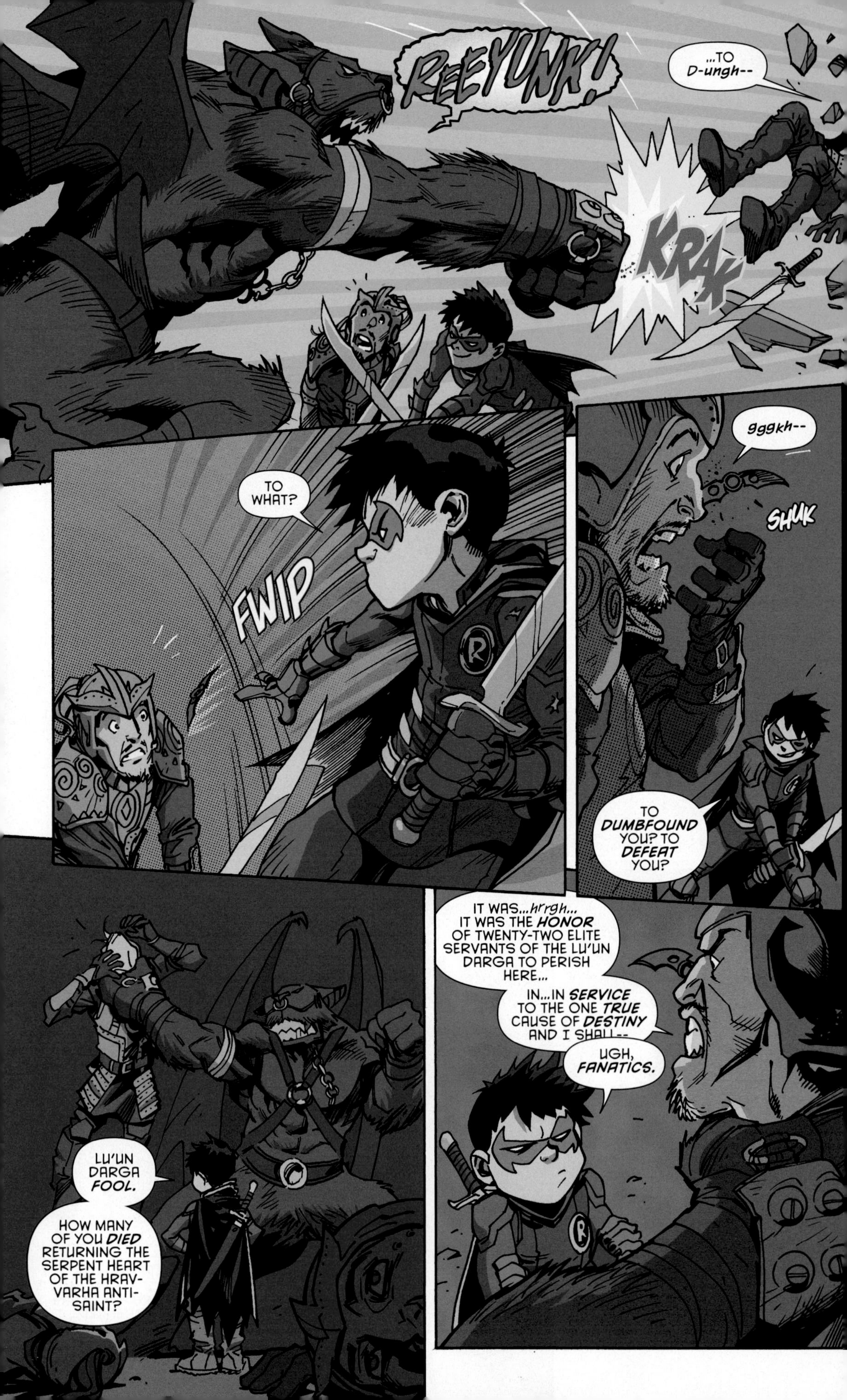
REEYUNK!
...TO D-ungh--
KRAK
TO WHAT?
FWIP
gggkh--
SHUK
TO *DUMBFOUND* YOU? TO *DEFEAT* YOU?
LU'UN DARGA *FOOL.*
HOW MANY OF YOU *DIED* RETURNING THE SERPENT HEART OF THE HRAV-VARHA ANTI-SAINT?
IT WAS...*hrrgh*... IT WAS THE *HONOR* OF TWENTY-TWO ELITE SERVANTS OF THE LU'UN DARGA TO PERISH HERE...
IN...IN *SERVICE* TO THE ONE *TRUE* CAUSE OF *DESTINY* AND I SHALL--
UGH, *FANATICS.*

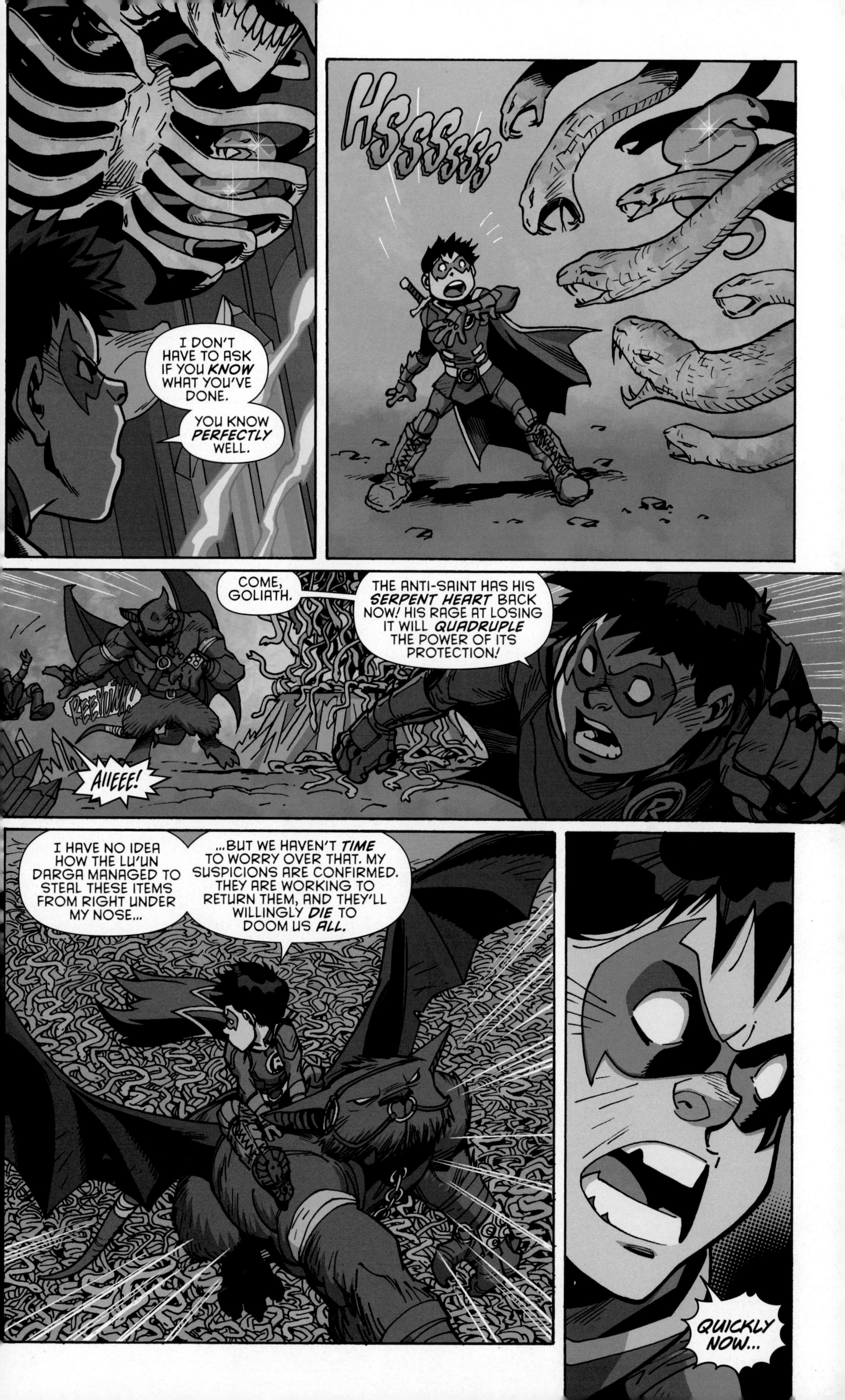
I DON'T HAVE TO ASK IF YOU KNOW WHAT YOU'VE DONE.
YOU KNOW PERFECTLY WELL.
HSSSSSS
COME, GOLIATH.
THE ANTI-SAINT HAS HIS SERPENT HEART BACK NOW! HIS RAGE AT LOSING IT WILL QUADRUPLE THE POWER OF ITS PROTECTION!
REEYOWW!
AIIEEE!
I HAVE NO IDEA HOW THE LU'UN DARGA MANAGED TO STEAL THESE ITEMS FROM RIGHT UNDER MY NOSE...
...BUT WE HAVEN'T TIME TO WORRY OVER THAT. MY SUSPICIONS ARE CONFIRMED. THEY ARE WORKING TO RETURN THEM, AND THEY'LL WILLINGLY DIE TO DOOM US ALL.
QUICKLY NOW...

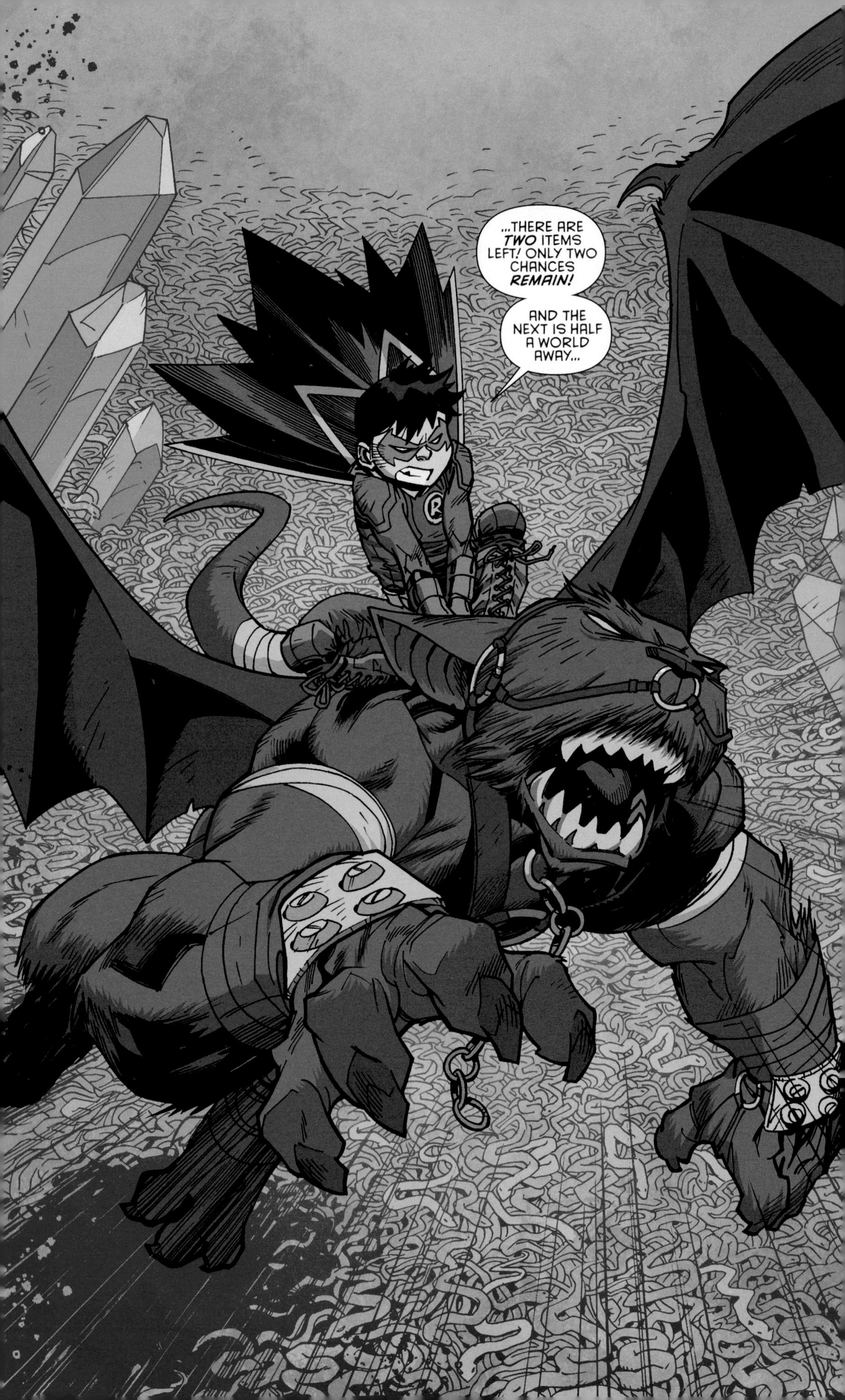
...THERE ARE *TWO* ITEMS LEFT! ONLY TWO CHANCES *REMAIN!*
AND THE NEXT IS HALF A WORLD AWAY...

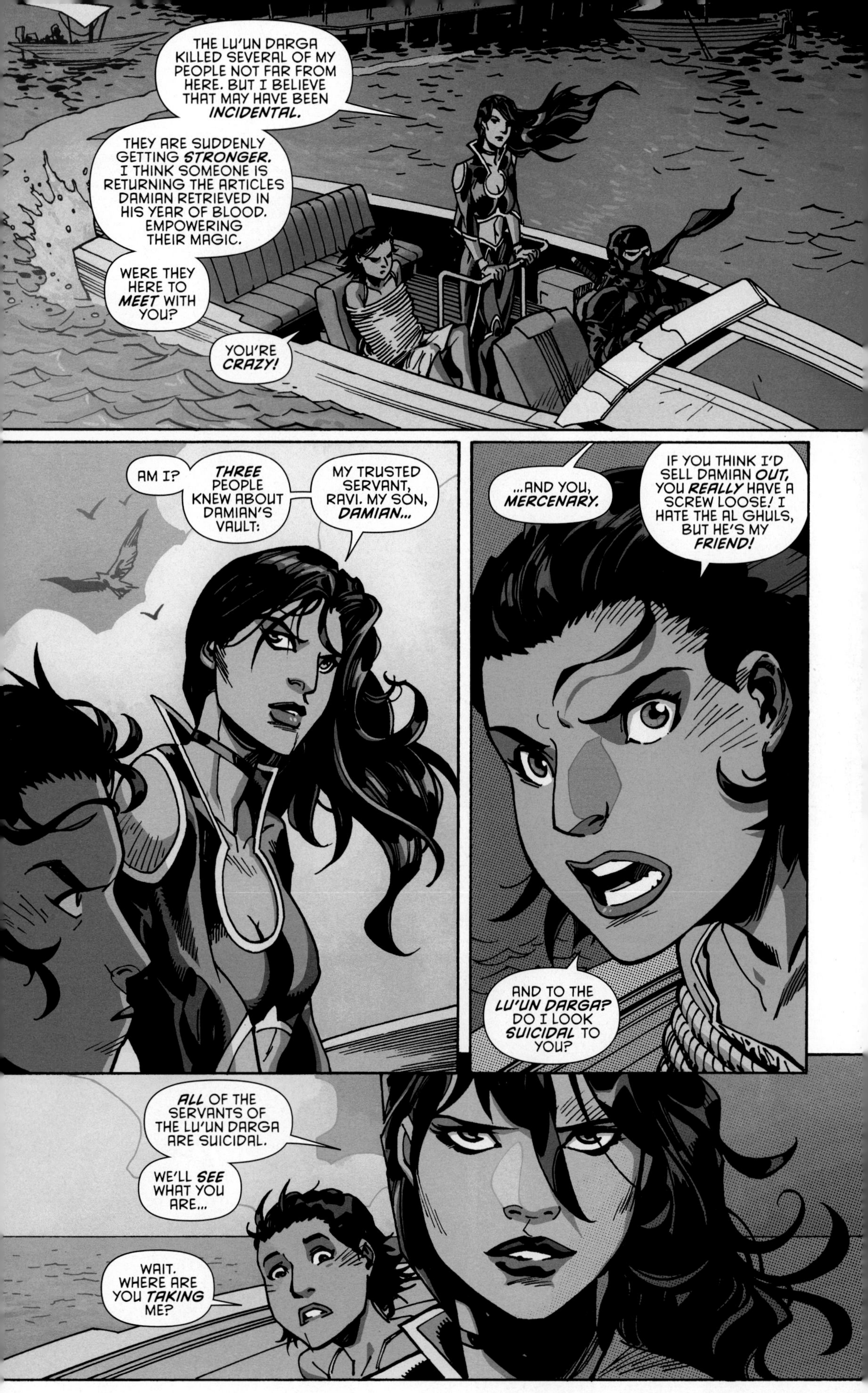
THE LU'UN DARGA KILLED SEVERAL OF MY PEOPLE NOT FAR FROM HERE. BUT I BELIEVE THAT MAY HAVE BEEN INCIDENTAL.
THEY ARE SUDDENLY GETTING STRONGER. I THINK SOMEONE IS RETURNING THE ARTICLES DAMIAN RETRIEVED IN HIS YEAR OF BLOOD. EMPOWERING THEIR MAGIC.
WERE THEY HERE TO MEET WITH YOU?
YOU'RE CRAZY!
AM I?
THREE PEOPLE KNEW ABOUT DAMIAN'S VAULT:
MY TRUSTED SERVANT, RAVI. MY SON, DAMIAN...
...AND YOU, MERCENARY.
IF YOU THINK I'D SELL DAMIAN OUT, YOU REALLY HAVE A SCREW LOOSE! I HATE THE AL GHULS, BUT HE'S MY FRIEND!
AND TO THE LU'UN DARGA? DO I LOOK SUICIDAL TO YOU?
ALL OF THE SERVANTS OF THE LU'UN DARGA ARE SUICIDAL.
WE'LL SEE WHAT YOU ARE...
WAIT. WHERE ARE YOU TAKING ME?

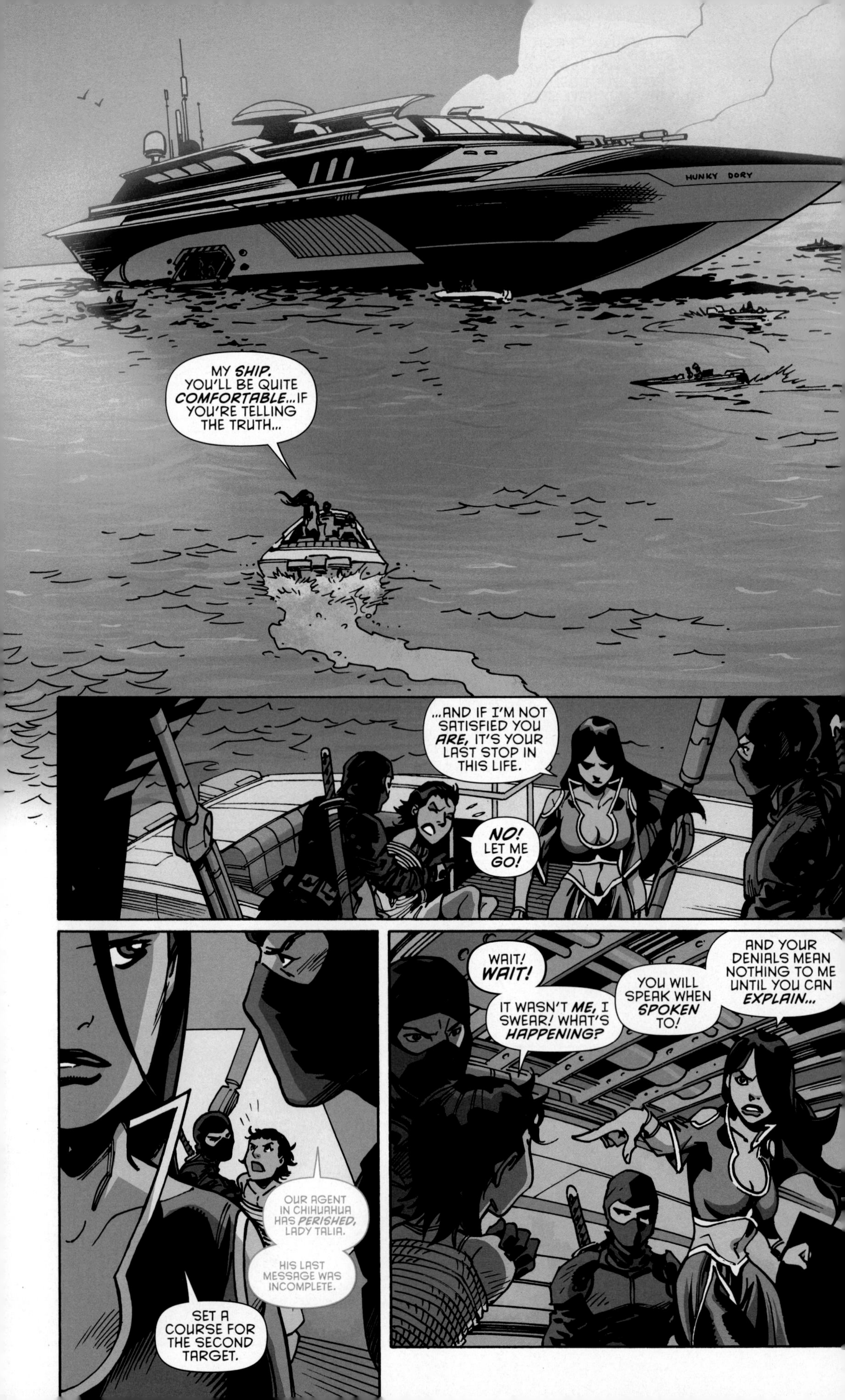

HUNKY DORY
MY SHIP. YOU'LL BE QUITE COMFORTABLE...IF YOU'RE TELLING THE TRUTH...
...AND IF I'M NOT SATISFIED YOU ARE, IT'S YOUR LAST STOP IN THIS LIFE.
NO! LET ME GO!
OUR AGENT IN CHIHUAHUA HAS PERISHED, LADY TALIA.
HIS LAST MESSAGE WAS INCOMPLETE.
SET A COURSE FOR THE SECOND TARGET.
WAIT! WAIT!
IT WASN'T ME, I SWEAR! WHAT'S HAPPENING?
YOU WILL SPEAK WHEN SPOKEN TO!
AND YOUR DENIALS MEAN NOTHING TO ME UNTIL YOU CAN EXPLAIN...

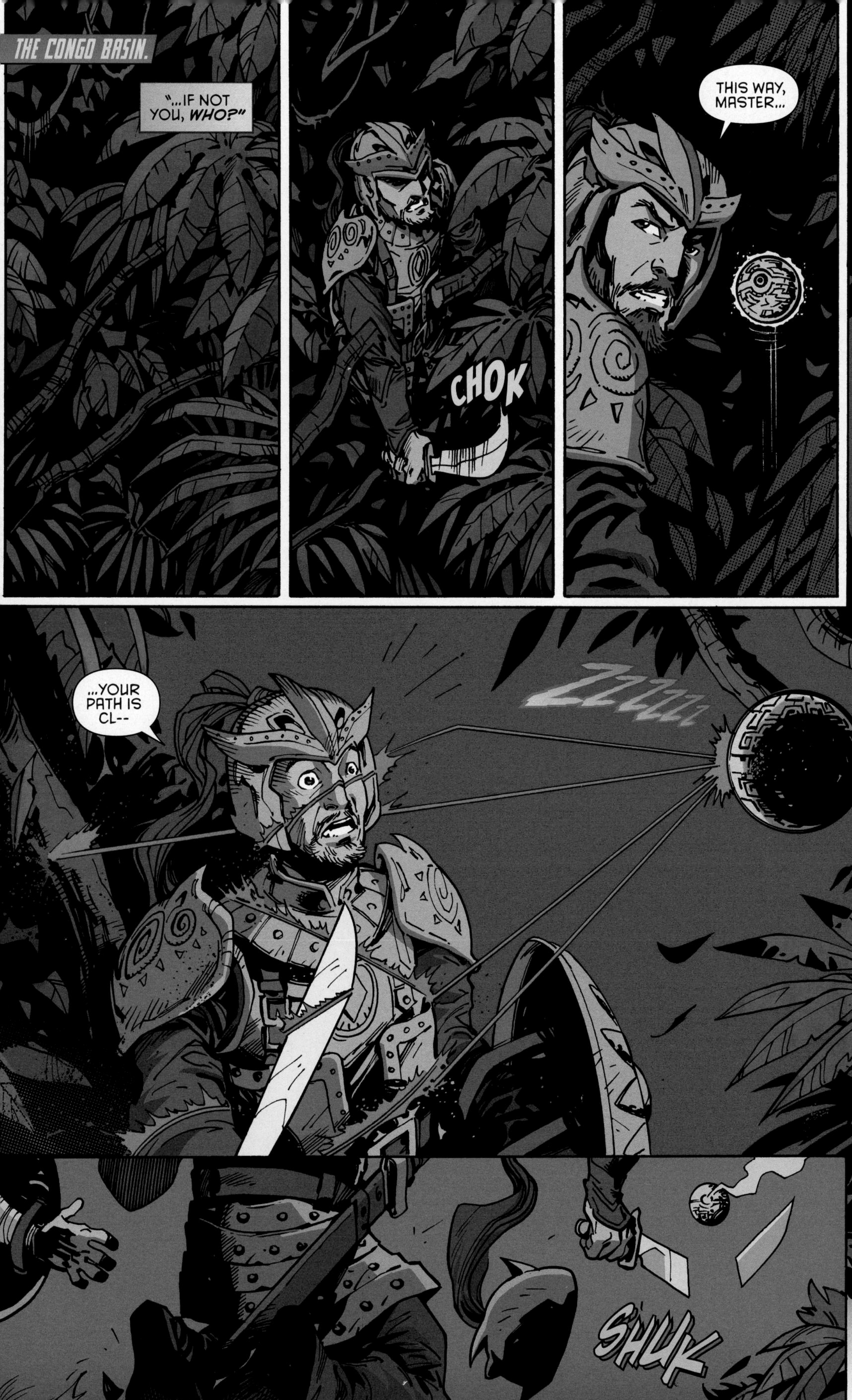
THE CONGO BASIN.
"...IF NOT YOU, WHO?"
CHOK
THIS WAY, MASTER...
...YOUR PATH IS CL--
ZZZZZZZ
SHUK

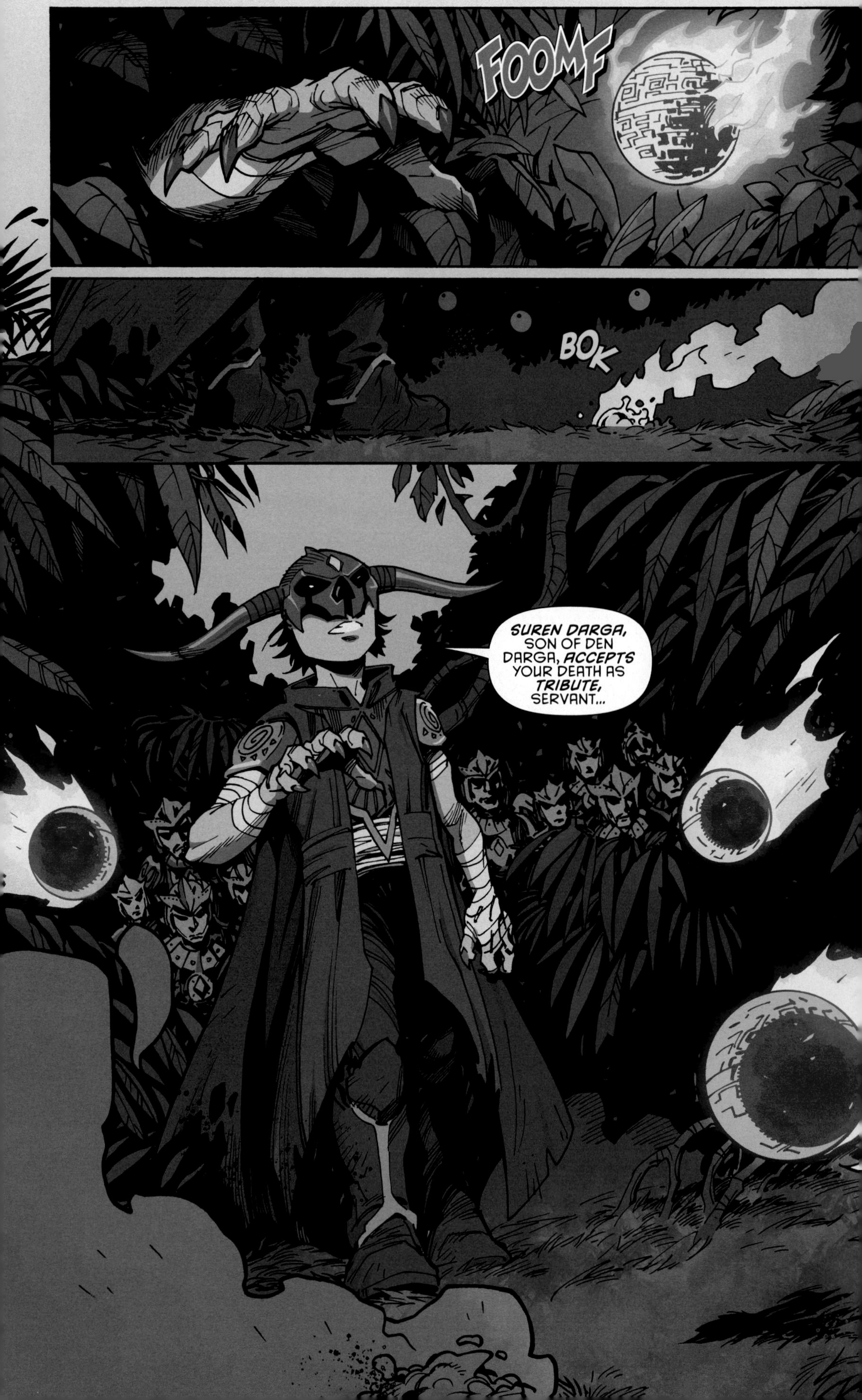
FOOMF
BOK
SUREN DARGA, SON OF DEN DARGA, ACCEPTS YOUR DEATH AS TRIBUTE, SERVANT...

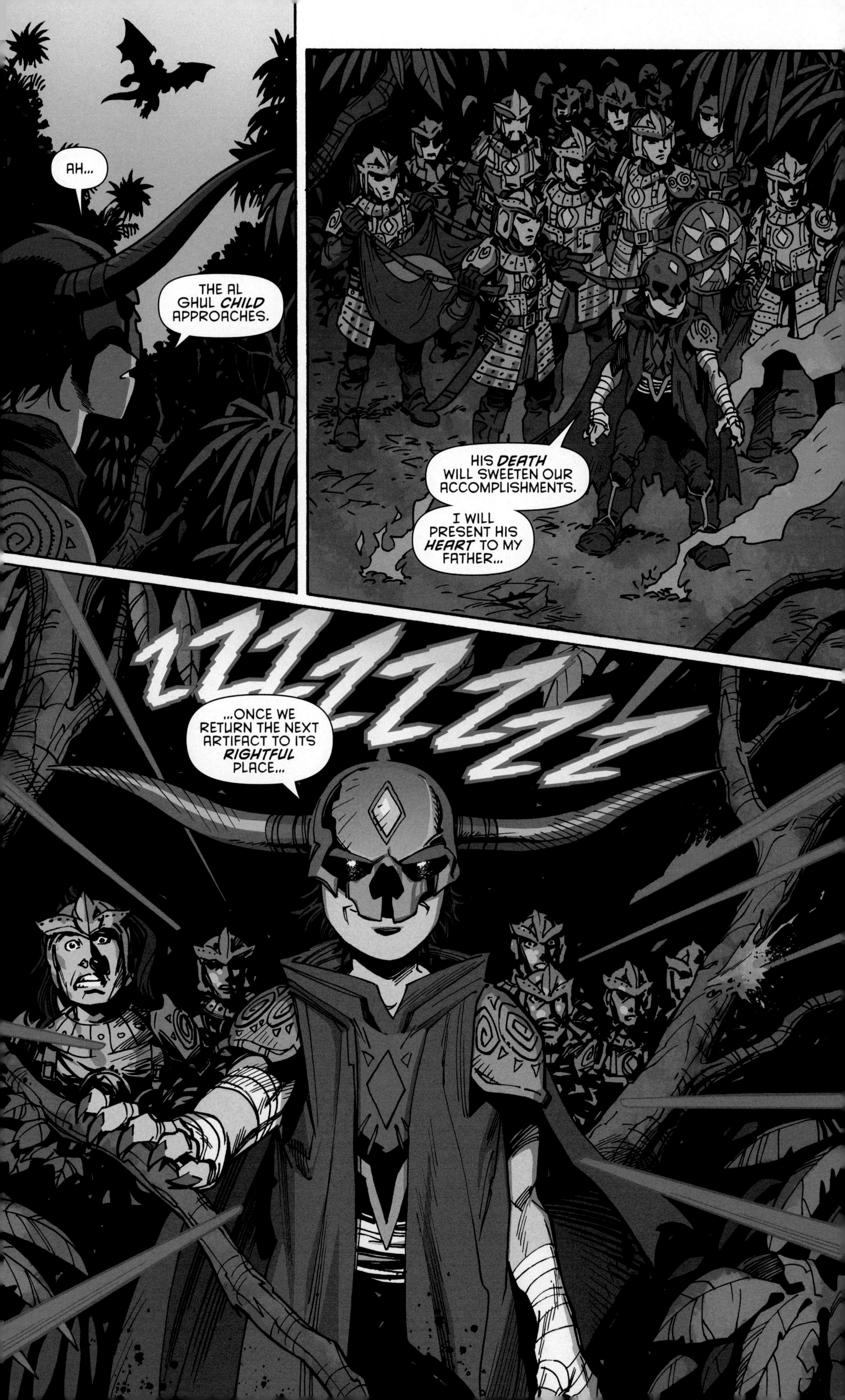
AH...
THE AL GHUL *CHILD* APPROACHES.
HIS *DEATH* WILL SWEETEN OUR ACCOMPLISHMENTS.
I WILL PRESENT HIS *HEART* TO MY FATHER...
ZZZZZZZZ
...ONCE WE RETURN THE NEXT ARTIFACT TO ITS *RIGHTFUL* PLACE...

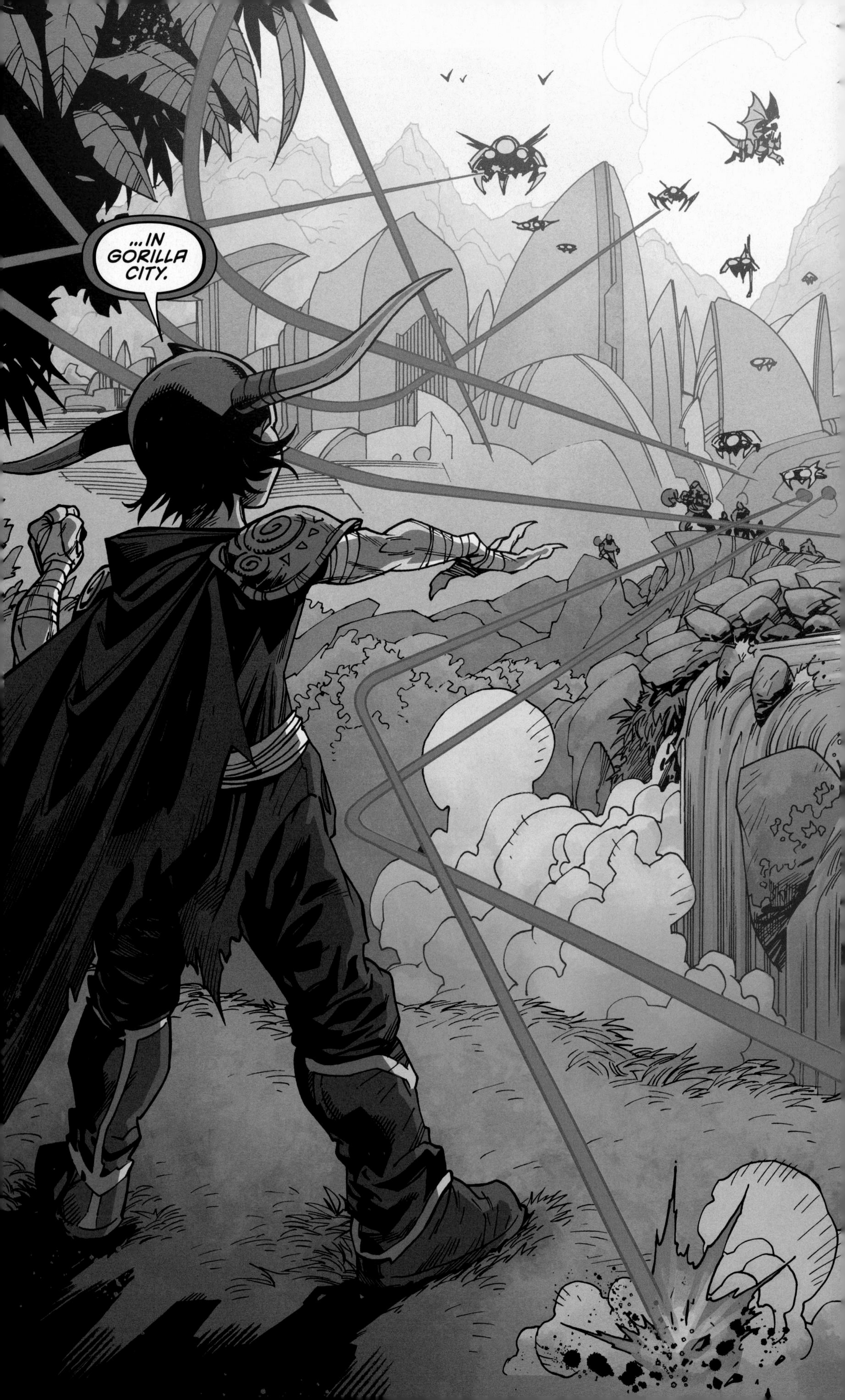
...IN GORILLA CITY.

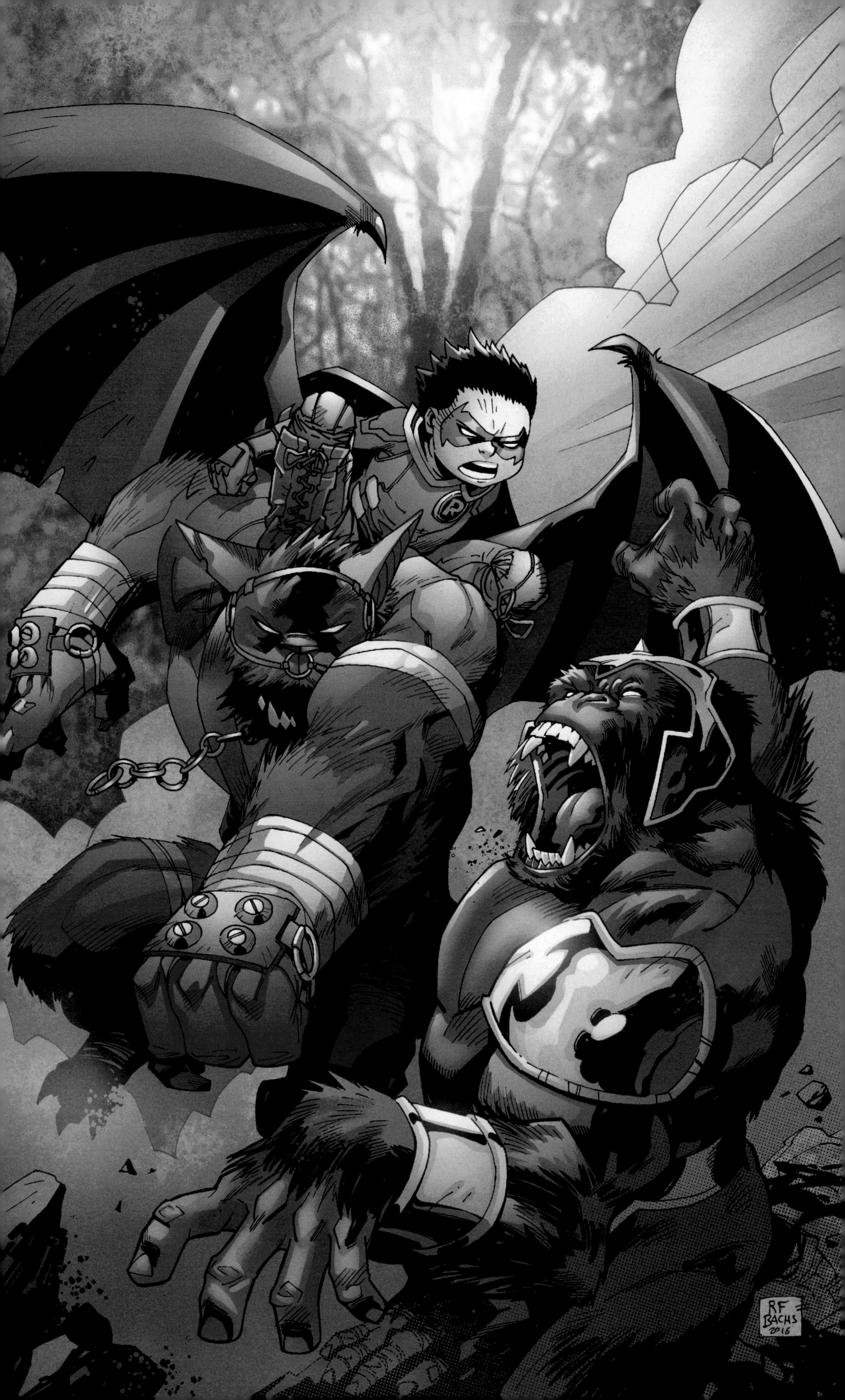
RF
BACHS
2016

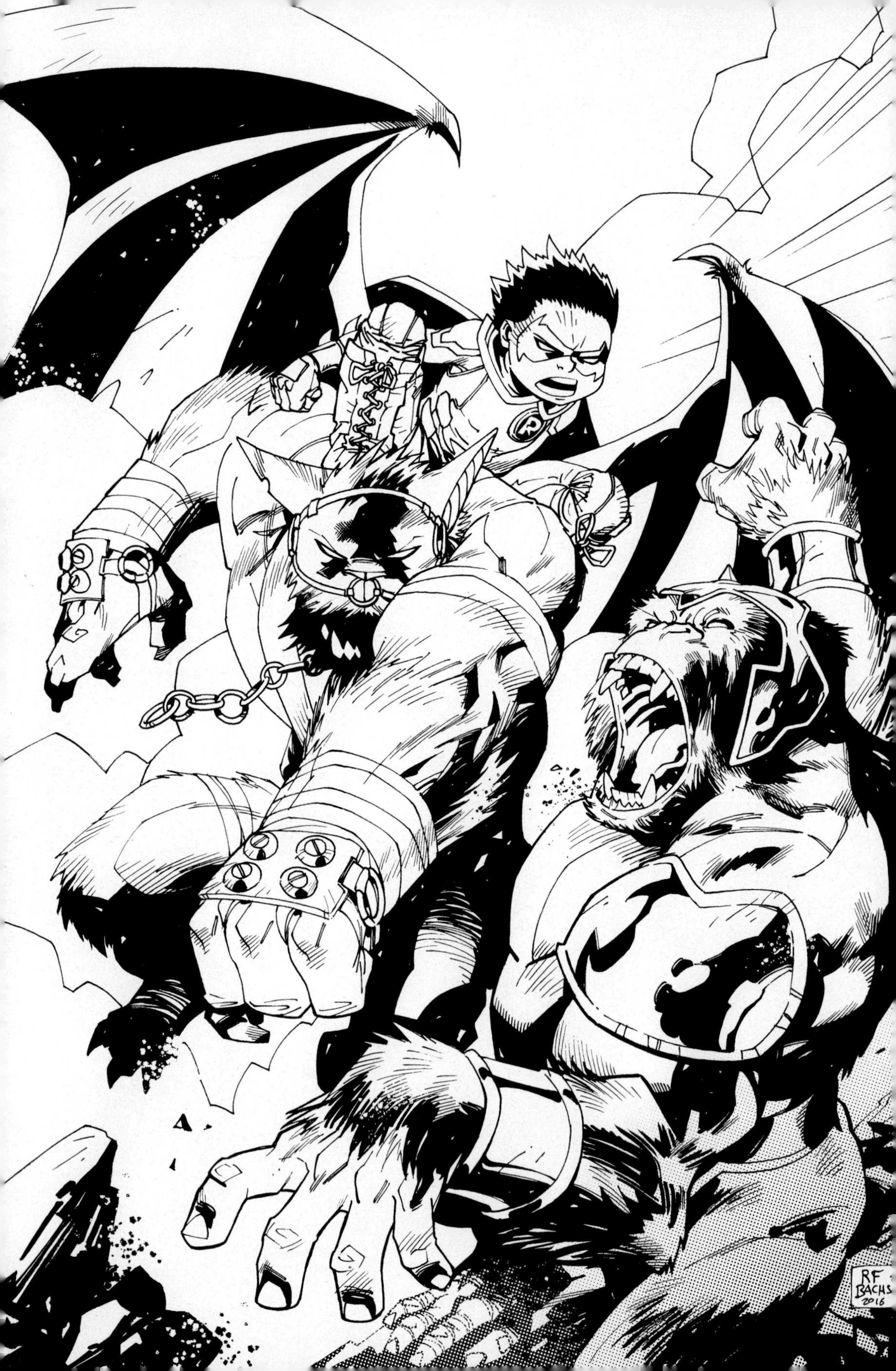
RF
BACHS
2016

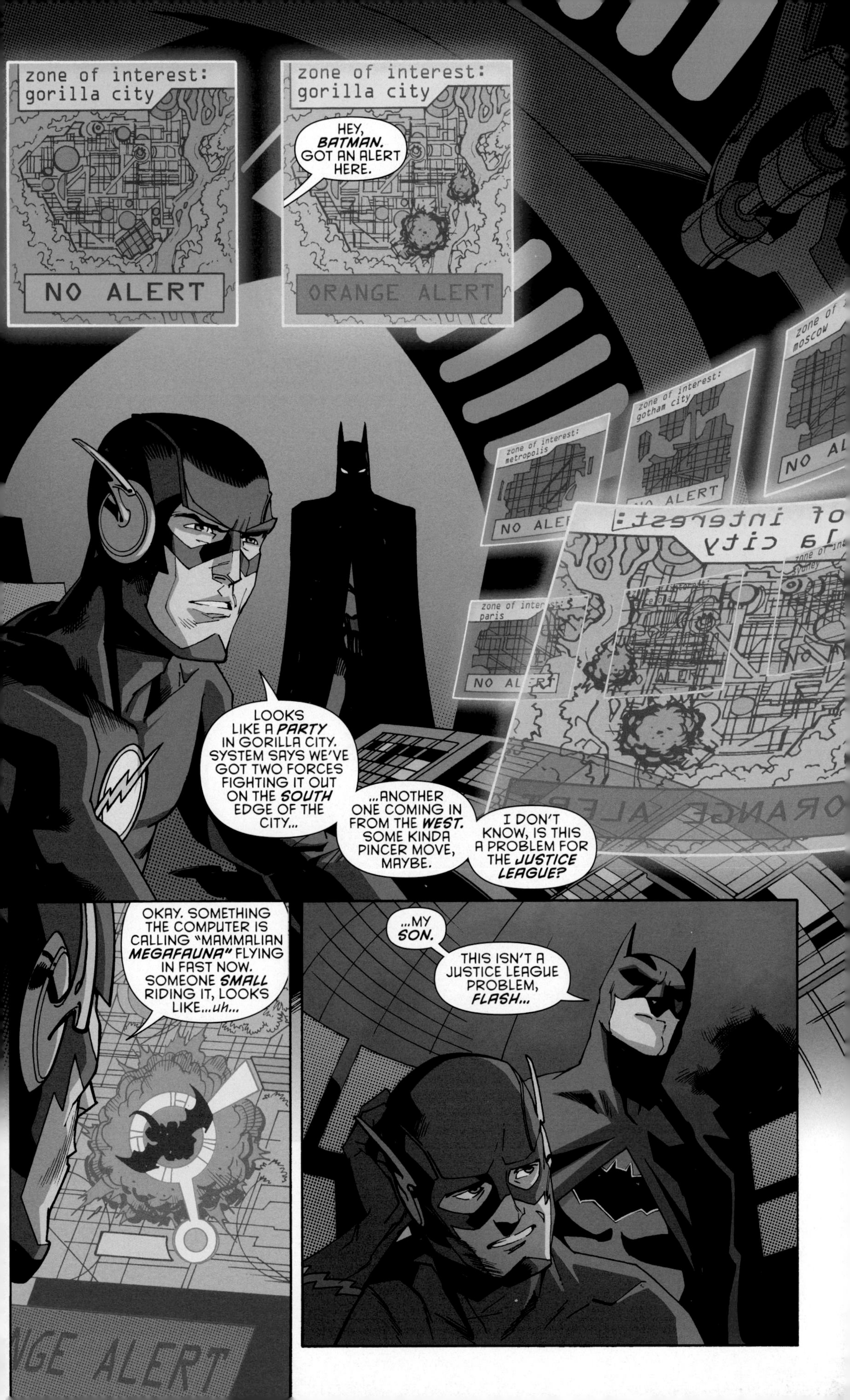
zone of interest: gorilla city
NO ALERT
zone of interest: gorilla city
HEY, BATMAN. GOT AN ALERT HERE.
ORANGE ALERT
zone of interest: metropolis
NO ALERT
zone of interest: gotham city
NO ALERT
zone of interest: moscow
zone of interest: paris
NO ALERT
LOOKS LIKE A PARTY IN GORILLA CITY. SYSTEM SAYS WE'VE GOT TWO FORCES FIGHTING IT OUT ON THE SOUTH EDGE OF THE CITY...
...ANOTHER ONE COMING IN FROM THE WEST. SOME KINDA PINCER MOVE, MAYBE.
I DON'T KNOW, IS THIS A PROBLEM FOR THE JUSTICE LEAGUE?
OKAY. SOMETHING THE COMPUTER IS CALLING "MAMMALIAN MEGAFAUNA" FLYING IN FAST NOW. SOMEONE SMALL RIDING IT, LOOKS LIKE...uh...
THIS ISN'T A JUSTICE LEAGUE PROBLEM, FLASH...
...MY SON.

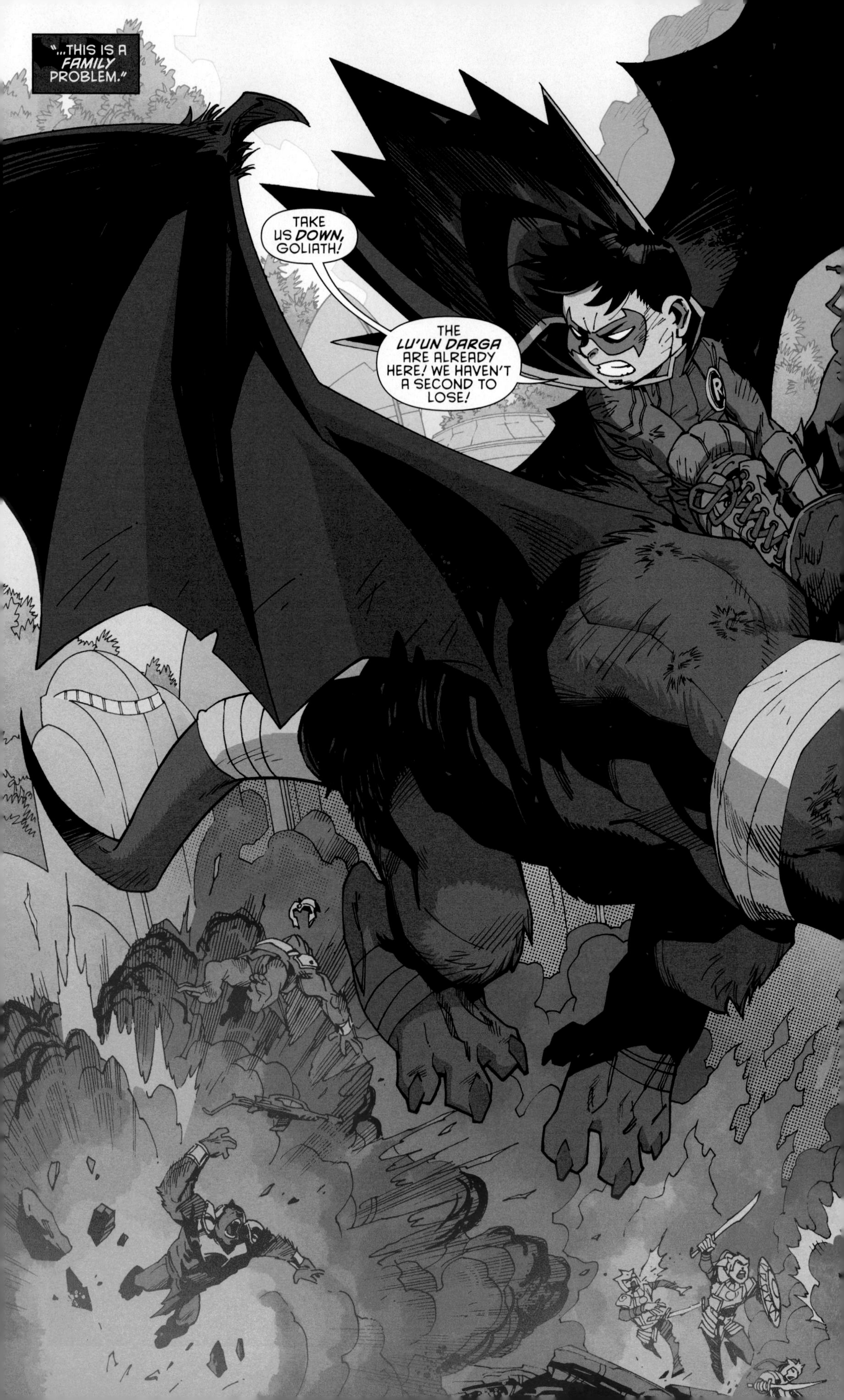
"...THIS IS A FAMILY PROBLEM."
TAKE US DOWN, GOLIATH!
THE LU'UN DARGA ARE ALREADY HERE! WE HAVEN'T A SECOND TO LOSE!

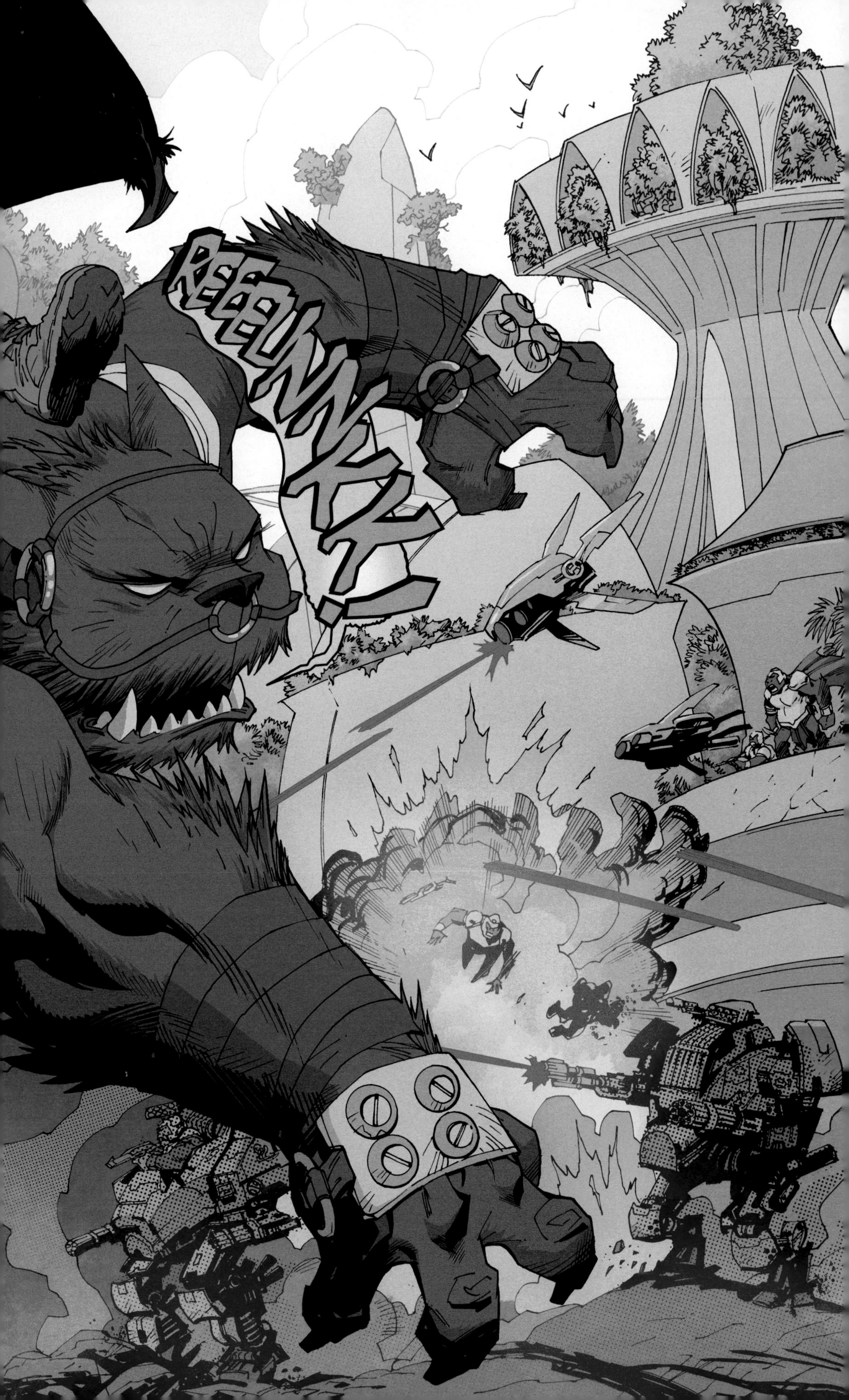
REELNNKK!

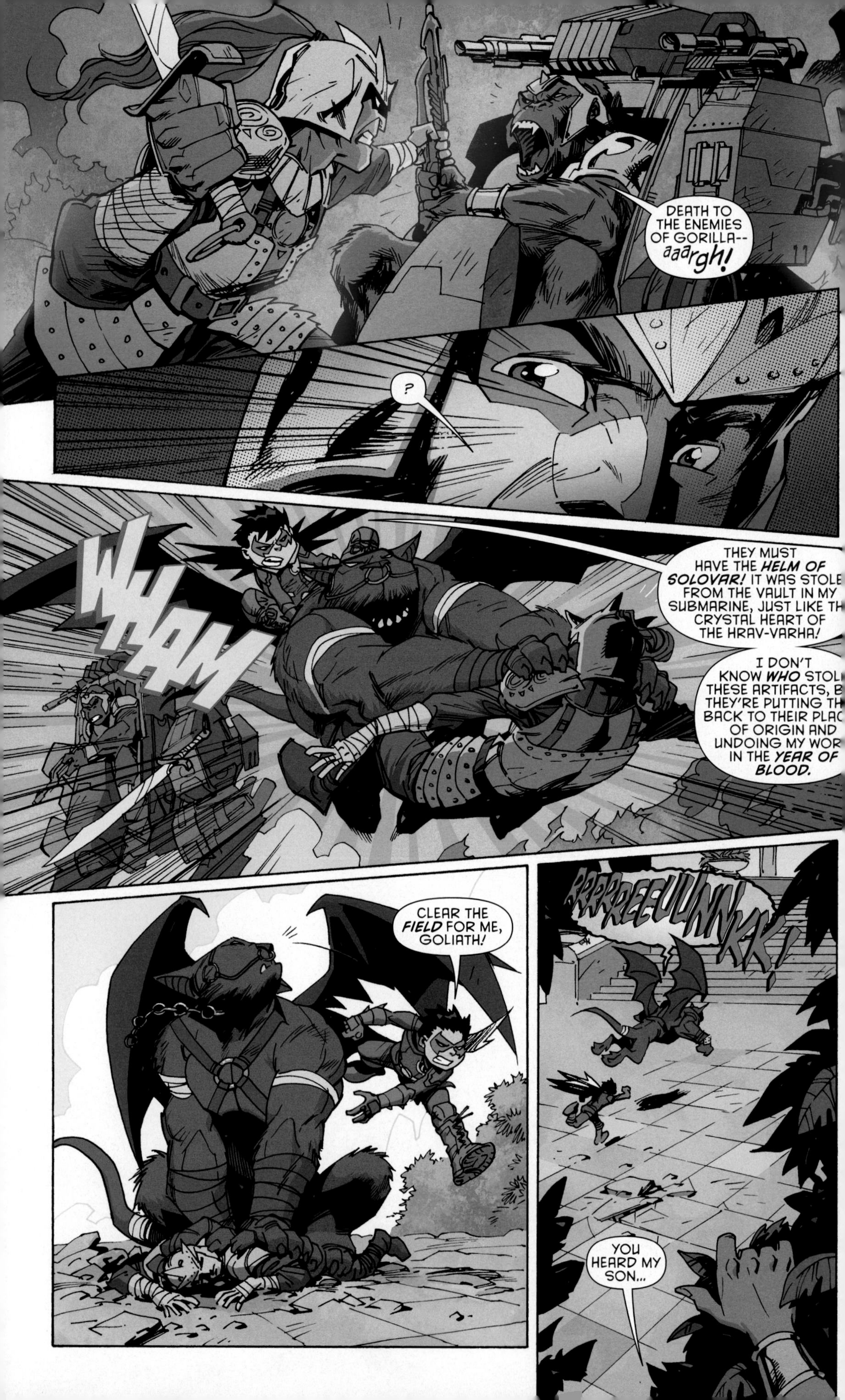
DEATH TO THE ENEMIES OF GORILLA-- aaargh!
?
WHAM
THEY MUST HAVE THE HELM OF SOLOVAR! IT WAS STOLE FROM THE VAULT IN MY SUBMARINE, JUST LIKE TH CRYSTAL HEART OF THE HRAV-VARHA!
I DON'T KNOW WHO STOL THESE ARTIFACTS, B THEY'RE PUTTING TH BACK TO THEIR PLAC OF ORIGIN AND UNDOING MY WOR IN THE YEAR OF BLOOD.
CLEAR THE FIELD FOR ME, GOLIATH!
RRRREEUUNNKK!
YOU HEARD MY SON...

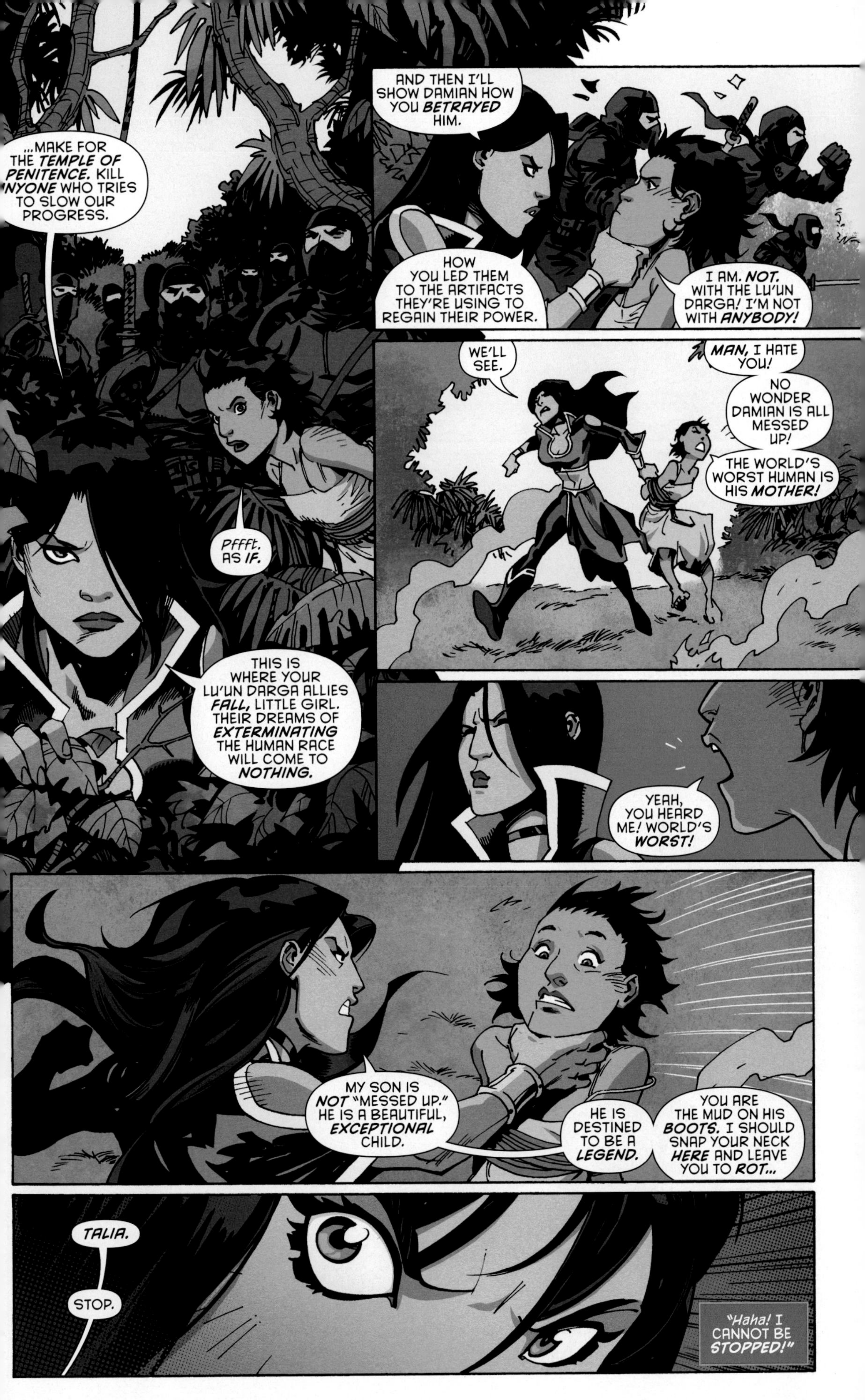

...MAKE FOR THE TEMPLE OF PENITENCE. KILL NYONE WHO TRIES TO SLOW OUR PROGRESS.
PFFFT. AS IF.
THIS IS WHERE YOUR LU'UN DARGA ALLIES FALL, LITTLE GIRL. THEIR DREAMS OF EXTERMINATING THE HUMAN RACE WILL COME TO NOTHING.
AND THEN I'LL SHOW DAMIAN HOW YOU BETRAYED HIM.
HOW YOU LED THEM TO THE ARTIFACTS THEY'RE USING TO REGAIN THEIR POWER.
I AM. NOT. WITH THE LU'UN DARGA! I'M NOT WITH ANYBODY!
WE'LL SEE.
MAN, I HATE YOU!
NO WONDER DAMIAN IS ALL MESSED UP!
THE WORLD'S WORST HUMAN IS HIS MOTHER!
YEAH, YOU HEARD ME! WORLD'S WORST!
MY SON IS NOT "MESSED UP." HE IS A BEAUTIFUL, EXCEPTIONAL CHILD.
HE IS DESTINED TO BE A LEGEND.
YOU ARE THE MUD ON HIS BOOTS. I SHOULD SNAP YOUR NECK HERE AND LEAVE YOU TO ROT...
TALIA.
STOP.
"Haha! I CANNOT BE STOPPED!"

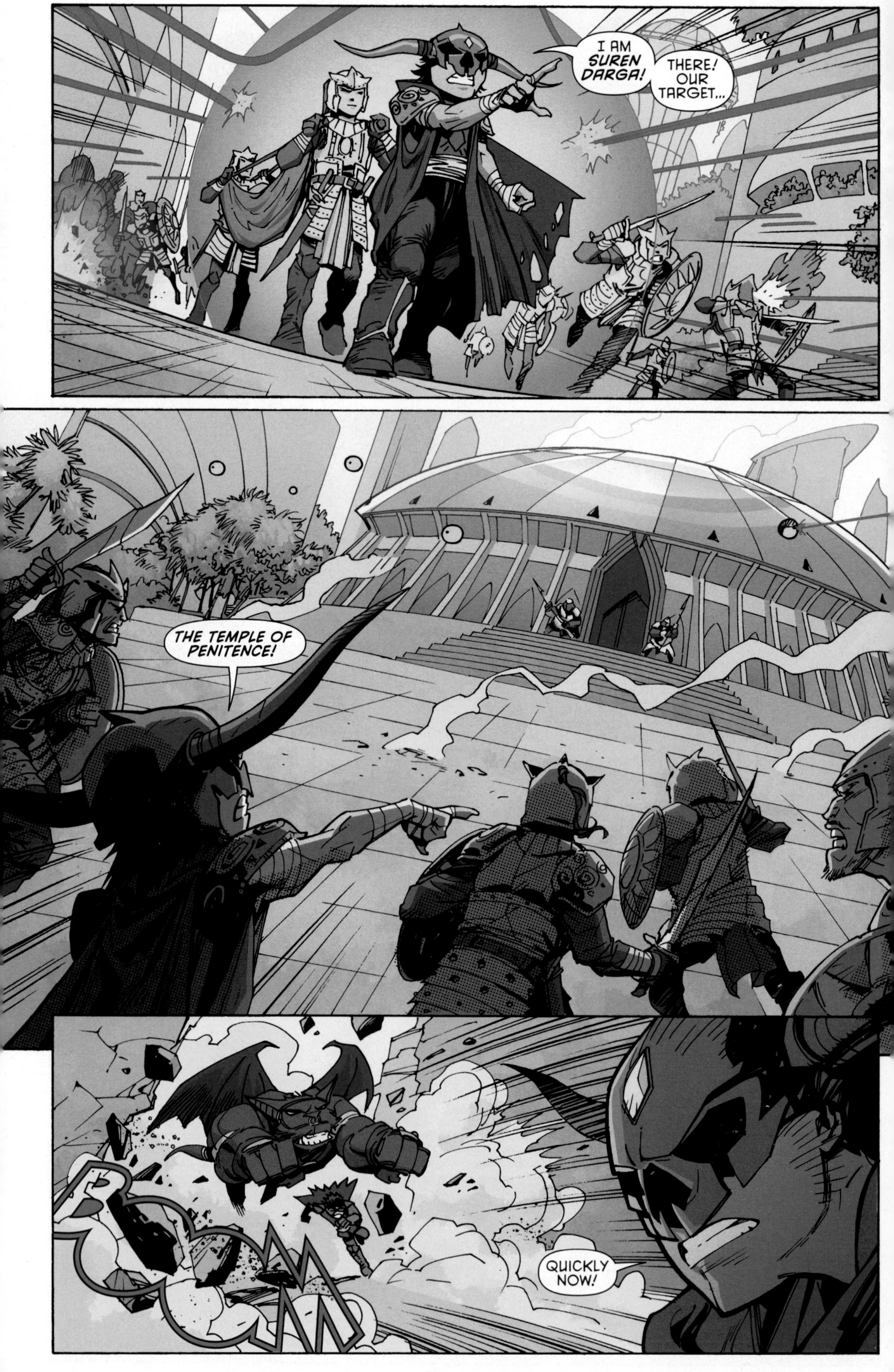
I AM SUREN DARGA!
THERE! OUR TARGET...
THE TEMPLE OF PENITENCE!
QUICKLY NOW!

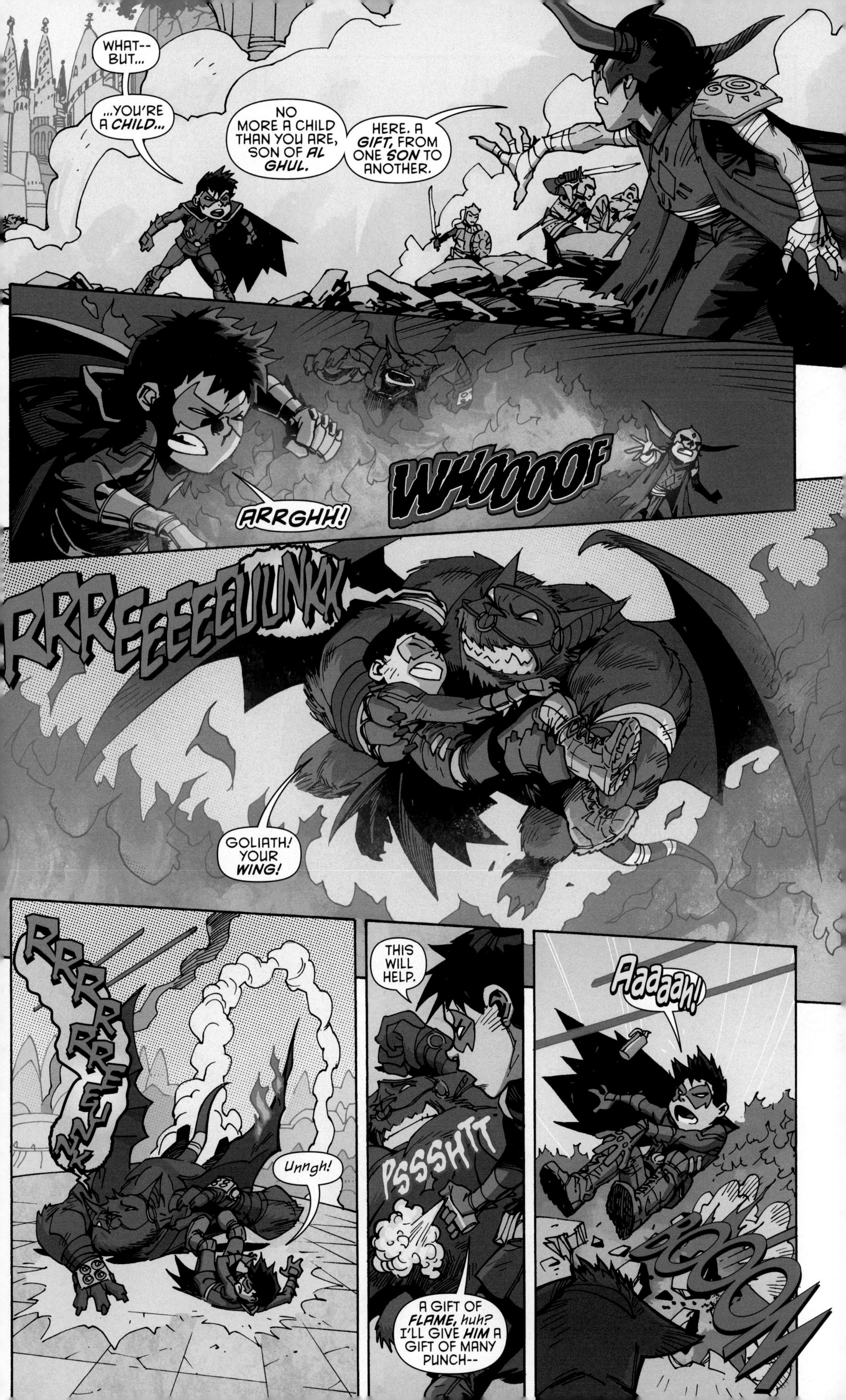
WHAT-- BUT...
...YOU'RE A CHILD...
NO MORE A CHILD THAN YOU ARE, SON OF AL GHUL.
HERE. A GIFT, FROM ONE SON TO ANOTHER.
WHOOOOOF
ARRGHH!
RRREEEEEEUUNKK
GOLIATH! YOUR WING!
RRRRRREEEUNK
Unngh!
THIS WILL HELP.
PSSSHTT
A GIFT OF FLAME, huh? I'LL GIVE HIM A GIFT OF MANY PUNCH--
Aaaaah!
BOOOM

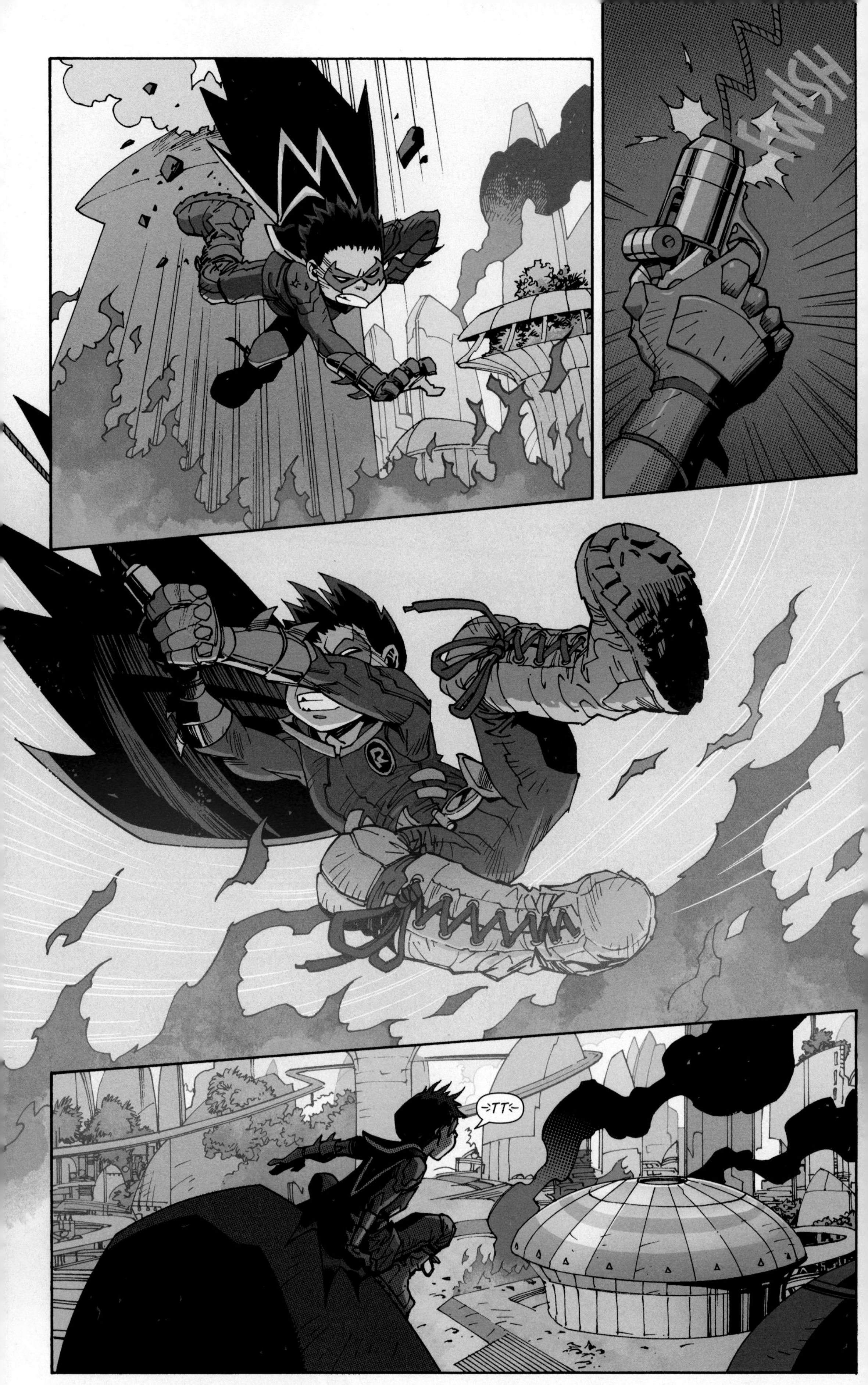
FWISH
TT

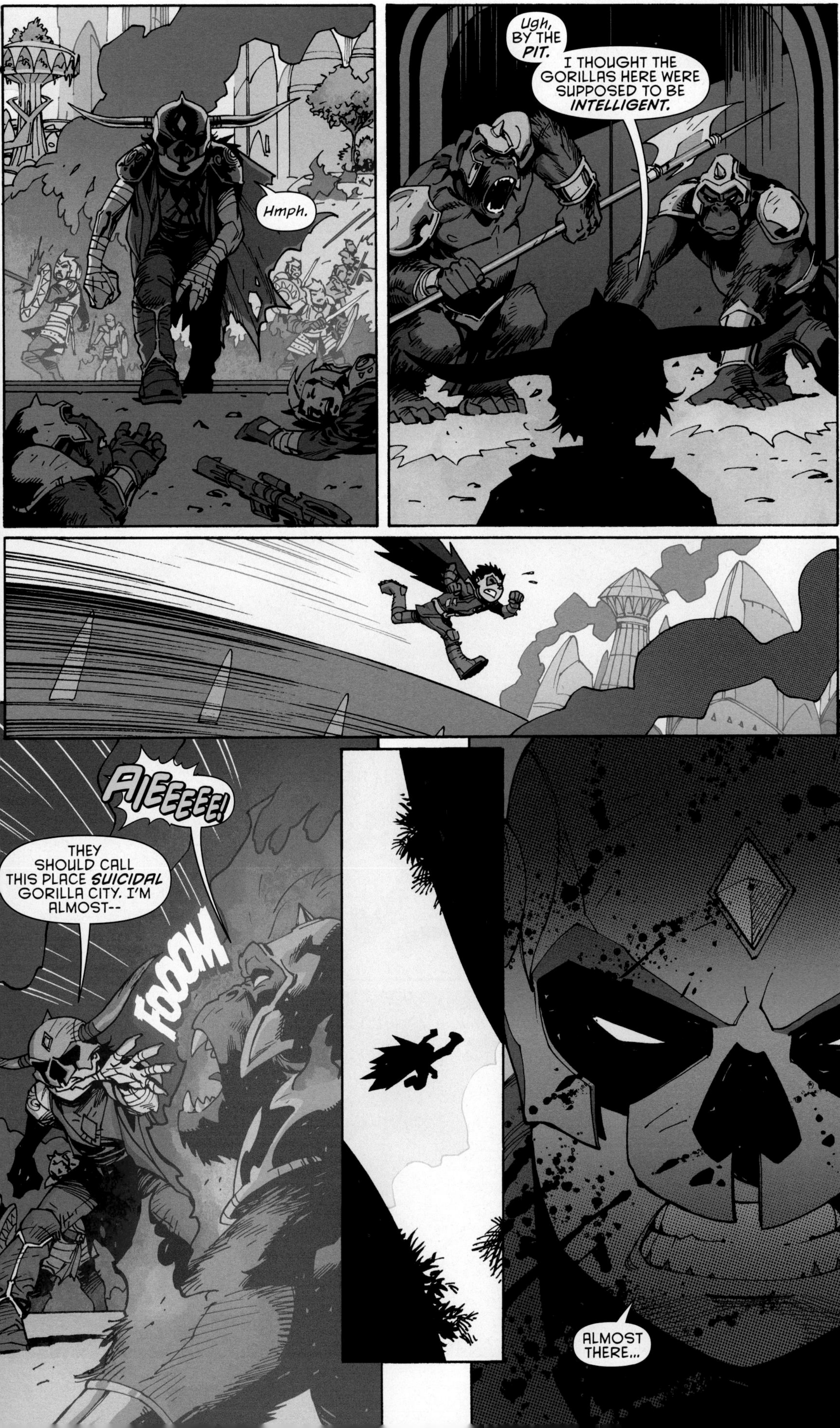
Hmph.
Ugh, BY THE PIT.
I THOUGHT THE GORILLAS HERE WERE SUPPOSED TO BE INTELLIGENT.
AIEEEEEE!
THEY SHOULD CALL THIS PLACE SUICIDAL GORILLA CITY. I'M ALMOST--
FOOOM
ALMOST THERE...

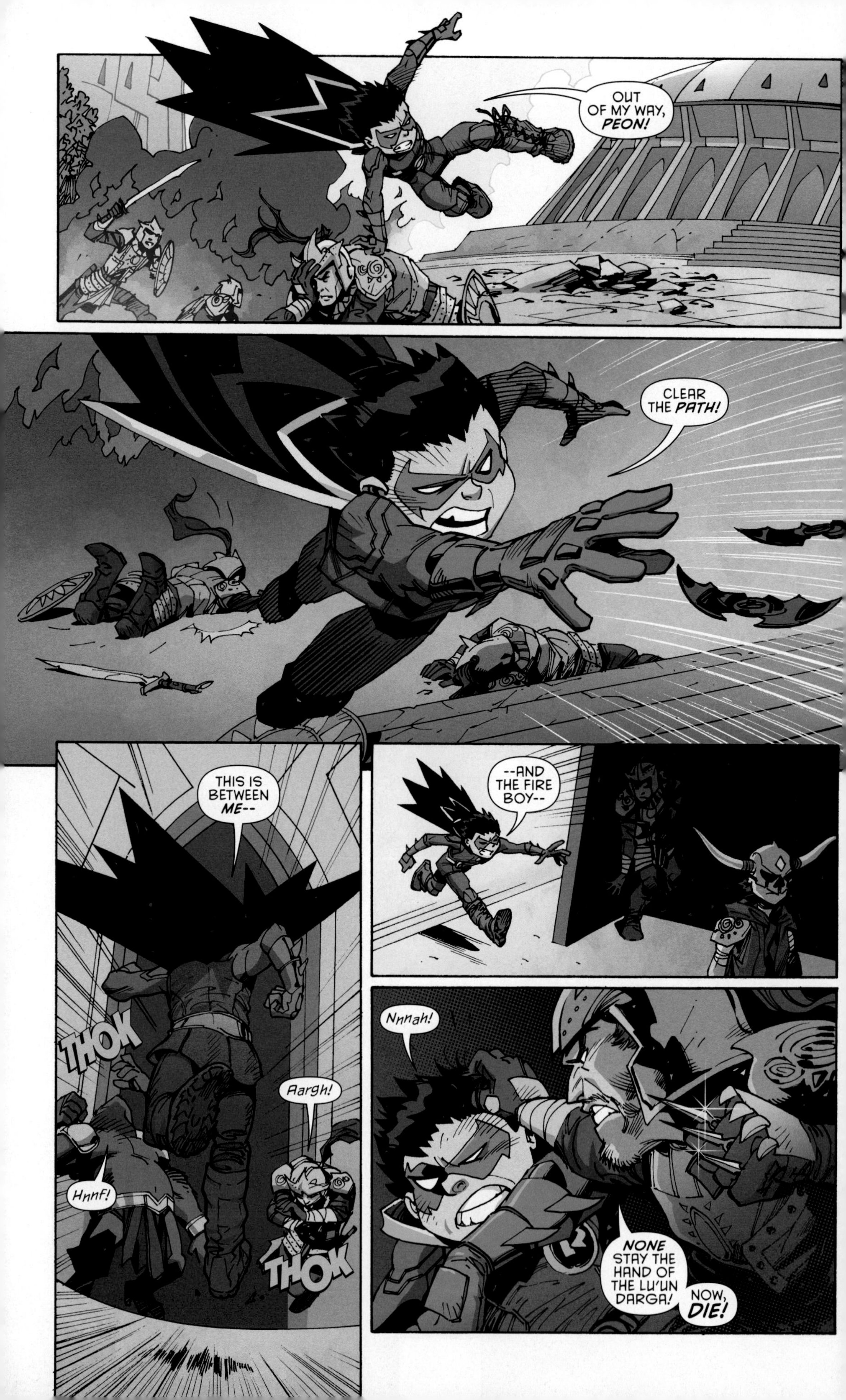
OUT OF MY WAY, PEON!
CLEAR THE PATH!
THIS IS BETWEEN ME--
THOK
Aargh!
Hnnf!
THOK
--AND THE FIRE BOY--
Nnnah!
NONE STAY THE HAND OF THE LU'UN DARGA!
NOW, DIE!

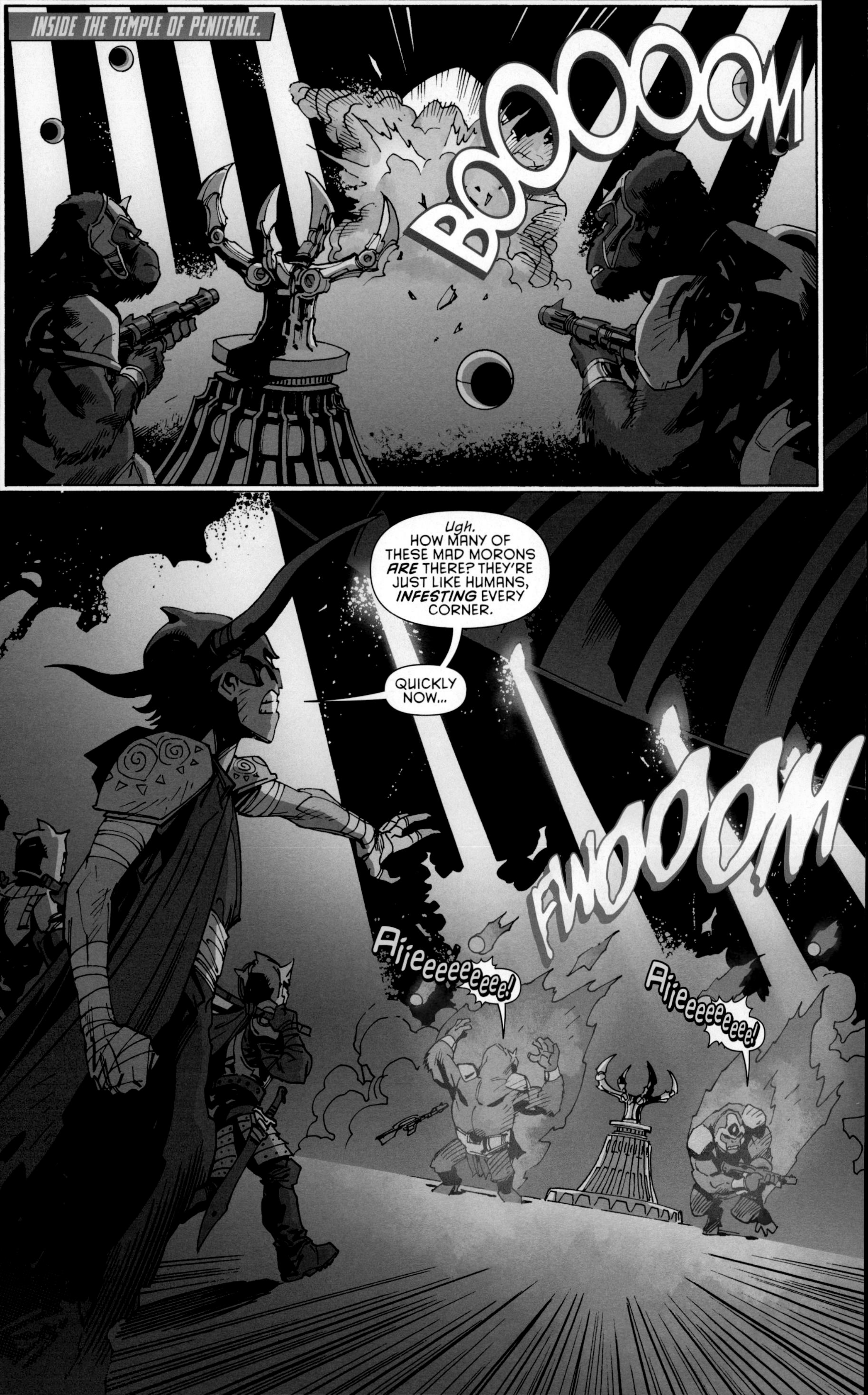
INSIDE THE TEMPLE OF PENITENCE.
BOOOOOOM
Ugh. HOW MANY OF THESE MAD MORONS ARE THERE? THEY'RE JUST LIKE HUMANS, INFESTING EVERY CORNER.
QUICKLY NOW...
FWOOOM
Aiieeeeeeeeee!
Aiieeeeeeeeee!

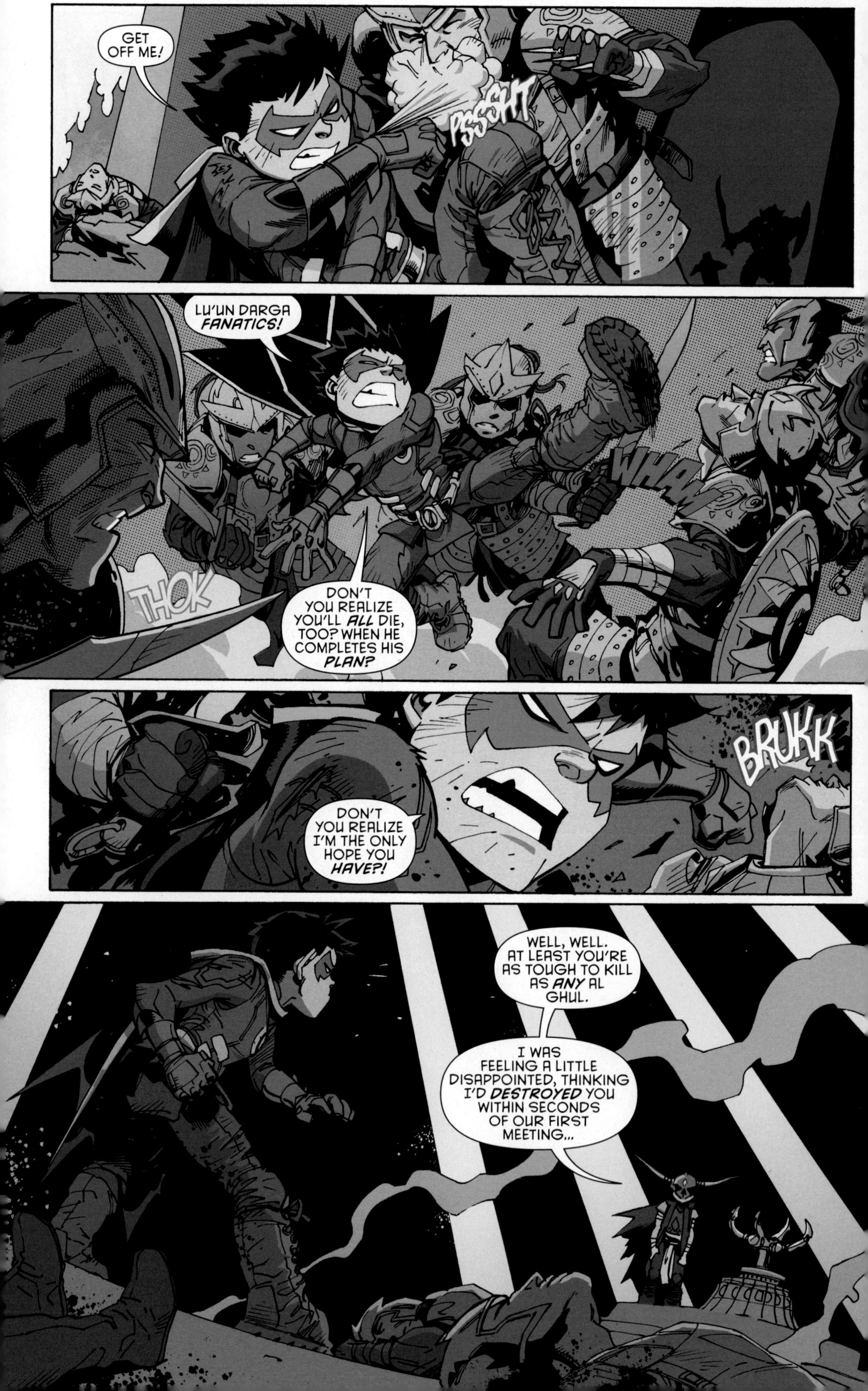
GET OFF ME!
PSSSHT
LU'UN DARGA FANATICS!
WHAM
THOK
DON'T YOU REALIZE YOU'LL ALL DIE, TOO? WHEN HE COMPLETES HIS PLAN?
BRUKK
DON'T YOU REALIZE I'M THE ONLY HOPE YOU HAVE?!
WELL, WELL. AT LEAST YOU'RE AS TOUGH TO KILL AS ANY AL GHUL.
I WAS FEELING A LITTLE DISAPPOINTED, THINKING I'D DESTROYED YOU WITHIN SECONDS OF OUR FIRST MEETING...

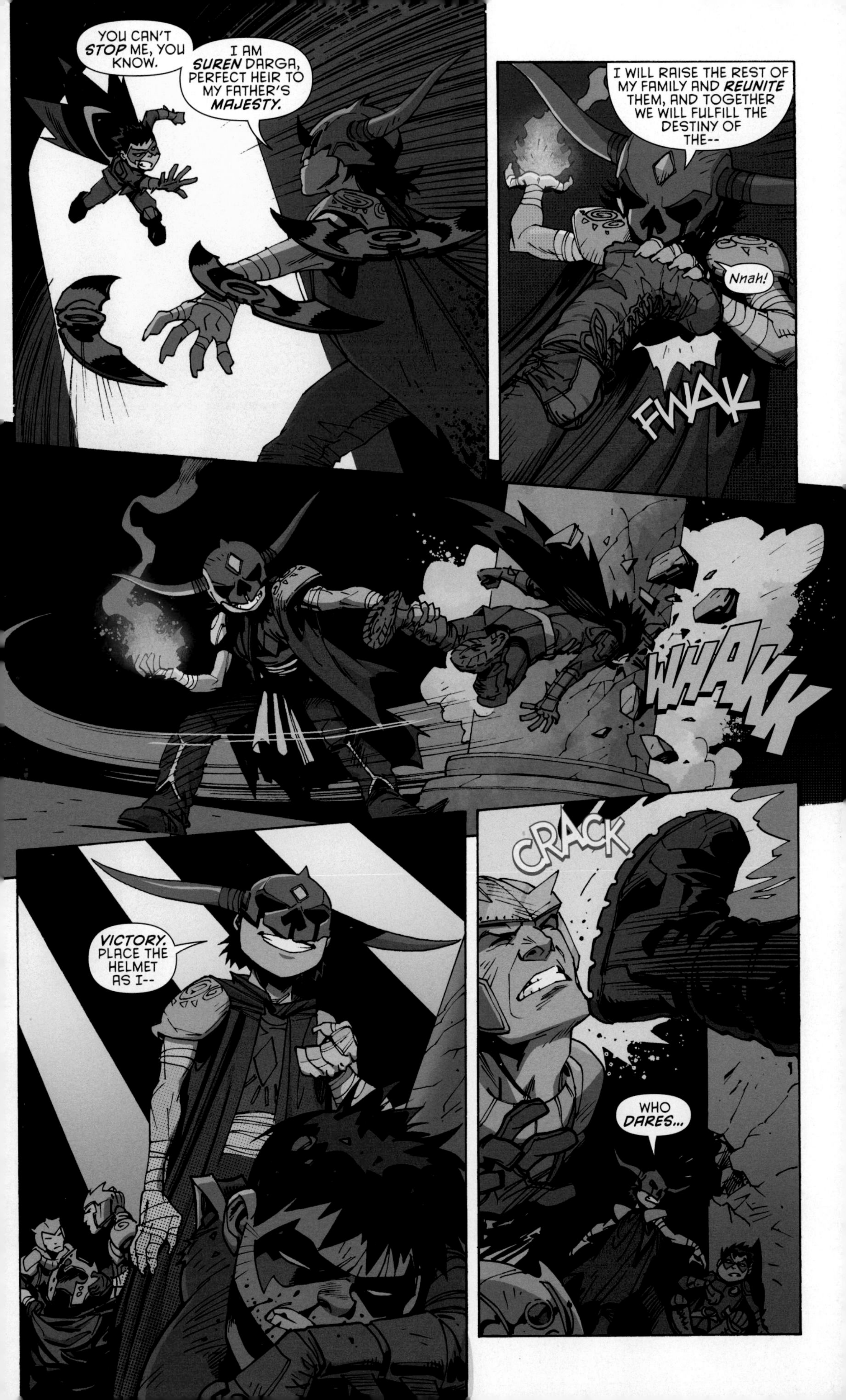
YOU CAN'T STOP ME, YOU KNOW.
I AM SUREN DARGA, PERFECT HEIR TO MY FATHER'S MAJESTY.
I WILL RAISE THE REST OF MY FAMILY AND REUNITE THEM, AND TOGETHER WE WILL FULFILL THE DESTINY OF THE--
Nnah!
FWAK
WHAKK
VICTORY. PLACE THE HELMET AS I--
CRACK
WHO DARES...

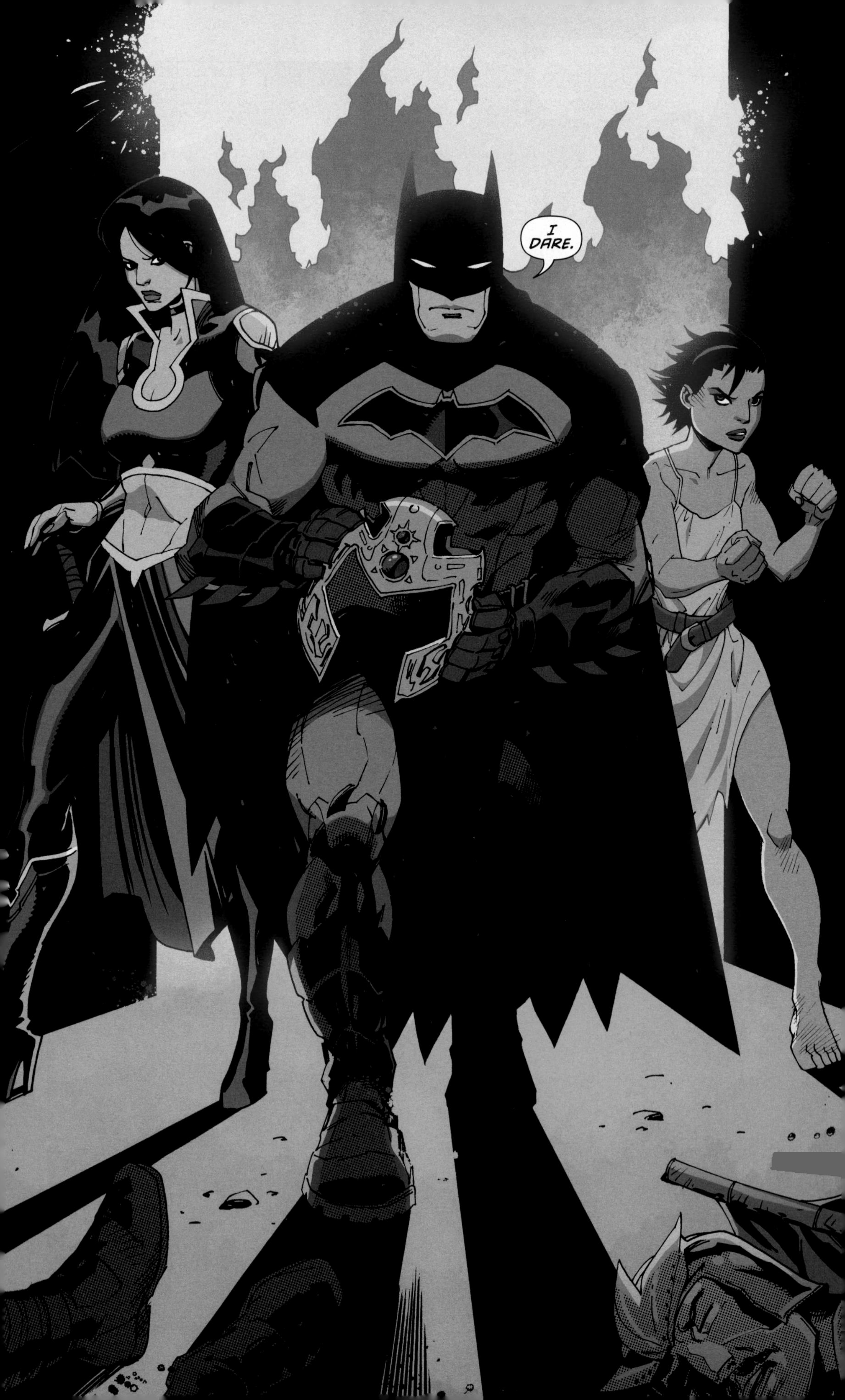
I DARE.

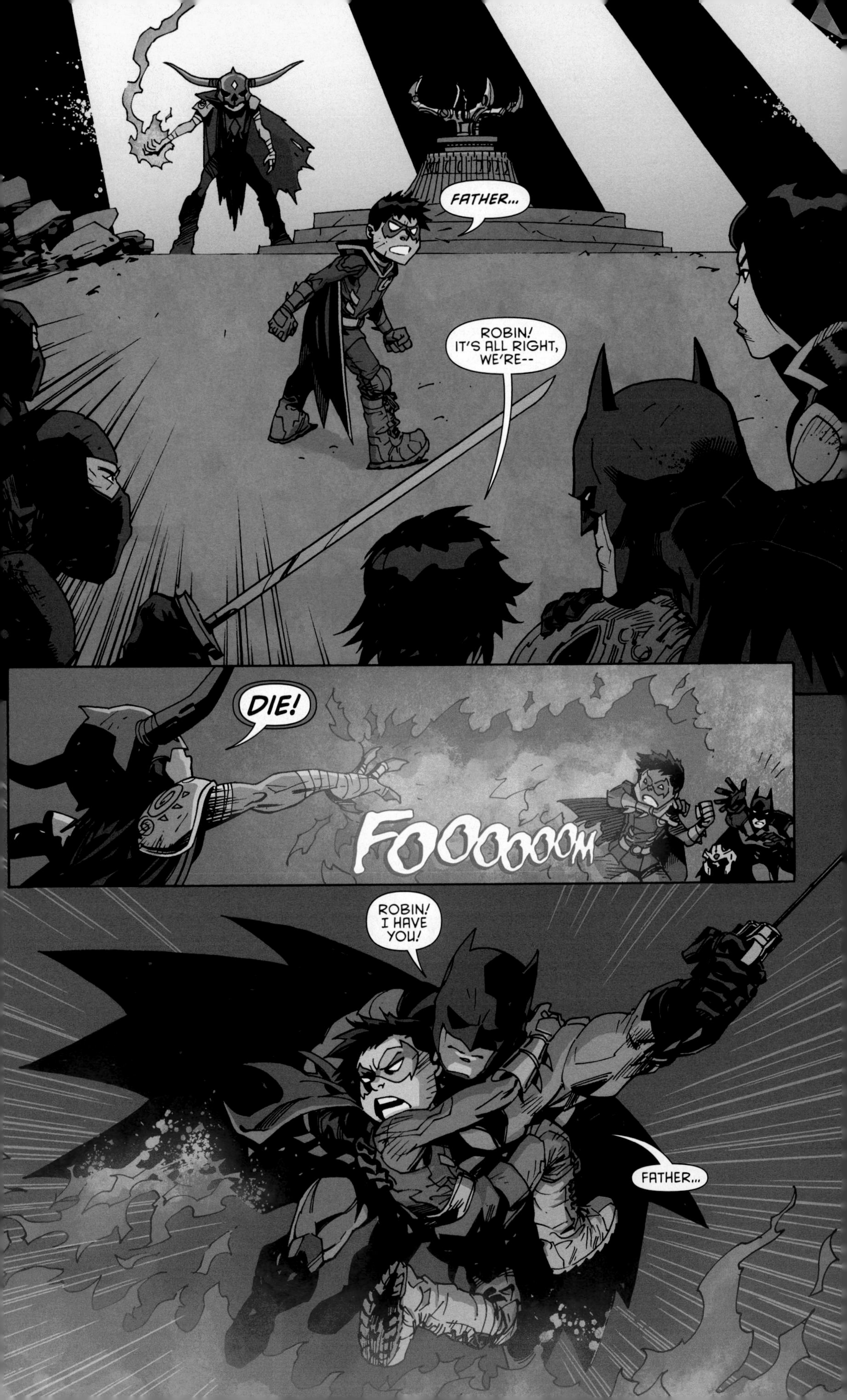
FATHER...
ROBIN! IT'S ALL RIGHT, WE'RE--
DIE!
FOOOOOOOM
ROBIN! I HAVE YOU!
FATHER...

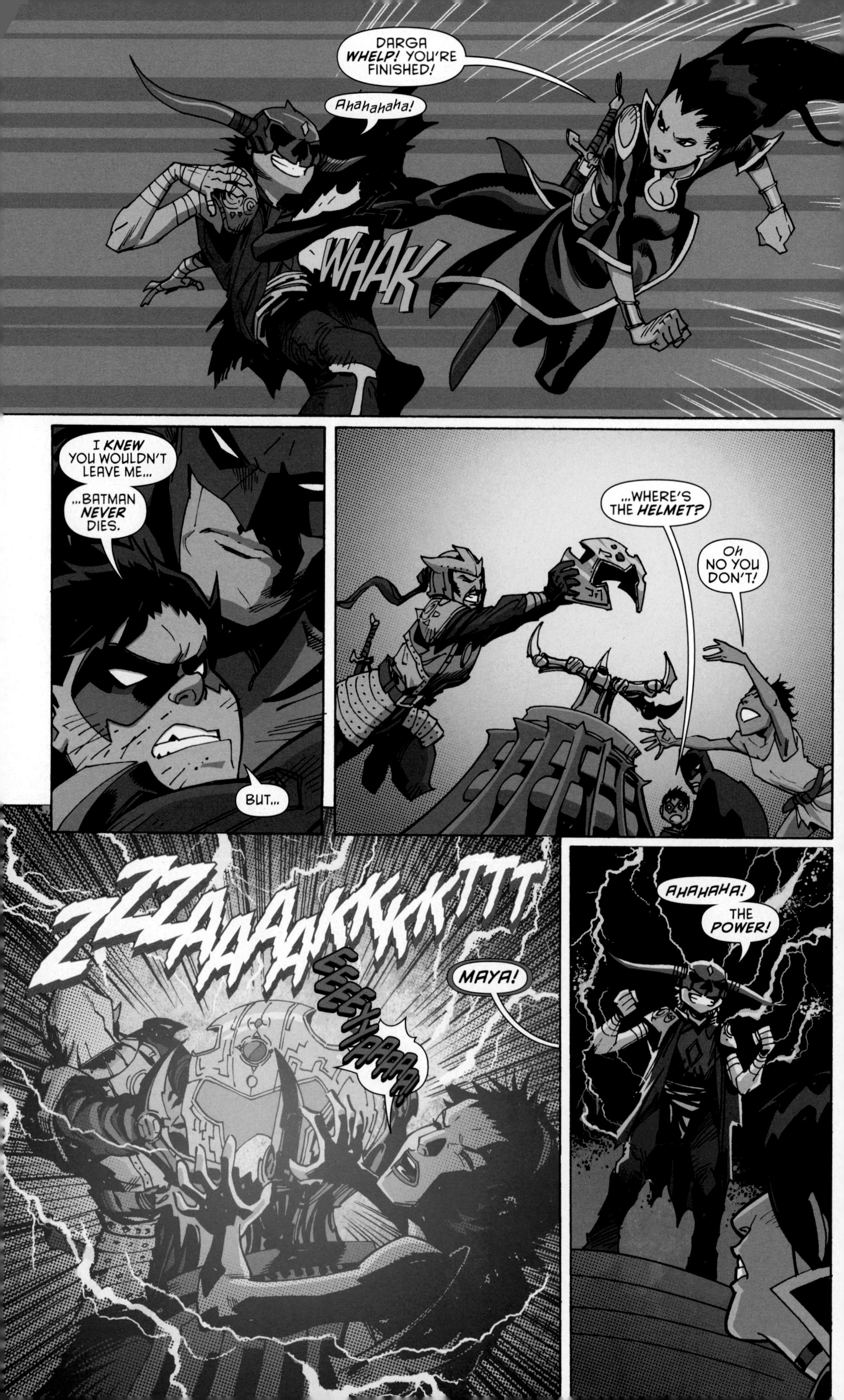
DARGA WHELP! YOU'RE FINISHED!
Ahahahaha!
WHAK
I KNEW YOU WOULDN'T LEAVE ME...
...BATMAN NEVER DIES.
BUT...
...WHERE'S THE HELMET?
Oh NO YOU DON'T!
ZZZAAAAKKKKTTT
EEEEYAAAA!
MAYA!
AHAHAHA!
THE POWER!

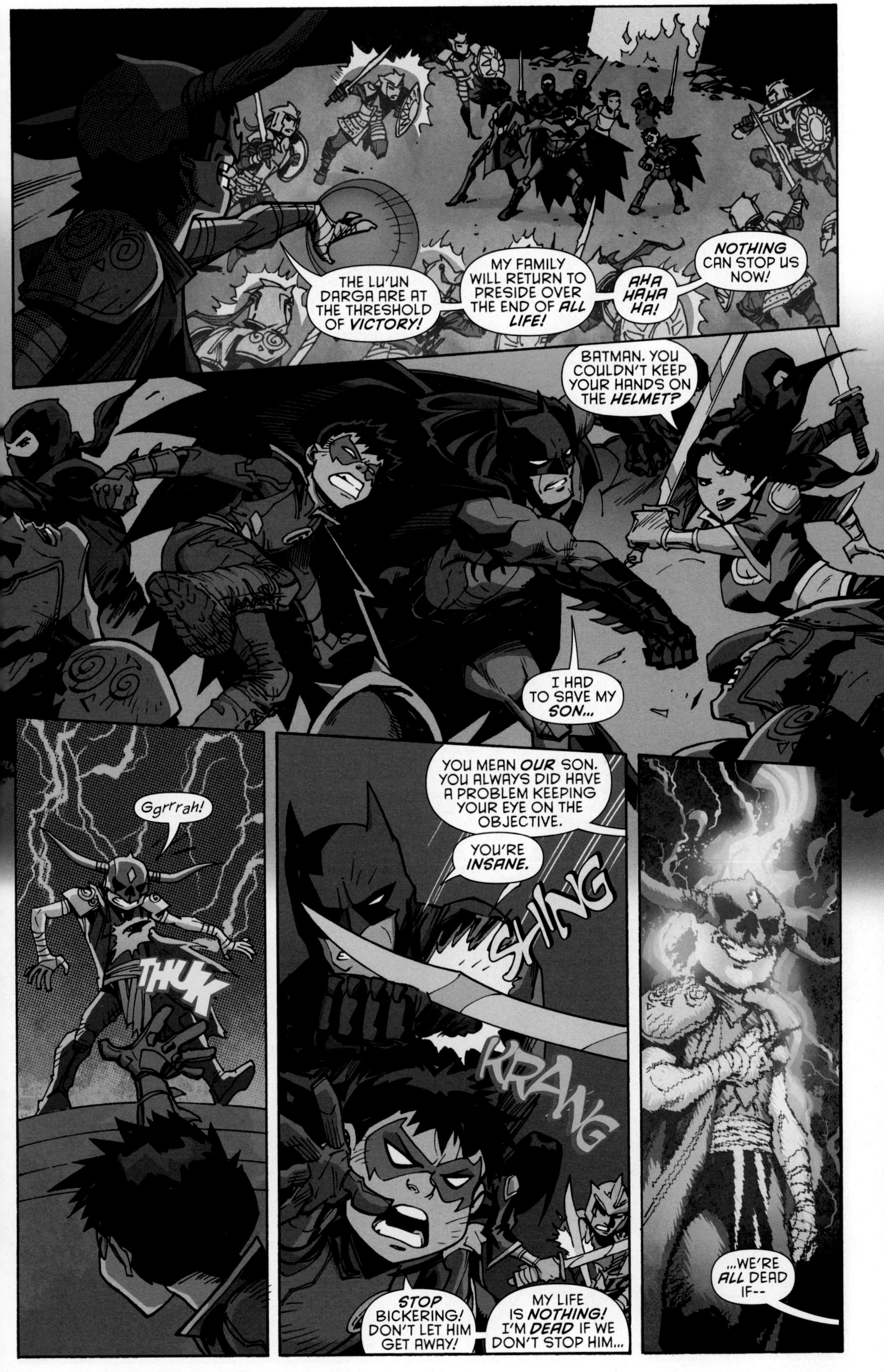
THE LU'UN DARGA ARE AT THE THRESHOLD OF VICTORY!
MY FAMILY WILL RETURN TO PRESIDE OVER THE END OF ALL LIFE!
AHA HAHA HA!
NOTHING CAN STOP US NOW!
BATMAN. YOU COULDN'T KEEP YOUR HANDS ON THE HELMET?
I HAD TO SAVE MY SON...
Ggrrrah!
THUK
YOU MEAN OUR SON. YOU ALWAYS DID HAVE A PROBLEM KEEPING YOUR EYE ON THE OBJECTIVE.
YOU'RE INSANE.
SHING
KRANG
STOP BICKERING! DON'T LET HIM GET AWAY!
MY LIFE IS NOTHING! I'M DEAD IF WE DON'T STOP HIM...
...WE'RE ALL DEAD IF--

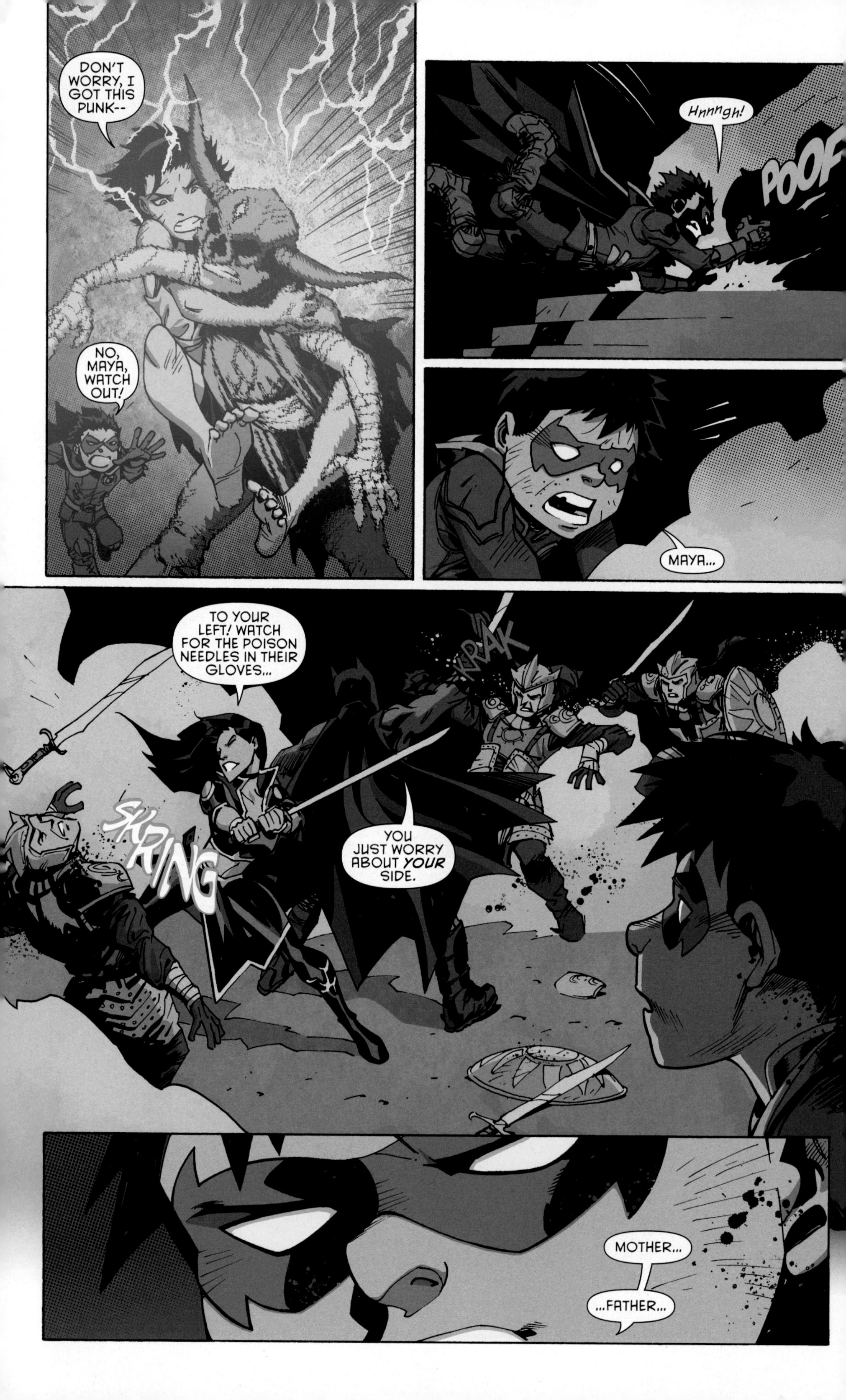
DON'T WORRY, I GOT THIS PUNK--
NO, MAYA, WATCH OUT!
Hnnngh!
POOF
MAYA...
TO YOUR LEFT! WATCH FOR THE POISON NEEDLES IN THEIR GLOVES...
KRAK
SKRING
YOU JUST WORRY ABOUT YOUR SIDE.
MOTHER...
...FATHER...

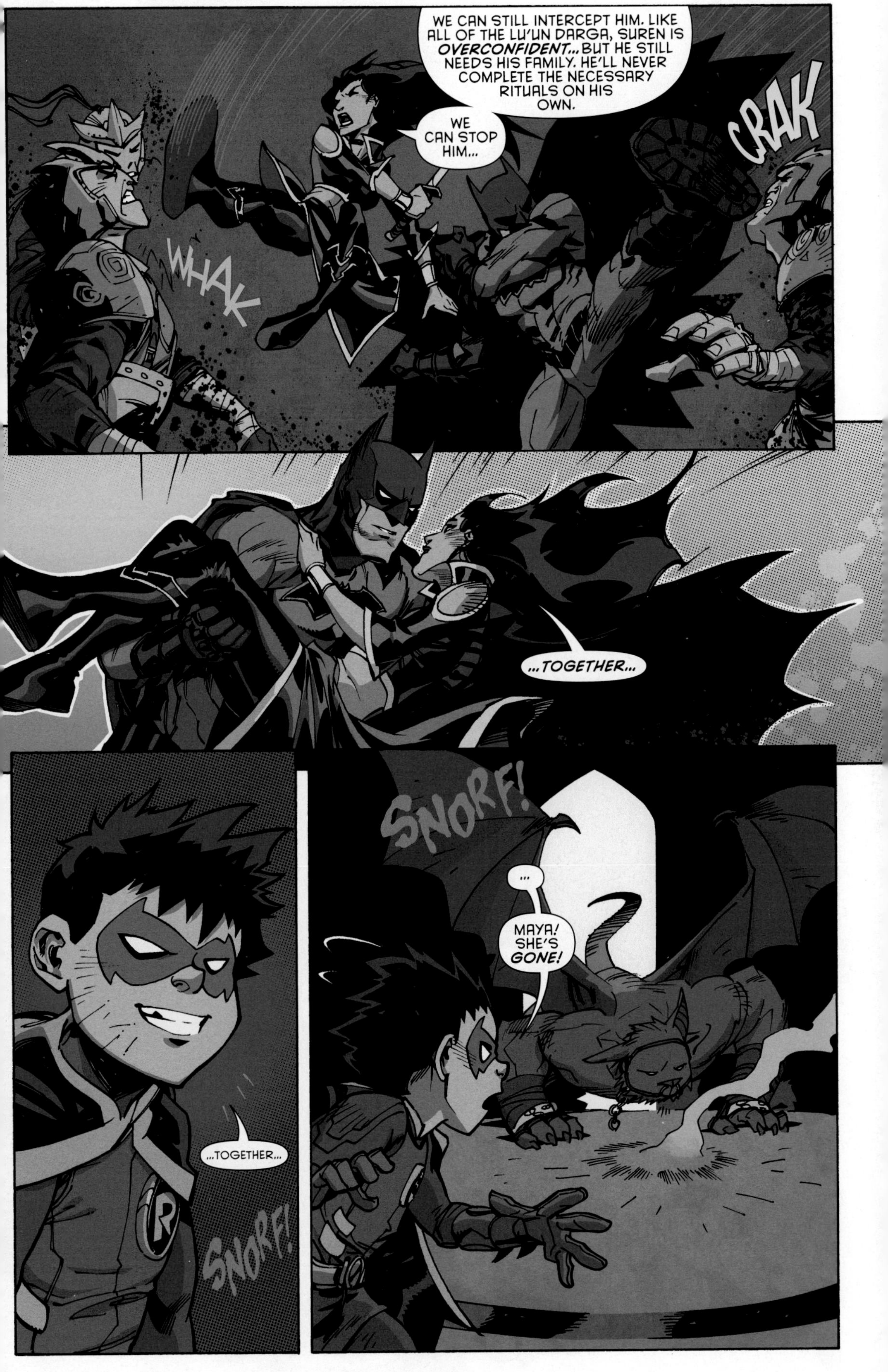
WE CAN STILL INTERCEPT HIM. LIKE ALL OF THE LU'UN DARGA, SUREN IS OVERCONFIDENT... BUT HE STILL NEEDS HIS FAMILY. HE'LL NEVER COMPLETE THE NECESSARY RITUALS ON HIS OWN.
WE CAN STOP HIM...
WHAK
CRAK
...TOGETHER...
...TOGETHER...
SNORF!
SNORF!
...
MAYA! SHE'S GONE!

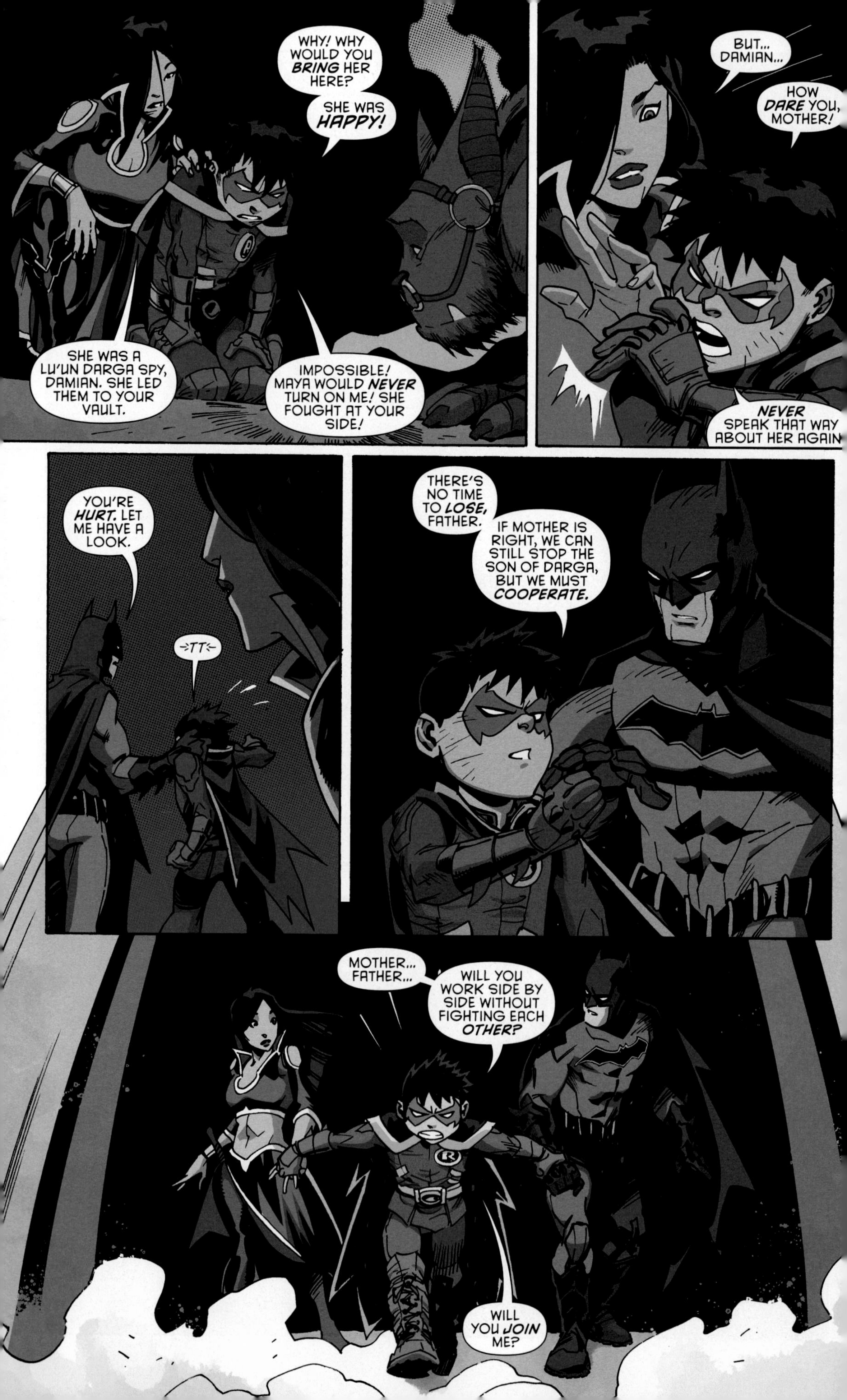
WHY! WHY WOULD YOU BRING HER HERE?
SHE WAS HAPPY!
SHE WAS A LU'UN DARGA SPY, DAMIAN. SHE LED THEM TO YOUR VAULT.
IMPOSSIBLE! MAYA WOULD NEVER TURN ON ME! SHE FOUGHT AT YOUR SIDE!
BUT... DAMIAN...
HOW DARE YOU, MOTHER!
NEVER SPEAK THAT WAY ABOUT HER AGAIN
YOU'RE HURT. LET ME HAVE A LOOK.
TT
THERE'S NO TIME TO LOSE, FATHER.
IF MOTHER IS RIGHT, WE CAN STILL STOP THE SON OF DARGA, BUT WE MUST COOPERATE.
MOTHER... FATHER...
WILL YOU WORK SIDE BY SIDE WITHOUT FIGHTING EACH OTHER?
WILL YOU JOIN ME?

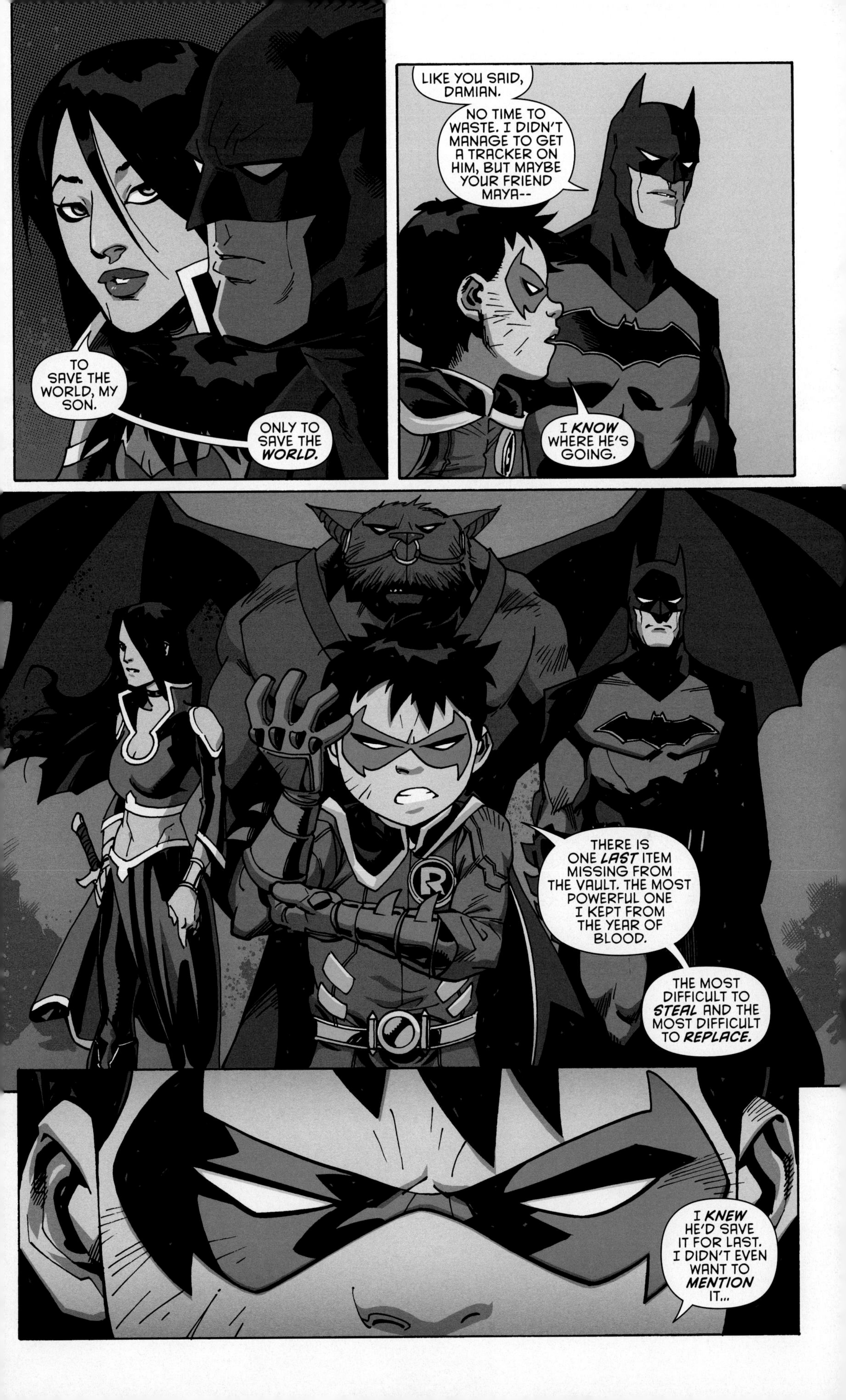
TO SAVE THE WORLD, MY SON.
ONLY TO SAVE THE *WORLD.*
LIKE YOU SAID, DAMIAN.
NO TIME TO WASTE. I DIDN'T MANAGE TO GET A TRACKER ON HIM, BUT MAYBE YOUR FRIEND MAYA--
I *KNOW* WHERE HE'S GOING.
THERE IS ONE *LAST* ITEM MISSING FROM THE VAULT. THE MOST POWERFUL ONE I KEPT FROM THE YEAR OF BLOOD.
THE MOST DIFFICULT TO *STEAL* AND THE MOST DIFFICULT TO *REPLACE.*
I *KNEW* HE'D SAVE IT FOR LAST. I DIDN'T EVEN WANT TO *MENTION* IT...

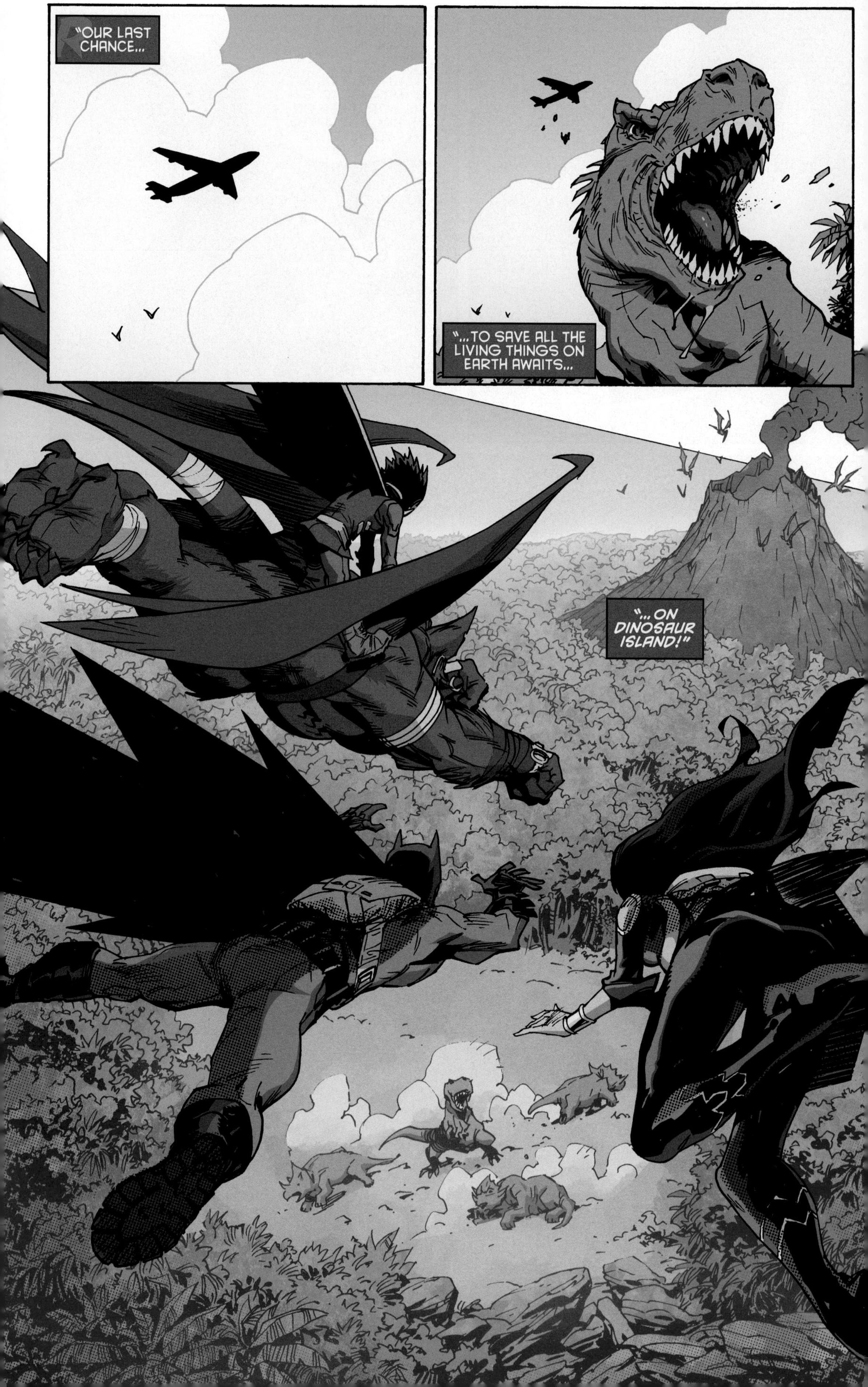
"OUR LAST CHANCE...
"...TO SAVE ALL THE LIVING THINGS ON EARTH AWAITS...
"...ON DINOSAUR ISLAND!"

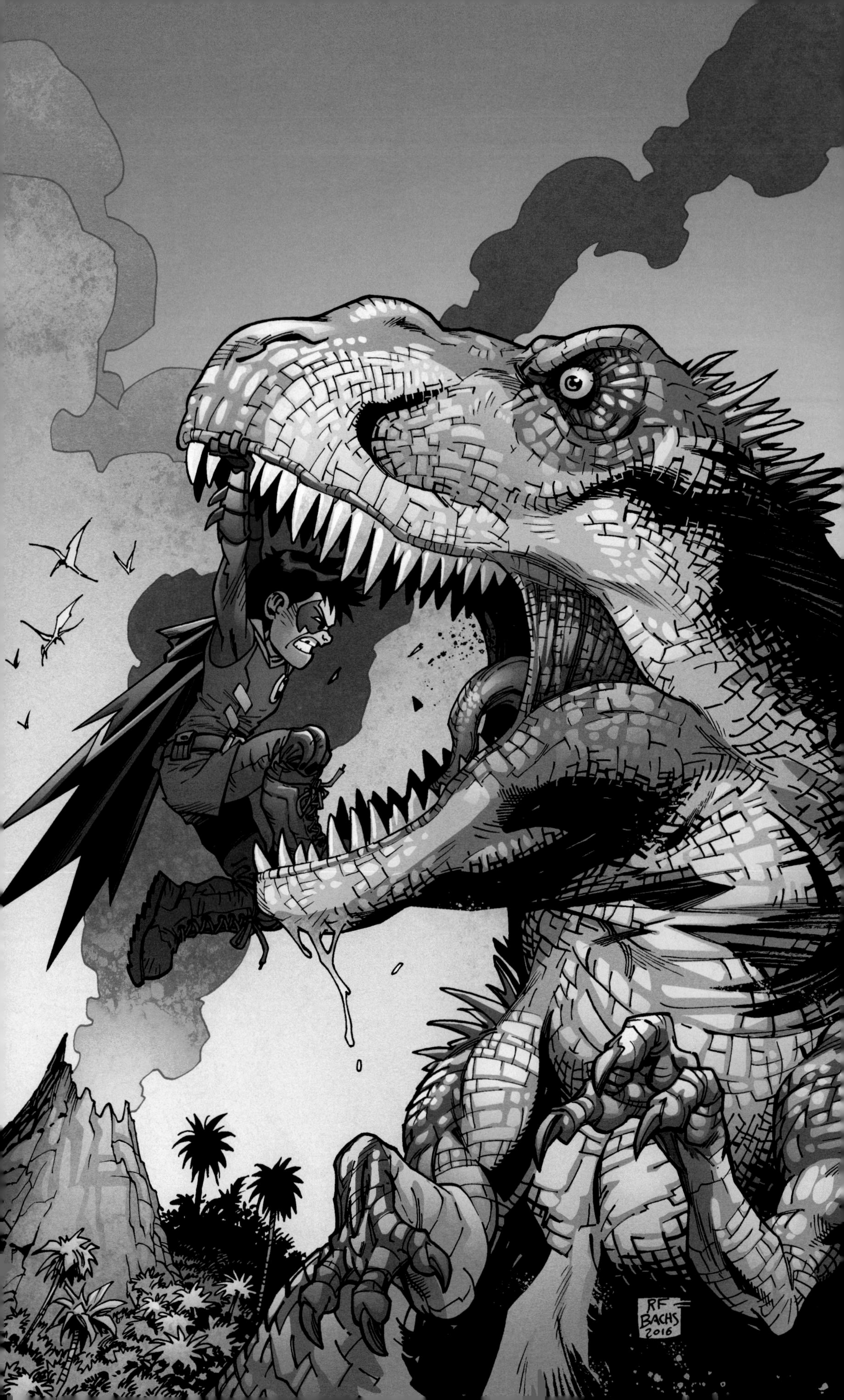
RF
BACHS
2016

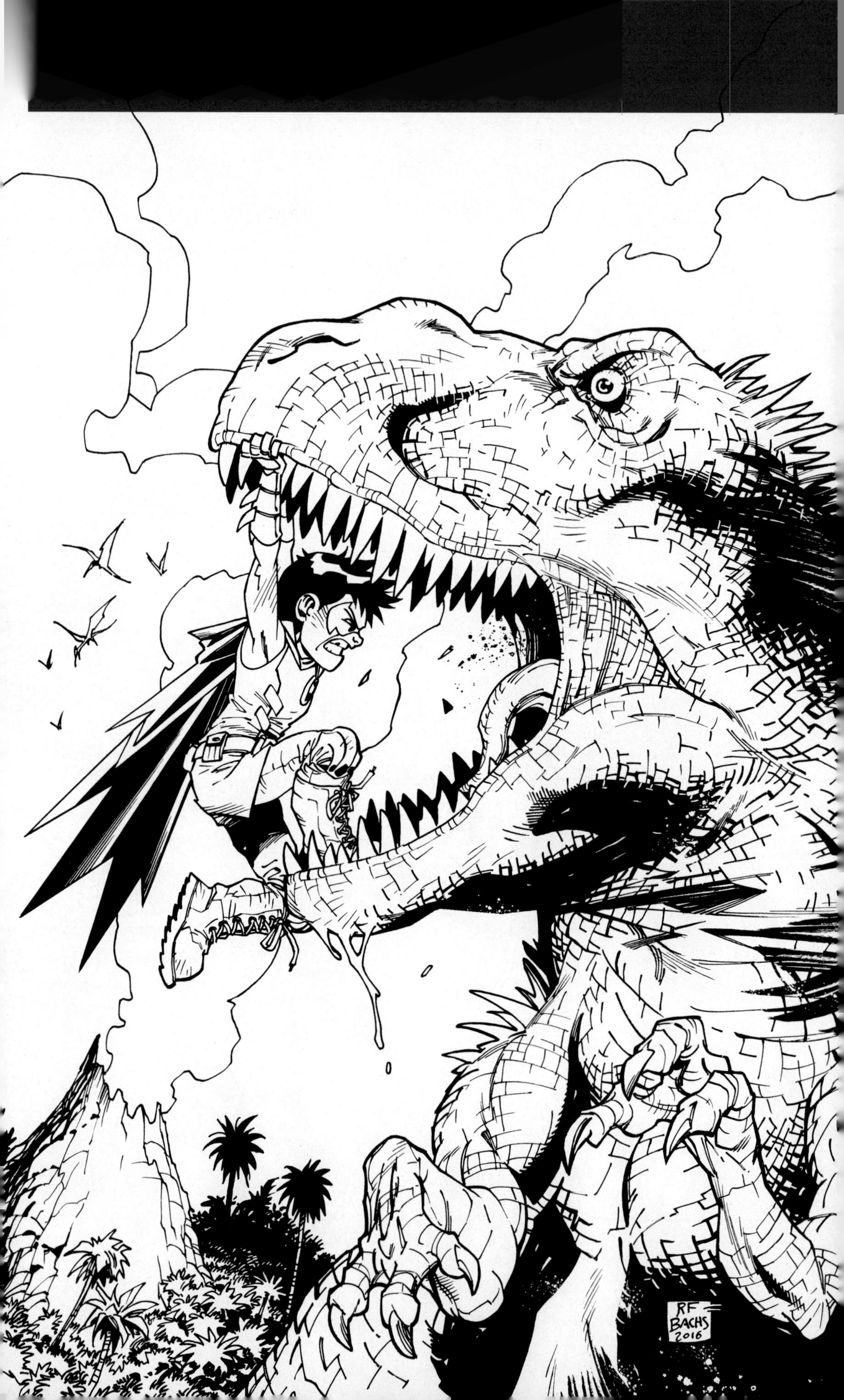
RF
BACHS
2016

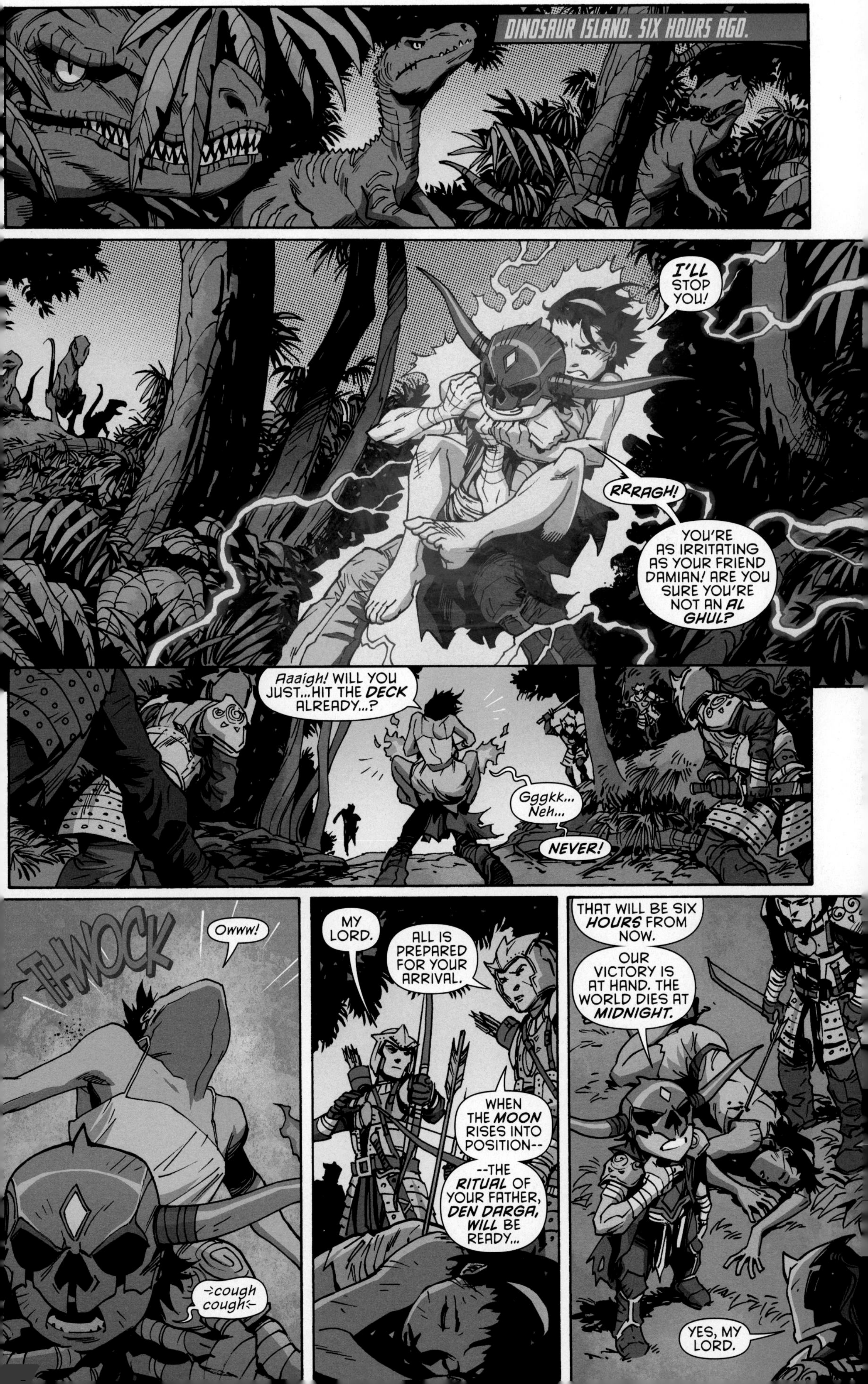
DINOSAUR ISLAND. SIX HOURS AGO.
I'LL STOP YOU!
RRRAGH!
YOU'RE AS IRRITATING AS YOUR FRIEND DAMIAN! ARE YOU SURE YOU'RE NOT AN AL GHUL?
Aaaigh! WILL YOU JUST...HIT THE DECK ALREADY...?
Gggkk... Neh...
NEVER!
THWOCK
Owww!
cough cough
MY LORD.
ALL IS PREPARED FOR YOUR ARRIVAL.
WHEN THE MOON RISES INTO POSITION--
--THE RITUAL OF YOUR FATHER, DEN DARGA, WILL BE READY...
THAT WILL BE SIX HOURS FROM NOW.
OUR VICTORY IS AT HAND. THE WORLD DIES AT MIDNIGHT.
YES, MY LORD.

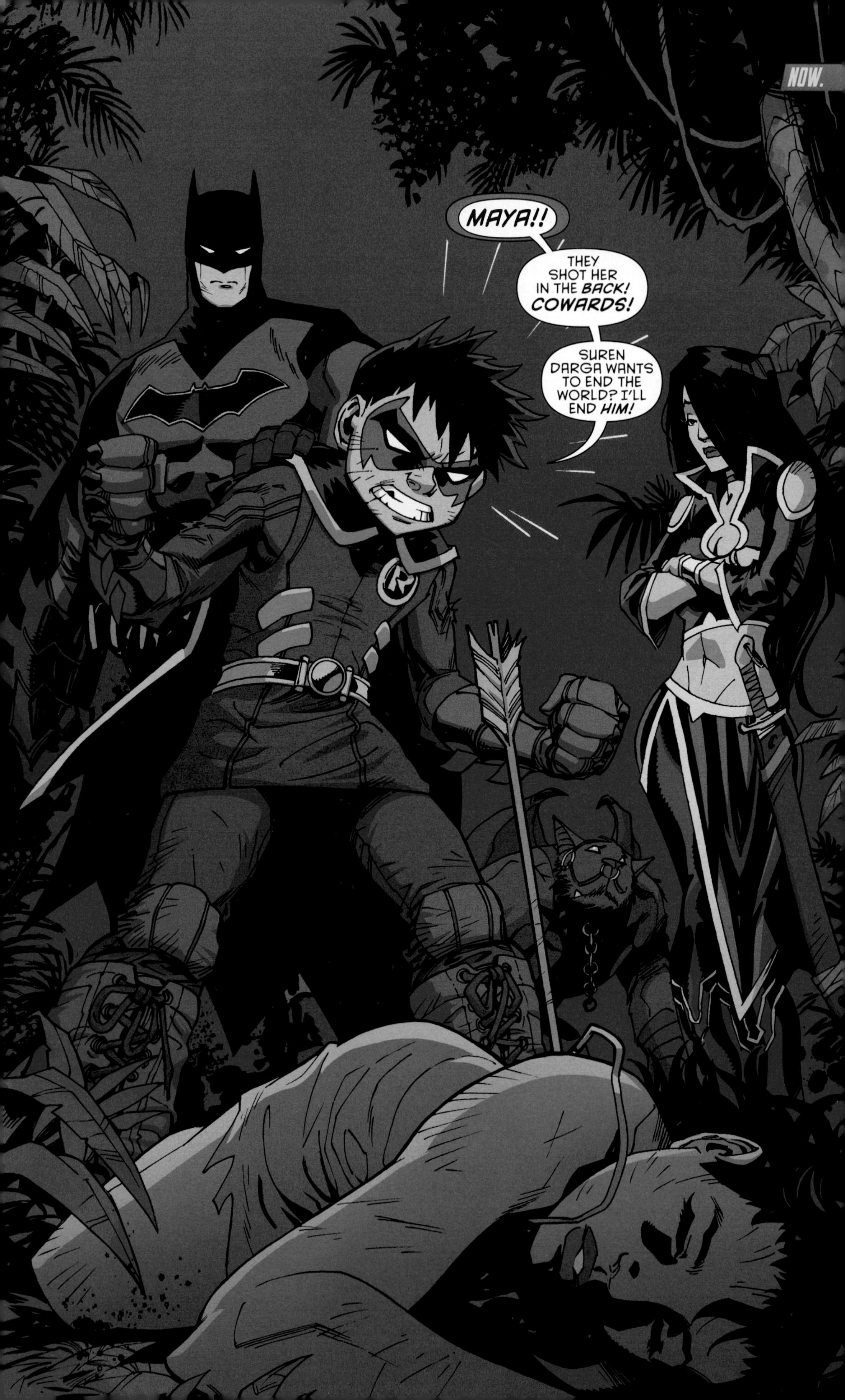
NOW.
MAYA!!
THEY SHOT HER IN THE BACK! COWARDS!
SUREN DARGA WANTS TO END THE WORLD? I'LL END HIM!

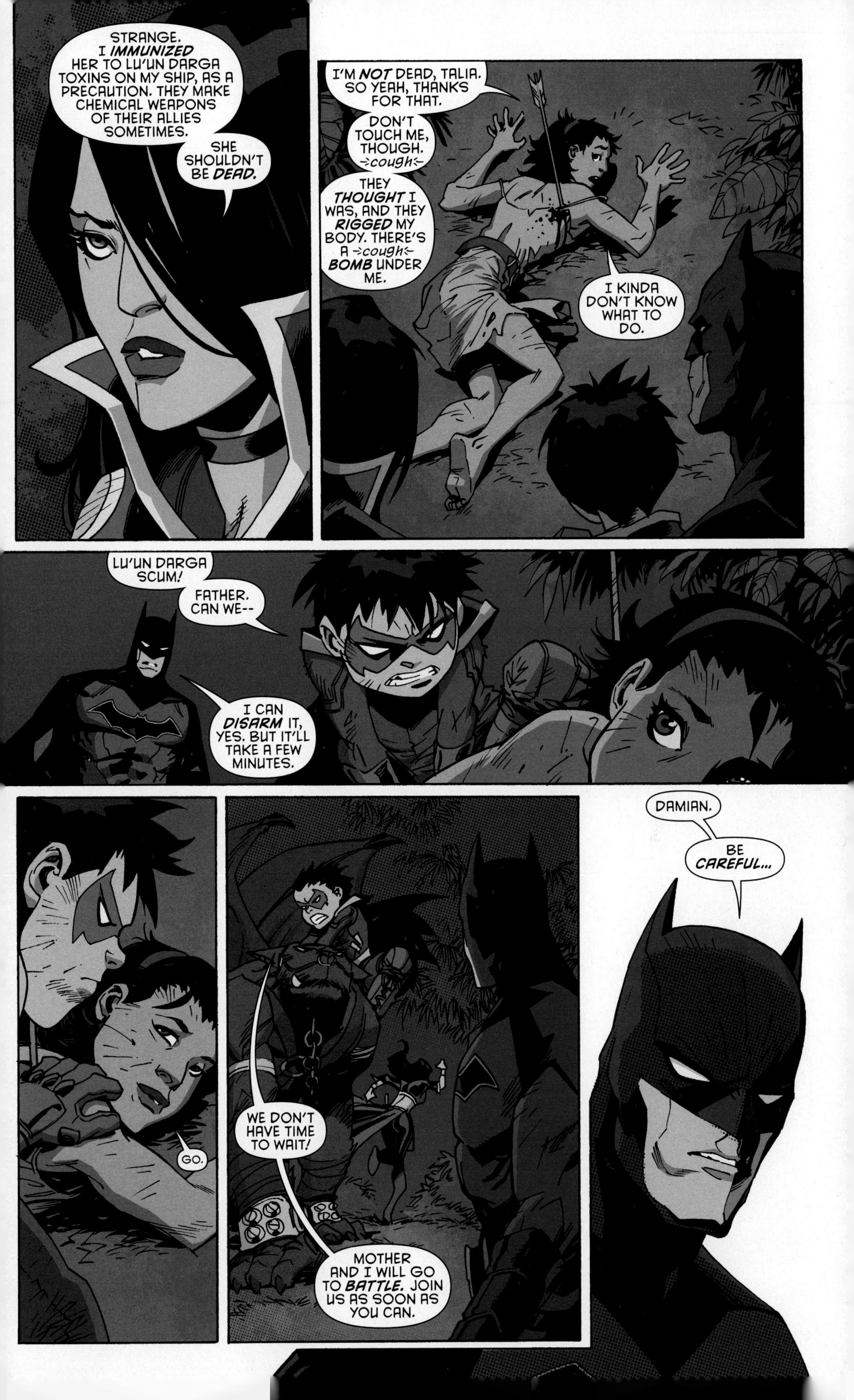
STRANGE. I IMMUNIZED HER TO LU'UN DARGA TOXINS ON MY SHIP, AS A PRECAUTION. THEY MAKE CHEMICAL WEAPONS OF THEIR ALLIES SOMETIMES.
SHE SHOULDN'T BE DEAD.
I'M NOT DEAD, TALIA. SO YEAH, THANKS FOR THAT.
DON'T TOUCH ME, THOUGH. -cough-
THEY THOUGHT I WAS, AND THEY RIGGED MY BODY. THERE'S A -cough- BOMB UNDER ME.
I KINDA DON'T KNOW WHAT TO DO.
LU'UN DARGA SCUM!
FATHER. CAN WE--
I CAN DISARM IT, YES. BUT IT'LL TAKE A FEW MINUTES.
GO.
WE DON'T HAVE TIME TO WAIT!
MOTHER AND I WILL GO TO BATTLE. JOIN US AS SOON AS YOU CAN.
DAMIAN.
BE CAREFUL...

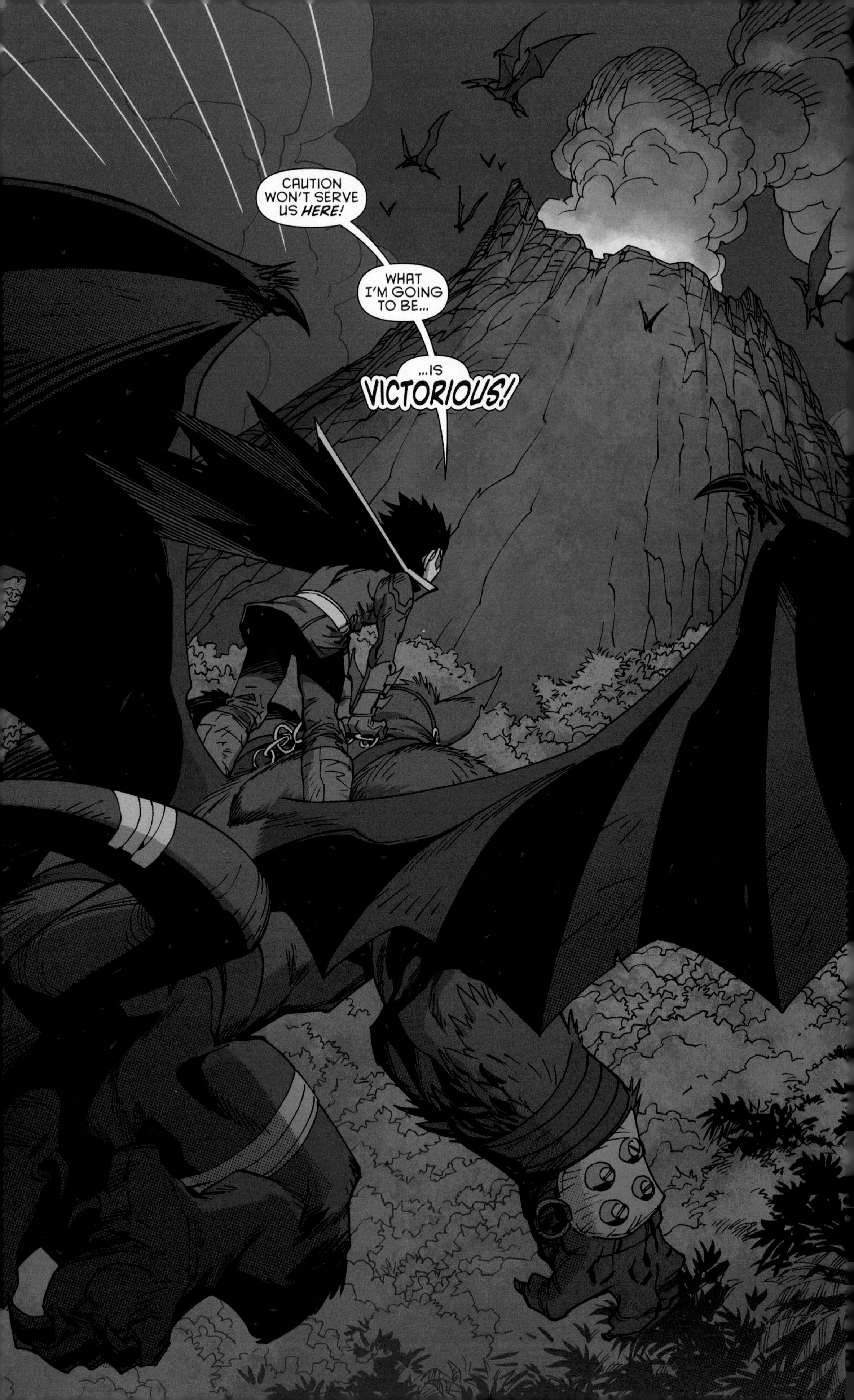
CAUTION WON'T SERVE US *HERE!*
WHAT I'M GOING TO BE...
...IS VICTORIOUS!

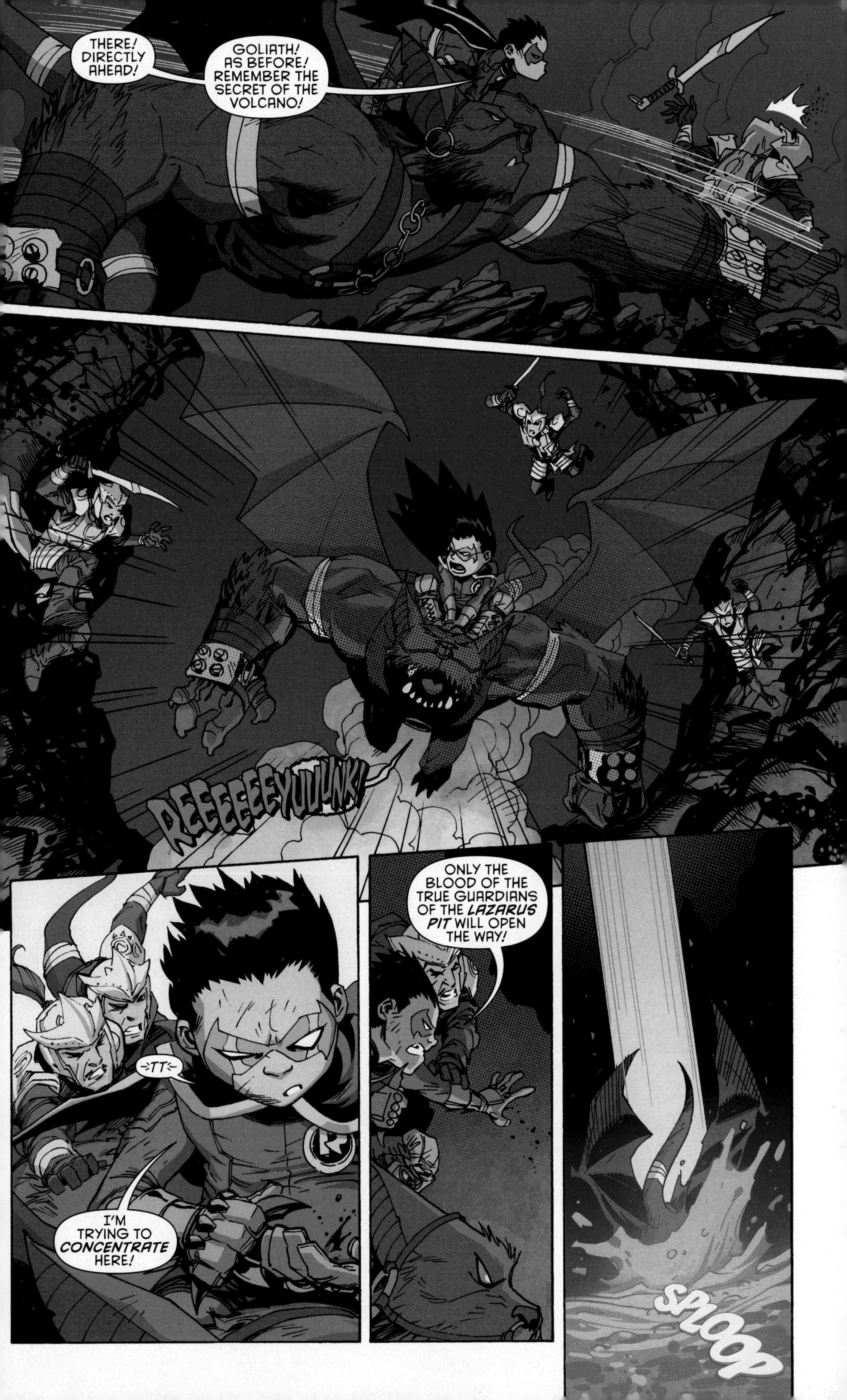
THERE! DIRECTLY AHEAD!
GOLIATH! AS BEFORE! REMEMBER THE SECRET OF THE VOLCANO!
REEEEEEYUUUNK!
~TT~
I'M TRYING TO CONCENTRATE HERE!
ONLY THE BLOOD OF THE TRUE GUARDIANS OF THE LAZARUS PIT WILL OPEN THE WAY!
SPLOOP

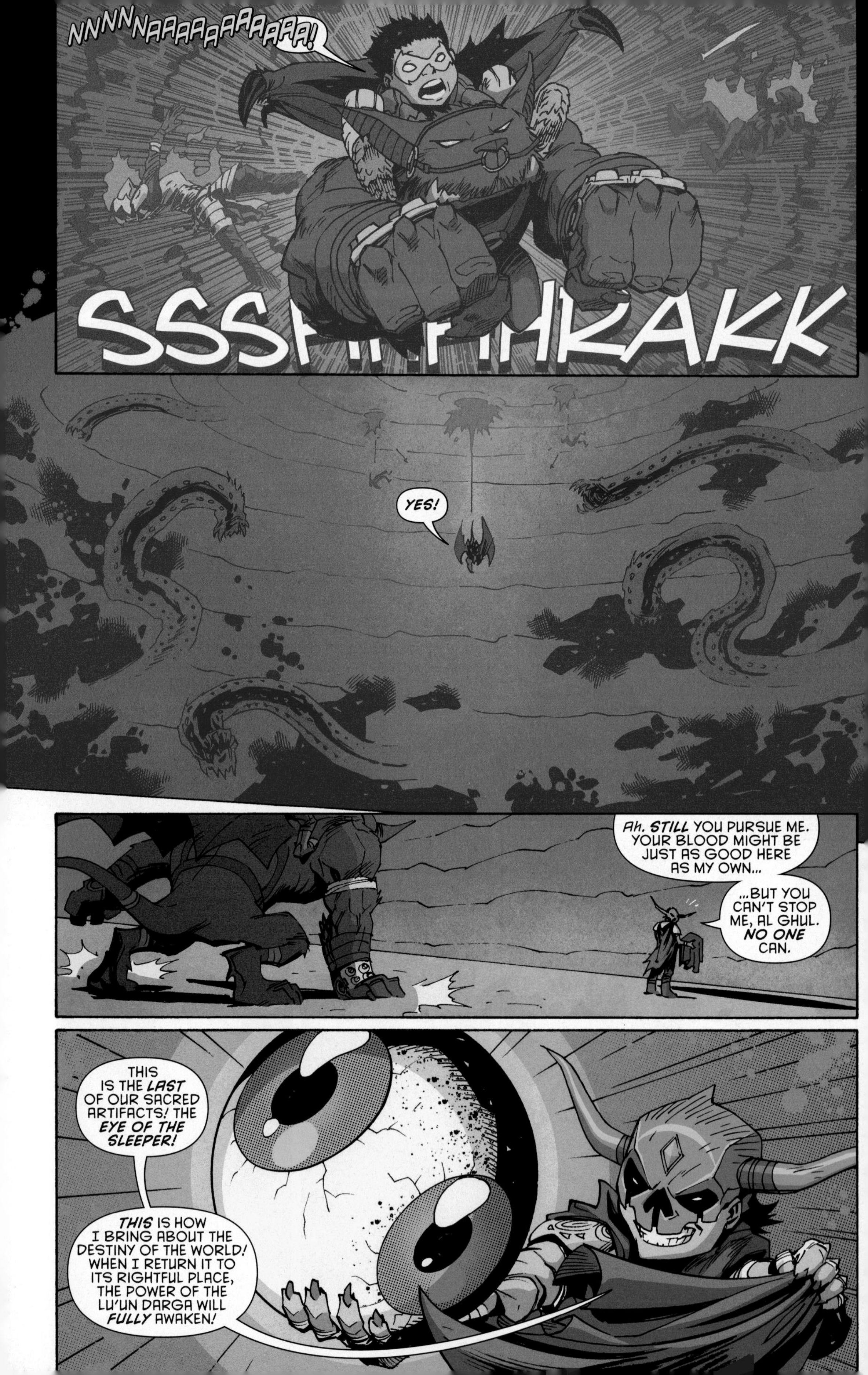
NNNNNAAAAAAAAAAA!
SSSHHHHRAKK
YES!
Ah. STILL YOU PURSUE ME. YOUR BLOOD MIGHT BE JUST AS GOOD HERE AS MY OWN...
...BUT YOU CAN'T STOP ME, AL GHUL. NO ONE CAN.
THIS IS THE LAST OF OUR SACRED ARTIFACTS! THE EYE OF THE SLEEPER!
THIS IS HOW I BRING ABOUT THE DESTINY OF THE WORLD! WHEN I RETURN IT TO ITS RIGHTFUL PLACE, THE POWER OF THE LU'UN DARGA WILL FULLY AWAKEN!

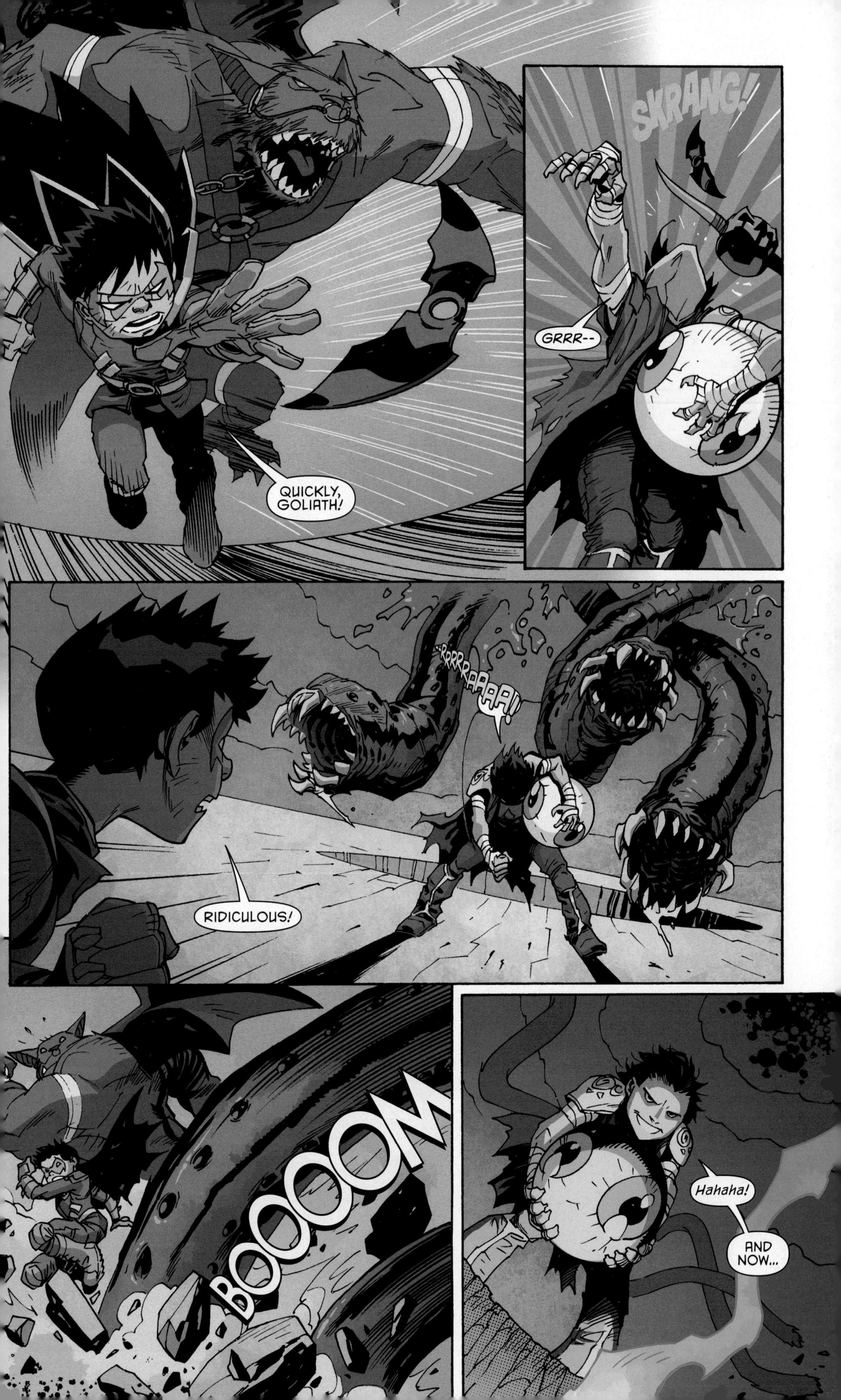
QUICKLY, GOLIATH!
SKRANG!
GRRR--
RRRRRAAAAA!!
RIDICULOUS!
BOOOOOM
Hahaha!
AND NOW...

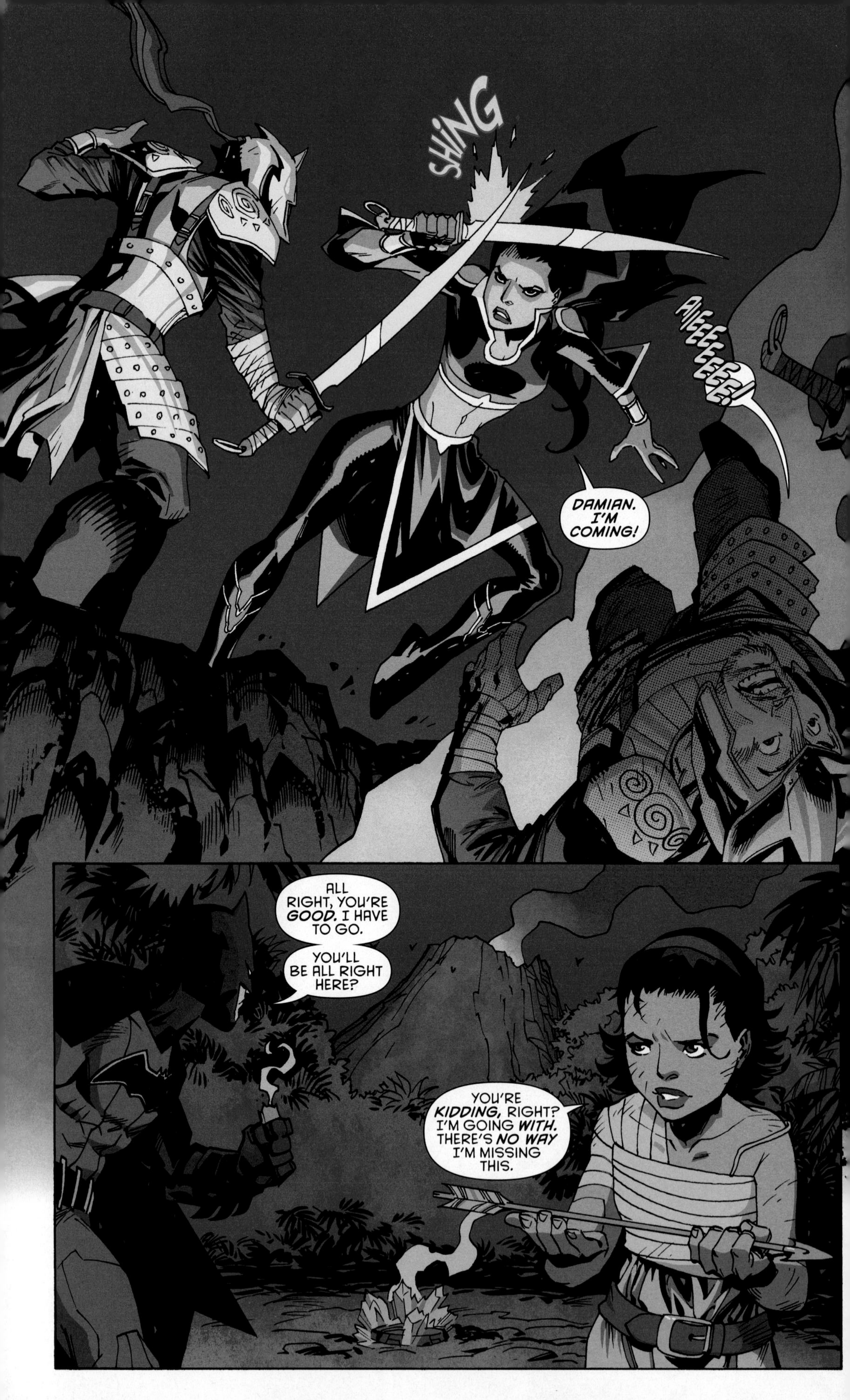
SHING
AIEEEEEEE!
DAMIAN. I'M COMING!
ALL RIGHT, YOU'RE ***GOOD.*** I HAVE TO GO.
YOU'LL BE ALL RIGHT HERE?
YOU'RE ***KIDDING,*** RIGHT? I'M GOING ***WITH.*** THERE'S ***NO WAY*** I'M MISSING THIS.

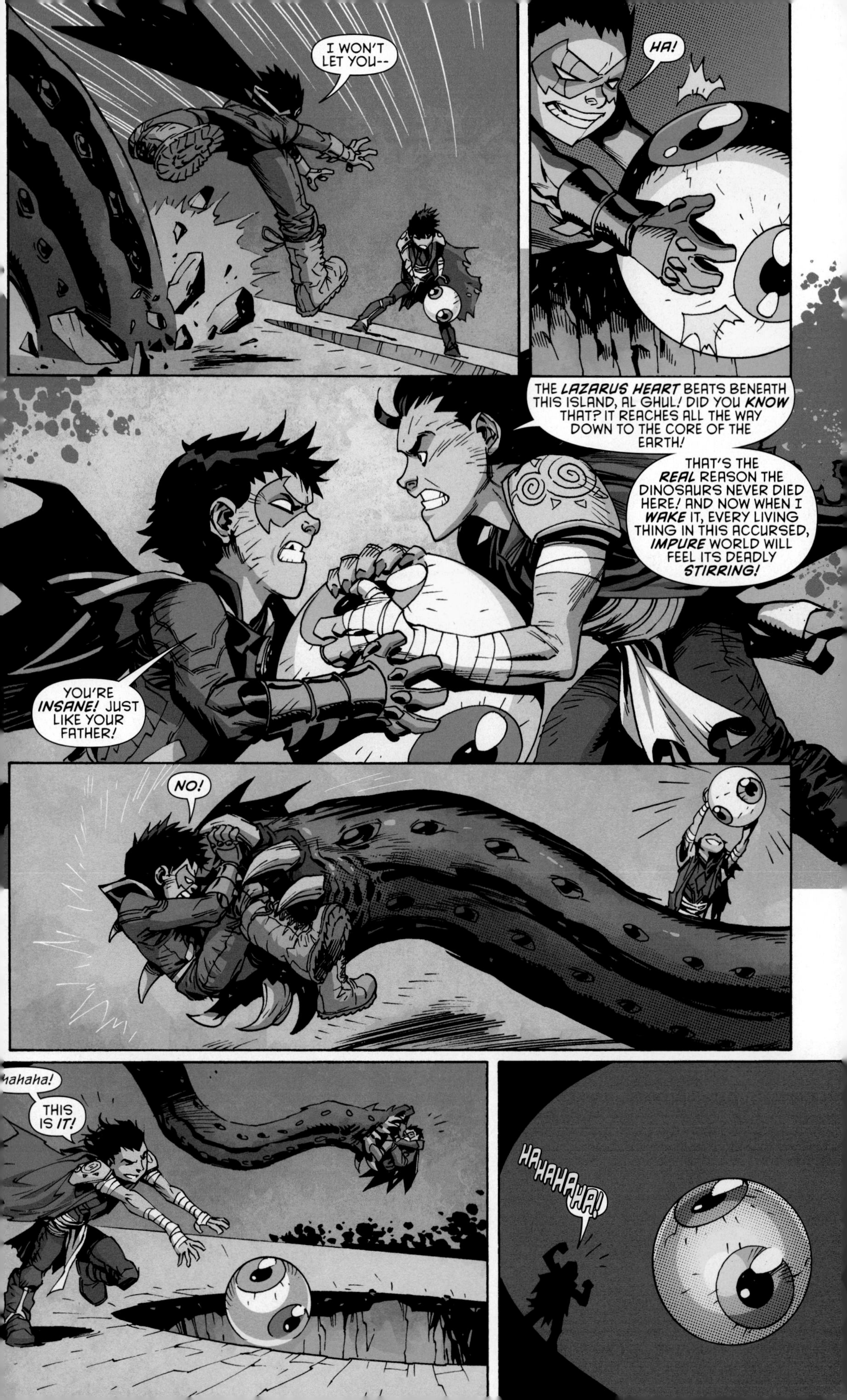
I WON'T LET YOU--
HA!
THE LAZARUS HEART BEATS BENEATH THIS ISLAND, AL GHUL! DID YOU KNOW THAT? IT REACHES ALL THE WAY DOWN TO THE CORE OF THE EARTH!
THAT'S THE REAL REASON THE DINOSAURS NEVER DIED HERE! AND NOW WHEN I WAKE IT, EVERY LIVING THING IN THIS ACCURSED, IMPURE WORLD WILL FEEL ITS DEADLY STIRRING!
YOU'RE INSANE! JUST LIKE YOUR FATHER!
NO!
hahaha!
THIS IS IT!
HAHAHAHAHA!

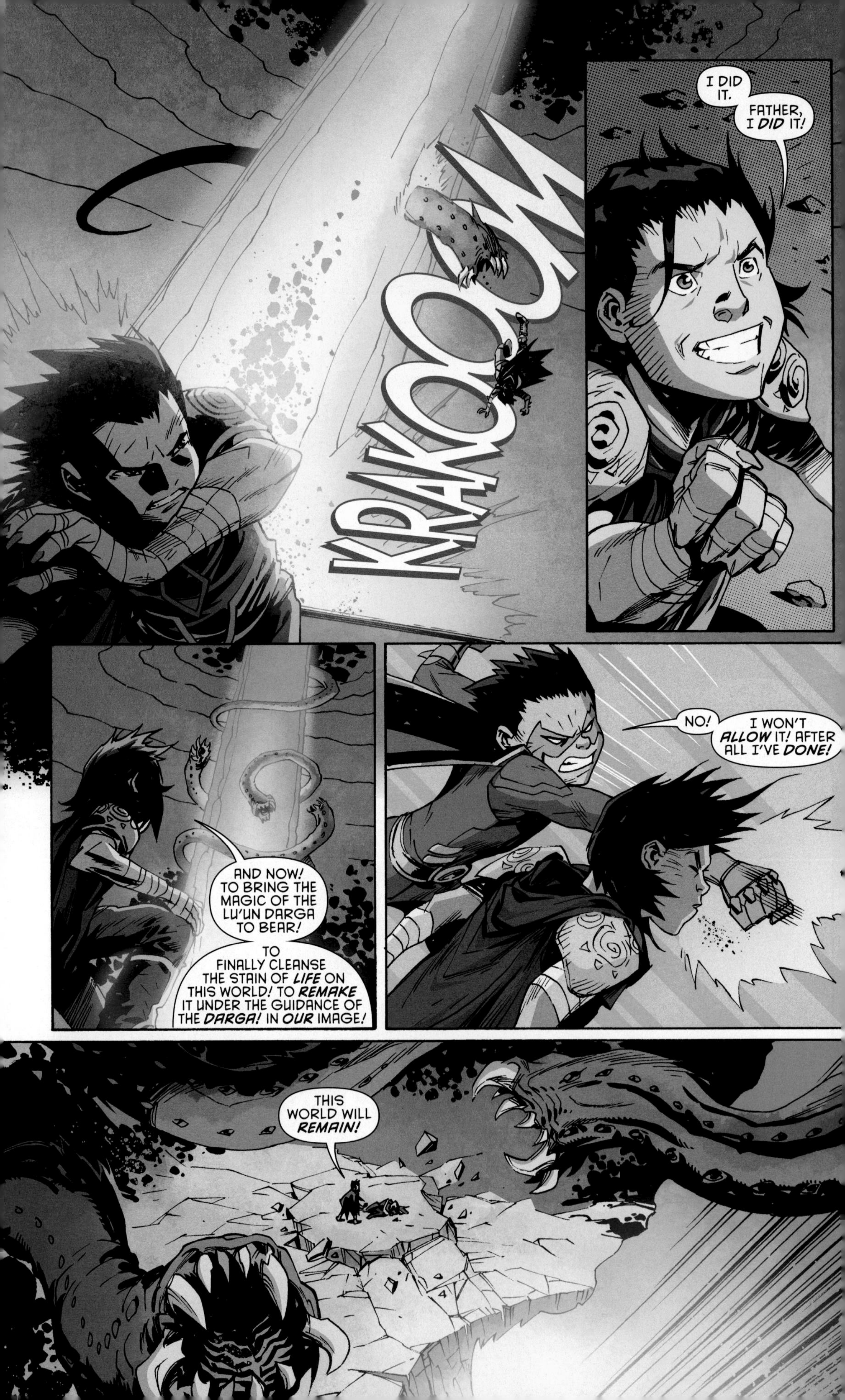
KRAKOOM
I DID IT.
FATHER, I DID IT!
AND NOW! TO BRING THE MAGIC OF THE LU'UN DARGA TO BEAR!
TO FINALLY CLEANSE THE STAIN OF LIFE ON THIS WORLD! TO REMAKE IT UNDER THE GUIDANCE OF THE DARGA! IN OUR IMAGE!
NO!
I WON'T ALLOW IT! AFTER ALL I'VE DONE!
THIS WORLD WILL REMAIN!

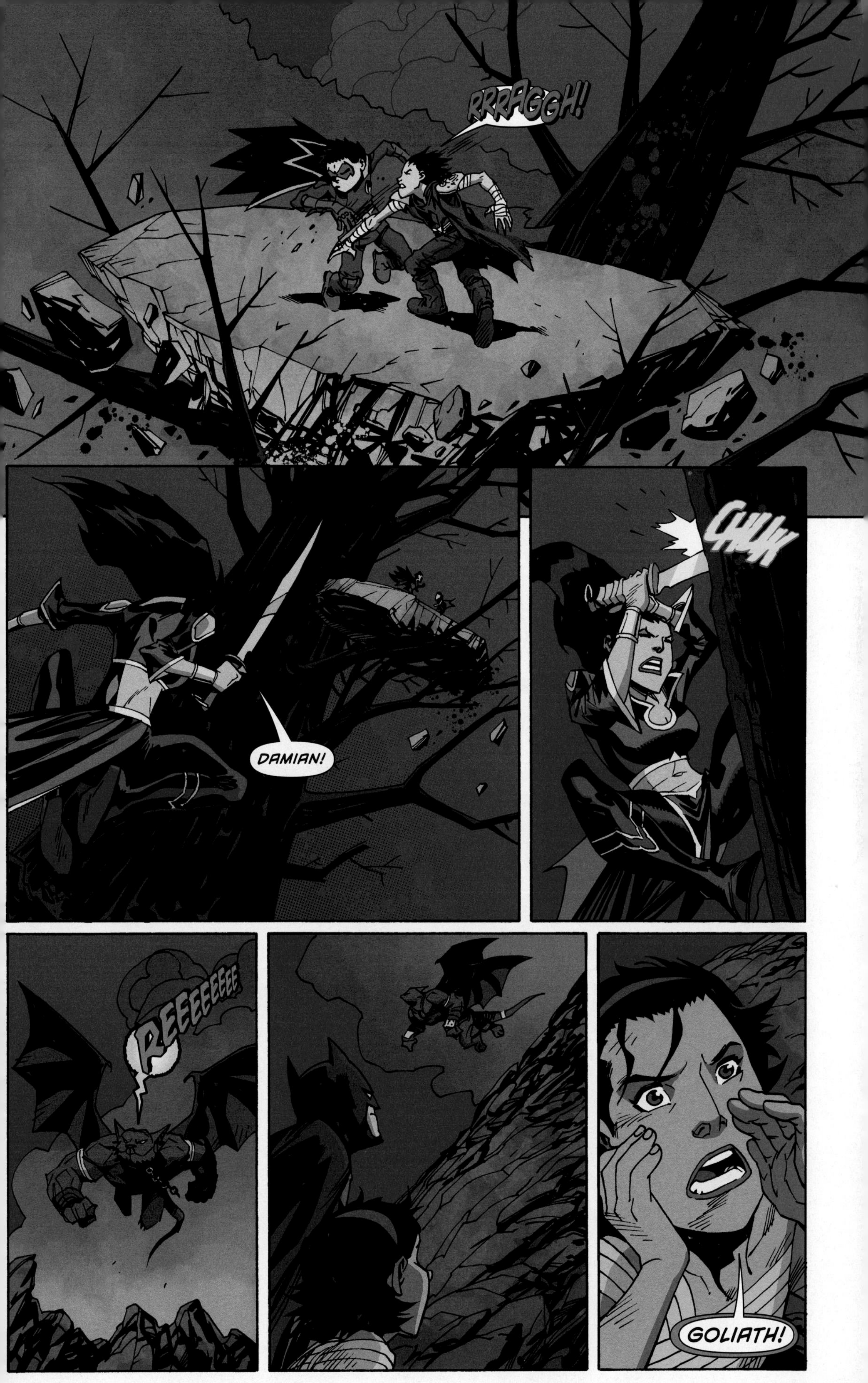

RRRAGGH!
DAMIAN!
CHUK
REEEEEEEE
GOLIATH!

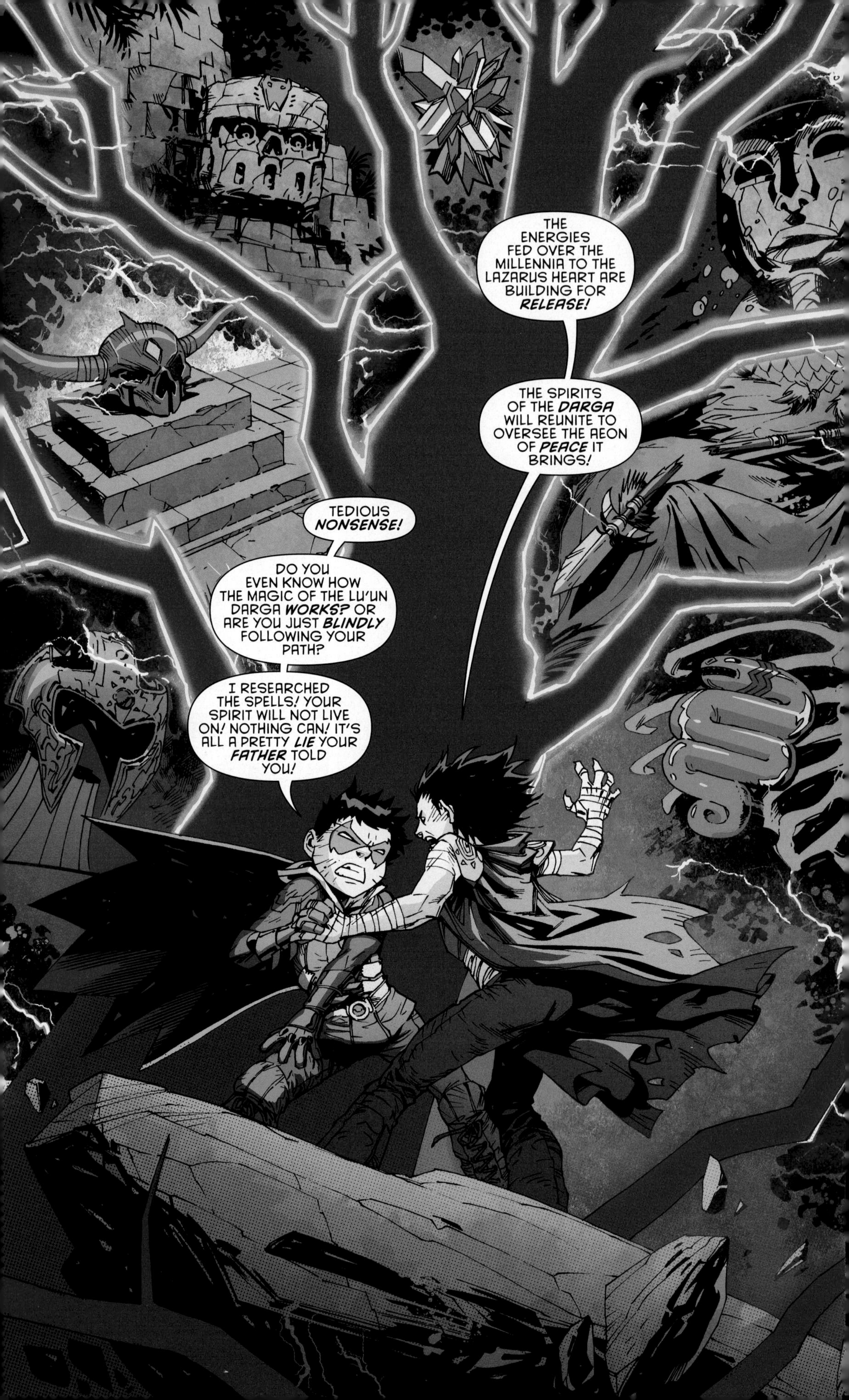
THE ENERGIES FED OVER THE MILLENNIA TO THE LAZARUS HEART ARE BUILDING FOR *RELEASE!*
THE SPIRITS OF THE *DARGA* WILL REUNITE TO OVERSEE THE AEON OF *PEACE* IT BRINGS!
TEDIOUS *NONSENSE!*
DO YOU EVEN KNOW HOW THE MAGIC OF THE LU'UN DARGA *WORKS?* OR ARE YOU JUST *BLINDLY* FOLLOWING YOUR PATH?
I RESEARCHED THE SPELLS! YOUR SPIRIT WILL NOT LIVE ON! NOTHING CAN! IT'S ALL A PRETTY *LIE* YOUR *FATHER* TOLD YOU!

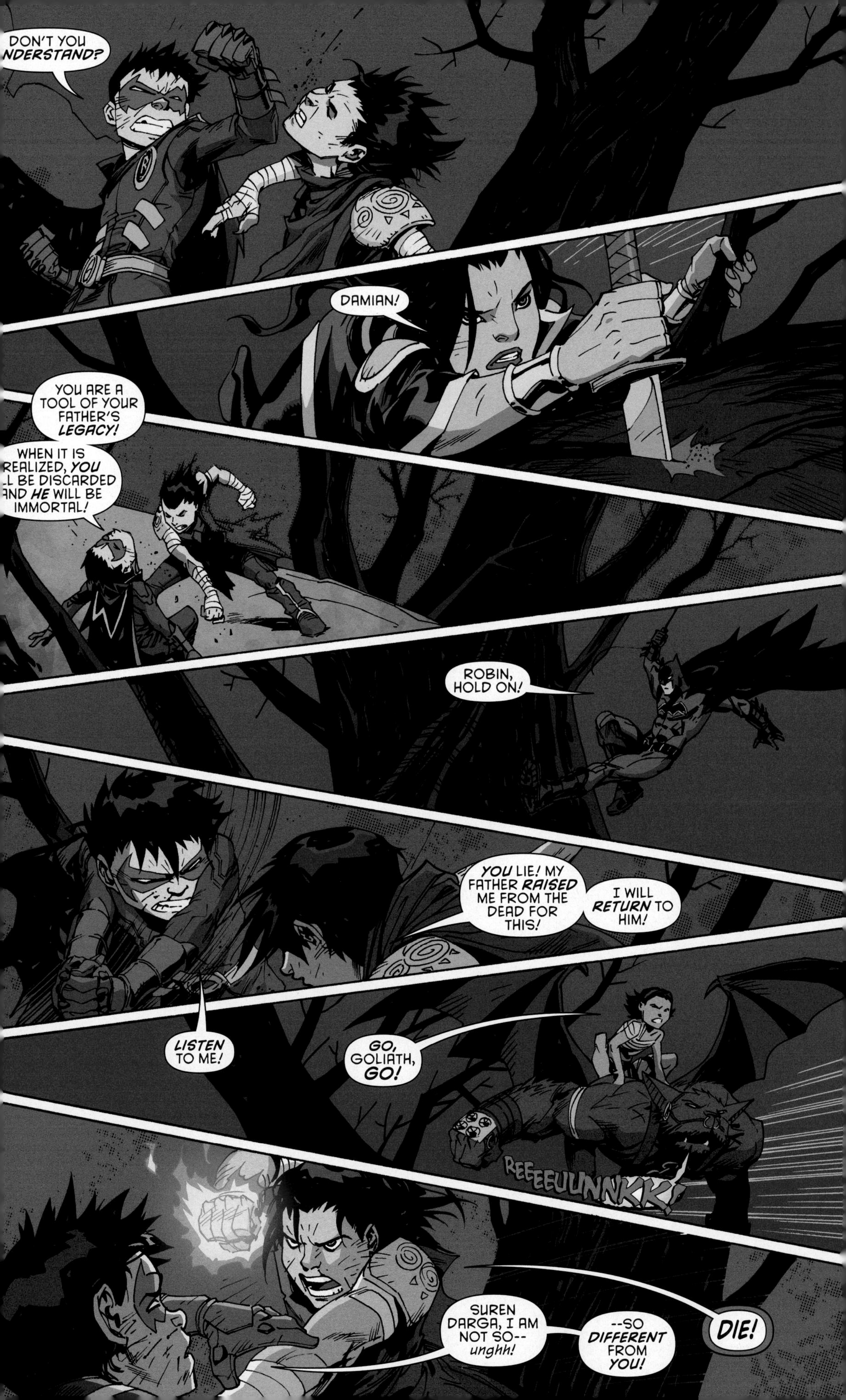
DON'T YOU
NDERSTAND?
DAMIAN!
YOU ARE A TOOL OF YOUR FATHER'S *LEGACY!*
WHEN IT IS REALIZED, *YOU* L BE DISCARDED AND *HE* WILL BE IMMORTAL!
ROBIN, HOLD ON!
YOU LIE! MY FATHER *RAISED* ME FROM THE DEAD FOR THIS!
I WILL *RETURN* TO HIM!
LISTEN TO ME!
GO, GOLIATH, *GO!*
REEEEUUNNKK!
SUREN DARGA, I AM NOT SO-- *unghh!*
--SO *DIFFERENT* FROM *YOU!*
DIE!

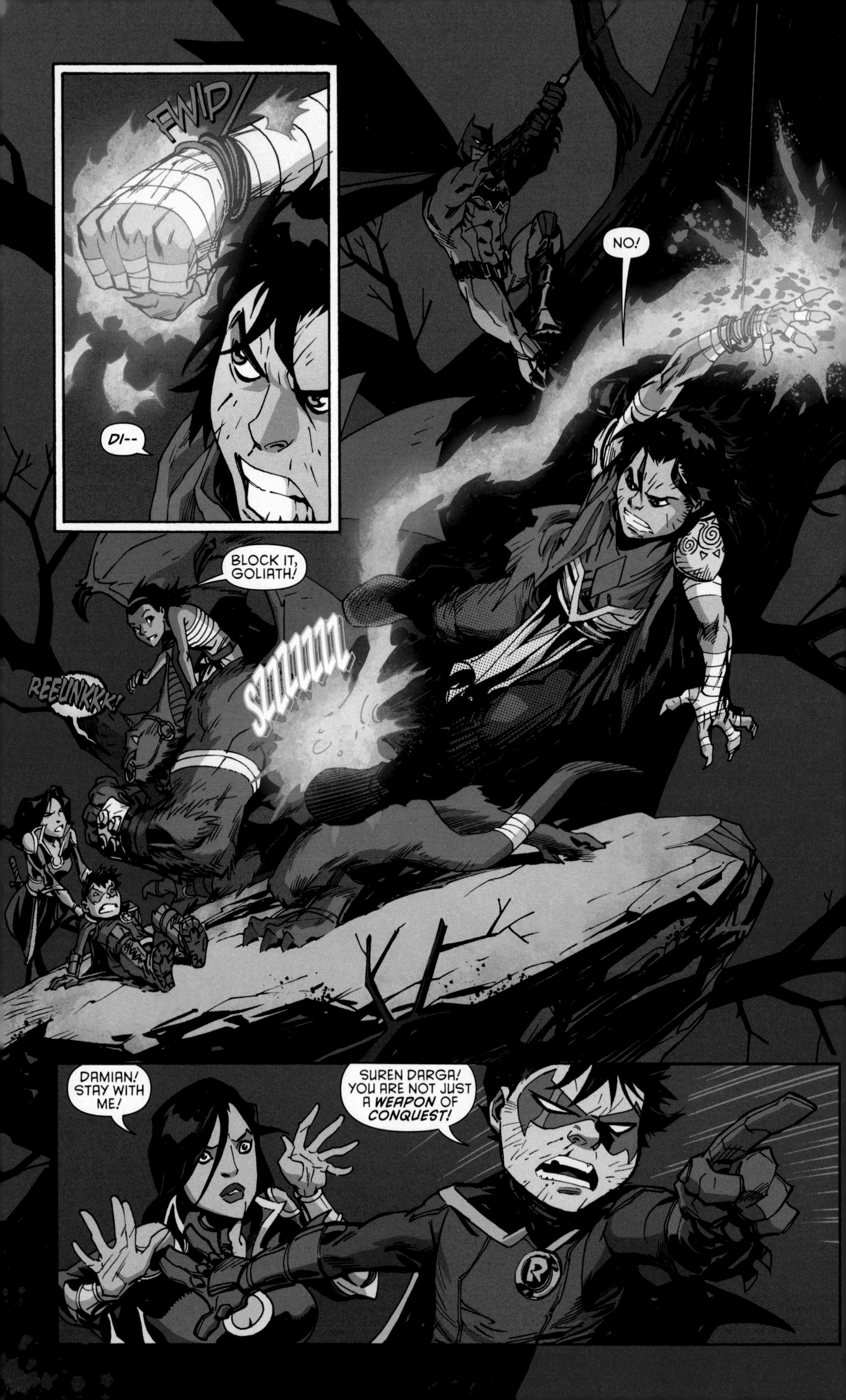
FWIP
DI--
NO!
BLOCK IT, GOLIATH!
SZZZZZZZ
REEUNKKK!
DAMIAN! STAY WITH ME!
SUREN DARGA! YOU ARE NOT JUST A WEAPON OF CONQUEST!

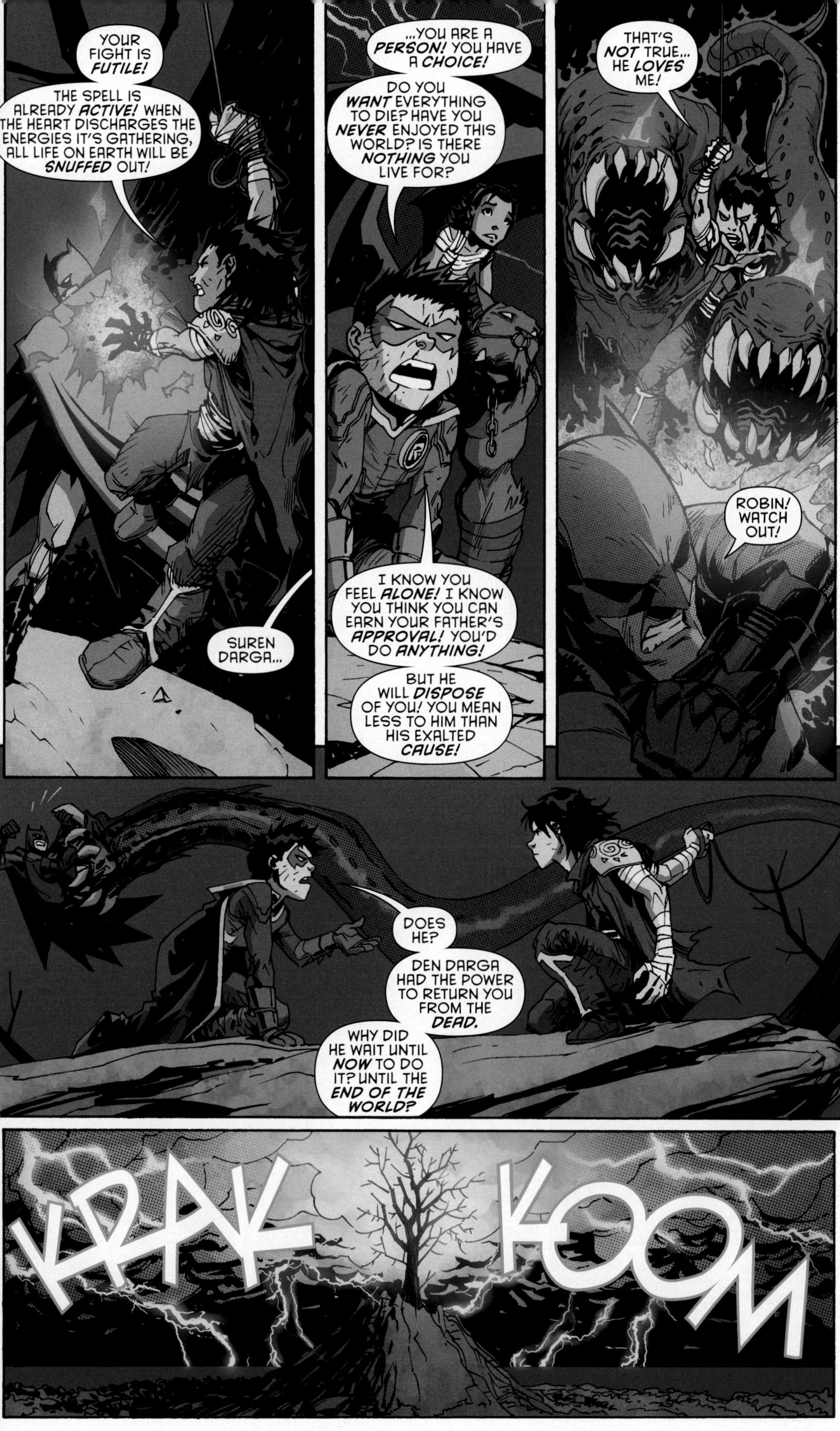

YOUR FIGHT IS FUTILE!
THE SPELL IS ALREADY ACTIVE! WHEN THE HEART DISCHARGES THE ENERGIES IT'S GATHERING, ALL LIFE ON EARTH WILL BE SNUFFED OUT!
SUREN DARGA...
...YOU ARE A PERSON! YOU HAVE A CHOICE!
DO YOU WANT EVERYTHING TO DIE? HAVE YOU NEVER ENJOYED THIS WORLD? IS THERE NOTHING YOU LIVE FOR?
I KNOW YOU FEEL ALONE! I KNOW YOU THINK YOU CAN EARN YOUR FATHER'S APPROVAL! YOU'D DO ANYTHING!
BUT HE WILL DISPOSE OF YOU! YOU MEAN LESS TO HIM THAN HIS EXALTED CAUSE!
THAT'S NOT TRUE... HE LOVES ME!
ROBIN! WATCH OUT!
DOES HE?
DEN DARGA HAD THE POWER TO RETURN YOU FROM THE DEAD.
WHY DID HE WAIT UNTIL NOW TO DO IT? UNTIL THE END OF THE WORLD?
KRAK
KOOM

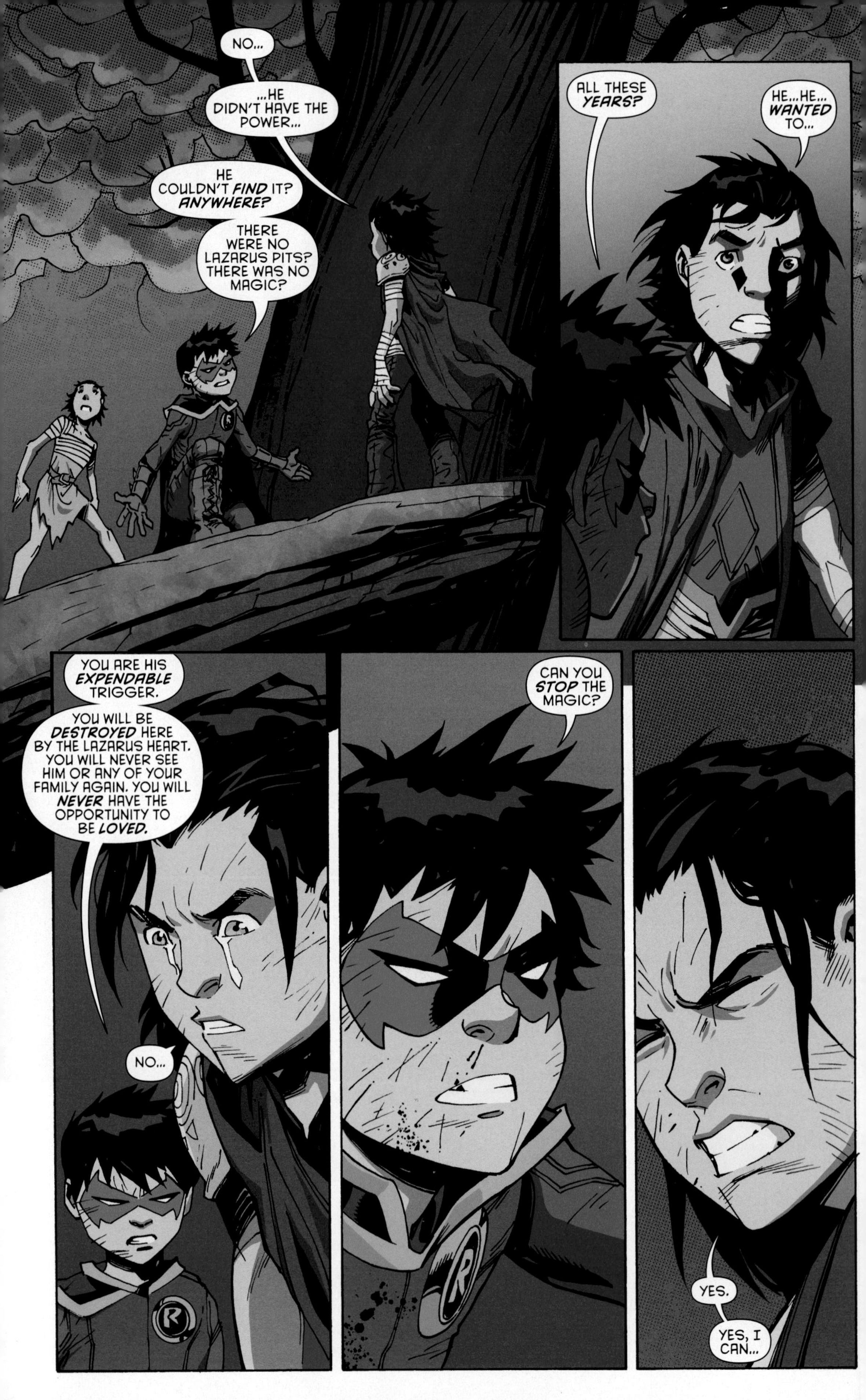
NO...
...HE DIDN'T HAVE THE POWER...
HE COULDN'T FIND IT? ANYWHERE?
THERE WERE NO LAZARUS PITS? THERE WAS NO MAGIC?
ALL THESE YEARS?
HE...HE... WANTED TO...
YOU ARE HIS EXPENDABLE TRIGGER.
YOU WILL BE DESTROYED HERE BY THE LAZARUS HEART. YOU WILL NEVER SEE HIM OR ANY OF YOUR FAMILY AGAIN. YOU WILL NEVER HAVE THE OPPORTUNITY TO BE LOVED.
NO...
CAN YOU STOP THE MAGIC?
YES.
YES, I CAN...

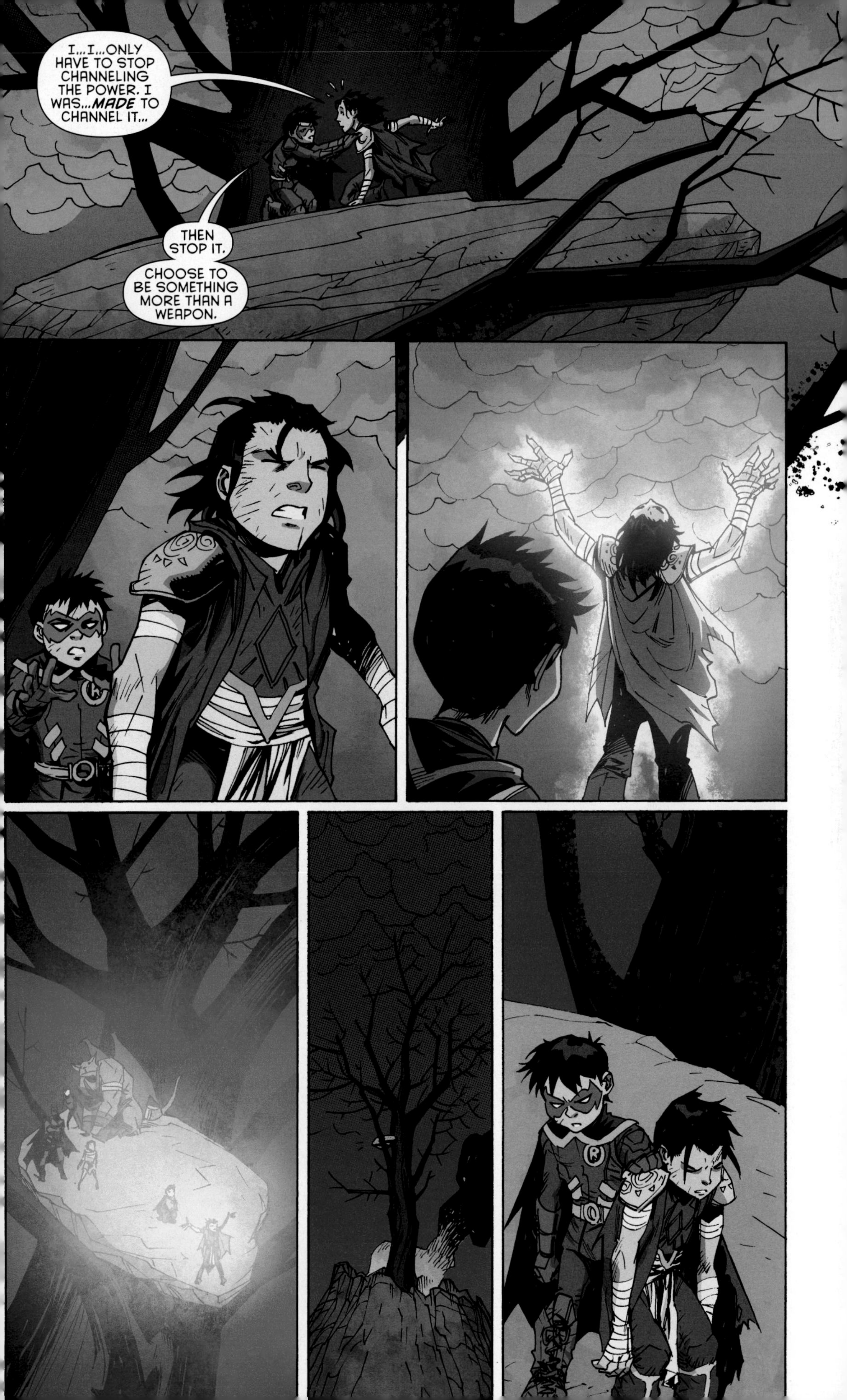
I...I...ONLY HAVE TO STOP CHANNELING THE POWER. I WAS...*MADE* TO CHANNEL IT...
THEN STOP IT.
CHOOSE TO BE SOMETHING MORE THAN A WEAPON.

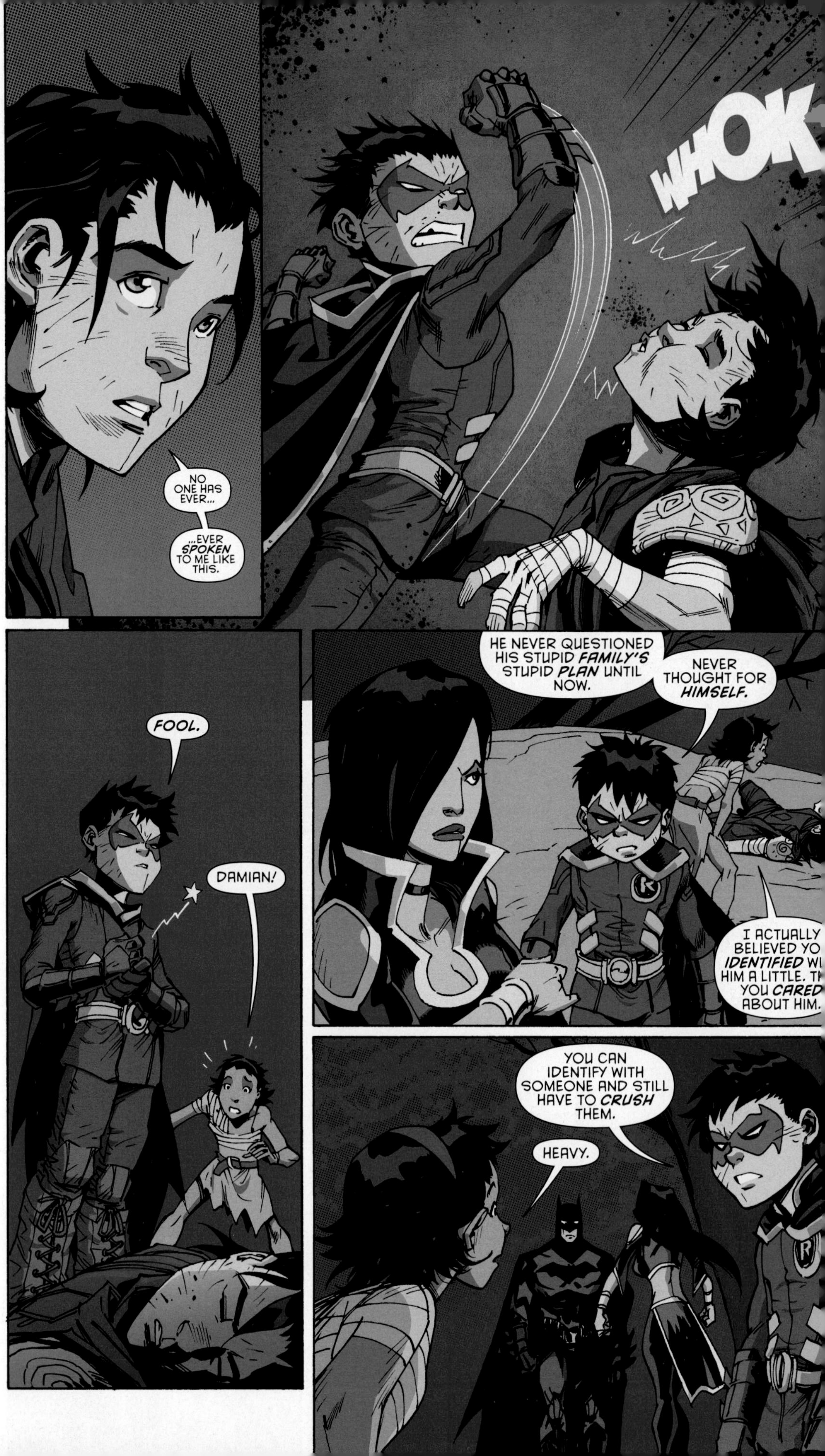
NO ONE HAS EVER...
...EVER SPOKEN TO ME LIKE THIS.
WHOK
FOOL.
DAMIAN!
HE NEVER QUESTIONED HIS STUPID FAMILY'S STUPID PLAN UNTIL NOW.
NEVER THOUGHT FOR HIMSELF.
I ACTUALLY BELIEVED YO IDENTIFIED WI HIM A LITTLE. TH YOU CARED ABOUT HIM.
YOU CAN IDENTIFY WITH SOMEONE AND STILL HAVE TO CRUSH THEM.
HEAVY.

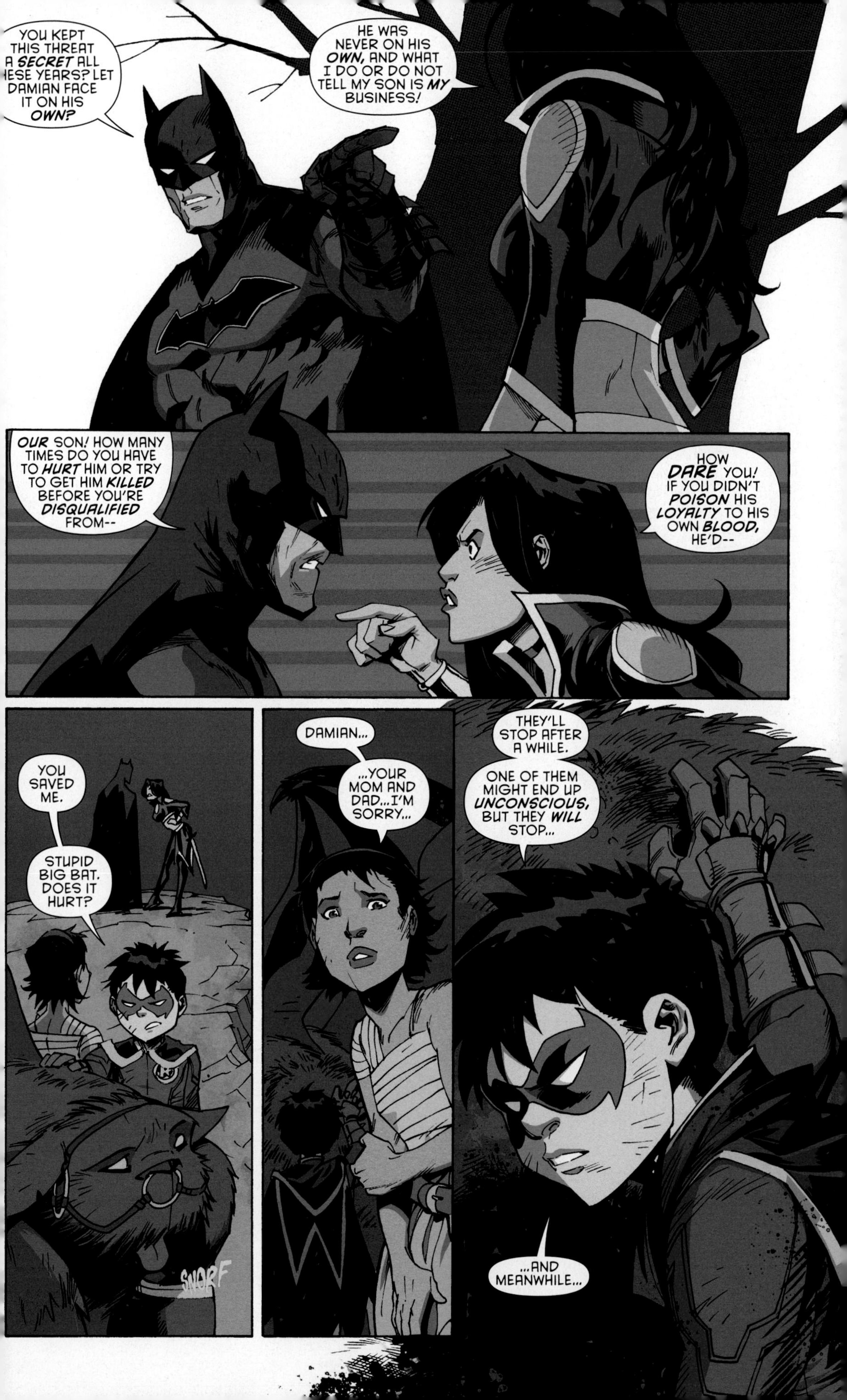
YOU KEPT THIS THREAT A SECRET ALL HESE YEARS? LET DAMIAN FACE IT ON HIS OWN?
HE WAS NEVER ON HIS OWN, AND WHAT I DO OR DO NOT TELL MY SON IS MY BUSINESS!
OUR SON! HOW MANY TIMES DO YOU HAVE TO HURT HIM OR TRY TO GET HIM KILLED BEFORE YOU'RE DISQUALIFIED FROM--
HOW DARE YOU! IF YOU DIDN'T POISON HIS LOYALTY TO HIS OWN BLOOD, HE'D--
YOU SAVED ME.
STUPID BIG BAT. DOES IT HURT?
SNORF
DAMIAN...
...YOUR MOM AND DAD...I'M SORRY...
THEY'LL STOP AFTER A WHILE.
ONE OF THEM MIGHT END UP UNCONSCIOUS, BUT THEY WILL STOP...
...AND MEANWHILE...

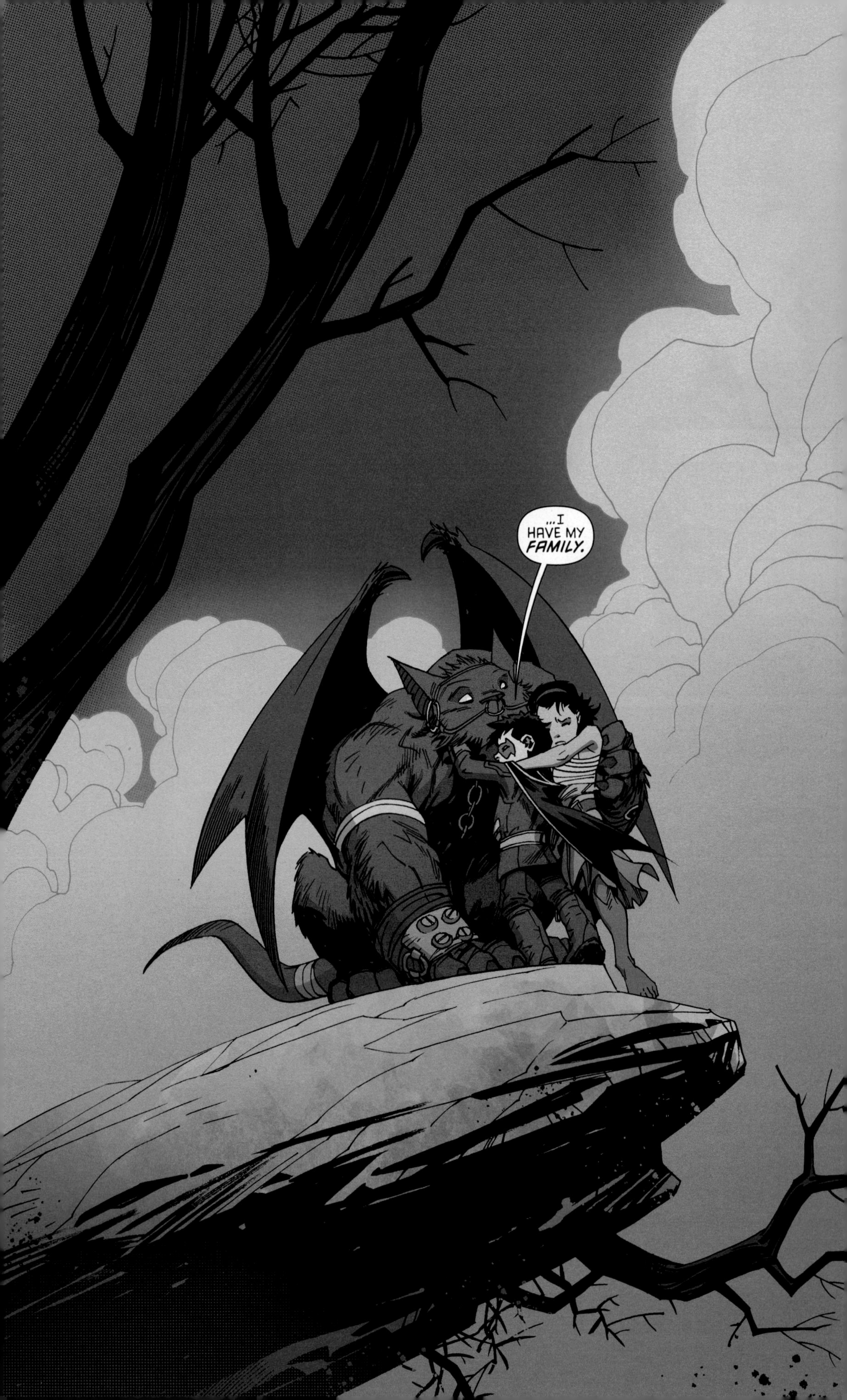
...I HAVE MY FAMILY.

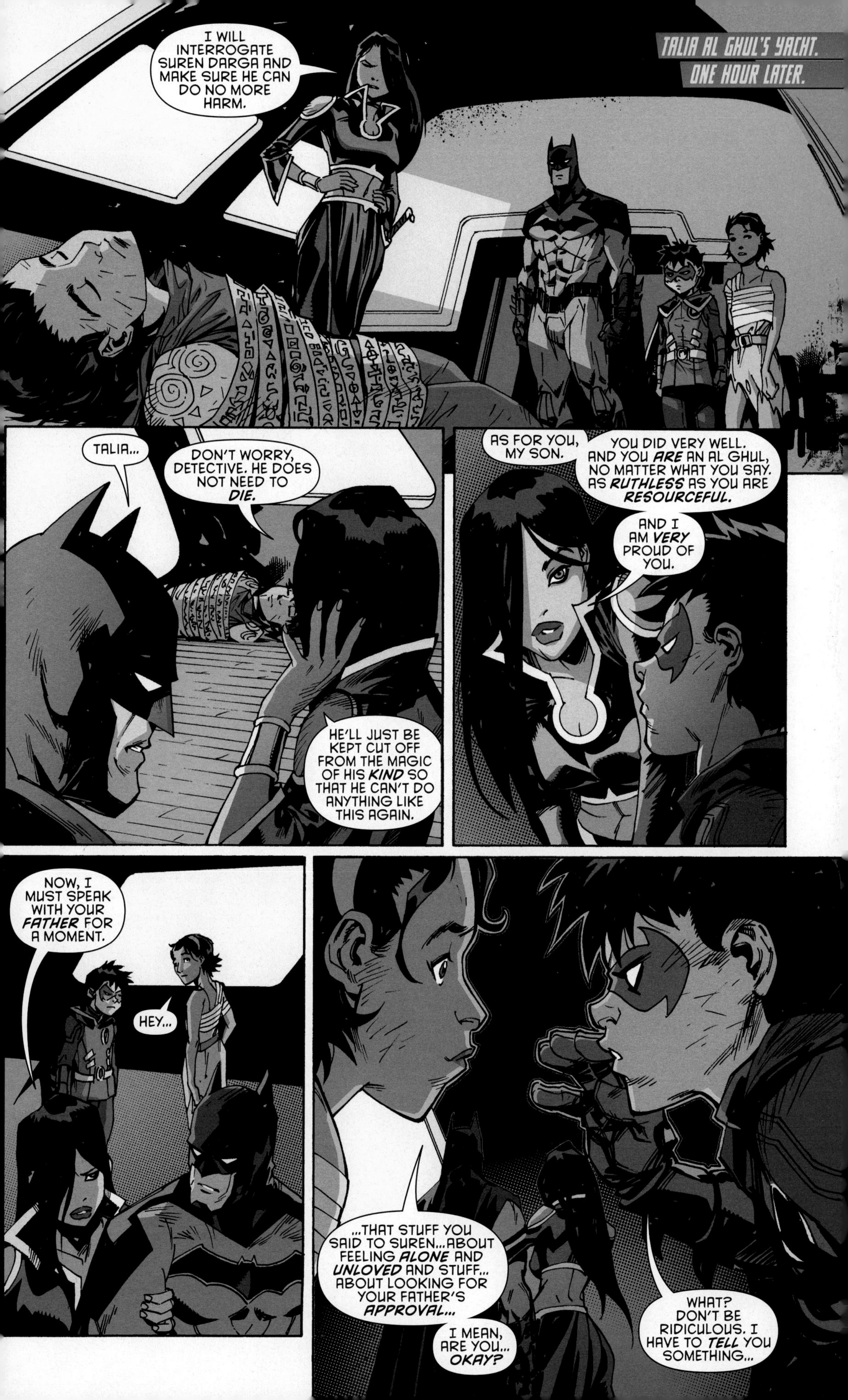

TALIA AL GHUL'S YACHT.
ONE HOUR LATER.
I WILL INTERROGATE SUREN DARGA AND MAKE SURE HE CAN DO NO MORE HARM.
TALIA...
DON'T WORRY, DETECTIVE. HE DOES NOT NEED TO DIE.
HE'LL JUST BE KEPT CUT OFF FROM THE MAGIC OF HIS KIND SO THAT HE CAN'T DO ANYTHING LIKE THIS AGAIN.
AS FOR YOU, MY SON.
YOU DID VERY WELL. AND YOU ARE AN AL GHUL, NO MATTER WHAT YOU SAY. AS RUTHLESS AS YOU ARE RESOURCEFUL.
AND I AM VERY PROUD OF YOU.
NOW, I MUST SPEAK WITH YOUR FATHER FOR A MOMENT.
HEY...
...THAT STUFF YOU SAID TO SUREN...ABOUT FEELING ALONE AND UNLOVED AND STUFF... ABOUT LOOKING FOR YOUR FATHER'S APPROVAL...
I MEAN, ARE YOU... OKAY?
WHAT? DON'T BE RIDICULOUS. I HAVE TO TELL YOU SOMETHING...

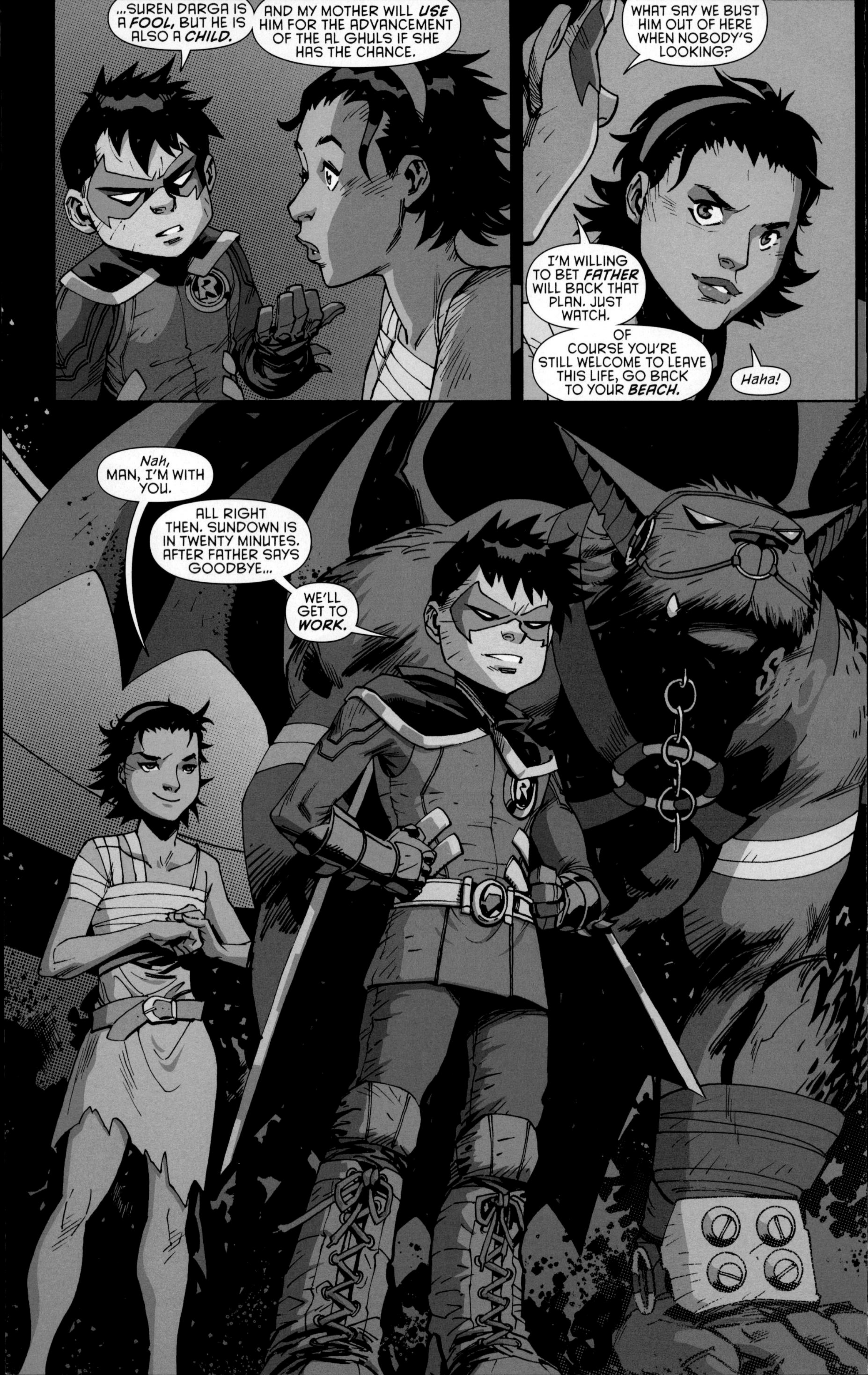
...SUREN DARGA IS A *FOOL*, BUT HE IS ALSO A *CHILD.*
AND MY MOTHER WILL *USE* HIM FOR THE ADVANCEMENT OF THE AL GHULS IF SHE HAS THE CHANCE.
WHAT SAY WE BUST HIM OUT OF HERE WHEN NOBODY'S LOOKING?
I'M WILLING TO BET *FATHER* WILL BACK THAT PLAN. JUST WATCH.
OF COURSE YOU'RE STILL WELCOME TO LEAVE THIS LIFE, GO BACK TO YOUR *BEACH.*
Haha!
Nah, MAN, I'M WITH YOU.
ALL RIGHT THEN. SUNDOWN IS IN TWENTY MINUTES. AFTER FATHER SAYS GOODBYE...
WE'LL GET TO *WORK.*

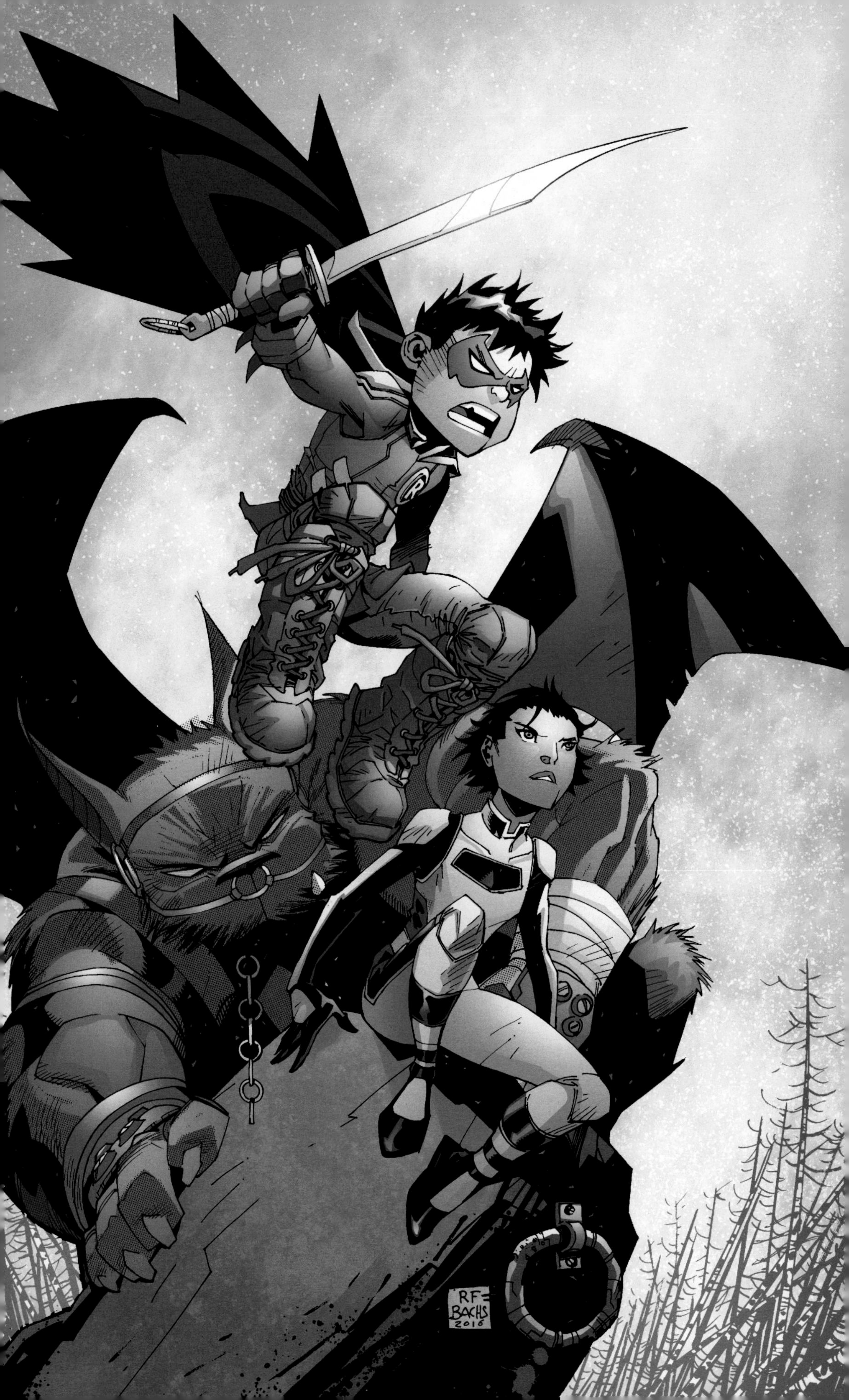
RF
BACHS
2016

IT *NEVER* ENDS

RAY FAWKES writer **RAMON BACHS** artist **MAT LOPES** colorist **DERON BENNETT** letterer **RAMON BACHS & JOHN KALISZ** cover

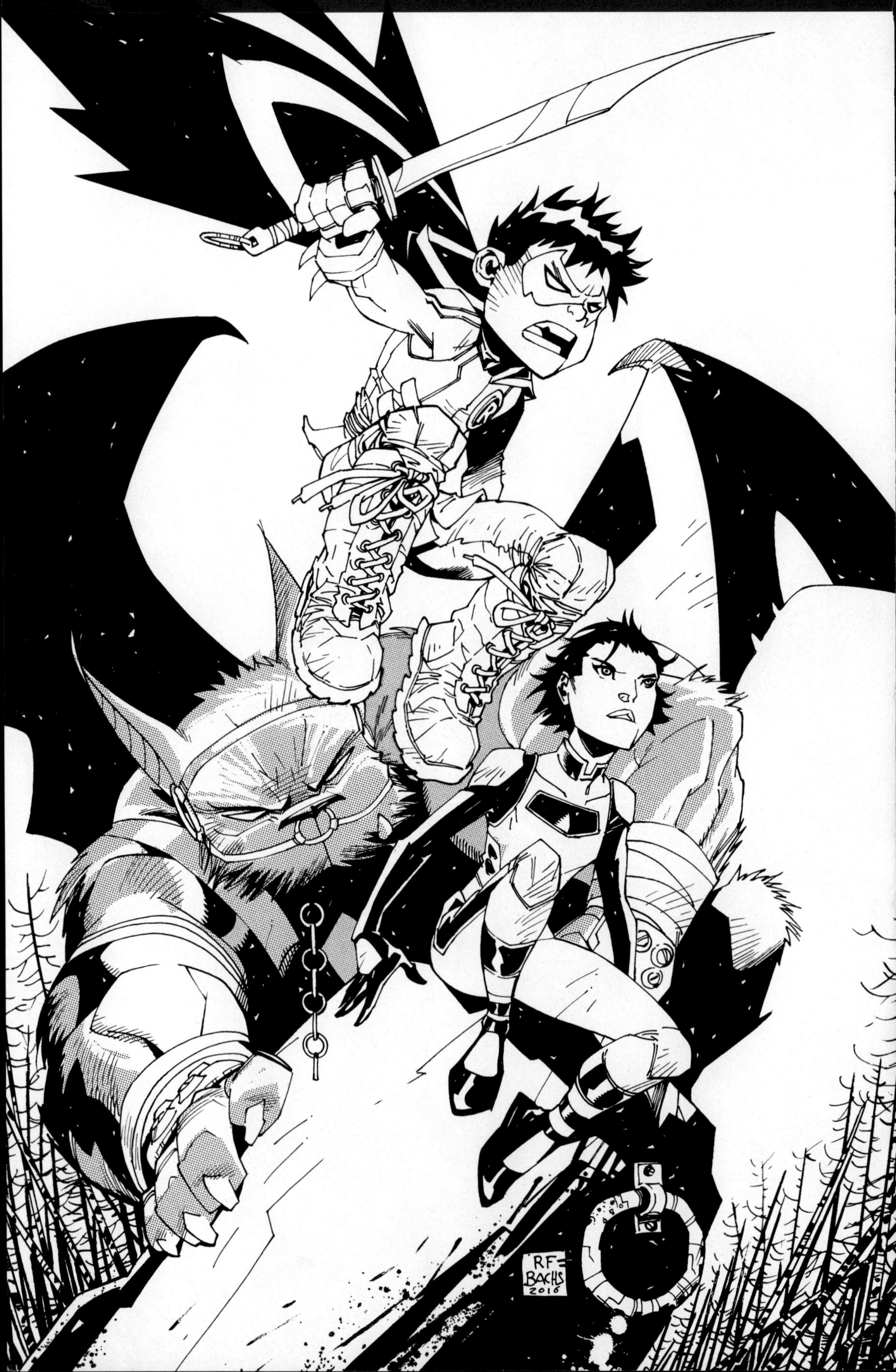
RF-
BACHS
2016

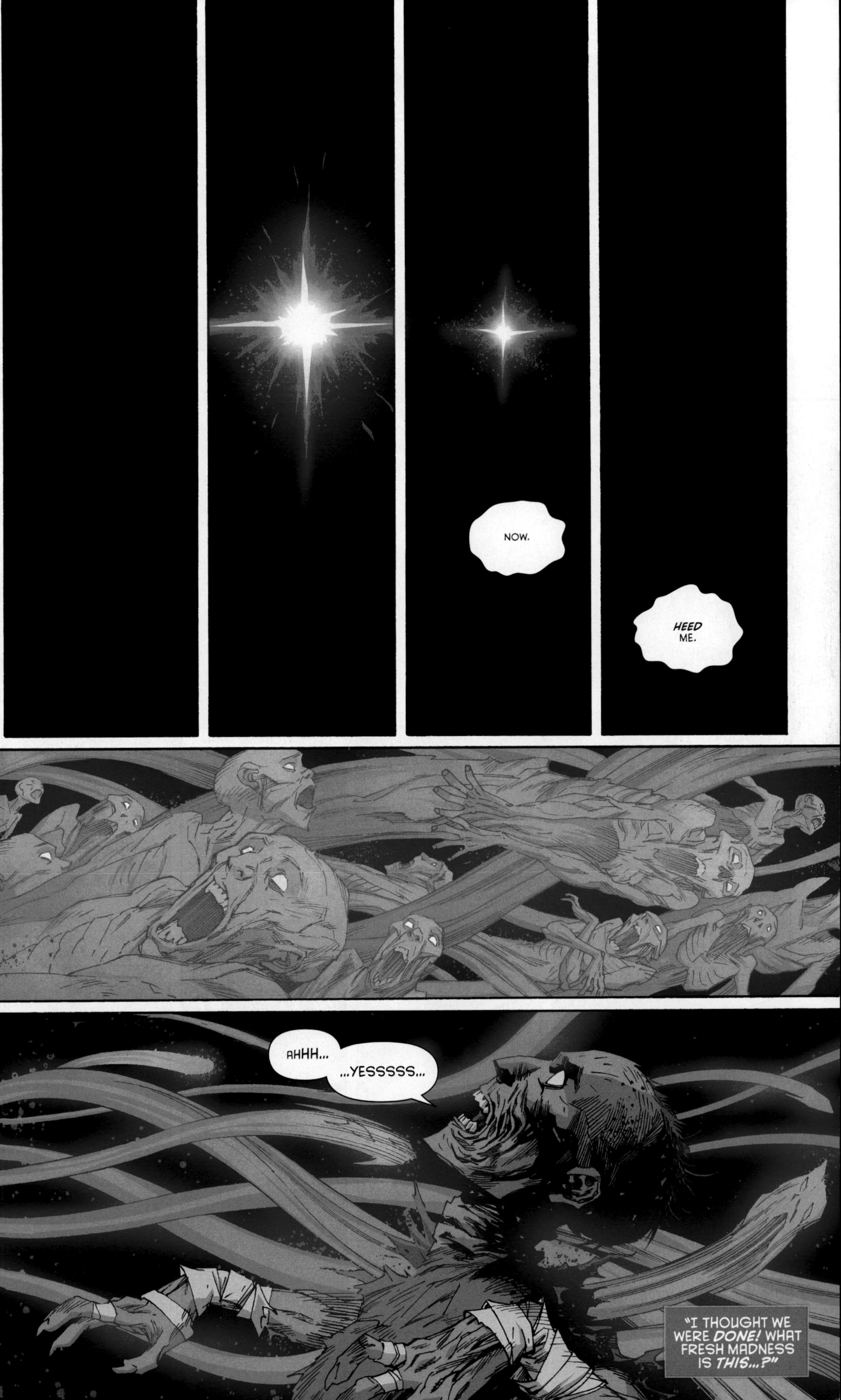
NOW.
HEED ME.
AHHH...
...YESSSSS...
"I THOUGHT WE WERE DONE! WHAT FRESH MADNESS IS THIS...?"

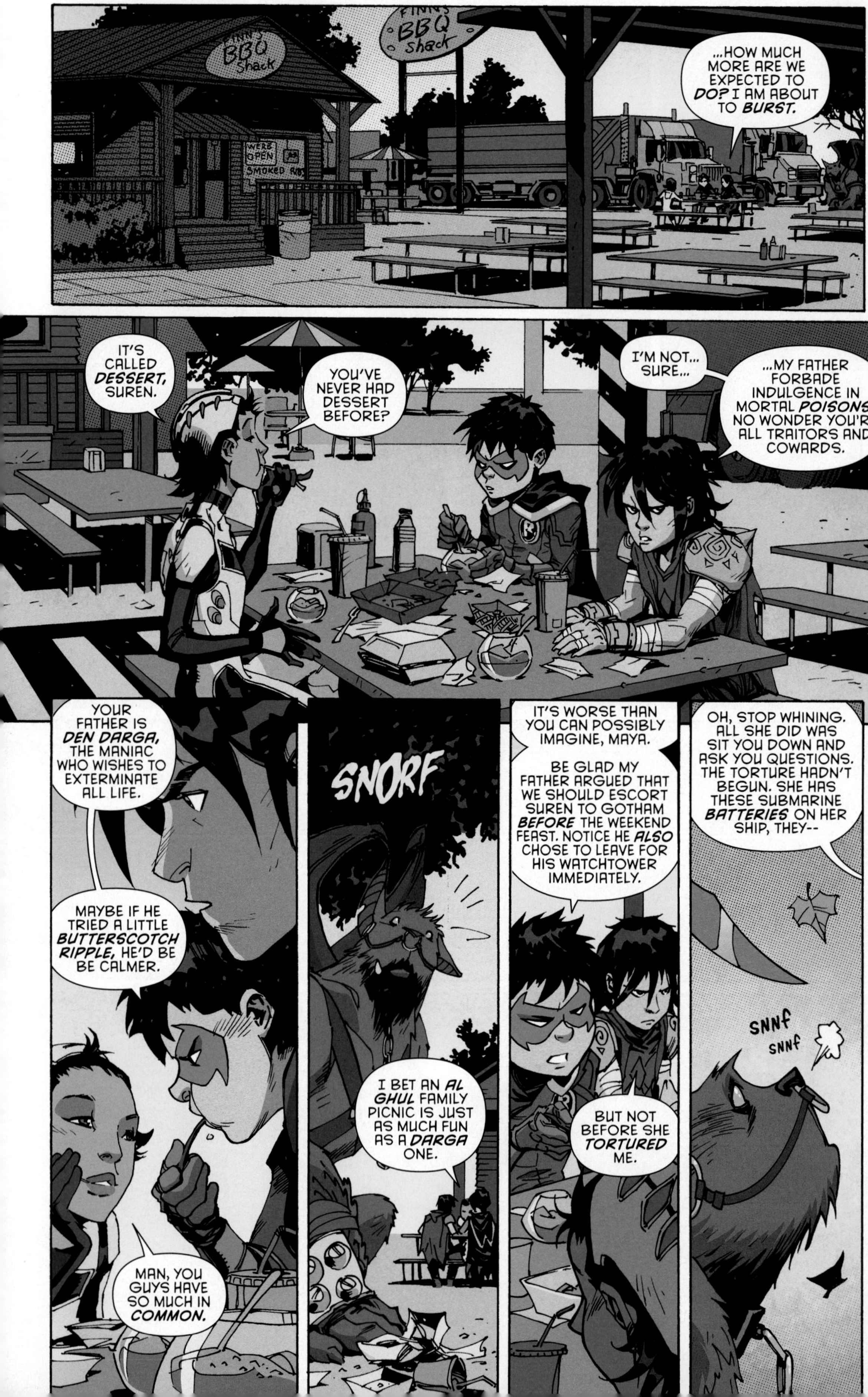
FINN'S BBQ Shack
FINN'S BBQ Shack
WE'RE OPEN
SMOKED RIBS
...HOW MUCH MORE ARE WE EXPECTED TO DO? I AM ABOUT TO BURST.
IT'S CALLED DESSERT, SUREN.
YOU'VE NEVER HAD DESSERT BEFORE?
I'M NOT... SURE...
...MY FATHER FORBADE INDULGENCE IN MORTAL POISONS. NO WONDER YOU'R ALL TRAITORS AND COWARDS.
YOUR FATHER IS DEN DARGA, THE MANIAC WHO WISHES TO EXTERMINATE ALL LIFE.
MAYBE IF HE TRIED A LITTLE BUTTERSCOTCH RIPPLE, HE'D BE BE CALMER.
MAN, YOU GUYS HAVE SO MUCH IN COMMON.
SNORF
I BET AN AL GHUL FAMILY PICNIC IS JUST AS MUCH FUN AS A DARGA ONE.
IT'S WORSE THAN YOU CAN POSSIBLY IMAGINE, MAYA.
BE GLAD MY FATHER ARGUED THAT WE SHOULD ESCORT SUREN TO GOTHAM BEFORE THE WEEKEND FEAST. NOTICE HE ALSO CHOSE TO LEAVE FOR HIS WATCHTOWER IMMEDIATELY.
BUT NOT BEFORE SHE TORTURED ME.
OH, STOP WHINING. ALL SHE DID WAS SIT YOU DOWN AND ASK YOU QUESTIONS. THE TORTURE HADN'T BEGUN. SHE HAS THESE SUBMARINE BATTERIES ON HER SHIP, THEY--
SNNf
SNNf

REEEEUUNK!

THE LU'UN DARGA HAVE FOUND US *AGAIN!*

WHAT ARE THERE, LIKE, *TEN MILLION* OF THESE GUYS?

YOUR DAD MUST'VE OFFERED SOME KINDA SWEET NINJA SIGNING BONUS, SUREN, OR—

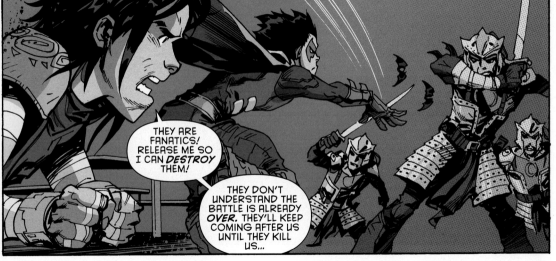

THEY ARE *FANATICS!* RELEASE ME SO I CAN *DESTROY* THEM!

THEY DON'T UNDERSTAND THE BATTLE IS ALREADY *OVER.* THEY'LL KEEP COMING AFTER US UNTIL THEY KILL US...

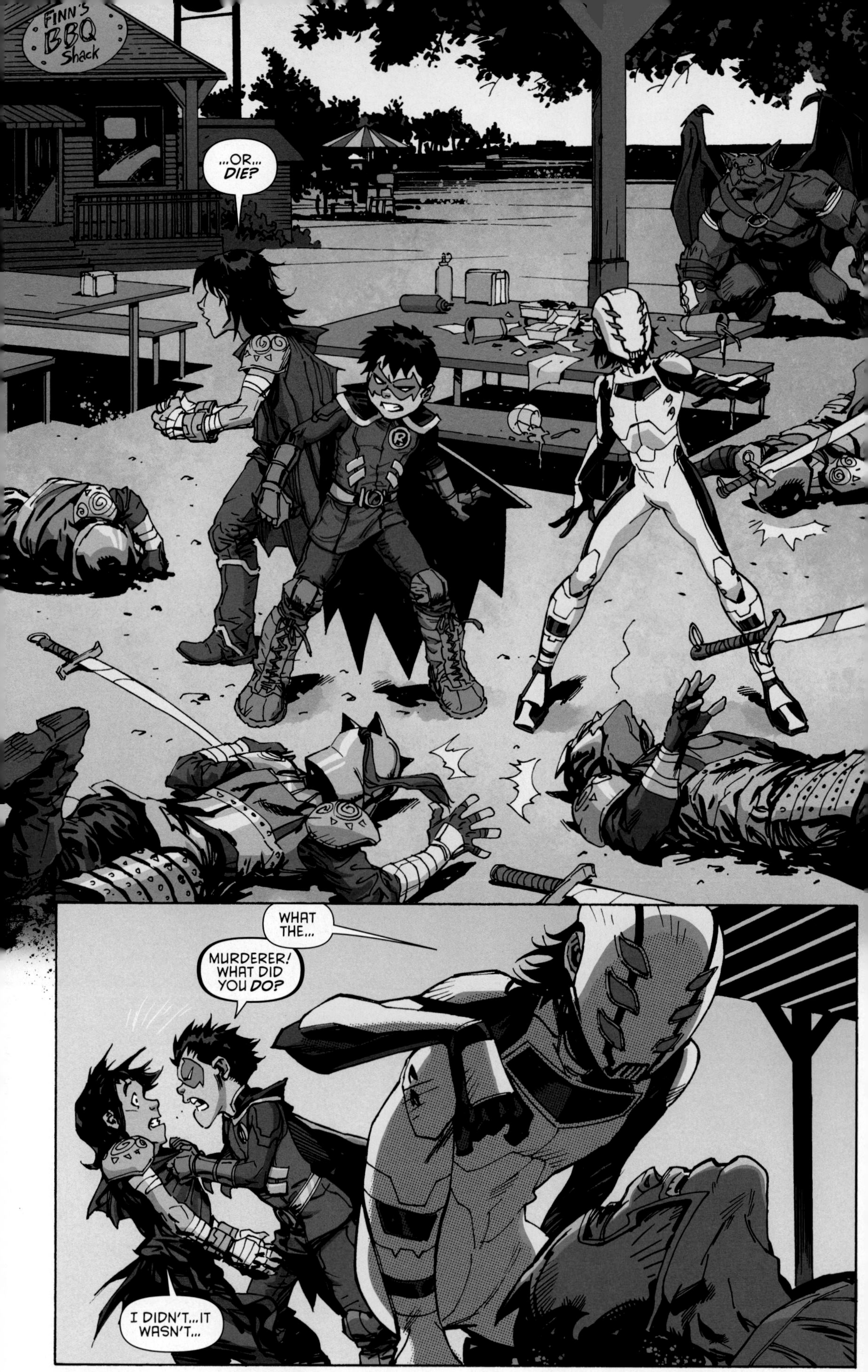
FINN'S BBQ Shack
...OR... DIE?
WHAT THE...
MURDERER! WHAT DID YOU DO?
I DIDN'T...IT WASN'T...

...Meeeee.

ROBIN! THERE'S SOME KINDA *ENERGY* DRAIN...

HERE. FREQUENCY DISRUPTER! THAT'LL KEEP HIM WITH US FOR NOW. CAN YOU CALL FOR HELP? YOUR *DAD* OR SOMEONE?

SLAP

MY COMMS ARE OFFLINE.

THIS IS *DARGA* SPIRIT MAGIC!

ONE OF SUREN'S FAMILY IS STILL *ACTIVE* SOMEWHERE. HE WAS WRONG. THIS BATTLE ISN'T OVER YET.

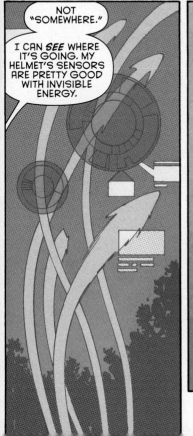

NOT "SOMEWHERE."

I CAN *SEE* WHERE IT'S GOING. MY HELMET'S SENSORS ARE PRETTY GOOD WITH INVISIBLE ENERGY.

THEN LET'S GO...

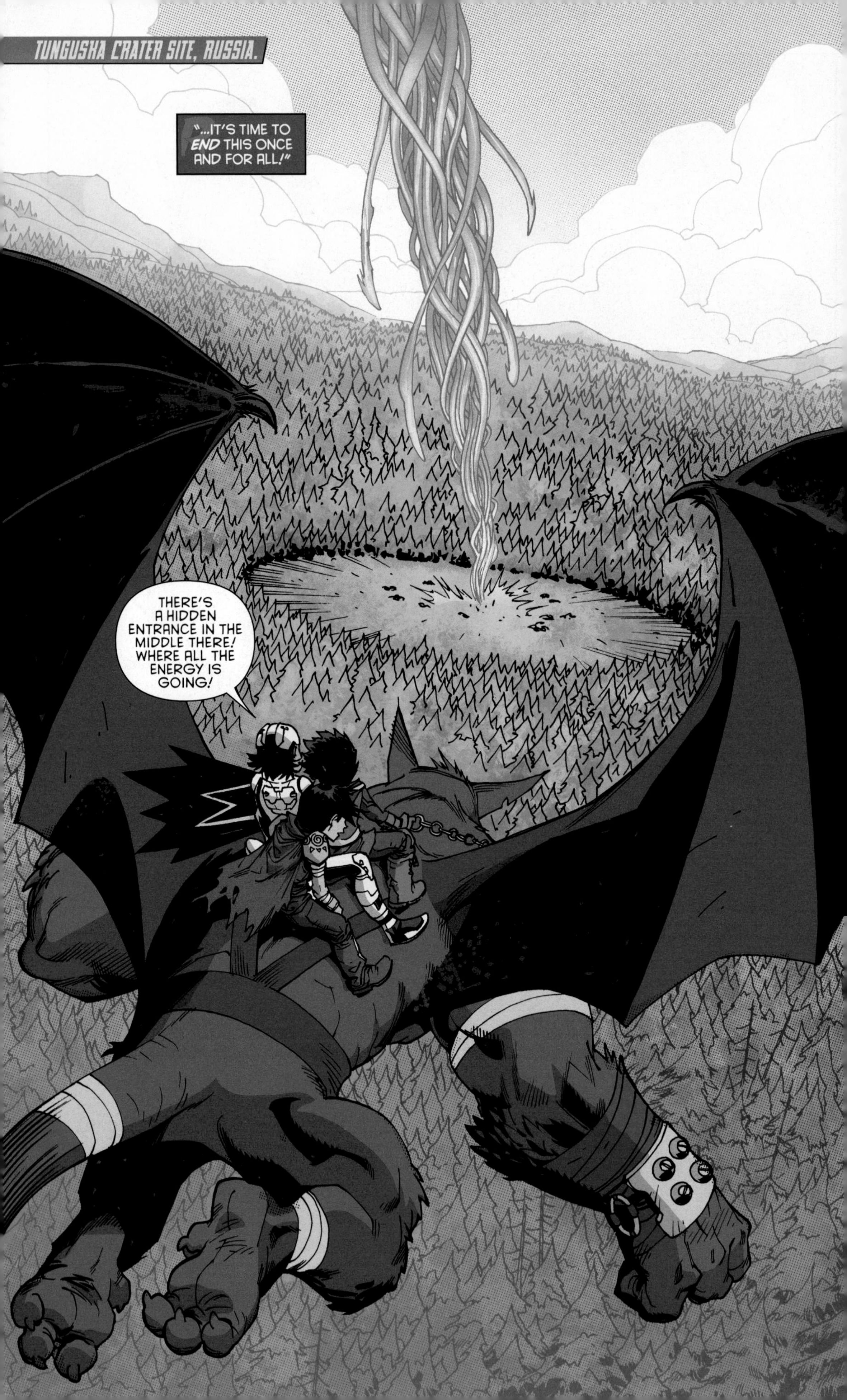
TUNGUSKA CRATER SITE, RUSSIA.
"...IT'S TIME TO END THIS ONCE AND FOR ALL!"
THERE'S A HIDDEN ENTRANCE IN THE MIDDLE THERE! WHERE ALL THE ENERGY IS GOING!

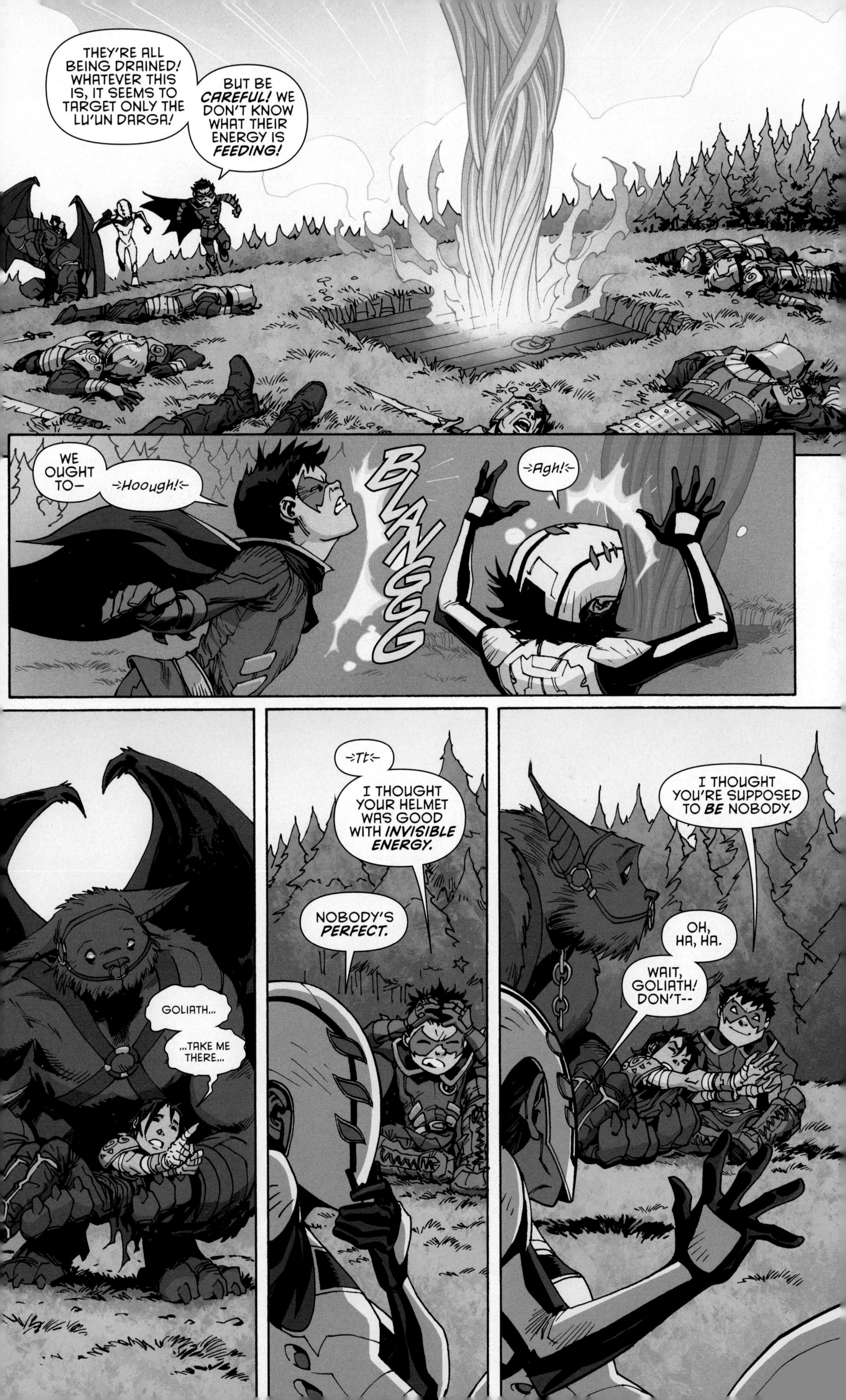
THEY'RE ALL BEING DRAINED! WHATEVER THIS IS, IT SEEMS TO TARGET ONLY THE LU'UN DARGA!
BUT BE CAREFUL! WE DON'T KNOW WHAT THEIR ENERGY IS FEEDING!
WE OUGHT TO—
Hooough!
BLANGGG
Agh!
GOLIATH...
...TAKE ME THERE...
Tt
I THOUGHT YOUR HELMET WAS GOOD WITH INVISIBLE ENERGY.
NOBODY'S PERFECT.
I THOUGHT YOU'RE SUPPOSED TO BE NOBODY.
OH, HA, HA.
WAIT, GOLIATH! DON'T--

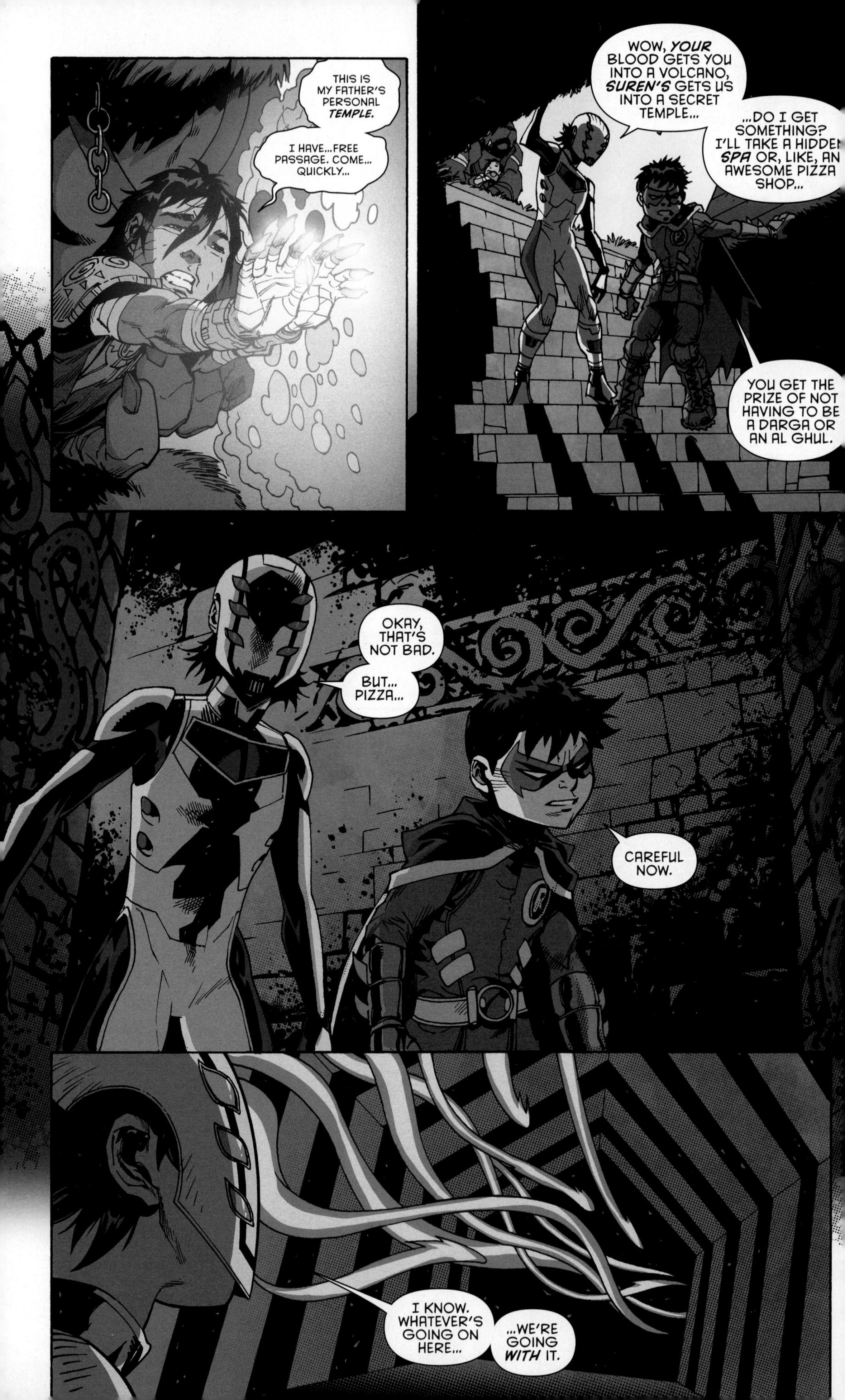

THIS IS MY FATHER'S PERSONAL TEMPLE.
I HAVE...FREE PASSAGE. COME... QUICKLY...
WOW, YOUR BLOOD GETS YOU INTO A VOLCANO, SUREN'S GETS US INTO A SECRET TEMPLE...
...DO I GET SOMETHING? I'LL TAKE A HIDDEN SPA OR, LIKE, AN AWESOME PIZZA SHOP...
YOU GET THE PRIZE OF NOT HAVING TO BE A DARGA OR AN AL GHUL.
OKAY, THAT'S NOT BAD.
BUT... PIZZA...
CAREFUL NOW.
I KNOW. WHATEVER'S GOING ON HERE...
...WE'RE GOING WITH IT.

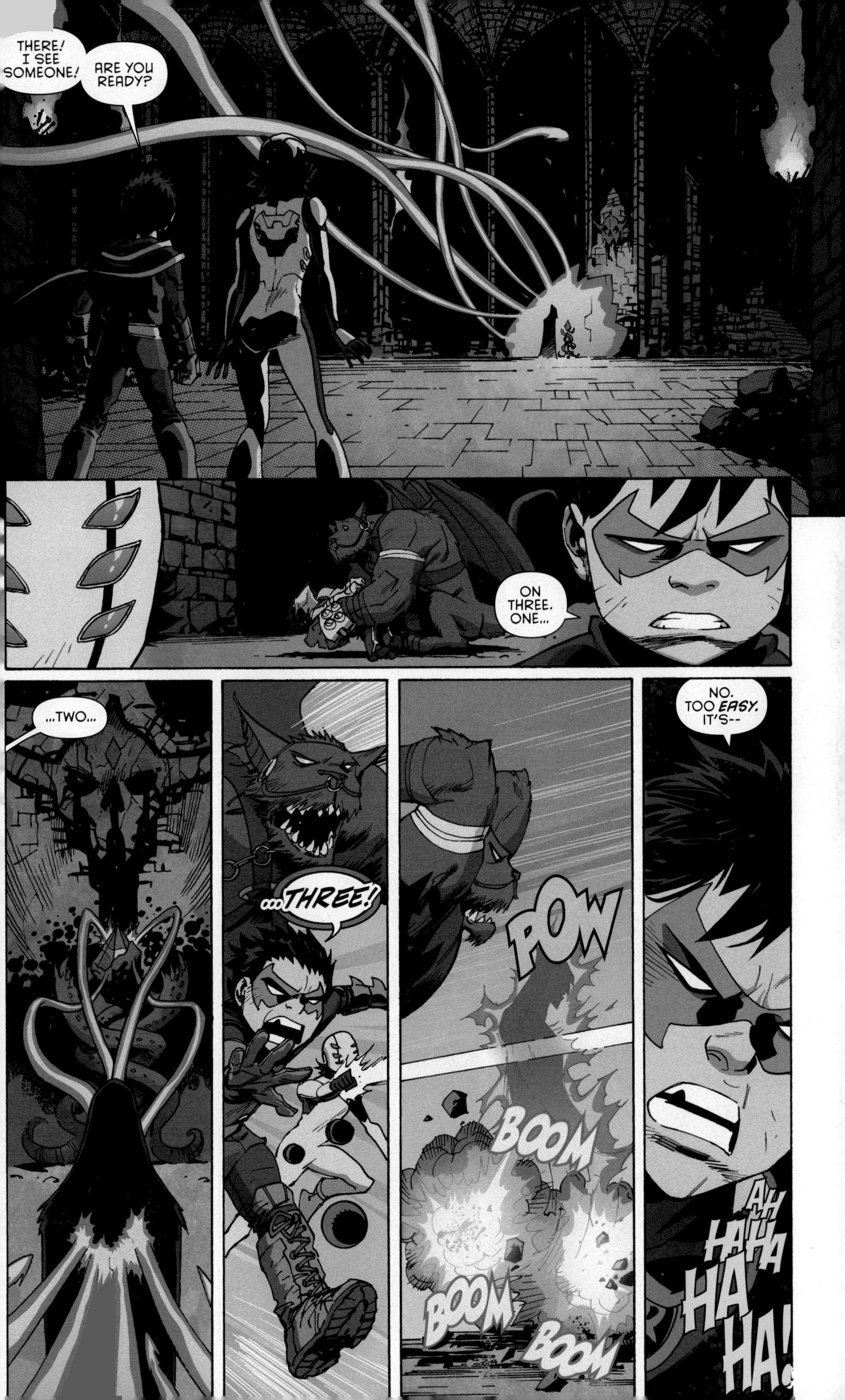
THERE! I SEE SOMEONE!
ARE YOU READY?
ON THREE. ONE...
...TWO...
...THREE!
POW
BOOM
BOOM
BOOM
NO. TOO EASY. IT'S--
AH HAHA HA HA!

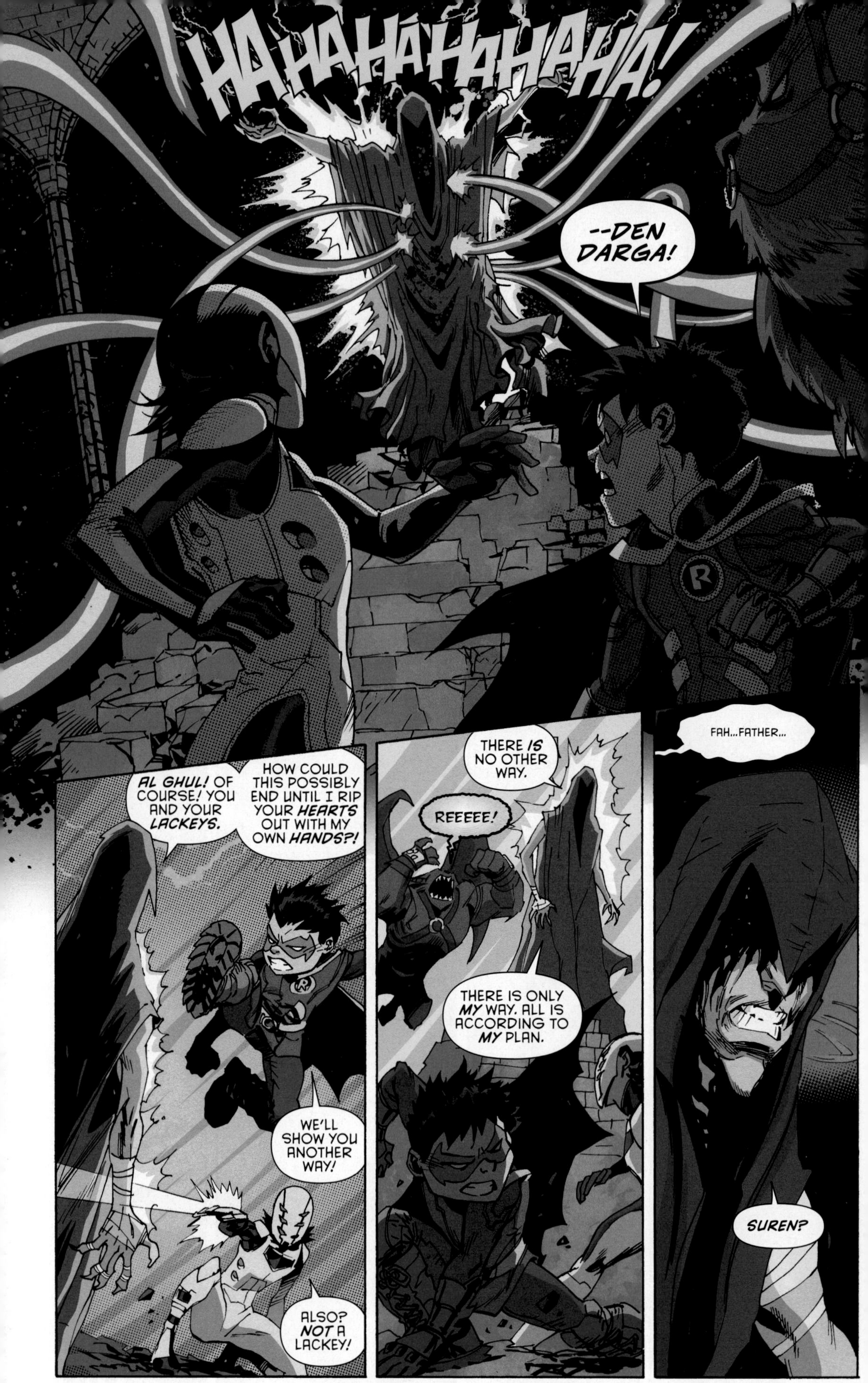
HAHAHAHAHAHAHA!
--DEN DARGA!
AL GHUL! OF COURSE! YOU AND YOUR LACKEYS.
HOW COULD THIS POSSIBLY END UNTIL I RIP YOUR HEARTS OUT WITH MY OWN HANDS?!
WE'LL SHOW YOU ANOTHER WAY!
ALSO? NOT A LACKEY!
THERE IS NO OTHER WAY.
REEEEE!
THERE IS ONLY MY WAY. ALL IS ACCORDING TO MY PLAN.
FAH...FATHER...
SUREN?

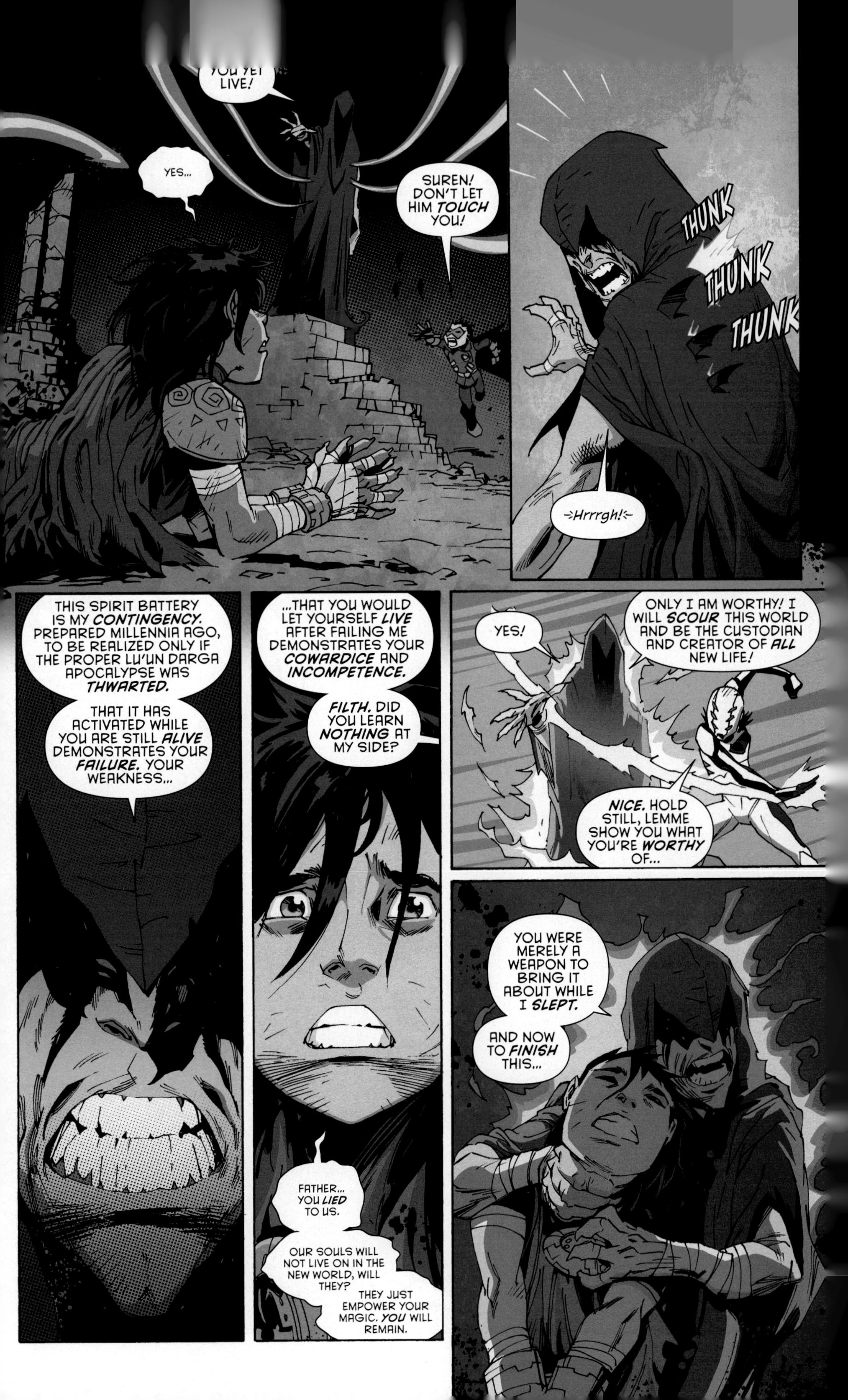

YOU YET LIVE!
YES...
SUREN! DON'T LET HIM *TOUCH* YOU!
THUNK
THUNK
THUNK
~Hrrrgh!~
THIS SPIRIT BATTERY IS MY *CONTINGENCY.* PREPARED MILLENNIA AGO, TO BE REALIZED ONLY IF THE PROPER LU'UN DARGA APOCALYPSE WAS *THWARTED.*
THAT IT HAS ACTIVATED WHILE YOU ARE STILL *ALIVE* DEMONSTRATES YOUR *FAILURE.* YOUR WEAKNESS...
...THAT YOU WOULD LET YOURSELF *LIVE* AFTER FAILING ME DEMONSTRATES YOUR *COWARDICE* AND *INCOMPETENCE.*
FILTH. DID YOU LEARN *NOTHING* AT MY SIDE?
FATHER... YOU *LIED* TO US.
OUR SOULS WILL NOT LIVE ON IN THE NEW WORLD, WILL THEY?
THEY JUST EMPOWER YOUR MAGIC. *YOU* WILL REMAIN.
YES!
ONLY I AM WORTHY! I WILL *SCOUR* THIS WORLD AND BE THE CUSTODIAN AND CREATOR OF *ALL* NEW LIFE!
NICE. HOLD STILL, LEMME SHOW YOU WHAT YOU'RE *WORTHY* OF...
YOU WERE MERELY A WEAPON TO BRING IT ABOUT WHILE I *SLEPT.*
AND NOW TO *FINISH* THIS...

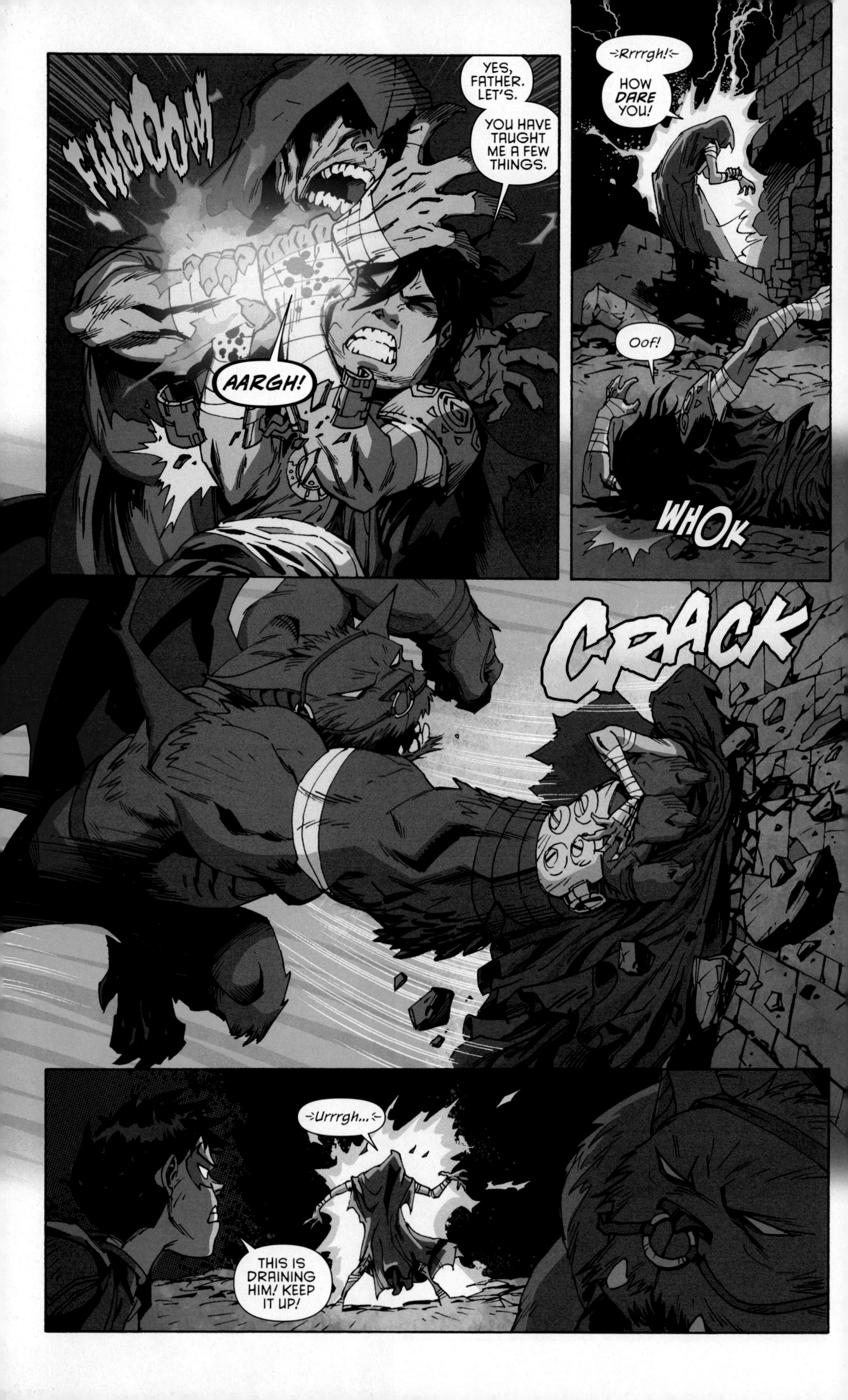
FWOOOM
YES, FATHER. LET'S.
YOU HAVE TAUGHT ME A FEW THINGS.
AARGH!
~Rrrrgh!~
HOW DARE YOU!
Oof!
WHOK
CRACK
~Urrrgh...~
THIS IS DRAINING HIM! KEEP IT UP!

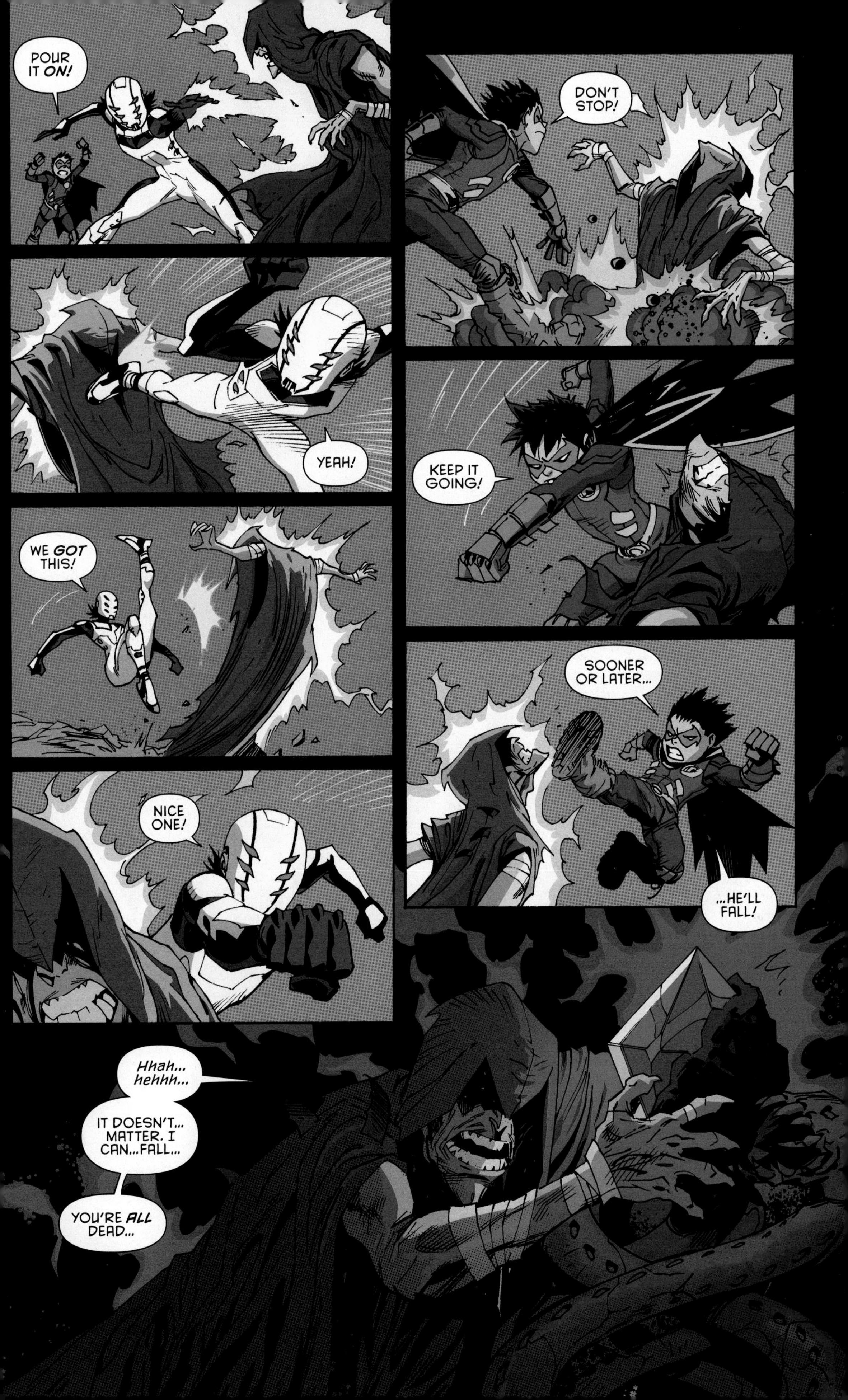
POUR IT ON!
DON'T STOP!
YEAH!
KEEP IT GOING!
WE GOT THIS!
SOONER OR LATER...
NICE ONE!
...HE'LL FALL!
Hhah... hehhh...
IT DOESN'T... MATTER. I CAN...FALL...
YOU'RE ALL DEAD...

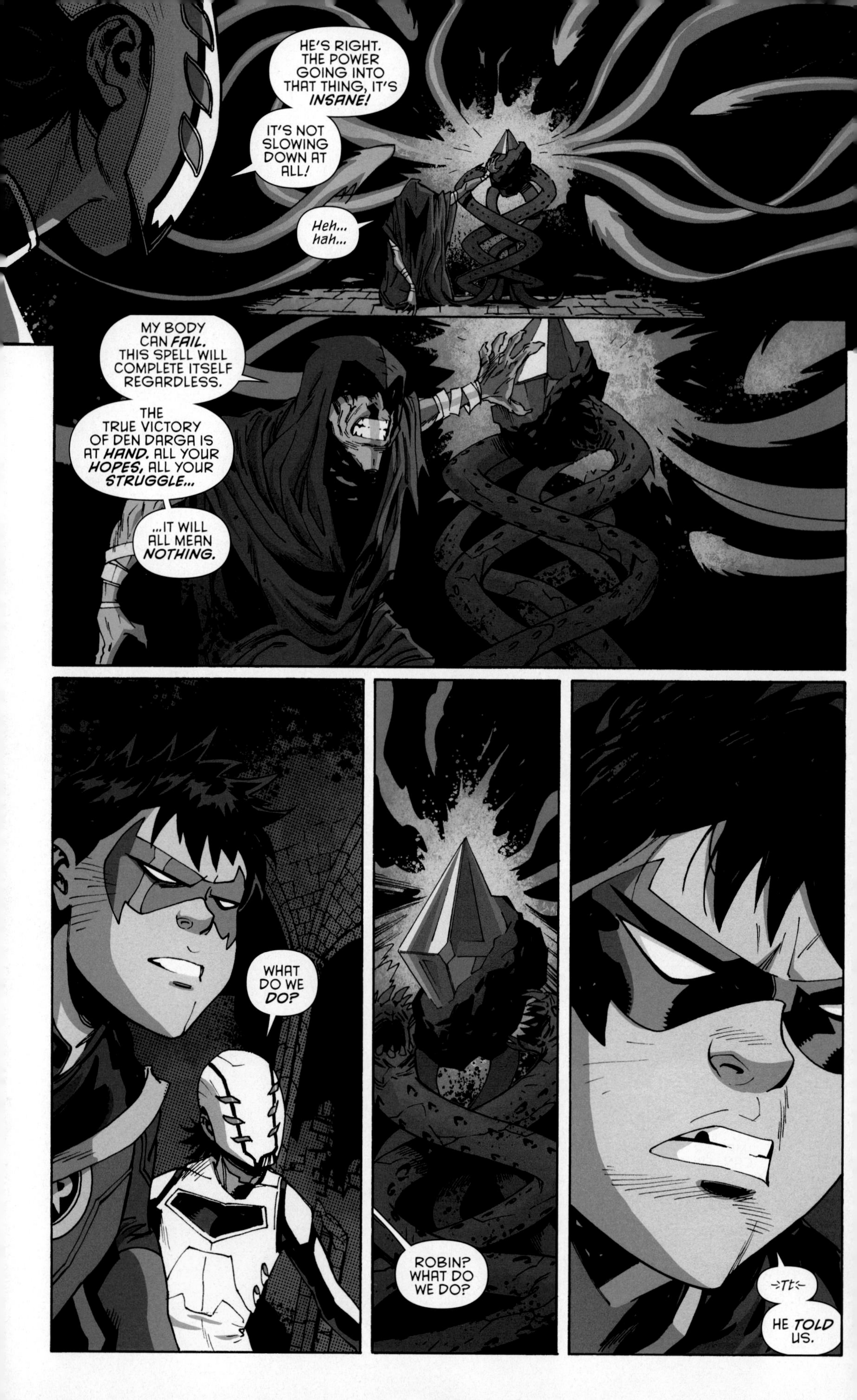

HE'S RIGHT. THE POWER GOING INTO THAT THING, IT'S *INSANE!*
IT'S NOT SLOWING DOWN AT ALL!
Heh... hah...
MY BODY CAN *FAIL.* THIS SPELL WILL COMPLETE ITSELF REGARDLESS.
THE TRUE VICTORY OF DEN DARGA IS AT *HAND.* ALL YOUR *HOPES,* ALL YOUR *STRUGGLE...*
...IT WILL ALL MEAN *NOTHING.*
WHAT DO WE *DO?*
ROBIN? WHAT DO WE DO?
-Tt-
HE *TOLD* US.

IT'S A *BATTERY*.

SUREN. DID YOU LEARN TO *PULL* SPIRITS LIKE YOUR FATHER CAN? *STEER* THEM?

A... LITTLE...

CRACK

GOOD.

WHAK

DO IT NOW! GUIDE THEM ALONG THESE *WIRES*!

WE CAN SHORT IT OUT!

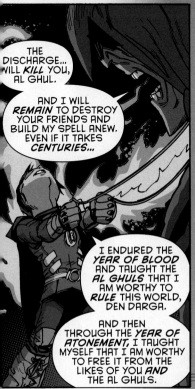

THE DISCHARGE... WILL *KILL* YOU, AL GHUL.

AND I WILL *REMAIN* TO DESTROY YOUR FRIENDS AND BUILD MY SPELL ANEW. EVEN IF IT TAKES *CENTURIES*...

I ENDURED THE *YEAR OF BLOOD* AND TAUGHT THE *AL GHULS* THAT I AM WORTHY TO *RULE* THIS WORLD, DEN DARGA.

AND THEN THROUGH THE *YEAR OF ATONEMENT,* I TAUGHT MYSELF THAT I AM WORTHY TO FREE IT FROM THE LIKES OF YOU *AND* THE AL GHULS.

NO!

THERE'S *GOT* TO BE ANOTHER WAY!

GOLIATH! ANYONE WHO TOUCHES ME... WILL CARRY THE SHOCK, TOO... STOP MAYA...

GO!

REEEEEUUNKK!

⌐Hnnf!⌐

KKKKKTTTTKKKT...

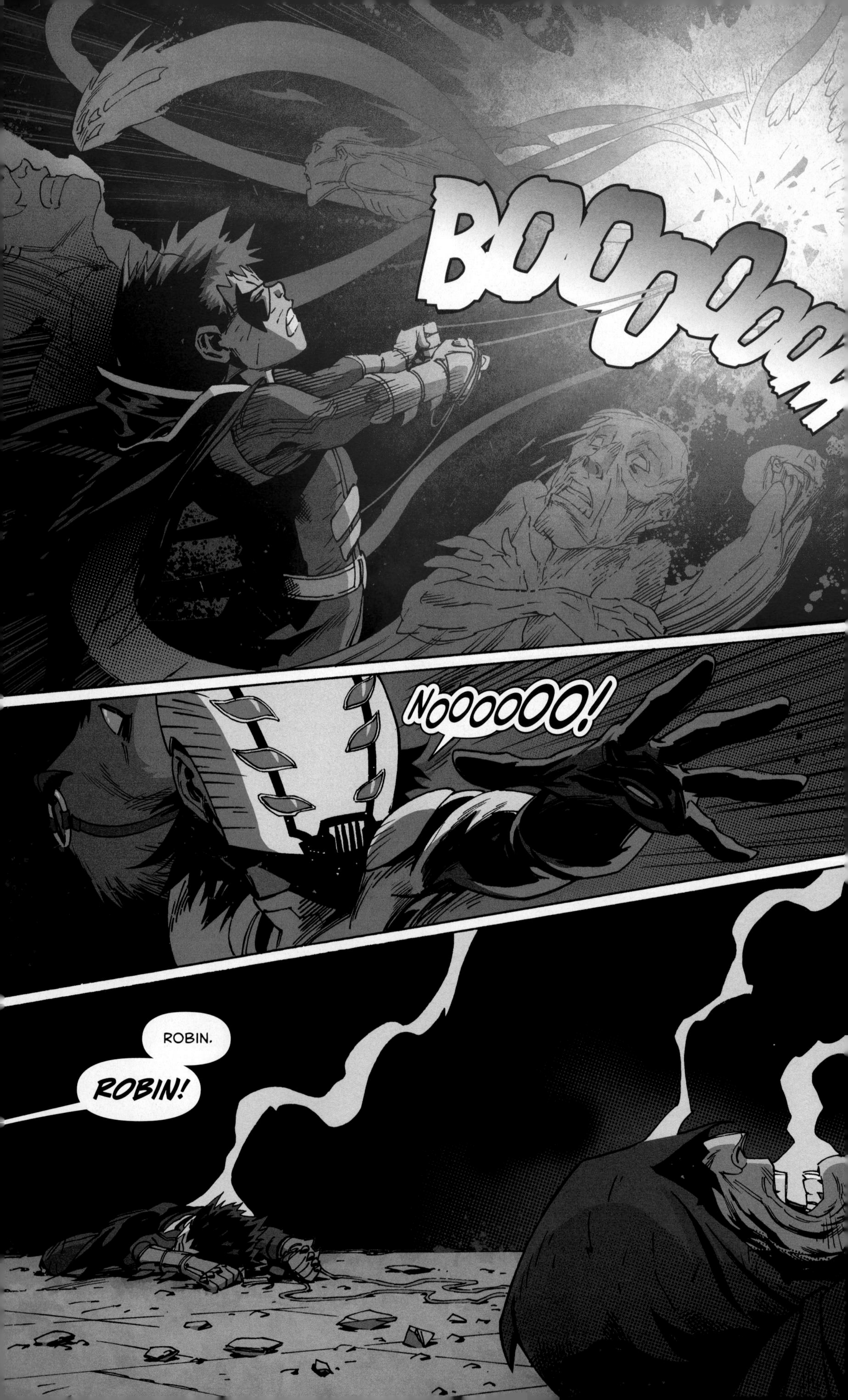
BOOOOOOM
NOOOOOO!
ROBIN.
ROBIN!

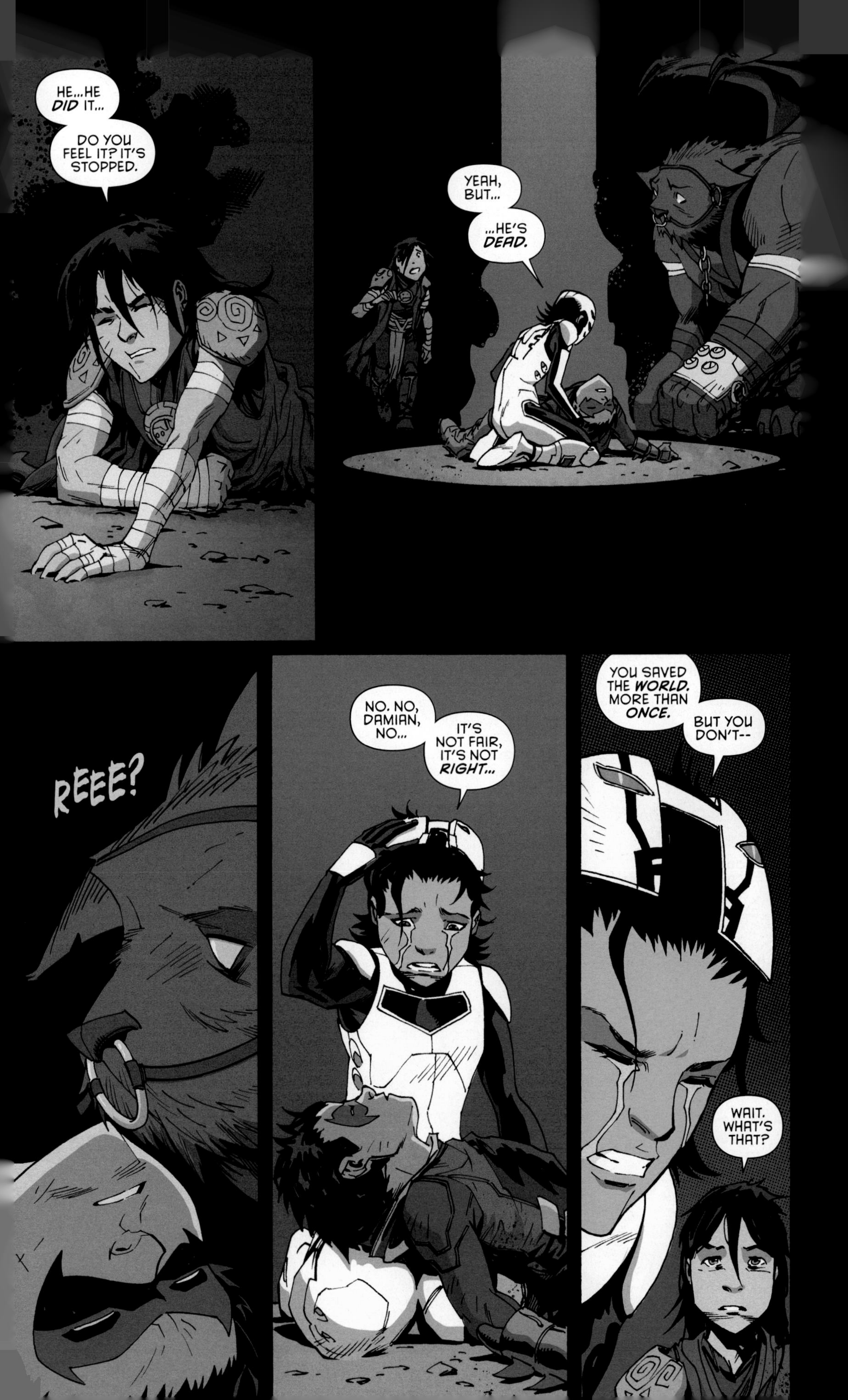
HE...HE DID IT...
DO YOU FEEL IT? IT'S STOPPED.
YEAH, BUT...
...HE'S DEAD.
REEE?
NO. NO, DAMIAN, NO...
IT'S NOT FAIR, IT'S NOT RIGHT...
YOU SAVED THE WORLD. MORE THAN ONCE.
BUT YOU DON'T--
WAIT. WHAT'S THAT?

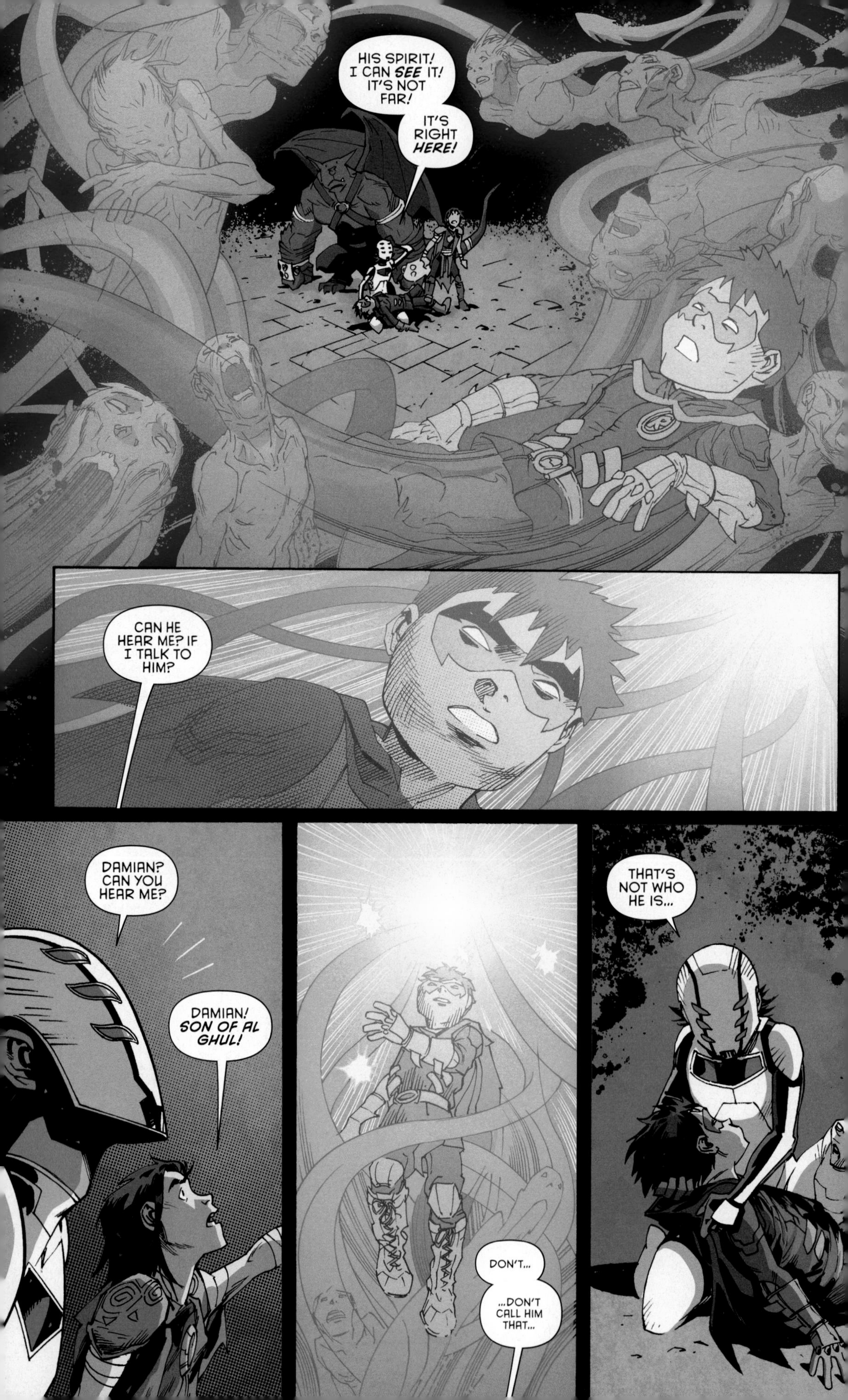
HIS SPIRIT! I CAN SEE IT! IT'S NOT FAR!
IT'S RIGHT HERE!
CAN HE HEAR ME? IF I TALK TO HIM?
DAMIAN? CAN YOU HEAR ME?
DAMIAN! SON OF AL GHUL!
DON'T...
...DON'T CALL HIM THAT...
THAT'S NOT WHO HE IS...

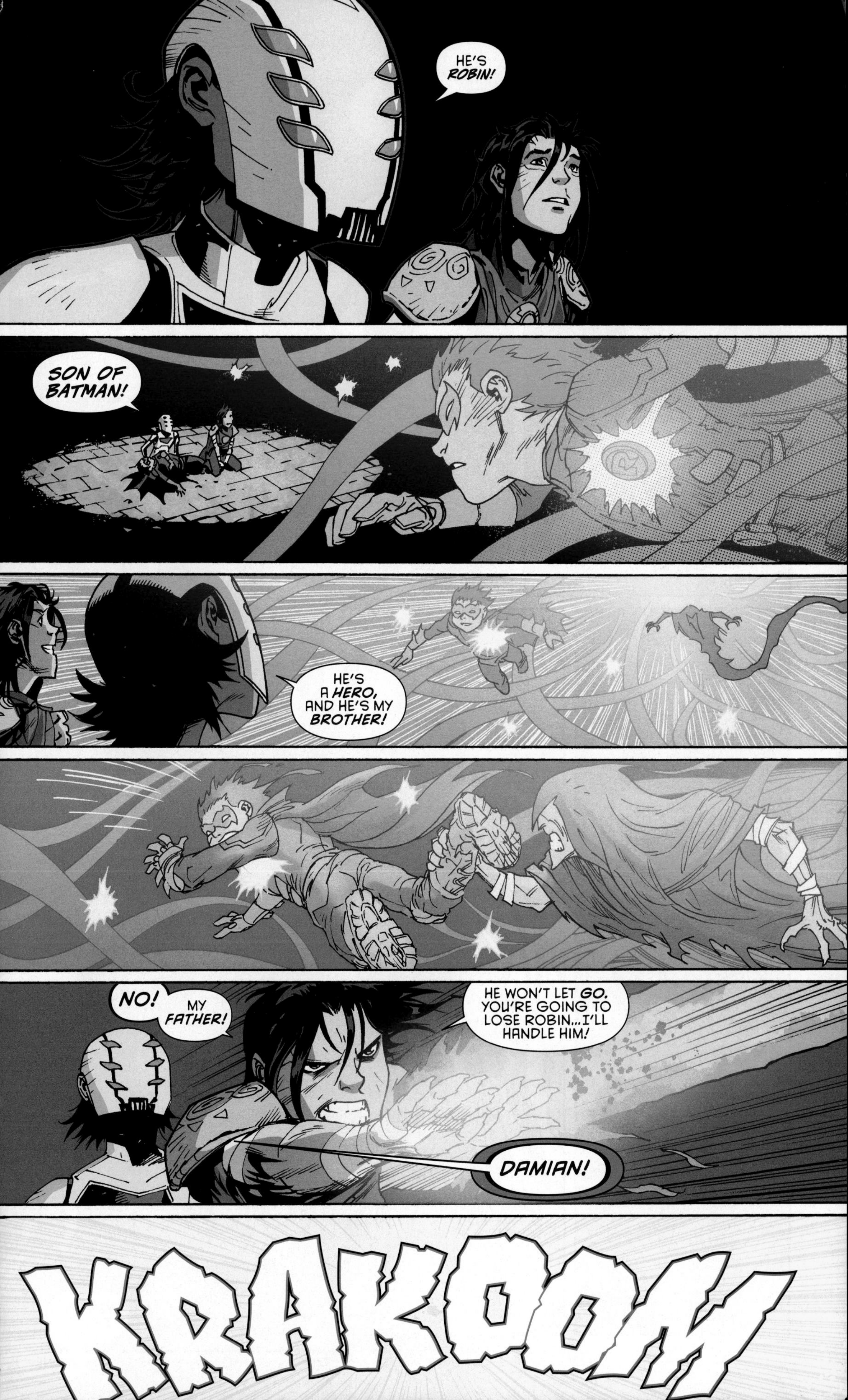
HE'S ROBIN!
SON OF BATMAN!
HE'S A HERO, AND HE'S MY BROTHER!
NO!
MY FATHER!
HE WON'T LET GO. YOU'RE GOING TO LOSE ROBIN...I'LL HANDLE HIM!
DAMIAN!
KRAKOOM

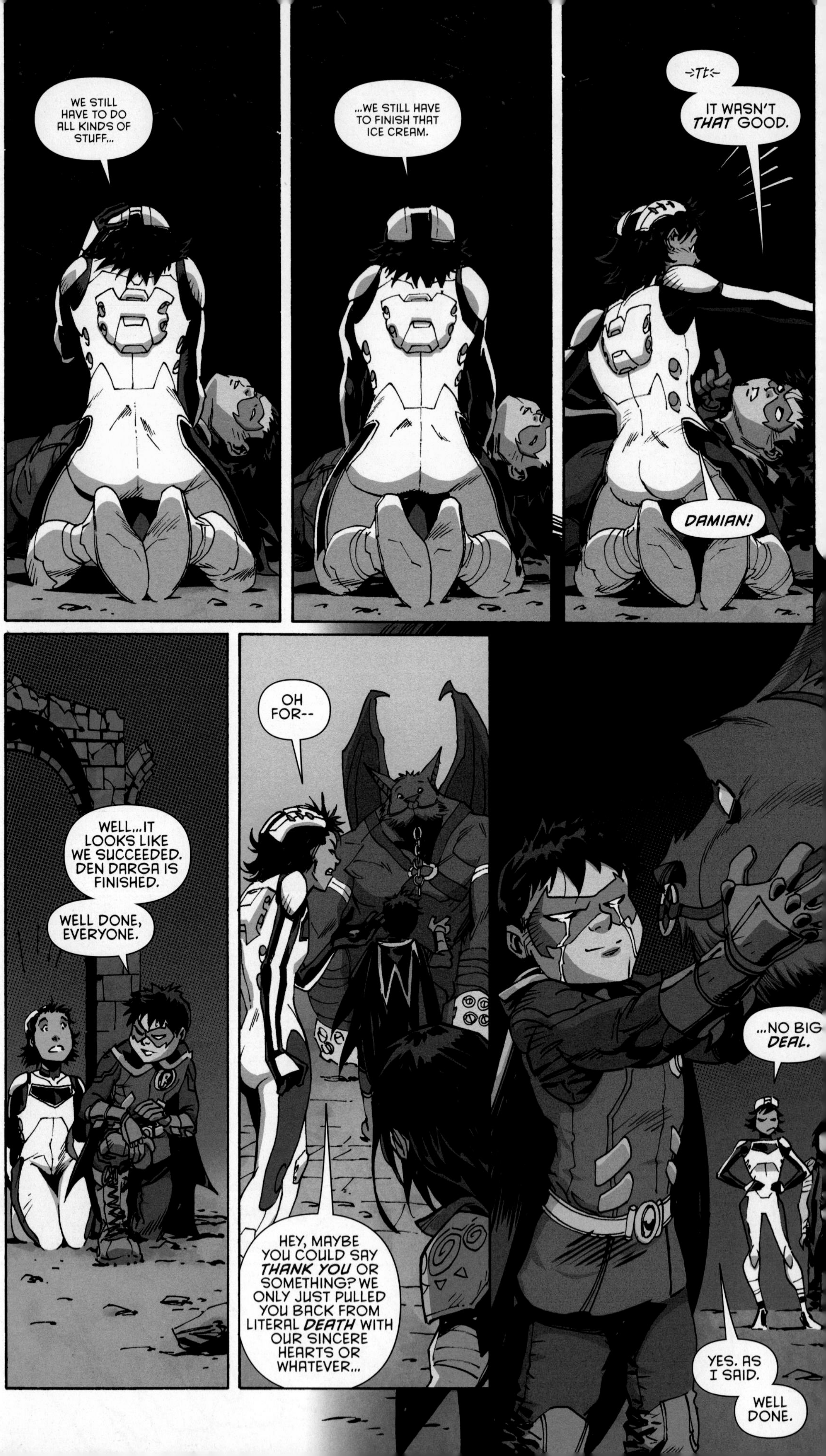
WE STILL HAVE TO DO ALL KINDS OF STUFF...
...WE STILL HAVE TO FINISH THAT ICE CREAM.
-TT-
IT WASN'T THAT GOOD.
DAMIAN!
WELL...IT LOOKS LIKE WE SUCCEEDED. DEN DARGA IS FINISHED.
WELL DONE, EVERYONE.
OH FOR--
HEY, MAYBE YOU COULD SAY THANK YOU OR SOMETHING? WE ONLY JUST PULLED YOU BACK FROM LITERAL DEATH WITH OUR SINCERE HEARTS OR WHATEVER...
...NO BIG DEAL.
YES. AS I SAID.
WELL DONE.

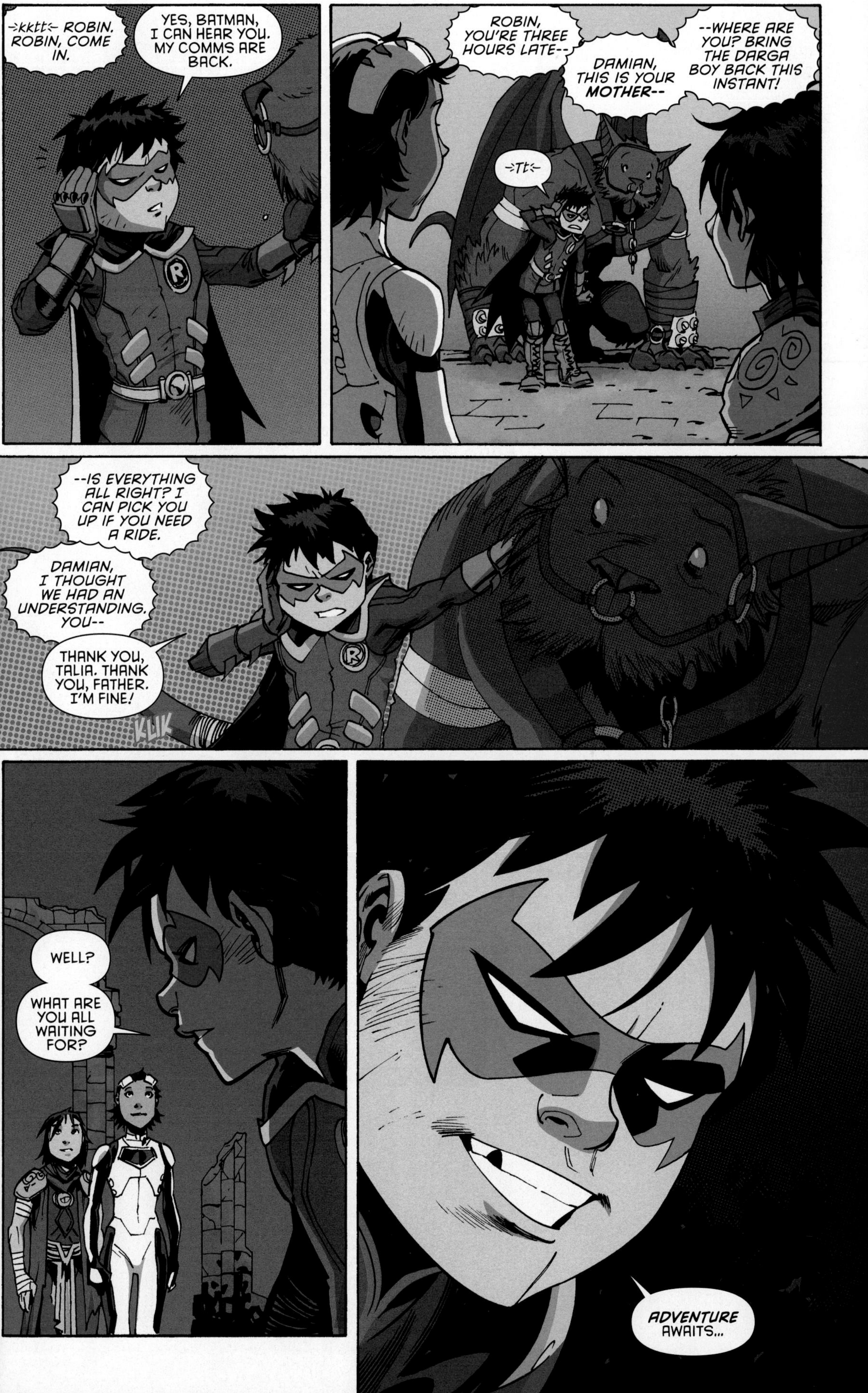
-kkt- ROBIN. ROBIN, COME IN.
YES, BATMAN, I CAN HEAR YOU. MY COMMS ARE BACK.
ROBIN, YOU'RE THREE HOURS LATE--
DAMIAN, THIS IS YOUR MOTHER--
--WHERE ARE YOU? BRING THE DARGA BOY BACK THIS INSTANT!
-Tt-
--IS EVERYTHING ALL RIGHT? I CAN PICK YOU UP IF YOU NEED A RIDE.
DAMIAN, I THOUGHT WE HAD AN UNDERSTANDING. YOU--
THANK YOU, TALIA. THANK YOU, FATHER. I'M FINE!
KLIK
WELL?
WHAT ARE YOU ALL WAITING FOR?
ADVENTURE AWAITS...

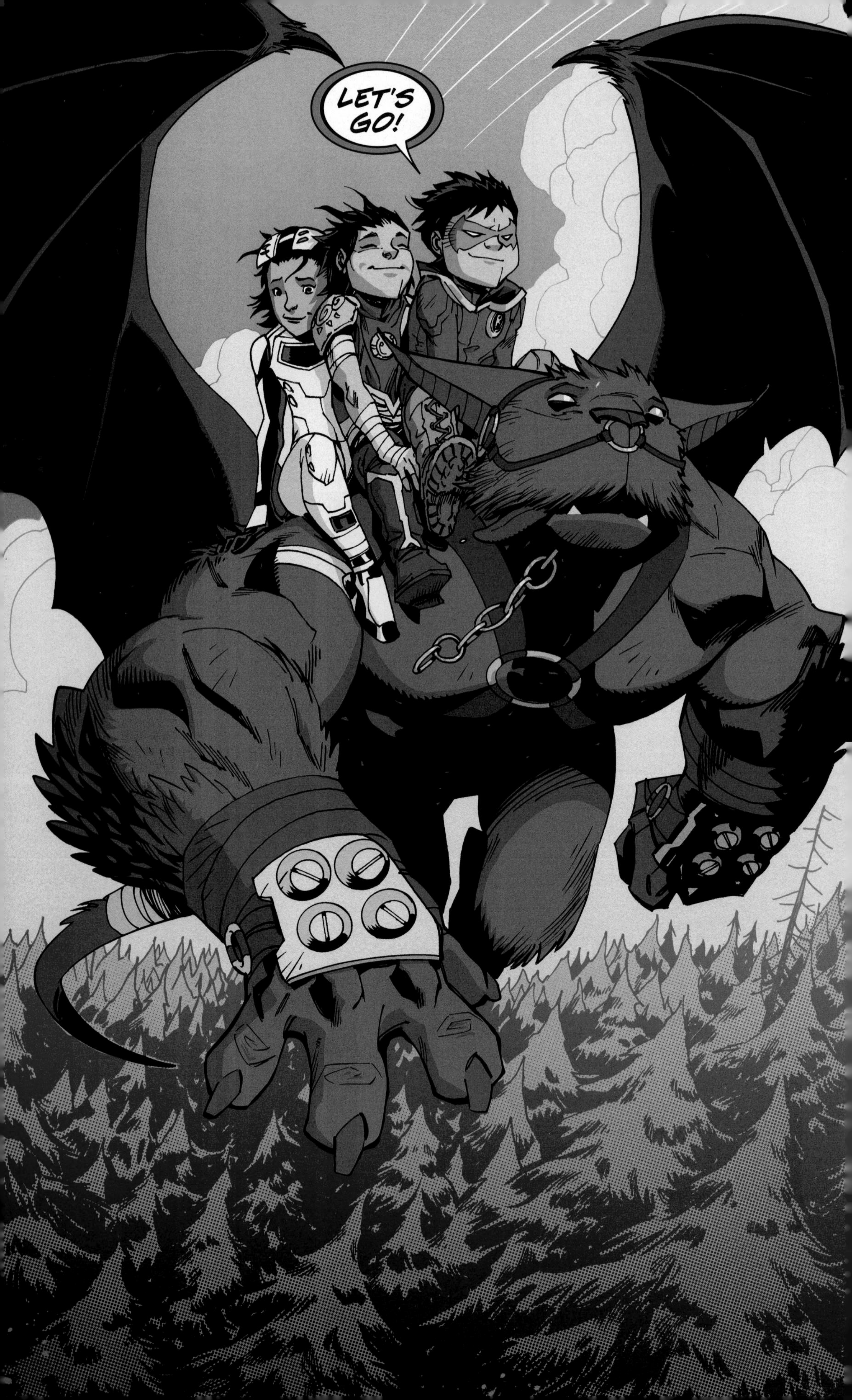
LET'S GO!

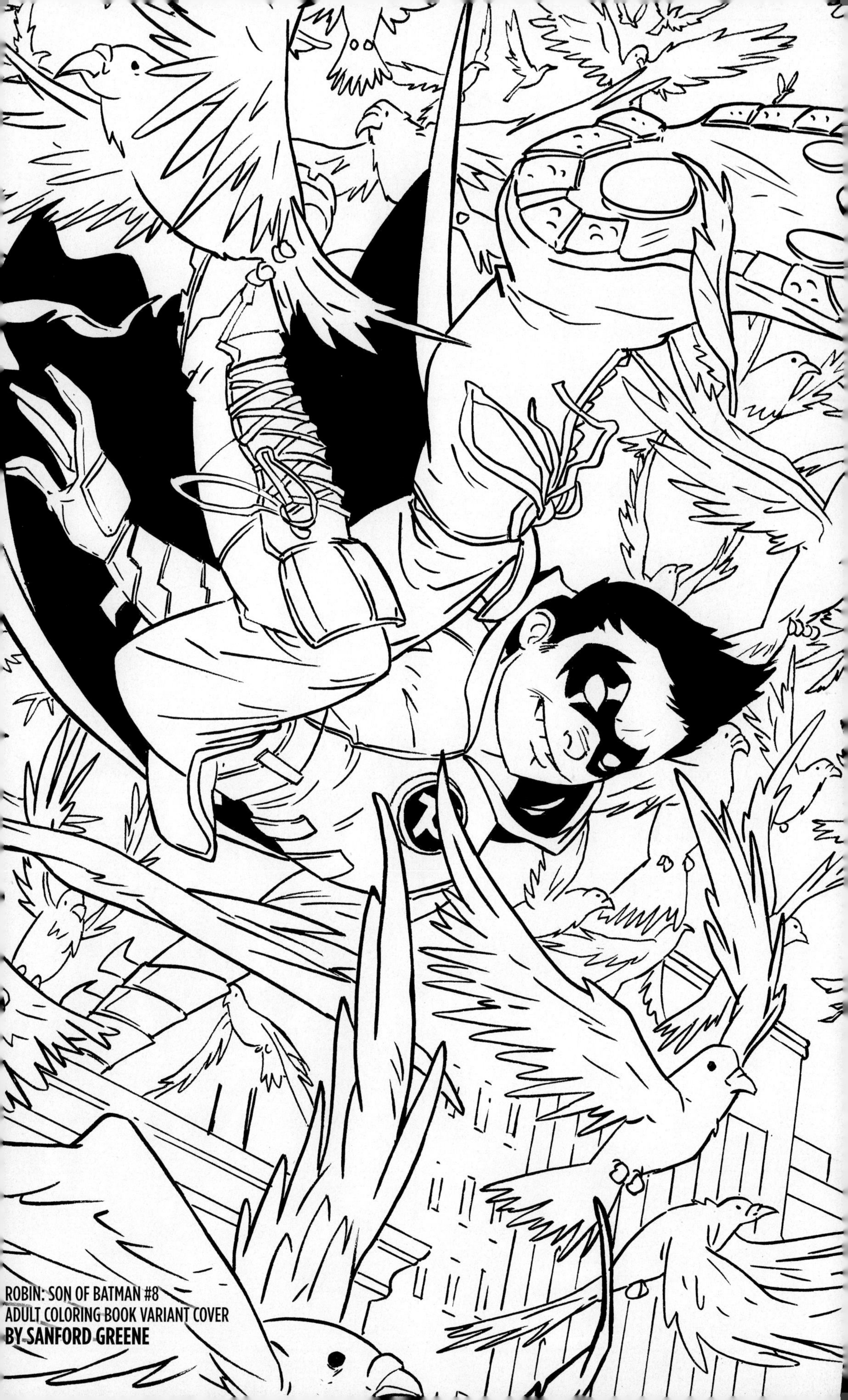

ROBIN: SON OF BATMAN #8
ADULT COLORING BOOK VARIANT COVER
BY SANFORD GREENE

ROBIN: SON OF BATMAN #9 VARIANT COVER

BY NEAL ADAMS, BILL SIENKIEWICZ & DAVE McCAIG

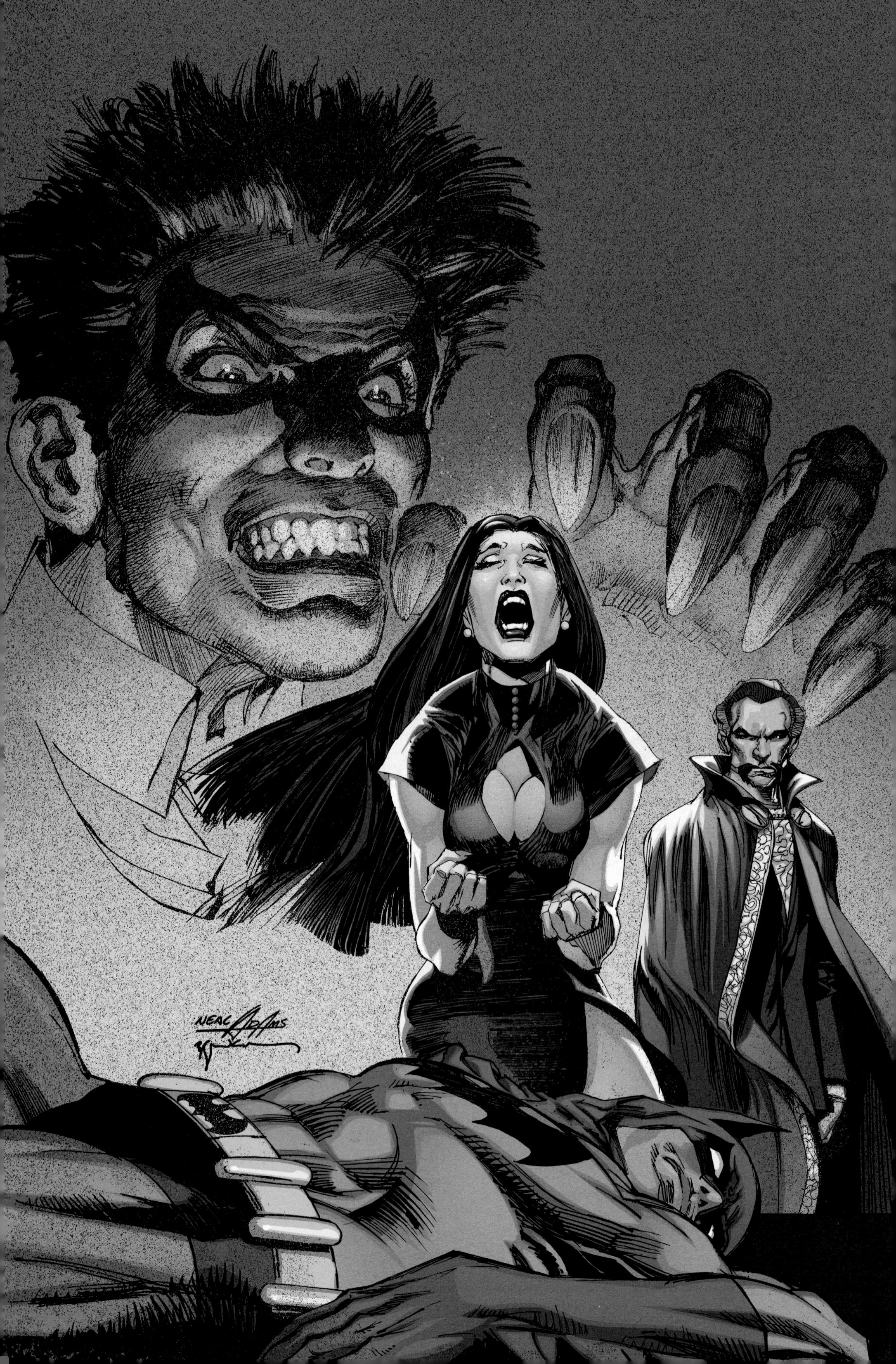

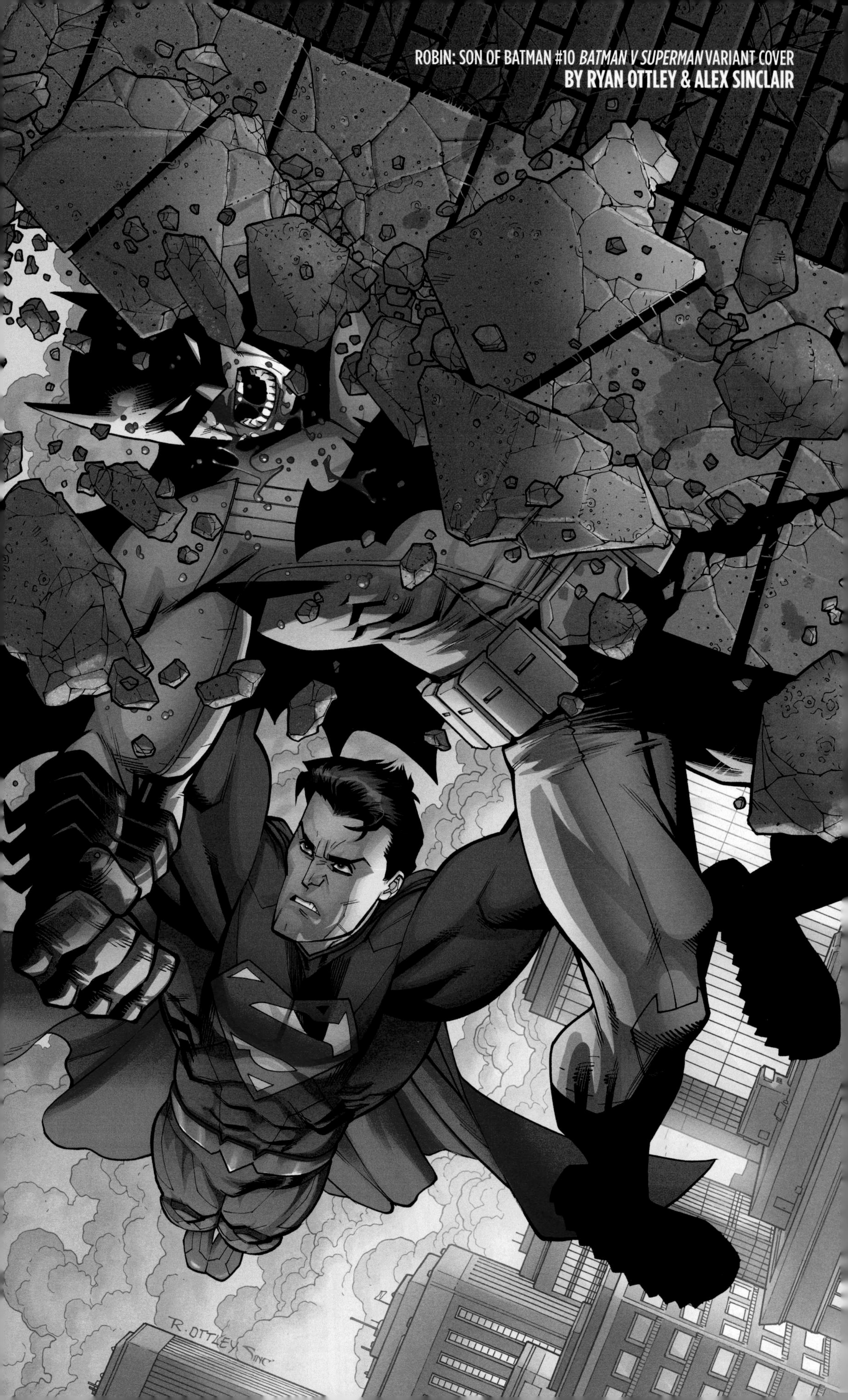

ROBIN: SON OF BATMAN #10 *BATMAN V SUPERMAN* VARIANT COVER
BY RYAN OTTLEY & ALEX SINCLAIR

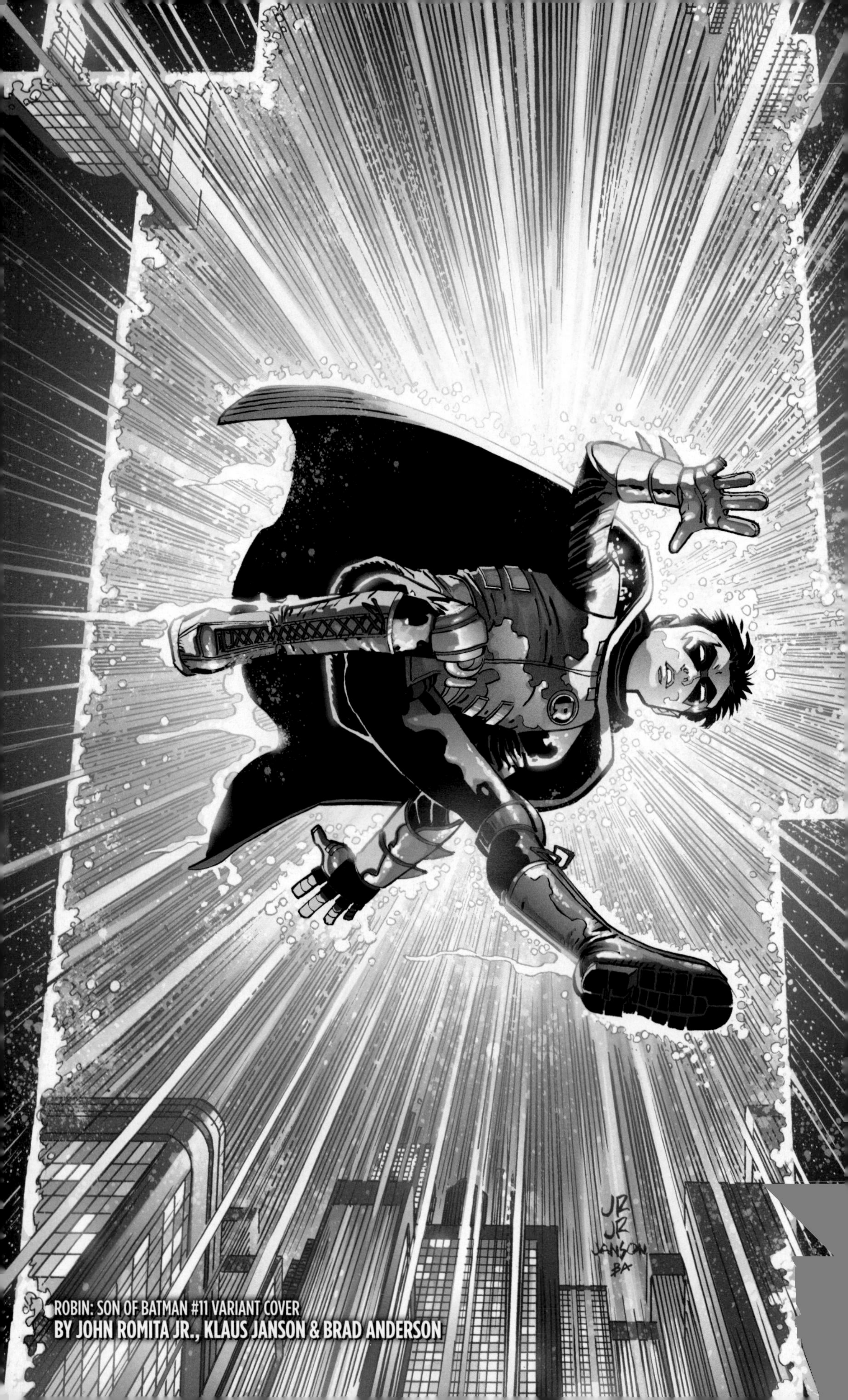
JR
JR
JANSON
BA

ROBIN: SON OF BATMAN #11 VARIANT COVER
BY JOHN ROMITA JR., KLAUS JANSON & BRAD ANDERSON